U0685722

海南旅游景区中英文导游词选编

The Selected Tour Commentaries in Chinese and English for Hainan Tourist Attractions

杨坤燕 张建强 编著

中国旅游出版社

项目策划：段向民
责任编辑：武　洋
责任印制：钱　宬
封面设计：温　泉

图书在版编目（CIP）数据

海南旅游景区中英文导游词选编 / 杨坤燕，张建强编著. -- 北京 : 中国旅游出版社，2024. 8. -- ISBN 978-7-5032-7437-4

Ⅰ. K928.966

中国国家版本馆 CIP 数据核字第 2024TG7655 号

书　　名：海南旅游景区中英文导游词选编

作　　者：杨坤燕　张建强
出版发行：中国旅游出版社
（北京静安东里 6 号　邮编：100028）
https://www.cttp.net.cn　E-mail:cttp@mct.gov.cn
营销中心电话：010-57377103，010-57377106
读者服务部电话：010-57377107
排　　版：北京旅教文化传播有限公司
经　　销：全国各地新华书店
印　　刷：北京工商事务印刷有限公司
版　　次：2024 年 8 月第 1 版　2024 年 8 月第 1 次印刷
开　　本：720 毫米 × 970 毫米　1/16
印　　张：24.25
字　　数：331 千
定　　价：59.80 元
ISBN　978-7-5032-7437-4

前　言

景区导游词是在旅游途中或景区向游客提供有关旅游目的地信息的讲解服务所使用的材料，其主要功能是帮助游客快速了解旅游景区的自然风光、民风民俗、本土特产、风味小吃、历史文化古迹与遗产等。是为了帮助游客在旅游的同时，能够更好地理解景点所包含的文化背景和历史意义；是为了让游客在欣赏赏心悦目的湖光山色的同时，对于其本身所蕴含的丰富文化内涵也能够具有一定的鉴赏能力。另外，景区导游词也是进行国际文化交流的重要手段和工具，尤其是英文导游词的质量好坏直接影响到海南旅游业在国际旅游市场上的形象。优秀而规范的英文导游词可以帮助提升景区的档次，会适当唤起外国游客心中的美感和向往，有助于他们领略海南独特的魅力，以吸引更多的外国游客。

海南山水秀丽、风光旖旎、历史文化旅游资源丰富，吸引着大批外国游客前来观光游览。自建立海南国际旅游岛特别是海南自由贸易港以来，海南的入境旅游业得到了较快发展，新冠疫情暴发前，入境游客逐年稳步增加。其中，以英语为母语和以英语为沟通语言的游客占海南入境旅游人数比重逐年增长。海南要在建立国际自由贸易港过程中，成为世界知名旅游目的地，就必须规范景区的英文导游词。

首先本书试着对海南近些年导游考试中出现的景区导游词进行中英文版本的创作，希望对有志于从事海南导游服务行业的旅游人有所帮助和启发。其次，一位优秀的讲解员在掌握高质量讲解词的同时，还少不了和观众进行必要的互动。虽然讲解人员在讲解过程中扮演的是讲述者，游客扮演的是聆听者，但这不应该是一成不变的，甚至在讲解过程中某些时候角色应该发生互换。共鸣是非常重要的，如果讲解员只是一味地讲，观众只是一味地听，那么可以说空气都会犯困。最后，因人施讲是讲解的最高境界。至圣先师孔子主张的“有教无类”，但要“因材施教”，被奉为教育行业的圭臬。其实讲解员和教师的身份在这方面是极为类似的。讲解员在景区会遇到各种各样的观众，但如果对每一位观众都以同样的讲解方式进行讲解，恐怕是不会受到欢迎和好评的。

本书由杨坤燕、张建强共同编写，共计 33.1 万字。由于时间紧迫以及编写人员的水平有限，书中难免出现疏漏之处，敬请专家和读者批评指正。

书稿在编写过程中参考、引用了许多景区讲解词，在此向各景区负责人的配合表示敬意和感谢。在初稿完成过程中，黄学彬教授与乔淑英教授给予了指导和帮助，海南热带海洋学院国际学院的本科生樊园渊、王雨飞、姜曼曼、刘毅、李佳琪、张子琦、李晓波、刘铸稻、杨可意、江万锂、沈融融、胡思婷、武颖、梁海佩、周博文、姬文娇、郑佩瑶、侯一鸣、李佳、王凯韬、暴鉴瑶等参与书稿的整理及编辑，在此一并表示感谢。

对本书的责任编辑付出的辛勤劳动表示由衷的感谢。

编者
2024 年 1 月

目 录

第一篇　海南旅游之路

1. 海南省简介……………………………………………………………… 2
2. 海口概览………………………………………………………………… 6
3. 三亚概览………………………………………………………………… 9

第二篇　A 级旅游景区

5A 级旅游景区 ……………………………………………………………14
1. 三亚大小洞天旅游区 ……………………………………………………14
2. 南山文化旅游区 …………………………………………………………21
3. 呀诺达雨林文化旅游区 …………………………………………………27
4. 分界洲岛旅游区 …………………………………………………………41
5. 海南槟榔谷黎苗文化旅游区 ……………………………………………42
6. 蜈支洲岛旅游区 …………………………………………………………56
7. 天涯海角游览区 …………………………………………………………62

4A 级旅游景区 ……………………………………………………………71
1. 兴隆热带植物园 …………………………………………………………71
2. 南湾猴岛生态旅游区 ……………………………………………………72

3. 中国雷琼海口火山群世界地质公园 …… 75
4. 博鳌亚洲论坛永久会址 …… 79
5. 三亚西岛海洋文化旅游区 …… 82
6. 鹿回头风景区 …… 85
7. 三亚水稻国家公园 …… 91
8. 海南儋州石花水洞地质公园 …… 95
9. 东坡书院 …… 98
10. 母瑞山革命根据地纪念园 …… 104
11. 椰子大观园 …… 107
12. 七仙岭温泉国家森林公园 …… 110
13. 海南文笔峰盘古文化旅游区 …… 114
14. 海口观澜湖旅游度假区 …… 116

3A 级旅游景区 …… 120
1. 五公祠 …… 120
2. 三亚凤凰岭海誓山盟景区 …… 122
3. 海口骑楼建筑历史文化街区 …… 130
4. 尖峰岭国家森林公园 …… 132
5. 霸王岭国家森林公园 …… 135

2A 级旅游景区 …… 139
1. 海瑞墓 …… 139
2. 红色娘子军纪念园 …… 140

第三篇　其他旅游景区

1. 三亚千古情 …… 146
2. 亚龙湾国家旅游度假区 …… 159

参考文献 …… 161

Part I Hainan Tourism Information

1. An Overview of Hainan Province …… 164
2. An Overview of Haikou City …… 170
3. An Overview of Sanya City …… 175

Part II A-rated Tourist Attractions

5A-rated Tourist Attractions …… 180
1. Daxiao Dongtian Tourism Zone …… 180
2. Nanshan Cultural Tourism Zone …… 190
3. Yanoda Rainforest Cultural Tourism Zone …… 199
4. Boundary Island Tourist Attraction of Hainan …… 217
5. Binglanggu Hainan Li & Miao Cultural Heritage Park …… 220
6. Wuzhizhou Island …… 240
7. Tianya Haijiao …… 247

4A-rated Tourist Attractions …… 259
1. Xinglong Tropical Botanical Garden …… 259
2. Nanwan Monkey Island …… 261
3. China Leiqiong Global Geopark Haikou Volcanic Cluster …… 264
4. Permanent Venue of the Bo'ao Forum for Asia …… 270
5. West Island …… 274
6. Luhuitou Park …… 278
7. Paddy Field National Park …… 285
8. Shihua Water Cave Geological Park …… 290
9. Dongpo Academy …… 296

10. Mu Rui Shan Revolutionary Base Area Memorial Park ······ 303
11. Coconut Grand View Garden ······ 308
12. Qixianling Hot Springs National Forest Park ······ 312
13. Hainan Wenbifeng Pangu Cultural Tourism Area ······ 319
14. Mission Hills Resort Haikou ······ 323

3A-rated Tourist Attractions ······ 328
1. Wugong Temple ······ 328
2. Phoenix Hill Park ······ 331
3. Historic Qilou Culture Streets ······ 342
4. Jianfengling National Forest Park ······ 345
5. Bawangling National Forest Park ······ 349

2A-rated Tourist Attractions ······ 354
1. Hai Rui Memorial Park ······ 354
2. Red Detachment of Women Memorial Park ······ 355

Part III Other Tourist Attractions

1. Sanya Romance Park ······ 364
2. Yalong Bay National Tourism Resort ······ 381

第一篇

海南旅游之路

1. 海南省简介

海南省位于中国最南端，北以琼州海峡与广东省划界，西隔北部湾与越南相对，东面和南面与菲律宾、马来西亚、文莱、印度尼西亚等隔海相望。海南省的行政区域包括海南岛、西沙群岛、中沙群岛、南沙群岛的岛礁及其海域，是全国面积最大的省。全省陆地（主要包括海南岛和西沙、中沙、南沙群岛）总面积 3.54 万平方千米，海域面积约 200 万平方千米。海岸线总长 1944 千米，有大小港湾 68 个。

截至 2022 年 12 月，海南省行政区划市级 4 个（地级市 4 个）、县级 25 个（市辖区 10 个、县级市 5 个、县 4 个、民族自治县 6 个）、乡级 218 个（街道 22 个、镇 175 个、乡 21 个）。其中地级市包括海口市、三亚市、三沙市、儋州市，县级市包括五指山市、文昌市、琼海市、万宁市、东方市，县包括定安县、屯昌县、澄迈县、临高县，自治县包括白沙黎族自治县、昌江黎族自治县、乐东黎族自治县、陵水黎族自治县、保亭黎族苗族自治县、琼中黎族苗族自治县。

截至 2022 年年末，海南省常住人口 1027.02 万人，比上年年末增加 6.56 万人。常住人口城镇化率为 61.49%，提高了 0.52 个百分点。汉族、黎族、苗族、回族是海南省的世居民族，其余民族是中华人民共和国成立后迁入的干部、职工和移民，分散于全省各地。黎族人民是海南岛上最早的居民。世居的黎、苗、回族，大多数聚居在中部、南部的琼中、保亭、白沙、陵水、昌江、乐东等自治县和三亚市、东方市、五指山市；汉族人口主要聚集在东北部、北部和沿海地区。

海南居民语言种类多，主要使用的方言有 10 种，包括：海南话、黎话、临高话、儋州话、军话、苗话、村话、回辉话、迈话及疍家话。海南话使用最广泛、使用人数最多，全省有 500 多万居民通用，主要分布在海口、文昌、琼海、万宁、定安、屯昌、澄迈等市县的大部分地区和陵水、乐东、东方、昌江、三亚等市县的沿海一带地区。在不同地方，海南话语音和声调有所不同，一般以文昌人的语音为标准口音。

海南省的自然资源丰富。它是全国最大的“热带宝地”，土地总面积

351.87 万公顷，占全国热带土地面积的 42.5%，人均土地约 0.44 公顷。由于光、热、水等条件优越，农田终年可以种植，不少作物年收获 2~3 次。粮食作物是海南种植业中面积最大、分布最广、产值最高的作物，主要有水稻、旱稻、山兰坡稻，其次是番薯、木薯、芋头、玉米、粟、豆等。经济作物主要有甘蔗、麻类、花生、芝麻、茶等。水果种类繁多，主要有菠萝、荔枝、龙眼、香蕉、柑橘、杧果、西瓜、阳桃、菠萝蜜、红毛丹、火龙果等。蔬菜则有 120 多种。同时，这里热带作物资源丰富，其中栽培面积较大、经济价值较高的热带作物主要有橡胶、椰子、槟榔、咖啡、胡椒、油棕、剑麻、香茅、腰果、可可等。海南的植被生长快，植物繁多，是热带雨林、热带季雨林的原生地。海南岛有维管束植物 4600 多种，约占全国总数的 1/7，其中 490 多种为海南所特有。海南陆生脊椎动物有 660 种，其中两栖类 43 种，爬行类 113 种，鸟类 426 种，哺乳类 78 种。在陆生脊椎动物中，23 种为海南特有。世界上罕见的珍贵动物有黑冠长臂猿和坡鹿、水鹿、猕猴、黑熊、云豹等。

海南的海洋水产资源具有海洋渔场广、品种多、生长快和鱼汛期长等特点，是国内发展热带海洋渔业的理想之地。海南岛近海已有记录的鱼类有 800 多种，南海北部大陆架海已有记录的鱼类有 1000 多种，南海诸岛海域已有记录的鱼类有 500 多种。同时，海南岛是理想的天然盐场，在三亚至东方沿海数百里的弧形地带上，许多港湾滩涂都可以晒盐。目前已建有莺歌海、东方、榆亚等大型盐场，其中莺歌海盐场最著名。海南矿产资源种类较多，全省共发现矿产 88 种，经评价有工业储量的矿种 70 种，其中已探明列入矿产资源储量统计的 59 种，产地 487 处。海南矿产资源主要包括石油、天然气、黑色金属、有色金属、贵金属、稀有金属、冶金辅助原料、化工原料、建筑材料、其他非金属矿、地下水、热矿水和饮用天然矿泉水等。

海南旅游资源丰富，极富特色，主要有以下几个方面：

海岸带景观

在海南岛长达 1823 千米的海岸线上，沙岸占 50%~60%，沙滩宽度短则百米，长则千米有余，向海面坡度一般为 5°，缓缓延伸；多数地方风平浪静，海水清澈，沙白如絮，清洁柔软；岸边绿树成荫，空气清新；海水温度一般为 18~30℃，阳光充足明媚，一年中多数时间可进行海浴、日光浴、沙浴和风浴。当今国际旅游者喜爱的阳光、海水、沙滩、绿色、空气这 5 个要素，海南环岛沿岸均兼而有之。自海口至三亚东岸线就有 60 多处可辟为海滨浴场。环岛沿海有不同类型滨海风光特色的景点，在东海岸线上，特殊的热带海涂森林景观——红树林，热带特有的海岸地貌景观——珊瑚礁，均具有较高的观赏价值。目前，当地已在海口东寨港、文昌清澜港等地建立了红树林保护区。

海岛

环海南岛有 100 余个岛屿，主要分布在东部和南部沿海。西沙群岛有岛屿 22 座，陆地面积 8 平方千米，其中永兴岛最大。这些岛屿地处热带，日照长，光能充足，四周海水清澈，水生资源丰富，非常具有旅游价值。已开展旅游项目的岛屿有蜈支洲岛、西岛、分界洲岛、西沙群岛等。

山岳、热带原始森林

海南岛有海拔 1000 米以上的山峰 81 座，绵延起伏，山形奇特，气势雄伟。颇负盛名的有山顶部成锯齿状、形如五指的五指山，气势磅礴的鹦哥岭，奇石叠峰的东山岭，瀑布飞泻的太平山，以及七仙岭、尖峰岭、吊罗山、霸王岭等，均是登山旅游和避暑的胜地。海南的山岳最具特色的是密布热带原始森林，有乐东尖峰岭、昌江霸王岭、陵水吊罗山和琼中五指山 4 个热带原始森林区，其中以乐东尖峰岭最为典型。

珍禽异兽

为了保护物种，利于观赏，海南已建立多个野生动物自然保护区和驯养场，包括昌江霸王岭黑冠长臂猿保护区、东方大田坡鹿自然保护区、万宁大洲岛金丝燕保护区、陵水南湾半岛猕猴保护区、屯昌养鹿场等。

大河、瀑布、水库风光

南渡江、昌化江、万泉河等河流，滩潭相间，蜿蜒有致，河水清澈，是旅游观景的好地方，尤以万泉河风光闻名全国。大山深处的小河或山间小溪密布，瀑布众多，其中太平山瀑布和琼中百花岭瀑布等久负盛名。海南岛上还有不少水库，特别是松涛、南扶、长茅、石碌等水库兼具湖光山色之美，不是湖泊胜似湖泊。

火山、溶洞、温泉

历史上的火山喷发，在海南岛留下了许多死火山口。最为典型的是位于海口的石山，石山有海拔200多米的双岭，岭上有2个火山口，中间连着下凹的山脊，形似马鞍，又名马鞍岭。石山附近的雷虎岭火山口、罗京盘火山口也保存得十分完整。海南还有不少千姿百态的喀斯特溶洞，其中著名的有三亚的落笔洞、保亭的千龙洞、昌江的皇帝洞等。岛上温泉分布广泛，多数温泉矿化度低、温度高、水量大、水质佳，属于治疗性温泉，且温泉所在区域景色宜人。兴隆温泉、官塘温泉、南平温泉、蓝洋温泉等，适于发展融观光、疗养、科研等为一体的旅游。

名胜古迹

海南具有历史意义的古迹主要有为纪念唐宋两代被贬谪来海南岛的李德裕等5位历史名臣而修建的五公祠，北宋大文豪苏东坡居琼遗址——东坡书院以及为纪念苏轼而修建的苏公祠，清代雷琼兵备道焦映汉所修建的琼台书院，明代名臣丘浚墓，明代大清官海瑞墓，相传受汉武帝派遣率兵入海南的将军马援为拯救兵马而下令开凿的汉马伏波井，以及崖州古城、韦氏祠堂、文昌孔庙等。

革命纪念地

海南的革命纪念地有中共琼崖一大旧址、琼崖纵队司令部旧址、红色娘子军纪念园、金牛岭烈士陵园、白沙起义纪念馆、陵水县苏维埃政府旧址等，还有宋庆龄祖居及陈列馆、张云逸大将纪念馆等。

民族风情

海南岛的世居少数民族有黎族、苗族、回族，至今保留着许多质朴敦厚的民风民俗和生活习惯，使海南的社会风貌显得独特而多彩。海南是全国唯一的黎族聚居区，黎族颇具特色的民族文化和风情，有独特的旅游观光价值。

热带作物及田园风光

海南岛上生长着大量的热带作物，极大地丰富了自然景观。游客上岛既可欣赏热带田园风光，增长见识，又可品尝热带水果，一饱口福。

2. 海口概览

海口，别称“椰城”，海南省辖地级市、省会，国家“一带一路”倡议支点城市，海南自由贸易港核心城市。海口地处海南岛北部，东邻文昌市，南接定安县，西连澄迈县，北临琼州海峡与广东省隔海相望。海口东起大致坡镇老村，西至西秀镇拔南村，两端相距 60.6 千米；南起大坡镇五车上村，北至大海，两端相距 62.5 千米。国土面积 2296.82 平方千米，海域面积 791 平方千米。

海口市地处热带，是一座富有海滨自然旖旎风光的南方滨海城市。同时，海南位于低纬度热带北缘，属于热带季风气候，自北宋开埠以来，已有上千年的历史，是海南省政治、经济、科技、文化中心和最大的交通枢纽。海口是一座富有海滨自然旖旎风光的南方滨海城市。1926 年 12 月 9 日，广东省批复设立海口市政厅，“习惯上始称海口市”。1929 年 8 月，改市政厅为市政局。1950 年 4 月 23 日，海口解放。1988 年 4 月 13 日，海南建省办经济特区，海口市成为海南省省会。2002 年，海口、琼山两市合并，海口市的发展翻开了新的一页。

行政区划

海口市辖秀英、龙华、琼山、美兰 4 个区（县级），下设 21 个街道、22 个镇、208 个社区、248 个行政村、3 个农垦居。截至 2021 年年末，全市常住人口 290.8 万人，聚居有汉族、黎族、苗族、回族、满族、瑶族、蒙古族、朝鲜族、土家族、布依族、傣族、侗族、壮族等 49 个民族，其中汉族人口占 98.61%，少数民族人口占 1.39%。海口市通用语言包括海南话、普通话、白话、军话、客家话、闽南话与四川、河南、湖南及其他地方话和各少数民族话等语种。

生态环境

海口生态环境优美，空气污染指数优于国家一级标准。这里气候舒适宜人，生态环境一流，常年位居中华人民共和国生态环境部发布的全国 168 个地级及以上城市空气质量排名榜单之首，城市绿化覆盖率达 43.5%，被世界卫生组织选定为中国第一个“世界健康城市”试点地。

海口拥有“中国魅力城市”“中国最具幸福感城市”“中国最具投资潜力城市”“中国优秀旅游城市”“国家环境保护模范城市”“国家卫生城市”“国家园林城市”“国家历史文化名城”“全国文明城市”“全国双拥模范城市”等荣誉称号，荣获了由住建部颁发的年度“中国人居环境奖”，2018 年还被联合国国际湿地公约组织评定为全球首批“国际湿地城市”。

自然风光

海口市北面临海，海域面积 830 平方千米，海岸线长 131 千米。大部分海底平缓，以软泥为主，泥沙次之；靠近沙滩海岸一带海底以细沙为主。大部分海岸坡度平缓，岸线开阔连绵，沙岸带沙细洁白，有热带海洋世界、假日海滩、白沙门海滩、西秀海滩、粤海铁路通道南站码头海滩、东寨港海滨海滩、桂林洋海滩等海滨风景区和游乐区。港湾与近海还有少许岛礁和潮滩。近海海水清澈，常年风轻浪平，有多处较为适宜的傍岸泳区。这里的蓝天、碧海、阳光、沙滩、椰树构成一幅迷人的滨海风光，让游客流连忘返。

历史遗迹

这里有始建于洪武年间（1368—1398 年）的古代军事遗址——明代海南卫所在地城门楼的府城鼓楼；为纪念明代琼籍名贤王佐而建于 1567 年的西天庙；为纪念为维护祖国统一、促进民族团结的历史名人冼英而始建于 1583 年的冼太夫人庙；为纪念明代琼籍清官海瑞而始建于 1589 年的海瑞墓园；为传播文化、培养海南子弟而始建于1710年的琼台书院；为纪念被贬谪来海南岛、传播文化推动海南文化发展和交流的唐代名臣李德裕和宋代名臣李纲、李光、胡铨、赵鼎而始建于 1889 年的“五公祠”。

这里还有为抵御外侮而于 1891 年建成，与天津大沽口、上海吴淞口、广州虎门炮台并称中国清末四大炮台的秀英炮台等历史古迹；有始建于 1919 年的中共琼崖党、政、军主要领导人冯白驹出生地的冯白驹故居；有 1926 年 6 月召开的中共琼崖第一次代表大会旧址；为纪念中国民主革命先行者孙中山而始建于 1926 年的中山纪念堂；为纪念长期坚持琼岛革命斗争和英勇渡海作战解放海南牺牲的 2 万多名烈士而建于 1951 年的海南革命烈士纪念碑；为纪念第二次国共合作时期琼崖红军改编为抗日独立队而始建于 1952 年的云龙改编旧址；为纪念解放海南渡海作战英雄烈士而建于 1957 年的金牛岭烈士陵园；为纪念土地革命战争时期赴琼指导武装斗争的中共广东省军委书记李硕勋而建于 1986 年的李硕勋烈士纪念亭等革命名胜。

节庆

近年来，各类民俗节庆活动逐渐成为海口市的一大亮点，其吸引了不少爱好者前来观摩或参与，使文化与旅游进一步融合。海口市大型传统民俗活动有正月十五闹元宵灯会和换花节、舞龙、舞狮活动，纪念冼夫人的军坡节等。大型节庆活动有欢乐节、万春会等。

民俗

海口市历经近千年的发展，在不同历史时期文化熏陶和特定社会环境的共同催化下，逐渐形成自身的一些民风习俗。1988 年海南建省办经济特区后，海口市迅速发展，移民日益增多，海口传统文化风俗与外来文化相互渗透并融合，形成以中华民族文化为主，兼容东西方文化，传统文化与现代文化相结合的民风习俗。琼剧为海口市主要地方剧种，椰雕、贝雕是海口市的主要地方传统手工艺品。海口原居民民风淳朴，保留了较多的民间习俗，例如除夕吃围炉，大年初一吃斋。农历正月十五日元宵节，海口人俗称小年，市民集聚府城、万绿园等地，相互送花、换花，传递友情，互祝好运，之后逐渐演变成为元宵换花节。农历二月初九至十二，这里有“闹军坡”、赶庙会的传统，以祭祀南北朝时期南方女英雄冼太夫人冼英，后来传统的祭祀也逐步演变成为每年在龙华区新坡镇主会场举办的海南冼夫人文化节。此外，海口人有喝“老爸茶”（又称大众茶）的习俗，这种花费 20 元左右，冲上一壶茶，配上一些小点心，边饮茶边叙情谊、谈家常、交流信息商情的大众茶在海口市随处可见。

3. 三亚概览

三亚又称“鹿城”，位于海南岛南端，东邻陵水县，西接乐东县，北毗保亭县，南临南海。1984 年 5 月，经国务院批准撤销崖县设立县级三亚市。1987 年，三亚升格为地级市。2014 年 2 月，国务院批复三亚市撤六镇新设四区。2015 年 1 月，三亚市新设立的四个区正式挂牌成立。

行政区划

三亚市全市辖海棠、吉阳、天涯、崖州 4 个行政区，陆地总面积 1921.4 平方千米，海域面积 3226 平方千米，共有居委会 57 个，村委会 92 个，自然村 491 个。海岸线长度 264.42 千米，大小港湾个数 19 个，主要岛屿 66 个。土地总面积 192151 公顷。其中，山地占地面积 64074 公顷，丘陵占地面积 48343 公顷，台地占地面积 34722 公顷，平原占地面积 44936 公顷，其他占地面积 75.71 公顷。2022 年全市年末户籍人口 731090 人，比上年年末增加 20191 人。其中，男性 366967 人，女性 364123 人。按民族分：汉族 457971 人，占总人口的 62.6%；黎族 244640 人，占总人口的 33.5%；回族 11697 人，占总人口的 1.6%；苗族 4370 人，占总人口的 0.6%；壮族 2804 人，占总人口的 0.4%；其他民族 9608 人，占总人口的 1.3%。全市年末常住人口 106.59 万人，其中，城镇人口 76.52 人，乡村人口 30.07 万人，城镇化率为 71.8%。

历史人文

三亚古称崖州，历史悠久，源远流长，人杰地灵。1992 年 10 月及次年 11 月，在三亚境内的落笔洞里，考古学家发现了一万年前的三亚人遗址，是目前已知海南岛最早的人类居住遗址，也是迄今为止我国旧石器文化分布最南的一处遗址，它把海南人类历史提前了二至三千年。早在西汉元封元年（公元前 110 年），三亚因其远离帝京、孤悬海外，自古以来三亚又被称为“天涯海角”，但溯自隋、唐以来 1400 年间，它与中原地区在政治、经济、文化等各个方面的联系从未中断。它曾是隋朝谯国冼太夫人的“汤沐邑”；唐朝大和尚鉴真漂流登岸和传道讲经之地；唐、宋两代曾有 7 位名相、名臣被贬到三亚。中原衣冠人物之南来，客观上在当地起了敷扬教化的作用，留下了诸多历史悠久的人文胜迹，沉淀了三亚灿烂的历史文化基础。据历史考究，延及宋、元、明朝时期，三亚的经济得以初步发展，棉纺业在全国居于领先地位，黄道婆早年向本地黎族妇女学纺织技术的故事就是历史的见证。明朝时期，这里还涌现出了“琼州三星”之一的岭南巨儒钟芳。三亚非物质文化遗产资源丰富且分布广泛。黎族打柴舞和崖城民歌于2006年入选国家级非物质文化遗产保护项目名录，黎族原始制陶等7项目分别于2007年和2009年入选省级非物质文化遗产保护项目名录，钻木取火等11项入选市级非物质文化遗产保护项目名录。

生态环境

三亚2022年全年空气质量达标（AQI ≤ 100）365天，空气质量达标率100%。细颗粒物（$PM_{2.5}$）平均浓度11微克每立方米，可吸入颗粒物（PM_{10}）平均浓度21微克每立方米。全市共有自然保护区7个，其中国家级1个，省级1个。自然保护区总面积12354.74公顷，其中国家级保护区8500公顷，省级保护区1844.60公顷。造林面积133.72公顷，其中，人工造林36.98公顷；更新造林96.74公顷。森林面积13.47万公顷，森林覆盖率70.1%，较上年提高1.2个百分点。曾经荣获“国家级生态示范区”“国家园林城市”“国家卫生城市”“中国人居环境奖”“美丽山水城市”等多项殊荣。

自然风光

三亚地理环境极为独特，是国内唯一一个可以同时领略热带雨林和海洋风光的城市。三亚三面环山，形成怀抱之势，山、海、河三种美景自然融合，众多山头也提供了眺望大海、河湾和城市景观的制高点。这里海水清澈、能见度高，水温适中，全年适合游泳；三亚市区有三亚东、西两条河流穿过，两岸自然生长的红树林绿影婆娑，四季常青，生机盎然，是著名的白鹭栖息之地。美丽的自然风光，优良的生态环境，造就了三亚人居、旅游、度假的美丽天堂。

革命传统

在1927年至1937年的土地革命战争时期，仲田岭作为崖县第一个革命根据地，为建立红色革命武装队伍，加强苏维埃政权建设奠定了坚实的基础。在抗日战争时期，在极其残酷的斗争环境下，根据琼崖特委的指示，中共崖县县委迁到梅山，建立起抗日游击根据地，发动组织人民群众与敌人进行殊死搏斗，成为一座众志成城的坚强战斗堡垒。仲田岭革命烈士纪念碑、梅山革命史馆等都是三亚宝贵的精神财富。

第二篇

A 级旅游景区

5A 级旅游景区

1. 三亚大小洞天旅游区

各位朋友，大家好，我是你们此次游览的导游杨洁，大家可以叫我小杨，为我们开车的师傅姓李，很高兴为大家服务，希望我们的服务能给各位带来温馨和快乐！非常欢迎各位来到我们国家首批 5A 级旅游风景名胜区——大小洞天旅游区！大小洞天依托浓厚的人文景观和优美的自然风光，成为三亚市首家挂牌全域旅游婚纱摄影拍摄基地、三亚首批全域旅游研学旅行实践教育基地。在出发之前请允许我提醒六点：第一，景区岔路较多，游人如织，请跟紧我以防迷路。第二，由于海边岩石光滑，大家在游览过程中禁止攀爬礁石，以防摔倒划伤。第三，景区为生态无烟景区，为了防止森林火灾，请勿吸烟。第四，三亚市目前正在大力开展全国文明旅游城市的工作，所以大家在游览过程中要遵守公共秩序，讲究公共卫生。第五，注意车辆来往，切勿横穿马路，步行请走人行道。第六，禁止下海游泳，采摘珊瑚，保护我们的海洋环境。在此谢谢大家的配合！好的！狮子滚绣球，好戏在后头！

我们现在所在的位置是椰林吧。椰林吧是本景区椰树最多的地方，椰风阵阵，海浪声声，最能体现海南岛的特色。这里是整个景区最大的休闲场所，不仅有凉亭摇椅，更有解渴消暑的椰子（椰子汁及椰肉含有大量蛋白质、果糖、葡萄糖、蔗糖、脂肪、维生素 E、钾、钙、镁等，是老少皆宜的美味佳果）和各种海南当地特色小吃（如清补凉），欢迎大家品尝。

大小洞天景区秉承道家“道法自然，天人合一”的发展理念，在景区开发过程中并未对自然环境进行过多的人为干预，这里的一草一木、一花一石都有其存在的价值。比如，大家现在看到的露兜树，它还有一个名字叫野菠萝。虽然其果实长得像菠萝，却不能食用。很多人认为它是没有价值的树，但仔细观察，其发达的根部能防风护堤、防止水土流失，这就是“天生我材必有用”。

朋友们知道吗？我们海南省有“两最之省”的美称。一是海洋面积最大（海洋面积为 200 多万平方千米），二是陆地面积最小（陆地面积为 3.54 万平方千米）。

朋友们都喜爱这湛蓝的大海，但大家知道多少关于海洋的知识呢？现在我们就先来了解一下大海吧。首先说海水，大家知道海水为什么是蓝色的吗？其实海水是无色透明的，而太阳光是一种复合光，是由红、橙、黄、绿、蓝、靛、紫七种颜色的光组成。当太阳光照射到大海上，红光、橙光这些光波较长的光，能绕过一切阻碍，它们在前进的过程中，不断被海水和海里的生物所吸收。而像蓝光、紫光这些波长较短的光，虽然也有一部分被海水和海藻等吸收，但是大部分光一遇到海水的阻碍就纷纷散射到周围了，或者干脆被反射回来了。我们看到的就是这部分被散射或被反射出来的光。海水越深，被散射和反射的蓝光就越多，我们看到的海水也越蓝。

海洋是生命的摇篮，为生命的诞生与繁衍提供了条件，对人类文明社会的发展进步有着巨大的影响。随着全球生态环境的恶化，海洋环境也面临着严峻的挑战。景区在三亚市人民政府等多家单位和企业的支持下，发起创建了“蓝丝带”海洋保护协会，通过各项公益活动，传递海洋保护理念，宣传海洋保护知识，让保护海洋计划从你我做起。在这里，我向大家倡议：不向海洋乱扔垃圾，不随意采摘珊瑚，让我们一起行动，保护海洋，爱护海洋，呵护我们共同的家园！

右边海面上有一座塔叫领海基点灯塔，从此基点塔向外延伸 12 海里为我国的领海，向外延伸 200 海里为专属经济区（1 海里 =1.852 千米）。领海基点塔不仅有导航的作用，也是我国宣示主权的标志，对于维护我国海洋权益、保护海洋环境、加强海洋管理等具有长远的战略意义和重大的现实意义。

海南岛的海岸主要可以分为：砂质海岸、基岩海岸、植物（红树林）海岸和珊瑚礁海岸四大类型。大家可以看到景区的海岸礁石众多，是典型的基岩海岸，主要为花岗岩风化形成的奇石景观，是海南著名风景区。岸边有一形似龙头的礁石，名曰“龙抬头石”。大家看是不是很像呀。尤其是涨潮时碧波荡漾，犹如龙的身子蜿蜒，龙头在湛蓝的海水中若隐若现。

请大家看这边，我们现在看到的是“鉴真登岸群雕”。大家知道鉴真大师五次东渡日本的事件吗？他第五次东渡即漂到这里。在唐玄宗天宝七年（748年）的六七月间，鉴真大师带着弟子和日本僧人荣睿、普照等十七人，外加水手十八人，从浙江绍兴出发，开始他们的第五次东渡日本，因遇上台风，帆船被毁，并将他们从东海刮到南海。鉴真一行人在海上漂流了整整 14 个日夜，才从崖州湾脱险登陆。唐代时期崖州一带称为临振，当时的临振知事得知大名鼎鼎的鉴真到此，立即命别驾冯某率四百人出城相迎。

鉴真大师登岸后，积极传播中原文化，并且修复大云寺，对海南本土文化的发展作出了巨大的贡献。大小洞天旁边有一港口叫大疍港，那里有一处叫“晒经坡”的地方，正是当年鉴真大师登岸晾晒经书之地。鉴真大师在此休整一年半，随后北上回扬州，于天宝十二年（753 年）第六次东渡日本获得成功。

“鉴真登岸群雕”是由著名雕塑艺术家林毓豪完成的，林毓豪是海南崖县人，其著名作品有《南京雨花台革命烈士纪念碑》《鹿回头》等。1994 年“鉴真登岸群雕”在大小洞天落成后，当地群众乃至国际友人纷纷前来拜谒凭吊。80 岁高龄的日本孝司夫妇前来拜谒并取了一袋土壤、石子带回日本以作纪念。已故中国佛教协会会长赵朴初专程前来凭吊并留下了三句话，即“想不到”“了不起”“功德无量”。

“鉴真登岸群雕”广场对面是由九只可爱的大龟和一只小龟构成的“九九归一”。九只大龟象征着过去的、老去的事物，那只小龟代表着欣欣向荣的新事物，这也预示着万物是周而复始、新旧交替、循环往复的，人的生命也是如此。万物的终点也是新的起点，不必执着于已逝的过去，要对未来抱有希望。

下面我们即将到达的地方是南海龙王别院，别院里面安奉着南海龙王——广利王的原身像。南海龙王源于中国古代对龙的崇拜，在中国的古典文化中，龙既代表阳刚进取精神，又体现出润物广利的品德。中国的龙起源于距今七八千年的新石器时代，是古人对各种动物和气象的变幻的敬畏，是通过模糊的印象集合而成的神物。相传三皇之一的伏羲氏集中了当时人们最喜爱的几种动物最占优势的那部分的特征，创造了马头、鹿角、蛇身、鱼鳞、虎掌、鹰爪等多种动物的综合体——龙，并将龙作为中华民族的族徽。从此，我们被称为龙的传人。

朋友们，我们现在到达的地方就是南海龙王别院广场了。

南海龙王别院由辅殿和正殿构成，内进三门。辅殿大门两侧有对联一副，内容是：

调风雨　欣谷畜　伏波安　澜厚泽　惠民黎

抟坎离　理阴阳　驱邪荡　灾重威　护国土

这副对联赞颂了龙王令人间风调雨顺、国泰民安的功德。别院辅殿正中有一玄珠台，玄珠台形状为二龙戏珠，两条白玉小龙托着一颗黑色的玄珠，此玄珠象征着博大精深的“道”。

随着台阶拾级而上，墙壁上有一“龍”字，是康熙皇帝的御笔。康熙皇帝执政期间，百姓安居乐业，国家强盛。他认为是得到龙王的庇佑，曾 11 次派大臣来此祭拜南海龙王，并不远千里将“龍”字带到此地。

往前走，我们即将看到的就是本景区的核心景点之一——小洞天。很多朋友都问，光有小洞天，那大洞天在哪儿呢？要回答这个问题，首先我们要先知道，什么是“洞天”。

“洞天”为道家术语，在道家文化中是指修道之人居住的名山胜地。洞天非洞，全称为“洞察天下”。它包括十大洞天、三十六小洞天和七十二福地，中国五岳则包括在洞天之内。

从起源角度看，道家洞天福地理论的产生与形成应与史前期及文明初期中国古代先民的山居习性有密切关系。对此，我们只要考虑“石室”“洞窟”在前道家时期和道家产生初期曾经充当过修道之士的基本居留场所就可明白。从宇宙论、存在论的角度看，道家洞天福地理论反映了修道之人观察天、地、人、物的独特视角，其中所隐含的天观、地观、人观、物观都是意味深长、发人深省的。它与我们通常看待存在、非存在、虚无、实体的看法都不相同，乃是以一种环环相套的圈层宇宙构成论为背景来解释天、地、人、物的存在形式。这与道家的根本道论有着内在的一致性。

南宋淳祐丁未年，时任古崖州郡守毛奎崇尚黄老之术，登南山时发现“小洞天”，遂认定这里是“洞天福地”，在洞口题刻“小洞天”三字，从此“洞天”胜迹开始闻名于世。这也是唯一一个直接用“洞天”命名的洞天福地。

据《崖州志》记载，小洞天附近还有一个“大洞天”。原文如下：“石船少南，有亭，匾曰‘大洞天’。亭四楹，大字刻对二。陈继统，港门人。雍正年间，往南山岭采樵，憩牛车山下，步入大洞天，见二叟对弈石上。”

因此，“大洞天”指的就是南山这个大的环境。“小洞天”指修道之人修炼的场所。

沿小道拾级而上，便进入洞天海景区，景区长约 3 千米的海岸线遍布着大大小小的垒石。此类海岸在地质学上属花岗岩滩涂，这里的岩石千奇百怪，鬼斧神工，也是我们景区独具特色的一道风景线。

走到这里，我们可以看到鳌山山海相接、风景奇丽、峰峦叠翠、碧波万顷，就像一幅无比优美的长卷画。据考证，景区共有 99 处石景，面对千奇百怪的石景，大家可以发挥自己的想象力，用心去感受，看看与我们日常生活中的哪些事物相似。

此地山水相融，是仁者、智者都喜欢的宝地。据《崖州县志》记载，毛奎任满离去时，来到小洞天，便不知所终。然而据当地百姓传说，毛奎并非不知所终，而是得道成仙了。毛奎成仙之日，在小洞天顶上飞身而去之时，被僚属们看到了，就一个个奔上去拉住他的脚，希望把他们也一起带到仙境去，但人多手杂，只扯脱了毛奎的一只鞋，落在小洞天背后的海滩化而为石，此石至今尚存，就是我们眼前不远处那块酷似鞋状的巨石，被人们称为“仙人足”。

再往前走，有一“灵应泉”，此处原有一水潭，潭中泉水很特别，涨潮时是咸水，退潮时是淡水，相传鉴真漂流上岸时，就是喝了这里的泉水得以解渴，此潭因年代久远，已经干枯，但此处仍为一历史古迹。“灵应泉”旁，有一状似抱拳的大石，好似对着苍天祈祷一样，我们称之为“祈福石”。

眼前的这个大石头就是著名的石景“鉴真沐海”，大家请看，整个石块就形似鉴真和尚安详地躺在海边，静听涛声，禅心入定。这不由使人想起 1200 多年前鉴真和尚及其弟子颠簸历险，登上宝岛海南的传奇经历。

家有梧桐树，引来金凤凰。此有刺桐树，招来孔雀栖。从“鉴真沐海”往前走有一巨石和一酸豆树组合而成的一组景观，俨然一只孔雀面向东南，凝望大海，不禁让人想起了《孔雀东南飞》中焦仲卿与刘兰芝的凄美爱情故事！而我们这里的孔雀石则是祥瑞之兆，是孔雀留恋此地美景故化而为石。

前面的巨石上有江泽民同志的题词：“碧海连天远，琼崖尽是春。”

放眼远眺，江泽民同志题词的旁边，有一形似仙桃的巨石，涨潮时漂在海中，退潮时又与陆地相连，这便是我们的“仙桃石”。不远处还有一巨岩，其形状酷似一浮在水面的牛头，对着仙桃，若有所思似的。

在仙桃石不远处的岸边，岩群连片，奇形怪状，无奇不有。有一巨石，头圆尾沉，程倾斜状，下面只有三个很小的支点撑着，看上去摇摇晃晃，实际上却纹丝不动，很有特色。这就是海蚀现象，我们称之为叠石。最远处便是风光迷人的“小月湾”，它呈现月牙形向前方延伸，就像一弯新月镶嵌在海天之间，“小月湾”也是海南最后一个“处女海湾”，这里的一草、一木、一石，甚至每一粒沙子都保持着最原始的面貌。这里的水是如此清澈，沙是如此柔软，林木是如此青翠，空气是如此纯净，云朵是如此轻悠……

现在我们所参观的景点是南极仙翁雕像。南极仙翁又叫“寿星”或“老人星”。

寿星老人为一白发老翁，鹤发童颜，面目慈祥，手捧寿桃，是吉祥长寿的象征。寿星的脑门儿突出也与古代养生术所营造的长寿意象紧密相关。比如，仙鹤的头部就高高隆起。因此本景区为了突出南山的长寿文化，在此以天然巨石雕刻出栩栩如生的目前为止最大的南极仙翁雕像，以体现景区的长寿文化。同时，在第五次全国人口普查时，南山一带百岁老人居全国之冠，南山也就有了“长寿之山，福泽之地”的美誉。

在小月湾的半山腰处，有一处由我国著名雕刻家何宝森大师所雕的老子望海，此雕像只显面部，而以山为其身体，体现了道家“大象无形，虚怀若谷”的奥义。面海而远眺，也展示了老子感悟水之要义的情景。

大家往上走不远处可看到一天然石块，长 4.5 米，尾宽 1.9 米，因形状酷似头尖尾宽的木船，所以人们把它称为“石船”。这个“石船”是我们景区最古老的一处石景，开发至今已有 800 多年的历史了，可以说是大小洞天的一个历史见证。相传是知军周康当年在此寻访山水时所得，他认为这是仙人乘坐的航船，是个神物。于是他派专人加以看护，后由于年代久远，隐没山野之中，便消失了几百年。一直到 1992 年，我们在开辟景区的时候根据史料记载细心寻找，终于让它重见天日。

前面这块石碑是慈禧太后御笔的“寿”字碑，是三亚的重点保护文物。其高 2.76 米，宽 1.1 米，厚 0.3 米。“寿”字阴刻于石碑正中，身高 1.45 米，宽 0.68 米。“寿”字顶额正中阴刻了五寸见方的慈禧玺印。“寿”字右边阴刻“光绪二十九年九月二十六日慈禧端佑康颐昭豫庄诚寿恭钦献崇颐皇太后六旬万寿御笔”。其右有一“赐”字，“寿”字下方阴刻碑记全文，“寿”字的左下边阴刻落款曰：“臣王亘。”

旁边巨石称为“石室”，上镌刻的“南山”二字为我国著名佛教协会会长赵朴初所题。南山因多奇石，沿山体分布，错落有致，远看有如集落村舍。当年郡守周康乘船沿近海巡视南山时，远眺山中，恍惚间以为山上住着人家，靠岸拜访时却发现原来是块大石。这块大石后被称为石室，现石壁上刻有“海陵周康其义，与郡僚王霈燃泽之，都邻周丕乘师武，淳熙丙午重九日来观石船，因览山水之奇，可为海邦之胜绝也”。此系周康手笔，字刻于南宋淳熙十三年（1186 年）。这是景区最早的摩崖石刻，是景区的历史里程碑。

再往上走，便进入南山不老松园。不老松又名龙血树，因其茎干肤色灰青，斑驳栉比状如龙鳞，而且又可分泌出鲜红的汁液，故而得其美名。此树原产于非洲西部的加那利群岛，生活在热带森林中，全世界共有 150 多种，我国南方的热带森林中有 5 种。龙血树是常绿乔木，一般高 10~20 米，主干异常粗壮，直径常达 1 米以上。其树上部多分枝，树态呈 Y 形，叶带白色，像锋利的长剑密密地倒插在树枝顶端，开白绿色花，结黄橙色浆果。

景区的优美风光吸引了无数文人墨客到此游览题咏，在不老松园我们可以看到许多名人的摩崖石刻。大家看到的“松”字便是清代著名书法家查士标的字。查士标（1615—1698 年），安徽休宁人，明末秀才，清初著名书画家。他的山水画笔墨疏简，气韵非凡。这个“松”字显示了他雄厚的草书功底，行笔俊逸豪放，让人感觉连绵不断，神韵深邃。

不老松上面的“寿比南山”四个字，相传是苏东坡当年被贬到海南，来此游览时所留下的真迹。大家在此拍照时，可以把“寿比南山”四个字和千年的不老松一块拍下来，正好就可以印证那句古话“寿比南山不老松”，希望大家都可以像“不老松”一样，青春永驻，活力十足。

好的，朋友们，欣赏了一路美景，相信大家对道家文化和民俗龙文化以及寿文化也有了一定的了解，我的讲解到此就圆满结束了，俗话说：“两山不能相遇，两人总能相逢！”我期待能再次见到大家，再次为大家服务！祝各位在新的一年里事事顺心，平平安安，旅途愉快，一路顺风！

2. 南山文化旅游区

各位朋友，大家好！我是大家的讲解员小刘，接下来由我带领大家游览。当你光临南山，自然而然就会想到“福如东海，寿比南山”这一流传千古、家喻户晓的吉言。尽管在我们中国，称为南山的，可谓甚多，但地属中国最南端的三亚南山，是名副其实的福泽之地，长寿之乡。不信，就请随我走进南山文化旅游区去感受一下南山之美、南山之奇吧！

三亚南山文化旅游区位于三亚市西南 20 千米处，于 1998 年 4 月建成并对外开放，目前由“三园一寺一湾一谷一区”七大部分构成，其中三园指的是“如意吉祥园”“慈航普渡园”“南山海上观音文化苑”，一寺是“南山寺”，一湾是“南山湾”，一谷是“长寿谷”，一区是大门景观区。我们现在所在的园区位置即南山佛教文化苑的第一个景点——大门景观区。

大家看到的这块花岗岩巨石，是经过南海风浪千百年洗礼的南山天然巨石，这上面镌刻的“南山佛教文化苑”七个字，是由原中国佛教协会会长赵朴初老先生亲笔题写的，在南山的开发与建设中赵朴初老先生是个举足轻重的人物，南山海上观音与南山寺就是由他亲自选址的。大家来到的是佛教圣地，那么什么是佛教？佛教的中心思想总结就是十二个字：诸恶莫作，众善奉行，自净其意。我们可以这样理解：一件事情是不分大小的，只要是有利于众生的事，我们就要努力去做，有害于众生的事，我们就要避免去做，这个社会环境是复杂的，我们需要自己去净化自己的心灵。所以说佛教是一种劝善的教育。好了，请大家把目光转移到巨石后方屹立着的九盏石灯，名为须弥莲花长命石灯，这是大乘佛教的代表性作品，也是南山的一件佛教艺术精品。它主要由三部分组成，从下往上看，底下的须弥山是佛教世界的中心山，山上有九山八海，山外有山、海外有海，是众天神居住的地方。中间共有33瓣莲花，表示观音普度众生所变现的33种化身。

接下来映入大家眼帘的是一座开阔的门楼，这是景区的大门——不二法门，整个门楼的建筑风格均是模仿我国魏晋南北朝风格的建筑，在古时称作“阙楼”，“阙”有宫阙的意思，在当时属于一种皇室建筑，是皇室贵族登高望远，开阔视野的场所；它在一个建筑群当中属于大门礼仪类建筑，在这里表示欢迎大家光临我们三亚南山文化旅游区的含义。门楼上正面的“不二”和背面的“一实”这四个大字都是我国著名书法家顾廷龙老先生在94岁高龄时专门为此所书。“不二”在佛教当中代表一种很高的悟道境界，在这里呢，就简单地为大家做个介绍。按佛教的理解，不二就是一实的意思。万事万物归根结底都是平等的，没有彼此之间的区别，就称为不二。比如，众生从表面上看有贫富贵贱的差别，然而每个人均有佛性，佛性在佛教中又叫菩提、本性。在儒家叫良心，表示的都是同一个含义。所谓公道自在人心。人人有个灵山塔，人人都有佛性，而佛性又是平等的，没有彼此之间的区别，就称为不二。“不二法门”中，法代表方法，门代表门径。

过了不二法门之后大家看到的便是一个大型园林景观——孔雀开屏，孔雀开屏，喜迎八方来客，不管大家来自哪个地区，有什么宗教信仰，今天能够相聚南山，说明就是有缘人。它展现了中国人，海南人，南山人热情好客的习俗，同时它也是中国园林艺术的体现，其采用的是传统的障景的构景手法，可以给人移步换景的感觉。在我们的右手方有个扇形的漏窗，后面有一棵开满鲜花的三角梅，这是中国园林艺术中的框景，也就是把远处的景物用一个框框起来，让这种美感可以更好地体现。孔雀也有吉祥福气的说法。这只“孔雀”形似中国家居布局中的屏风，有阻邪气进屋和防止福气外流的作用。

海上观音

在中国、日本、韩国，观音可谓家喻户晓的一位佛教人物，在都市，乡村，船上，有人烟的地方都会有人供奉，观音是民间流传最广的佛教人物，走进了所有佛堂庙宇之中，也走进了千家万户，在文学、绘画、音乐、雕塑等艺术领域，无不渗透着观音。观世音菩萨顾名思义就是观照我们人世间痛苦之人发出的声音，观音菩萨其实早就成佛了，正法明如来就是它的法号，因为看出我们众生都生活在痛苦之中，为了让众生得到解脱，观音菩萨倒驾慈航来到我们这个娑婆世界里，帮助释迦牟尼佛推行教化。每年农历的二月十九、六月十九、九月十九，这三天被人们俗称为“观音节”，各寺院道场都会举行观音法会，民众也会相携至寺院礼拜，以感怀菩萨的大慈、大悲。

现在我们大家到达的位置是海上观音景点，海上观音景点由普门经幢、观音赋、禅观桥、弘愿大道、八正道堂、许愿台、观音圣像等组成。

首先映入眼帘的便是广场的大门——普门经幢，它是佛教道场的一种建筑，佛教道场的建筑有寺院、石窟、佛塔、石灯、经幢，在南山园区，除了石窟没有，经幢象征佛的智慧，能降服一切烦恼，在佛教中有驱邪降魔的说法，经幢由多块石刻堆建而成，为八角形。

接下来我们大家迎面看到并排三座桥，这三座石桥是禅观桥，中间的是慧观桥，对应持箧观音，左边是净观桥，对应持莲观音，右边是真观桥，对应持珠观音。栏杆上刻着六字真言，六字真言又叫六字大明咒，大家一路上听到的音乐与看到许多建筑装饰中就有不少是这一句，此咒汉传的读音为“唵嘛呢叭弥吽”，藏传的读音为“唵嘛尼贝美吽”。此咒即观世音菩萨的微妙本心，观音菩萨持此咒而成佛，所以又称正法明如来。

通往拜佛广场的中央大道叫弘愿大道，两边种有很多木棉树，木棉可做枕芯被褥，木棉袈裟也是由此得来，黎族人通常用木棉的棉毛做成黎锦。

沿着大道前行即可看到广场的核心区域——礼佛台和许愿台，此区域是进行观景、礼佛祈愿、拍照等活动的最佳地点。拜佛广场是朝拜观音的最佳地点，面积为6500平方米，可容纳几千人同时拜佛。拜佛广场石阶上的门个瑞兽浮雕，左边从上往下依次刻的是象、牛、麒麟，是佛教、道教、儒教的吉祥代表。象为佛教里的瑞兽，相传佛祖释迦牟尼的母亲摩耶夫人曾梦六牙白象入怀而生佛祖。牛是道教的象征，传言中，牛是太上老君的脚力，老子骑青牛出函谷关，留下了五千余言的《道德经》后，即不知所终。麒麟则蕴含儒教的特色，象征人们祈求安居乐业的生活寓意。右边从上往下依次刻的是龙、凤、狮子，是中国传统民俗文化的吉祥物。狮为“百兽之王”，是力量的象征。龙、凤是中国特有的传统文化图腾，寄予了人们对吉祥福瑞的祈求。

这六个瑞兽表明佛教包容万法，圆融一切。

接下来大家看到的就是海上 108 米观音圣像的全景，南山海上观音圣像造型设计既符合佛教教义，体现了观音无缘之慈和同体之悲的大慈大悲形象，又应信息时代之变，具备当今美学、建筑学、雕塑学、佛像艺术、科学技术的时代特色。

观音像是在 1999 年动工兴建，于 2005 年建成完工。总工期六年时间，总投资 8 亿元人民币。观音像高 108 米，是目前为止世界上最大的一尊露天海上观音圣像，比美国自由女神像还高出 14.4 米。观音像主体材料采用航天材料钛合金，采用钛合金材料是为了增强雕像抗腐蚀、抗风、抗震的能力，因为雕像是修建在海岛当中的，而取“白色”则是为了让圣像与蓝色海水形成对比，增强视觉效果。赵朴初亲自为圣像题写了“南山海上观音”。

观音像在造型设计上采用一体三尊的造型，也是目前世界上最具有创新意义的三面观音，从每一面看均是一尊观音圣像，环绕一周方可看清三尊观音像的全貌。三尊观音像的手势各异，分别为持箧、持莲、持珠。

三尊观音像代表观音菩萨的不同形象，是观音化身和观音法门的综合体现，表现出观音“大慈能予一切众生乐、大悲能拔一切众生苦”的大慈大悲形象。

另外为什么要将观音像的高度定位成 108 米的高度呢？一百零八下的规则与“九”有关，因为在我国古代，认为“九”具有极高、吉祥之意。而“九”的十二倍正是“一百零八”，是把“九”的意境推向极致；“凡撞钟一百零八声以应十二月，二十四节气，七十二候（五天为一候）之数”合为一百零八，其象征一年轮回，天长地久；佛教认为人有一百零八种烦恼，敲一百零八下便能解除忧愁。

南山寺

南山寺，一是依地取名，二是为了纪念鉴真和尚，鉴真和尚所崇属“律宗”，又名“南山宗”，同地名巧合，故称。唐代鉴真和尚为了弘扬佛教文化曾率弟子五次东渡日本，但是五次东渡均以失败告终，第五次因台风原因漂流至南山周边地区，然后在此修建大云寺传法布道一年半之久，于第六次东渡日本终获成功，当时他双目已失明，但是意志坚定，被日本人尊称为“过海大师”和“唐大和尚”。后来鉴真在日本奈良东大寺筑坛传戒，成为日本律宗的初祖，对中日文化的交流做出了极大的贡献。

南山寺主要包括仁王门、兜率内院、金堂、观海平台四大部分。

下面就请大家跟随我步入南山寺的山门殿——仁王门。古时候很多寺庙都是建在深山老林中的，因此寺庙的第一重殿称为山门，同是因为山门一般为三开门，所以也称“三门”。按照佛教的说法，世间众生都生活在痛苦之中，要想摆脱这些痛苦，只有修行佛道才行，也只有入佛门，修行佛道，才能彻底断除一切烦恼，得到最大的解脱，最后实现清净自在，进入最高的境界——涅槃，而在达到这一最高目标的过程之中必须经过三个解脱门才行，寺院建门三座，就象征着这三个解脱门，中间的门叫空解脱门，俗称空门，左门叫无相门，右门叫无作门，但是这里应当说明的是有一些寺庙只有一个门洞，而不是三个，这时候，这个门仍然代表着三个解脱门，所以还是叫作三门。

进了三门殿，大家看到左右两边这两位护法善神，就是密迹金刚和那罗延金刚，因护持佛法，被佛封为仁王，为的是保国泰民安。所以，南山寺的山门殿称为“仁王门”。

在三门殿的两边有很多塑像，这些都是佛教的护法神，佛教称之为“天龙八部”，又称为“龙神八部”“八部众”，是指以天龙为首的八部鬼神。

走出山门殿，我们继续向前走，这是南山寺的第二重殿——兜率内院。兜率是界名、天名，即为兜率天（相当于地方名称），是佛教欲界六重天中的第四重天，其分为内院和外院。外院是众天神的欲乐处，而内院为弥勒菩萨之净土。大家首先看到正中的主尊佛像，就是天冠弥勒了，左右胁侍分别为大妙相菩萨和法苑林菩萨，四周便是四大天王。

大家接下来看看四大天王的形象。四大天王是印度佛教中保护天下的天神，他们住在须弥山的半山腰，各护持一方。东方为持国天王，南方为增长天王，西方为广目天王，北方为多闻天王。这些天王的形象因时代的不同而形态各异，而且持的法器也不一样，近代寺庙天王的形象多是明清时代的形象，塑像高大威猛，而且大多数为坐姿。

走出兜率内院，悬立在两座建筑物之间的是钟楼和转轮藏。而立在我们眼前的便是南山寺正殿——金堂。大家现在看到的金堂里供奉着的这三尊主像，便是代表着空间上的“横三世佛”。中间这尊便是婆娑世界，也就是我们这个现实世界的佛教创始人——释迦牟尼，释迦牟尼是梵语的音译，意译为“能仁”“能儒”“能忍”“能寂”等，即能以仁慈之心怜悯众生，合称为“释迦族的圣人”，这是佛教弟子对佛的尊称，在释迦牟尼背光上有三尊佛像，象征着释迦三圣，中间是释迦牟尼佛，其左胁侍为文殊菩萨，其右胁侍为普贤菩萨。释迦牟尼的两旁立着两大弟子，年长的尊者为大弟子迦叶，号称头陀第一，年轻英俊的尊者为二弟子阿难，号称多闻第一。

左边这尊主像，便是东方净琉璃世界的教主药师佛了，药师佛背光上有三尊佛像，象征着东方三圣教主是药师佛，其左胁侍为日光菩萨，其右胁侍为月光菩萨。药师佛于过去世行菩萨道时曾发下十二大愿，要满足众生一切愿望，拔除众生一切痛苦，使其解脱。大家不妨看他的手印，左手为施无畏印，表示劝慰鼓励众生不要害怕，可以帮助你们解除痛苦。右手托着药钵，用以解除众生苦痛，整尊佛像形象告诉了世人，不要畏惧生死，佛的智慧能帮助众生战胜畏惧生死的烦恼与痛苦。

右边这尊主像就是西方极乐世界教主阿弥陀佛了。阿弥陀佛背光上有三尊佛像，象征着西方三圣教主是阿弥陀佛，左胁侍为观世音菩萨，右胁侍为大势至菩萨。

金堂两旁便是十六尊者了，十六罗汉是中国流传最早的罗汉群。

大家可以自由观赏，请香拜佛。然后我们再到观海平台，去领略南山寺作为中国最南端的寺庙与其他寺庙不同的特色。

下面请随着我到观海平台，领略南山寺依山面海、观潮听涛的胸襟和气势。

转过照壁，眺望眼前南中国海，眺望海上观音，遐想吧，海比天高，海天一色，海阔天空，这不仅是视觉上的享受，也是心灵上的震撼啊！

各位贵宾，今天小刘的讲解就到此结束了，接下来是大家自由活动的时间。在自由活动期间，请保管好您的随身物品并注意安全，欢迎您再次光临，再见！

3. 呀诺达雨林文化旅游区

尊敬的贵宾朋友，今天我们要去游览呀诺达雨林文化旅游区。您知道呀诺达吗？呀诺达原是海南本土方言，是数字一、二、三的意思。它表示此“呀诺达”是海南的，意在弘扬根植在海南岛厚土中的本土文化，以及孕育了本土文化的源远流长、博大精深的中华传统文化。在这里，我们赋予它新的独特的含义：“呀”表示创新，“诺”表示承诺，“达”表示践行。我们将立足实践，履行承诺，通过不断的创新，创造出一个前所未有的绿色主题文化旅游园区，助推海南旅游进入一个全新的境界；“呀诺达”又表示欢迎、您好的意思，祝福大家一生平安、两全其美、三道圆融！下面，我们向每一位来到这里的客人深情地问候一句“呀—诺—达！”就让我们一起期待将来开启的神奇、神秘、神圣的呀诺达雨林之旅吧！

尊敬的贵宾朋友，在您观赏车窗外景色的同时，让我为您介绍一下热带雨林吧。什么是热带雨林呢？在围绕地球赤道的周围，有一条特殊的生物带，虽然这条生物带的陆地面积只占地球的8%左右，但是生物种类却占地球上生物种类的一半以上；这里气候潮湿，终年高温，没有明显的季节变化，与温带和寒带有着很大的区别；它还源源不断地向大气中输送氧气，被称为“地球之肺”，这就是热带雨林。热带雨林主要分布在南美洲的亚马孙河流域、亚洲的东南亚一带和非洲刚果盆地这三大区域。其中，南美洲的雨林面积最大，非洲雨林最小，亚洲的雨林大多在一些大岛屿上。不过，无论是哪里的雨林，虽然动植物的种类会有些不一样，但是它们的内部结构都非常相似。我们知道，三叶虫和初期那些巨型的爬行动物非常古老，但是热带雨林中的森林要比它们更加古老。

中国的热带雨林主要分布在台湾、云南和海南。海南有着我国纬度最低，面积最大的热带雨林，物种非常丰富，已发现各类木本植物4200多种，其中630多种为海南独有。全岛有药用植物2500多种，是我国南药的重要产地之一，被誉为“天然药库”。所以我们说，作为三亚后花园、地处北纬18° 的呀诺达雨林，是真正的热带雨林，也是海南五大雨林精品的浓缩，是最具观赏价值的热带雨林自然博览馆，堪称“中国钻石级雨林”。

来，现在大家来听听这首歌曲（歌词：有一个美丽的地方，人们都把她向往……那里四季常青，那里鸟语花香……它的名字叫香巴拉，传说是神仙居住的地方……），这首歌叫《香巴拉并不遥远》，当您听到这首美妙动听的歌曲时，是不是对“香巴拉”产生了无限的遐思呢？“香巴拉”，也叫“香格里拉”，那里有峡谷、森林、草甸、湖泊、雪山和纯净的空气，是人们追求和向往的地方。呀诺达被誉为海南岛的“热带香巴拉”。那“呀诺达”真的像香巴拉一样美丽吗？当您在这里畅游过之后，一定会有自己的感受。

说到这儿，想必您已经迫不及待地想了解神奇、神秘、神圣的呀诺达雨林了吧，别着急，为了您平安顺利地游览，在这里有几点温馨提示与您分享一下：

（1）珍爱雨林植被，护花爱草，不攀树摘花；

（2）珍爱雨林新鲜空气，不吸烟，不使用明火；

（3）珍爱雨林环境，垃圾随身带走；

（4）珍爱雨林人格，说到做到，做高素质的文明游客。好，相信您做到以上几点一定是没有问题的，非常感谢您的支持与配合！

尊敬的贵宾朋友，下车后请直接前往服务区，不要在停车场停留，谢谢您的配合。

景区 Logo

尊敬的贵宾朋友，现在请您往右手边欣赏石头上面所雕刻的图案，这就是呀诺达 Logo。景区 Logo“Yanoda”以藤、木、鸟、蛇等雨林生物形态作为构图主体，体现其独特的雨林文化；中文“呀诺达”则模拟海南黎锦的工艺特征，映射黎族人载歌曼舞的欢庆生活场景，充满动感与野趣，凸显本土生态人文。标志颜色选取叶绿、天蓝、明黄和朱红四种，分别标志生态、海岛、人文和快乐。标志图案和色彩搭配和谐、明朗欢快，将雨林生态、民俗风情和旅游属性有机巧妙结合；Logo 别出心裁、独树一帜，契合呀诺达雨林的独特魅力和文化内涵，彰显呀诺达昂首阔步迈向世界的创新、承诺和实践的 Yanoda 精神。好，景区 Logo 就为您介绍到这儿，请您继续向前游览。

千年根吊石

尊敬的贵宾朋友，现在我们来到了吉祥台，四周望去，一派山清水秀的景色，顺着吉祥梯拾级而上，最引人注意的就是这棵像巨伞一般的大榕树了，我们来看它，高约 40 米，树龄超过 1000 年，庞大的根系，将中间这块巨石团团抱住吊起。树下长着众多蒲葵和海芋，都被大榕树伸出的强健枝条“揽在怀中”，就这样撑起了一片自己的天空。在历经千年的风雨后，整棵树和巨石几乎融为一体，树根的错综复杂、树干的枝繁叶茂，都堪称大自然生命的奇迹。

这棵树当地人叫它“峒【dòng】主神树”，峒主，是黎族人的山神，在黎族人的眼中，每一片天地，都有山神掌管，一切山川、河流、湖泊、树林、飞禽走兽均由山神统领，自然界是由山神统治的，肆意地闯入山神的领地砍伐和狩猎，都将遭到山神的惩罚。呀诺达之所以生态保持这么完整，与黎族人对山神的敬奉是分不开的。

黎族人认为，山神是由山里最古老、最神奇的那棵大树化身而成。祈愿的时候，他们通过将愿望写在红布上或者刻到木牌上，再扔到神树上来祈祷实现，据说非常灵验。神树下也是青年男女定情的地方，每年的三月三，黎家的姑娘小伙就会成双成对地在神树下祈福、宣誓，并将刻上两人姓名的小木牌扔到神树上挂起来，象征两人的山盟海誓，对爱情的忠贞不渝。好，请您继续向前游览。

雨林射击馆

尊敬的贵宾朋友，一路走来，青山绿树，山涧鸟鸣，参天古树，令人心驰神往。在这洋溢着神秘气息的绿色地带，你是否想起曾经在丛林中野战的敌后游击队，他们秘密又快速地穿梭在这繁密又幽静的山林中，展示出了自己的武装力量。现在，我们已经来到了雨林射击馆，穿过万里长城，走过长征二万五千里的宣传板，一排排的高仿枪械、霰弹枪、高速机枪、狙击枪，当然还有丛林里捕猎不可少的弓箭等映入眼帘，我们似乎又回到当年的战场，现在大家可以亲临战场，感受一下高仿枪炮射击的快感，重温子弹弹出那一刻的震撼!

橡胶林

尊敬的贵宾朋友，这里有一片奇怪的树林，我们叫它“千刀万剐树”，它就是橡胶树，您看到了吗？它属于大乔木植物，原产地在巴西，我国在20世纪初引进并种植成功。

橡胶树从种植到可采集一般需要6年的时间。未开割的胶园要经过5~8年的精心管护，就进入了开割期。那么您知道一般在什么时候割胶吗？割胶工人一般在凌晨4点开始割胶，温度越低，越有利于胶水的流出，胶水的产量才会多，太阳出来后，他们就收工了，可想而知，割胶工作异常辛苦。

天然橡胶是一种世界性的大宗工业原料，也是战略物资，其地位非常重要，因其具有很强的弹性和良好的绝缘性、可塑性、隔水隔气、抗拉和耐磨等特点，应用非常广泛。中国是世界上第二大橡胶消费国，自产的天然橡胶和合成橡胶都不能满足消费的需求，所以我国的公用橡胶大多是从国外进口的。好，请您继续向前游览。

兰花溪

尊敬的贵宾朋友，您现在来到的是雨林中的世外桃源——兰花溪。这里有各种各样的野生兰花，您不妨仔细找一找，兰花小巧玲珑，形态多样，有的呈序状，像一串晶莹的绿珍珠；有的舒展，仿佛飞燕张开的金翅膀。最迷人的一种洁白如玉，一个柄上并开两朵一模一样的花，宛若一对天生丽质的孪生姐妹。您看到了吗？全世界有大约两万种兰花，根据其栖息方式可分为陆生、附生或腐生。而这里常见的兰花有石斛兰、血叶兰、高脚兰等近三十种。

在这里，您还可以看到一些微缩的热带景观：一些叫不出名字的奇花异草、极具特色的茅草屋、长藤下的树桌树椅等。幽静的雨林中，突然出现了这样一片别致的景色，定让您有些惊喜。这里的花、这里的水、这里的桥、这里的树都有些熟悉的感觉，但又有些不太一样，经典的中国传统造园技巧与热带雨林文化如此巧妙地结合，更增添了雨林独有的魅力。好，兰花溪就为您介绍到这儿，请您继续向前游览。

黑桫椤

尊敬的贵宾朋友，我们前方路边有一棵树一米多高，树叶像孔雀尾巴，它叫黑桫椤（suō luó），您看到了吗？它可不是树，而是一种蕨类植物。大约在 1.8 亿年前，桫椤曾经是地球上最繁盛的植物，与恐龙一样，都属于“爬行动物”时代的标志。然而经过漫长的变迁，地球上的桫椤大都死亡，现在世界上只有极少数地方才能看到，它主要生长在山沟的潮湿坡地和溪边阳光充足的地方，被称为“活化石”，已被列为我国一类保护植物之首。尊敬的贵宾朋友，我们今天能在呀诺达看到桫椤是非常不容易的。所以，我们应该重视每一棵树、每一株草的生命，它们为我们创造了和谐的生存空间，我们只有一个家园，失去了将不会再有，保护环境，是我们每一个人的责任！您说对吗？好，请您继续向前游览。

蟒蛇馆

尊敬的贵宾朋友，为了保护野生动物，体现人与自然、动物与人和谐相处，我们专门为景区内的“雨林精灵”建造了一个家。现在请您往右手边看，眼前这椭圆形像个巨蛋一样的就是“雨林精灵”的家了。在“雨林精灵”里面最让人感到恐惧的要数蟒了。谈到蟒，很多朋友就有恐惧感，其实它们并不是大家想象的那样冷酷无情，在这就由我详细地为您介绍一下吧。蟒是最为原始且最大种类的蛇，常栖息在水源丰富，植被茂密的原始森林之中，也有部分生活在沙漠地带。而在中国只在南方特别是海南部分地区有分布，一般生活在热带雨林和亚热带潮湿的森林中。

瞭望台

尊敬的贵宾朋友，呈现在您眼前的这个平台叫瞭望台，这是整个雨林谷中的最佳观景平台，站在这里举目瞭望，可以看到整个雨林谷的景观，远山近树尽收眼底，群山环绕，一水相拥，一棵棵槟榔树笔直挺立，亭台、小桥、流水点缀其中。下雨的时候，站在茅屋下往外看去，整个雨林谷沐浴在雨雾中，形成一幅云在山中，山在云中的独特的热带雨林画卷。

请看这里的地形，整个雨林谷坐东北朝西南，前面视野开阔，远处有青山，还有一片水域，青山绿水，山环水绕，空气清新，气候宜人。风水学上称之为“龙臼”。因此这里是非常适合生活和居住的。香港著名风水大师李居明称呀诺达雨林为“天然富氧聚宝盆”。好，请您继续向前游览。

桐亭

尊敬的贵宾朋友，您还记得唐朝诗人王维的诗歌《相思》吗？“红豆生南国，春来发几枝？愿君多采撷，此物最相思。”在这个亭子的周围就有几棵海南红豆，您看到了吗？红豆也叫相思豆，历来被视为爱情的象征和信物。人们将红豆串成项链、手链等首饰，送给亲朋好友，来表达爱情和友谊。相传，古时候有位男子出征，他的妻子每天站在高山上为他祈祷。有一天，她太思念丈夫，忍不住哭了。但是眼睛里流出来的却不是眼泪，而是一粒粒鲜红的血滴。血滴变成红豆，生根发芽，长成了大树。春去秋来。当她的丈夫回到她身边时，大树上结满了美丽的红豆，人们就把红豆叫作相思豆。海南红豆红得像宝石，有的上面还有一个黑点，就像恋人的相思泪滴。有的是心形的，像恋人们那一颗颗火热的心！玲珑的红豆仿佛在告诉我们，相思是既苦又甜的，而珍惜人与人之间的感情，才是最美的！好，请您继续向前游览。

祈愿风铃

尊敬的贵宾朋友，现在映入我们眼帘的就是祈愿风铃了。中国古人悬挂风铃，实用性高过装饰性，是以风吹玉振的声音，达到警示、静心养性、祈福的目的。现在在家中挂上一串风铃，是利用风铃声的“好韵”，改变环境空间磁场，招来好运，因此风铃象征吉祥，也是家庭中常见的装饰物。风动清凉，听其声能让人心宁气静、神清气爽。游客可把风铃悬挂在呀诺达的幸福天道上，并在风铃上亲手写上一则祈福短文——祈福全家平安、健康；祈福生意兴隆财源广进；祈福事业顺利有贵人相助；祈福儿女学业有成，工作顺利，吉祥如意！

幸福天道

尊敬的贵宾朋友，我们即将抵达幸福天道，它是由景区最长的吊桥构成。在这长长的幸福天道上，有着四道门：第一道叫友情门，结伴而来的朋友们一定要并肩走过友情门，友谊就会天长地久；第二道叫爱情门，我们的恋人们走过这道门时，一定要记得牵手哦，这样相爱的人便能携手共游人间；第三道门叫亲情门，穿过了友谊门，走过了爱情门，所有的感情在这里变成了浓浓的亲情；到最后我们就会抵达最后一道幸福门，在这里，我们所有的朋友都会收到来自黎家人的祝福，黎族人在欢迎客人的时候，会用一种很特别的方式来进行表达，大家可以先猜猜看是什么。而且在您收到祝福的那一刻，还将会有我们的摄影师为您留下最美最动人的一刻，所以大家在经过幸福门的时候一定摆个最美的姿势，露出最幸福的微笑。好，请您继续向前游览。

岔道景观：野生绿萝

尊敬的贵宾朋友，眼前的这片植物您是不是非常的熟悉呢？在您的家里或是办公桌上是不是养着一盆或是几盆呢？对的，这就是绿萝。这里就是呀诺达景区的野生绿萝观赏区。

尊敬的贵宾朋友，您知道绿萝的别称吗？您是不是会惊叹，呀，绿萝也和我们一样有小名的？没错的哦，绿萝又叫黄金葛，是天南星科常绿藤本植物，喜欢湿热，易繁殖。它的缠绕性强，气根发达，可以攀附在其他树木的枝干上，我们看到的很多“空中花园”，这些花园中就有绿萝的影子。

绿萝能净化空气，在家里的厨房、洗手间门角边摆放一盆绿萝，可以有效地吸收空气内的化学物质，也可以吸收新房装修后残留下来的气味，同时它能向空气中散发水分，补充湿度。好，绿萝就说到这，请您慢慢参观。

岔道景观：野牡丹

尊敬的贵宾朋友，您看周围有很多美丽的花朵。其中有几棵野牡丹您可以欣赏一下。野牡丹和牡丹是不一样的，野牡丹属于灌木，因为花朵大，被誉为“野生牡丹花”。如果说牡丹是花中之王，那么野牡丹就应该是野花之王了。这里有两种野牡丹，一种叫毛叶牡丹，另一种叫光叶牡丹。野牡丹是华南地区常见的野生观赏植物。同时，它也是中国常用的草药，可以治疗消化不良、腹泻及痢疾，其叶子还可以用于外伤止血。好，请您慢慢参观。

灵芝保护区

游客朋友，我们都知道“北有人参，南有灵芝”，您现在所在的位置就是野生灵芝保护区。灵芝，素有“仙草”之称，中华传统医学长期以来一直视其为滋补强壮、固本扶正的珍贵中草药。它对于提高机体抵抗力有着巨大作用。它不同于一般药物对某种疾病起治疗作用，也不同于一般营养保健食品只对某一方面营养素的不足进行补充和强化，而是在整体上双向调节人体功能平衡，调动机体内部活力，调节人体新陈代谢功能，提高自身免疫能力，促使全部的内脏或器官功能正常化。换句话说，灵芝虽不能用来治病，却能调节整体平衡，使人不容易生病。目前真正的野生灵芝已经越来越稀少，许多菌种都面临灭绝的危机。虽然国内有不少人工栽培的灵芝，但也只是“得其形而失其实”，药用效果远远不能和野生灵芝相媲美。因为大自然有大自然的规律，灵芝作为天然的产物，天然的环境不是人工可以复制的。好，请您继续向前游览。

碧玉亭

尊敬的贵宾朋友，前方有个亭子，叫碧玉亭，如果您走累了，可以去那儿休息一会。好，现在先来看身边的这一片竹林，在我们的印象中，竹子应该是碧绿的，可您看眼前的竹子却是金黄色的，中间还带有绿色条纹，很少见到吧？这叫黄金间碧玉竹，象征着金玉满堂，福寿安康，在这里也祝愿大家节节高升，财源滚滚。

老茎生花和结果

尊敬的贵宾朋友，通常我们见到的植物都是花朵开在枝条上，果子也是如此。而进入热带雨林后，您是否发现：一簇簇的花开、一串串的果结在粗大的树干上，有的甚至长在树干的基部。这种与众不同的现象，就是“老茎生花和老茎结果”。那为什么花会开在树干上呢？这种现象与热带雨林的环境有关。因为热带雨林的乔木，根据树冠所占据的垂直空间，一般可以分为上、中、下三个层次。层次太多，问题就来了，这些树木都需要昆虫授粉才能结成种子，如果花朵开在密集的枝条上，昆虫就不太容易接近它们了。而将花开在比较开阔的树干或基部，就容易被昆虫发现和光顾，授粉的机会就多些。所以大自然总是在无情地淘汰那些不能适应环境的物种，适者生存才是不变的定律。好，请您慢慢欣赏这些奇妙的景观吧。

野生桄榔林

尊敬的贵宾朋友，现在我们已经进入了桄榔林景观区，桄榔是海南特有的棕榈科树种，树形高大，叶片婆娑优美，是一种观赏性很强的植物。成龄树高 20 多米，树干直径 50 厘米以上，有近百条像羽毛一样的枝叶。桄榔一般在丛林中分散生长，但在这桄榔林区内，有上万株，面积之小，桄榔却如此密集，实属国内外罕见。

尊敬的贵宾朋友，您看树上那一束一束翠绿色的就是桄榔的花柄，一个花柄上有无数串花，每一串上又有数十个花朵紧紧挤在一起，我们如果把花絮戳破，就会有汁液流出，这种汁液经过收集蒸发之后就变成了砂糖，所以人们也叫它砂糖椰子，一株桄榔树每年可以产糖约 20 千克。而这一串串像大葡萄一样的就是桄榔果了，每株育龄桄榔，果实颗粒成千上万，最多一束重达半吨。有的朋友可能要问了，这么漂亮的果实，可以吃吗？告诉大家，鲜果是不能吃的，吃了会让人有头晕、呕吐、醉酒的感觉。但经过煮沸、浸泡等加工，把毒素去除干净后是可以食用的。好，桄榔就介绍到这儿，请您继续向前游览。

相思索桥

尊敬的贵宾朋友，我们现在所到达的就是呀诺达的“情人谷”了。面前这座桥叫“相思索桥”，是由“情缘桥”“情定桥”“情锁桥”三部分组成。接下来我们的情侣、夫妻之间可以手牵着手一起走过，在走过情缘桥时可以回想一下初次相识的那段缘分；走过情定桥时可以想一下他向您表白求婚时的场景；走过情锁桥时一定要紧紧拉住对方的手，并且锁住对方的心。走完相思索桥祝您和您的家人开开心心、快快乐乐、圆圆满满、和和美美，最后也祝愿有情人终成眷属。

好，相思索桥就介绍到这，请您继续向前游览。

根石雨林

尊敬的贵宾朋友，现在我们来到了根石雨林区，这里是一个河床遗址，在山岳形成的时期，由于地壳挤压，海底隆起形成高山，原来的一些河流也被逐渐抬高，形成了这样的河床遗址。这里的森林具有原始森林特征，还有石洞、暗河等景观。由于这里的地质由花岗岩巨石组成，山泉水流入石下深处，明河就转为暗河。在此还能听到暗河轰鸣，可是想要寻找水源却很不容易。这里的主要树种是梧桐、青皮硬杂木和高山榕树，灌木大多是非洲茉莉、藤竹、过江龙、红黄藤、刺藤等。

尊敬的贵宾朋友，一路上我们在雨林中行走，抬头仰望，您是否常常看到，在十几米高的半空，会有一座座郁郁葱葱的“空中花园”呢？“空中花园”也叫“树冠花园”，实际上就是雨林里奇异的寄生和附生现象。热带雨林有丰富多样的乔木，在高温潮湿的环境里，这些乔木一般高达三四十米，最高的有七八十米，这样大的垂直空间，为不同的附生、攀缘植物提供了多样化的落脚地，多姿多彩的“空中花园”就是这样生成的。

那么，您可能会有疑问：悬在半空中那么高，这些植物又是靠什么来维持生命呢？是不是靠吸收它附生的这棵树的养分呢？不是的。附生植物有气生根，什么是气生根呢？植物的根一般都长在地下，从土壤中吸收营养。但是有的根可以生活在空中。这种根有呼吸功能，像一条条绳子，有的紧贴在树干上或枝条上，有的悬挂在空中，能吸收空气中的水分，这就是气生根。除了气生根，附生植物的植株可以贮存较多的水分，有的叶片肥厚，有的覆盖着一层蜡质，可以帮助减少水分的蒸发。同时，有一些树木，如重阳木、榕树等，树皮粗糙，且含有较多的鞣酸，适合附生植物生长，因此，它们总是高朋满座，花枝招展。好，空中花园就说到这儿，请您继续向前游览。

千年灵芝洞

尊敬的贵宾朋友，道路的前方是一个古洞，叫千年灵芝洞。洞里有一棵木化了的千年灵芝，只有在经过的时候才能看到，您一会儿不要错过了哦。洞内不高，请您小心通过，千万不要碰头。在中国，灵芝是吉祥和长寿的象征，常常被运用到绘画、刺绣和建筑中去。中华传统医学中灵芝是滋补强壮、固本扶正的中草药，古人称之为仙草。

尊敬的贵宾朋友，呀诺达雨林里有很多野生灵芝，您在游览的途中会不时地看到，但还是那句话，可以看，可以拍照，但不能触摸，更不能摘走，感谢您的合作。好，请您继续向前游览。

雨林登峰景观区、野生芭蕉林

尊敬的贵宾朋友，在栈道的两侧，遍布着一种大叶子的树木，叫野芭蕉树。在成熟的季节，会有大片金灿灿的野芭蕉。芭蕉是我们远古祖先的食物之一，一直伴随着人类生命的进程。野芭蕉也是猕猴的主要食物，如果有缘的话，我们还会在这里看到猕猴的踪迹呢。在传统文学中，芭蕉经常与秋雨联系在一起，被做入诗画中，代表离别和愁绪。最出名的诗句大概算得上“红了樱桃，绿了芭蕉”。江南丝竹的《雨打芭蕉》曲，表达了凄凉的意境。其实，芭蕉被种在庭院的一角或者窗前墙边，营造出的是一种闲适与清凉。在夜里听听雨打芭蕉，我们的烦恼就会随着风、随着雨飘散而去。好，我们再来看栈道的右侧，有一种叶子像大象耳朵的植物，叫海芋，您看到了吗？它也叫观音芋或者瓣莲。海芋在雨林区比较多见，喜欢阴暗的地方，有的还寄生在粗壮的大树上。海芋作为药材，有解毒、消肿等功效。您看海芋的大叶子，是不是很有趣呢？在雨季，当地人们常常会站到下面躲雨。海芋芭蕉都是巨大的叶子，大叶子有什么好处呢？那就是能捕捉到更多的光线，有利于生长。好，我们继续向前游览。

八榕观景台

尊敬的贵宾朋友，我们已来到了八榕观景台，在这里有八棵巨大的榕树。相传有一年这里刮起了台风，在这八棵榕树中，有一棵三分之二的树根已经被风拔起离开了地面，巨大的树干瞬间砸了下来。就在此时，旁边的一棵榕树用自己的肩膀在狂风中扛住了大树倒下的身躯，直到现在，您还可以在两棵树的交会处，寻找到岁月留下的痕迹。八榕古树形象地演绎了世间真情，我们称这组榕树为友情树。在这里您还可以看到很典型的热带雨林画面，根石相拥，古榕相抱，静坐在这里，您是否已经感受到呀诺达雨林的神秘、神奇、神圣了呢？

藤龙闹海

尊敬的贵宾朋友，虽然各种森林里都有藤本植物，但热带雨林中的藤本植物种类最多，个体最大。植物学家认为，它们是雨林中最顽强的生命，它们占据各层空间，利用一切可能的机会攀爬生长，形成了一道道“古藤缠树”

的雨林奇观，我们看这里一根根、一条条，交叉在一起，盘根错节，密如蛛网，像游龙闹海一般。不远处还有几株巨树，像定海神针般插在这森林中。您是否看过美国电影《人猿泰山》，影片中主人翁泰山就是利用了像绳索一样的古藤，在大树之间和峡谷里飞来飞去。走在这藤龙闹海之中，您是否也有这种身临其境的感觉呢？好，请您继续向前游览。

双亭谷

尊敬的贵宾朋友，我们来看眼前的这两个亭子：一个叫一柱亭，它就像一棵雨林里的野生灵芝；另一个亭子叫封侯亭。您可以在亭子里休息一会儿，我来讲讲原因吧。武侠小说中经常提到一些暗器，上面涂有剧毒，人要是被击中，就会中毒。世界上真有这样的东西吗？确实有，亭子边上有棵树叫箭毒木，也叫“见血封喉”，它的乳白色汁液含有剧毒，当这些毒汁由伤口进入人体时，就会引起肌肉松弛、血液凝固、心脏跳动减缓，最后导致死亡。封侯亭就是根据这棵神奇的植物而得名，同时因为封喉与诸侯的“侯”谐音，故名封侯亭。我在这里祝福各位领导游完景区后加官晋爵、步步高升。好，双亭谷就介绍到这，请您慢慢游览。

船形屋、千年夫妻榕

尊敬的贵宾朋友，我们看一下眼前的这个建筑，像不像一只倒扣的船？它叫“船形屋”，是海南黎族人的传统民居。离船形屋不远处的那棵大榕树，是具有上千年树龄的黄葛榕，其（前方不远处）旁边还有一棵黄葛榕，您看到了吗？它们交相呼应，所以叫“千年夫妻榕”。您看这棵榕树，树根呈八字形，这种根是雨林的一大特色，叫板状根，形状像板墙，又像大鹏展翅，向四周延伸，牢固地支撑着巨大的身躯，象征夫妻间爱情坚贞、不离不弃、相互支撑、百年好合。您是否注意到，在这榕树底下形成一道树门，由于榕树的“榕”与神龙的“龙”谐音，所以叫它“龙门”，穿过这“龙门”，预示着我们在今后的人生道路上将飞黄腾达。好，请您继续向前游览。

观音莲座蕨（绿萝保护区）

尊敬的贵宾朋友，在栈道下方有一棵国家二级保护植物，叫观音莲座蕨，通过说明牌，您应该可以找到，它高约1.5米，属于大型陆生蕨，因为它的根部形状像一个莲花座，所以叫观音莲座蕨。莲座蕨可以入药，有疏风祛瘀、清热解毒、凉血止血、安神补脑的功效。我们人类与蕨类植物有着非常密切的关系，燃烧的煤炭就是由古代蕨类植物，在地下经过漫长的地质变迁形成的。现代蕨类植物也有很高的经济价值，根状茎含有丰富的淀粉，我们叫它蕨粉，营养价值不亚于藕粉，不但可以食用，还可以酿酒；像这种观音莲座蕨的根状茎最重的可达二三十公斤。另外啊，蕨的嫩叶用泔水或者清水浸泡几天，除去有毒成分后，有着特殊的清香，美国的很多高级餐厅，经常用嫩蕨叶做成高级食品。好，观音莲座蕨就说到这儿，请您继续向前游览。

五榕迎宾

尊敬的贵宾朋友，眼前这五棵榕树构成了一个奇特的景观，您看它们根连着根、枝挽着枝，就像一把张开的巨大绿伞，为您的到来挡风遮雨，我们叫它“五榕迎宾”。您仔细看看，能不能分出这些枝干分别是哪棵榕树的？是不是很难分辨呢？其实它们不分彼此，融为了一体，支撑着同一片天空，并搭建起一方小天地，这不就是和谐社会的最佳典范吗？

天蟾桥

尊敬的贵宾朋友，我们看眼前这座桥，是由八只神态各异的蟾蜍雕塑组成，叫“天蟾桥”。蟾蜍是海南黎族的图腾之一，据说走过天蟾桥，考场得意，情场甜蜜，官场有戏，还有做不完的生意。好，请您继续向前游览。

大果安息香

尊敬的贵宾朋友，现在在我们的前方有棵大叶子的树，结着绿色的小果实，叫大果安息香，您找到了吗？这棵树看着不起眼，但它可是国家珍稀濒危植物。在呀诺达有好多棵大果安息香，后面的游览中还可以看到。它可以作开窍药，也可以治疗风湿关节痛，还能提取香料。尊敬的贵宾朋友，在这里，我们见到了很多珍稀濒危植物，其实，大自然的一草一木，无论珍稀与否，都应该受到保护，您觉得呢？好，请您继续向前游览。

槟榔苑

尊敬的贵宾朋友，您听过这首《采槟榔》的民歌吗？这首歌为我们展现了一幅阿哥与阿妹情意切切采摘槟榔的画面。现在我们来到了槟榔苑，这些高大挺拔的树，便是槟榔树。结的果子叫槟榔，槟榔可以入药，是我国四大南药之首，可以驱蛔虫、打积食、止痢疾等，应用十分广泛。

蝴蝶树

尊敬的贵宾朋友，您见过蝴蝶，但见过蝴蝶树吗？这里有一棵非常珍稀的树木，叫蝴蝶树，又名加卜，在呀诺达景区中只有这一棵，您可以通过说明牌去找找看。蝴蝶树喜欢气温高、土壤肥厚的静风湿润环境。它对生长环境的要求相当严格，也就是说，凡是有它在的地方，生态环境一定是绝佳的。因此，呀诺达景区这棵蝴蝶树的存在，说明了这里自然环境一流，是几乎没有受到污染的世外桃源，您在这里可以多做深呼吸，感受一下呀诺达“天然富氧聚宝盆”的魅力。

蝴蝶树的材质非常好，抗压抗拉，在已知的海南用材树种中名列前茅，是名贵的造船和上等的家具材料。其还具有很高的药用价值，可清热利湿，消肿解毒，治传染性肝炎、膀胱炎、咽喉肿痛、湿疹等疾病。可惜的是，由于蝴蝶树本身的分布区狭小，又遭到过度砍伐，目前资源已日渐枯竭。您眼前的这棵树曾差点遭到盗伐，树顶有折断的痕迹也就是这个原因。在此，我倡导您和我一起：爱护花草树木，做绿色生态公民。好，请您继续向前游览。

尊敬的贵宾朋友，从这里到景区大门服务区，大约需要 15 分钟的时间，乘车时请您坐稳扶好，注意安全。呀诺达景区即将开放一个新景点，叫三道谷，那里有着奇特的地质构造和丰富的药材资源。里面的石头，有的像月球表面一样奇幻，有的如人工切割般平整，有的像画板一般多姿多彩。河水清澈见底，碧绿中透着湛蓝，各种奇怪的花朵竞相开放，三道谷完全是一个深藏山中的香巴拉，到时您就可以去探寻这个神秘世界了。

好了，前面就要到达大门服务区了，等车停稳后，请带好您的随身物品，依次下车。很高兴今天能为您服务，下车后请您将导游机退还。本次讲解由呀诺达雨林文化旅游区提供，我们期待您的下次光临，最后再次祝愿您一生平安，两全其美，三道圆融。

4. 分界洲岛旅游区

亲爱的游客朋友们，今天我们将参观的是海南分界洲岛旅游区，它是中国首家（无居民）海岛型国家 5A 级旅游景区，位于海南岛东南海面，坐拥热带原始岛屿特有地貌和稀有的海洋生物资源。该区面积约 0.41 平方千米，海拔最高约为 100 米。距海南岛最近海岸约 1.2 海里，乘船单程只需要 10 分钟左右。岛上年平均气温约 25℃，常年气候宜人，是海南最适宜潜水、观赏海底世界的海岛之一。

分界文化

这座浮在南海上的美丽小岛，因其地理位置，形成了特有的分界文化。分界洲岛与对面的牛岭山脉一起形成了海南南北气候的分界线，经常出现“牛头下雨牛尾晴”的气候景观；在古代，这里也是黎苗聚居区与汉族区域的人文分界线，今天，这里依然是陵水县与万宁市两地的行政分界线。当然，这里不仅仅是气候与行政的分界线，也被人们誉为是调换心情、感悟人生的“心灵分界线”。

海洋文化

这里有在纯自然条件下，规模较大、独具观赏特色的野生海洋动物剧场，您不仅可以观看海豚、海狮的精彩表演，还可以与海豚、海狮以及海龟进行亲密互动，还可观看活体珊瑚与珊瑚标本。该珊瑚区沿着岛屿海岸、依靠礁石而建，占地面积约 2900 平方米。游客在观赏的同时，可以进行一场有意义的海洋科普教育。

南海海捞瓷文化（海捞瓷）区

这里有跨越北宋、元、明、清初等历史年代的多种瓷器，是对海南南海文明的一种梳理与展示，是中国陶瓷文化史与海洋文明史的一个展示窗口。

生态“极潜岛”

潜入海底后您可以看到，除有大量保育良好的活体珊瑚礁群外，还有神秘的古代沉船、七福神像、海底村庄和多彩的海洋生物等。在这里，您不仅可以体验浮潜、堡礁潜水、远海潜水这类大众体验式潜水，还可以报名参加PADI-OW和PADI-AOW等专业潜水培训课程；当然对于持证的潜水达人们，分界洲岛还有更加神秘、更加刺激的自由潜点等待您来探索！

开心“梦幻岛”

你可以变身水上飞龙感受上天入海的刺激，也可以背上拖伞像海鸟那样翱翔，还可以坐上跳跃在浪尖上的香蕉船，抑或体验海上速度与激情的动感飞艇。这里海上娱乐项目多样化，竞技体育、冲关赛道、娱乐体验等元素得以融为一体，使得分界洲岛的旅游产品向休闲体育、运动娱乐等多个方向发展，适合不同年龄层的游客畅享体验。

彩虹“无忧岛”

除了热闹刺激的海上娱乐项目之外，您还可以漫步山间，寻一处凉亭小坐，点上一杯香醇的咖啡，放飞思绪，抑或躺在木屋的阳台。这里有原生态的自然风光，有一望无际的南海。您可以在这里静心梳理思绪，忘却所有的烦恼，自由自在度过一段没有尘嚣打扰的海岛曼妙时光。

浪漫“婚庆岛”

来分界洲岛，与单身分界！分界洲岛是海南省“十大浪漫景区”之一。是三亚、海口及周边市县婚纱摄影机构指定的婚纱拍摄基地。独特的“山、海、岛”等自然元素，以纯粹自然的符号融入浪漫的互动体验，特色的海岛风情微婚礼、浪漫温馨蜜月房，让分界洲成为海南独具特色浪漫型海岛。

舌尖“口福岛”

分界洲岛的美食与这里的景致一样令人回味。海南“陆产千名，海产万类”，这里除了有海南本土的餐饮美食，还有全国各地的风俗小吃，丰富的美味佳肴令游客在游览风光之余，味蕾也可以享受到一次快乐。

5. 海南槟榔谷黎苗文化旅游区

久久不见久久见，久久见过还想见！亲爱的游客朋友们，习近平总书记这样一句问候令海南民歌唱响全国，今天阿弟和阿妹也唱响这首歌热情地欢迎大家来到美丽的槟榔谷参观做客。作为传承海南黎苗文化的景区，槟榔谷一直秉承着挖掘、保护、传承、弘扬海南黎苗文化，并使其生生不息的使命，因而也成了海南民族文化的活化石。

在这块文化大地上，槟榔谷景区从 1998 年开园至今，凭借着浓厚的民族文化和槟榔谷人的不懈努力，成为中国首家民族文化 5A 级旅游景区，也是国家非物质文化遗产生产性保护示范基地，更获得了由国务院授予的全国民族团结进步模范集体称号。我们的大型实景演出《槟榔·古韵》获得国家六部委颁发的国家文化出口重点项目。此外，槟榔谷获得的荣誉还有很多。原住民怀传世艺，槟榔谷存千古情！今天就让我们一起用心去参观和了解这里，好好感受一下这个伟大民族的文化，做一回真正的黎家人，度过一个开心难忘的文化之旅。

出发前，教大家一个打招呼的方式，因为这里有些老人这辈子几乎没有走出过大山，听不懂普通话，所以等下我们见到当地的黎家人怎么打招呼呢？就是竖起右手大拇指，说一声：波隆！波光粼粼的波，生意兴隆的隆！波隆是黎语槟榔的意思，因槟榔是我们黎家人平时交友、婚庆、佳节必不可少的赠品，蕴含着幸福、吉祥、美好之意，竖起大拇指寓意着你好，你很棒，同时表达了祝福对方平安幸福吉祥的美好心愿。大家学会了吗？

景区大门

景区大门高 16.9 米、宽 30 米，是一个以黎族的代表图腾“大力神”和神牛、船形屋三要素构建而成的图腾形象大门。“大力神”是黎族人心目中的万能之神，他庇护和镇守村寨，保佑风调雨顺、五谷丰登。黎族人有自己的信仰和崇拜，主要有自然崇拜、祖先崇拜和图腾崇拜，其中“大力神”就是黎族信仰的最大崇拜。关于“大力神”的故事有很多，到达村子里会为大家详细介绍。而“牛”是苗族人的生死伴侣，苗家人的牛文化广泛蕴藏在建筑、服饰、舞蹈、节日、祭祀活动、饮酒习俗以及乡规民约中，他们认为世上水牛是威力最大的，故常用水牛来辟邪，它也象征着财富和权力，大门的主体构造由大力神、牛、船形屋图腾构成，寓意万能的大力神驾着神牛来到黎族的凡间，庇佑这一方的黎民。大家再注意看大门的底部结构，主要是用石头和木柴组合而成，代表着时来运转和财源广进，祝愿从这里跨过去的朋友们，“石”来运转，“柴”源滚滚。

我们现在看到的是一棵百年仙人掌，会开花、结果，有一百多年的历史。它寓意着仙人下凡，有仙人为我们黎族人指路和撑腰，也象征着我们黎族人坚韧不拔的精神。仙人掌旁边是一块龙船石，这块石头是2015年建设景区新大门时，在这个地方发现的，它没有经过任何人工雕琢，是经过大自然千百年来鬼斧神工的塑造，其远远看去就像一艘船，就好像是我们槟榔谷的宝石船，当年我们黎族祖先就是乘着独木舟来到海南岛，成为海南岛上最早的原住民，所以它也象征着我们黎族祖先的独木舟和生存智慧。

非遗村

我们游览的第一个区域是非物质文化遗产村，这里为游客朋友们展示了黎族几千年来的文化传承，是黎族文化中最绚烂的一部分。目前黎族拥有一项世界级和九项国家级非物质文化遗产保护项目［黎族打柴舞、黎族原始制陶技艺、黎族传统纺染织绣技艺（世界级）、黎族树皮布制作技艺、黎族钻木取火技艺、黎族“三月三”节、黎族竹木器乐、黎族船形屋营造技艺、黎族服饰、黎族民歌］，而且这里还有非常多的省级非物质文化遗产保护项目。

船形屋

居住是人类物质文化的一个重要组成部分。黎族村落的选址位置通常视地形、地势而定——平原村落都建在小山坡上，以防洪水侵袭，居民一般饮井水或河水；山区村落一般建造在山脚下，有利于防台风袭击，居民多饮山泉水。茅草屋以茅草盖顶、以竹木为架，主要有船形屋和金字屋两种样式，以船形屋最具代表性。传统船形屋的营造技艺不仅是原住民智慧的结晶，也体现了原住民浓郁的民族风格。

隆闺

黎族的男子和女子，一般长到十三四岁时就不再跟父母家居住，男子会自己上山备料盖“隆闺”，女子则由父母帮助盖“隆闺”。“隆闺”一般建在父母家旁边或在村边。“隆闺”是一间只有 8~10 平方米的小房子，且“隆闺”有男女之别，是男女青年居住、社交、吹奏乐器和对歌定情的场所。

黎族历史沿革（观景平台处）

早在 3000 多年以前，南方少数民族“百越”的一个叫作“骆越”的分支民族，由于不堪战争的迫害和侵扰，漂洋过海来到当时蛮荒的海南岛，成为岛上最早的居民。黎族现有人口 140 多万人，主要聚居在海南岛的中南部山区。因居住环境、生活习俗、服装服饰以及语言方面的差异，黎族内部又分为“哈、杞、润、赛、美孚”五大方言区。几千年来，勤劳智慧的原住民祖祖辈辈繁衍生息在这片热土上，创造出了丰富多彩、独具本民族特色的物质文化和精神文化，而槟榔谷就是这一灿烂文化的缩影。

五大方言服饰

想要了解一个民族，首先从它的服装、服饰开始，现在展现在大家眼前的是黎族五大方言区的服饰。一个民族的服饰能反映出这个民族的生产生活、宗教信仰、富裕程度等相关情况，首先我们看到不同方言区因为从事的生产生活劳动不一样，为适应自身的生活方式，他们在服饰上也有很大的差异，耕种为主的方言区服饰要更加精细，狩猎为主的方言区服饰要相对粗犷。在整个中华文化发展的过程中，我们的一些习惯也是根据生产劳作而来的。古时候在汉族有很明显的男尊女卑的现象，据统计南北方在这一点上没有太大的区别，这是源于中国社会自古就是一个以农耕为主的社会体制，相比之下，男性在生产劳动创造价值方面，对家庭、社会的贡献更大，慢慢就形成了男性为主的社会关系，再加上数千年的封建统治历史，使得汉族社会中重男轻女的现象较为严重，但是我们黎族在这一点上和汉族是不一样的，黎族社会男女关系非常平等，甚至在情感上，女性在家族中的位置要远远高于男性，这是由黎族的男人和女人在生产生活中的贡献差别决定的，男人负责狩猎或者耕种，女人负责纺染织绣，织锦成衣，另外女性在民族中是生育后代，让家庭人丁兴旺的主要力量，所以在黎族社会关系中，男性对于女性是非常尊重的。今天来到我们黎家，您可以目睹到集纺、染、织、绣四大技艺于一身的龙被，这是在黎族历史上女性创造出的最伟大的艺术宝藏。

黎族传统服饰图案多样、内容丰富、色彩斑斓、精美秀丽。主要是利用海岛棉、麻、木棉、树皮纤维织制缝合而成。黎族传统的四大工艺——纺、染、织、绣技艺是黎族传统服饰形成的重要基础。黎族传统服饰是黎族社会历史经过漫长的发展、演变、积淀而形成的，它根植于黎族的社会生活中，凝聚着黎族人民的智慧，具有鲜明的民族特色、地方特色以及丰富的民族文化内涵，是黎族历史的“活化石”，对于探讨海南黎族的社会发展历史、文化艺术、民俗形态、宗教信仰、生产生活等，具有极其重要的研究价值。中国古代有一个词叫穿金戴银，这是后人在表述时产生了偏差，这个词真正的意思是穿“锦”带银，在古代能身穿锦服的都是有着极高身份的人，所以我们常说锦衣玉食，衣锦还乡。在织锦技术没有普及之前黎民百姓所穿大多为麻衣，只有真正有身份的人才能穿锦衣，但是黎族确实是最早穿锦带银的民族。黎族各方言区的传统服饰，主要的色彩以黑色或深蓝色为其本色调，以七彩颜色作为辅助色，色彩搭配协调、工艺精巧。其中，润方言的服饰最为独特，富有本民族的风格和特点。筒裙短而窄，长度仅 20 厘米，是黎族五大方言筒裙款式最短的，故称为“超短裙”。（五大方言服饰笼统介绍，重点讲解熟悉服饰特点）

文化长廊

文身习俗

黎族文身，历史悠久。自汉代开始，已经有文字记载。在世界的民族族群中是一种罕见的文化现象。

文身，作为一种传统文化，是黎族母系氏族社会的遗存，是母权制的产物，是原始宗教——自然崇拜、祖先崇拜、图腾崇拜的艺术结晶，是黎族历史上凝聚力、号召力、生命力的标志。今天，黎族少数老年妇女身上还保留着文身的历史印痕，这些用血肉彩绘出的斑斓图画，为黎族的历史增添了璀璨的色彩。

黎族的绣面文身是一种古老的习俗，也是一笔极其宝贵且正在逝去的文化，它表现了黎族人对祖先的崇拜和敬畏之心。汉族有句古话叫“不识祖不以为人”，就是说连祖宗都不认了，就不配当人。黎族是中国以人类皮肤作为载体来记录民族符号，并将祖先启示传承下去的民族之一，他们将氏族的符号、崇拜的图腾纹在躯体上，饱含了原住民对生命的祈求、对幸福的祈祷、对灾难的回避以及对美的追求。小阿妹一般在 12 岁左右开始文身，在结婚前一定要完成。文身时，需要先用带有药性的植物颜色在要文的部位画好，再用藤刺在身上并沿着画好的图案敲打，文身完成后通常一辈子都洗不掉。那么黎族女人在以前为什么要文身呢？据说女人若不绣面、文身，死后先祖就不会相认，这是源于血缘氏族的说法。另一方面，又因各个方言部落之间图案花纹各不相同，便诞生了以绣面、文身来方便种族之间辨认，避免近亲结婚，以保障子嗣繁衍。另外，文身对于以前的黎族妇女来说也是一种美，文得越多就越漂亮。后来，由于审美观的改变以及习俗的变化加之文身在一定程度上会影响身体发育，所以这一习俗在中华人民共和国成立后就被废除了，现在年轻的小阿妹都不再文身。待会阿弟（阿妹）会带大家去看我们的文身阿婆，她们是最后一代的“活化石”，再过二三十年，咱们只能在历史和图片中去缅怀这一古老的习俗了。黎族文身作为一种文化现象，体现了族源意识、图腾崇拜和祖先崇拜，我国著名社会学家、民族学家和教育家吴泽霖教授说：“文身是海南岛黎族的‘敦煌壁画’，保存了 3000 多年，至今还能找到它的遗存，实在是一个奇迹。”

饮食习惯

鱼茶

把生肉或生鱼，混炒米粉，加入少许的食盐，用陶罐封存，发酵一个月后打开即食。黎语称“祥”。“祥”是黎家腌制一种味道甜酸可口的酸菜。

黎族人民积累了许多利用野生植物进行保健的经验，饮食疗法甚至成为黎族人民治疗疾病的重要方法。

Biang 酒

在黎族人们的日常生活中，酒是不可或缺的饮料。不管是在重大节日，还是在婚丧嫁娶等活动中，大家都会大摆宴席饮酒。在平常的生活中，若有远方客人到家中做客，主人都会盛情款待客人，其中是少不了饮酒的环节。黎族人不仅热情好客，且有着自己民族的酒文化。

千年黎医、百年苗药

黎族是一个没有文字的民族，传承医药的方法都是通过口传心授，从不向外人透露。一部“口书”就是几代黎医的行医宝库，极为珍贵。在旁人看来，黎医们口述的草药、验方就是无字“天书”！海南岛物华天宝、人杰地灵，蕴含着丰富的热带药用植物资源。黎族是一个非常善于识别和利用天然药用植物的民族，在信仰上有植物崇拜的习俗，所以黎族医生治病疗伤主要是以草药为主，所用药材，大都常见易得，一般是植物的根茎、花叶、果皮等直接用药。

此外，黎医强调人的肉体、言论、情欲和精神都必须有所制约。身体、精神健康的人平常应选择适宜的行、坐、卧等，不要随便佩戴铜钱、红线作护身符。他们认为人都应当尊老爱幼，团结邻居，因为只有行为高尚的人，才能健康、愉快、长寿。

苗族来到海南岛距今已经有400年的历史，在这个发展过程中通过传统岭南苗药与当地热带雨林资源的融合，独树一帜地形成了更具科研价值的海南苗药文化。

阿婆织锦

大家看到的这些阿婆，是掌握黎锦技艺最精湛的一代人。阿婆们就是这样每天身体呈90°，坐在地上靠脚和腰去织，一坐就是一天，一织就是一辈子，到了晚上就会腰酸背痛，所以现在几乎没有小阿妹愿意去学这项技艺了，而这项技艺现在也面临失传。阿婆用的这个工具叫距腰织机，就是由几根竹子和几根木头做的，它是我们中国最古老的纺织工具，但是黎族阿婆却能用它织出一百多种花纹图案，而且不需要看任何图案和样稿，全凭想象力，所以世界上任何一条黎锦都是独一无二的。这一条黎锦，阿婆在农闲的时候要织6~8个月，在农忙的时候要织8~12个月，在织之前要把棉花脱籽捻线，然后染成自己想要的颜色，之后坐在地上织，织好后还要绣花，非常烦琐复杂，它对阿婆身体和技艺的要求特别高，每一幅黎锦都是织锦阿婆一生故事的浓缩，是一个民族文化的传承，黎族人至今还保留着这种艺术形式来推动民族文化的发展，所以我们黎族传统纺染织绣技艺在2009年被联合国教科文组织列为世界级的非物质文化遗产保护项目，现在的黎锦具有很高的历史价值、文化价值、艺术价值、欣赏价值和收藏价值。大家如果觉得阿婆不容易，真心喜欢黎锦，今天可以收藏一条阿婆纯手工织的黎锦，留作纪念。

四大馆讲解

无纺馆

树皮布是人类重大发明之一，它的出现使人类摆脱了赤身裸体的尴尬，得以遮身保暖，成为早期人类文明的见证。它是人类服饰的始祖、活化石。2006 年 5 月，黎族树皮布制作技艺入选第一批国家级非物质文化遗产名录。

麻纺馆

麻纺织工艺是纺织业的里程碑，可以说没有原始的麻纺织工艺就不可能有闻名遐迩的黎锦。黎族先民从山里采集野生的麻作为原料，经过剥麻皮、去外层皮、煮麻皮、晒干、浸泡、捶打、搓麻线等工序，最后制成麻衣。

棉纺馆

黎族是最早种植和使用棉花的少数民族，黎族的纺织历史悠久，可追溯到的有文字历史记载的是春秋和战国时期。黎族很早就懂得利用当地野生的木棉来纺织制作各种服饰，原始的棉花分两种：一种是木本的攀枝木棉，俗称“红木棉”；一种是草本木棉，海南棉，统称中棉。

龙被馆

龙被，是海南黎族传统纺、染、织、绣工艺中的最为璀璨的一朵奇葩，是纺、织、染、绣四大工艺过程中难度最大，文化品位最高，技术最高超的织锦工艺美术品，也是黎族进贡历代封建王朝的珍品之一。

龙被馆内珍藏了几十幅珍贵的龙被作品，其中包含被世界纪录协会评定为“世界最大的黎族龙被”的龙腾祥云、麒麟双凤吉祥图龙被。

黎族纺染织绣技艺

在黎族地区有句谚语，“无黎无贝，无黎无榻”，其中“贝”和“榻”都是黎语，“贝”指的是“棉花”，“榻”指的是“棉布”。这句话的意思是：没有黎族人就没有棉花，没有黎族人就没有棉布。因为黎族是一个只有语言没有文字的民族，其手工技艺传承有着极大的难度，所以黎锦技艺就变得极其宝贵。据史料记载，至少在3000年前的商周时期，黎族妇女就已经懂得利用棉花来纺织棉布，经过千百年的摸索创新，逐渐形成了黎锦纺、染、织、绣四大传统工艺流程。其中“纺”为四大传统工艺流程之首。

黄道婆

黄道婆是宋末元初著名的棉纺织家，由于其传授先进的纺织技术以及推广先进的纺织工具而受到百姓的敬仰。在清代的时候，她被尊为布业的始祖。她一直生活在黎族姐妹中，并跟着黎族人学会了运用制棉工具和织崖州被的方法。黄道婆最突出的贡献在对纺纱技术的改进上，她把纺麻的脚踏车改造为三锭脚踏式纺车，使纺纱效率提高了3倍，这种新式纺车在浙江一带迅速得到推广。据说这种纺车在当时也是世界上最先进的纺织工具。在宋末元初，黄道婆由于封建婚姻的迫害逃至崖州生活了30多年，学习黎族织锦工艺并加以改进和推广，其晚年回到上海老家后将所学的棉纺织工艺传播于长江中下游一带，使得棉纺织业得到迅猛的发展，从而成为我国著名的女纺织家。

雨林苗寨

苗族

海南苗族是海南岛第二大少数民族，大约有8万人口，和黎族一样只有语言没有文字，海南苗语属于汉藏语系苗瑶语族中的瑶语支。全岛苗族语言统一，没有方言差异。海南苗族自称“金门”或“金第门”，“苗”是他称。苗族迁移海南岛始于明嘉靖至万历年间，他们从广西等地作为士兵被朝廷征调到海南，撤防后一些苗族士兵落籍海南，也有一部分因谋生而移居海南岛，至今已有400多年的历史，所以海南岛才有了苗族。

苗族人英勇善战，他们被称为勇士、战士，世世代代生活在大山里，靠狩猎为生。苗族的祖先是蚩尤，是与炎帝、黄帝齐名的部落首领。海南岛的苗族属于黑苗，以黑为美、以胖为美。苗族的药材、蛊术、蜡染、银饰、三色饭都非常有名。

现在是少数民族黎苗一家亲时代，一起在大山里和谐相处，创造了丰富多彩的文化产业。我们即将前往的就是谷银苗家，展示的就是黎苗族同胞一家亲的和谐场景。沿途您将看到谷银苗家的大门，这个大门通体全黑，两只银色的蝴蝶图案分立两侧。蝴蝶被视为苗族的图腾，黑色代表不能忘却苦难，银色代表幸福和美好，银黑搭配体现了苗族人不管生存环境多么恶劣、困苦，他们都要像银色一样百毒不侵，健康幸福。苗族人的祖先蚩尤，是中华三祖之一，传说中蚩尤是一个勇猛善战及制作各种兵器的能手，后人奉其为兵祖和战神。苗族人常年游走在海南中部崇山峻岭上，过着伐林为园，倚种山稻，一年一徙，林茂复归的生活，所以他们非常崇拜牛，以牛作为图腾，祈求带来平安、财富和地位，现在大家看到的就是苗家人的牛魂柱图腾。这一路上一个个挂满银饰的雕塑，就是海南原始的椰雕，在这些雕塑中大家能看到黎苗一家亲的和谐场景，你看他们那挂满银色的挂饰，在清风吹拂下奏响一曲民族大团结的新篇章。另外这里地处北纬 18° ，有含氧量极高的新鲜空气，大家可以尽情地感受这次难忘之旅。

黎族的祭祀习俗

黎族的祭祀习俗，反映了人与自然的关系，“万物有灵”的观念使黎族社会盛行自然崇拜、图腾崇拜和祖先崇拜。

自然崇拜指的是直接对自然实物进行崇拜，其等级最高的是石崇拜，如石祖崇拜、灵石崇拜等。其他还有天、地、风、树和雷公、山、水、火等的崇拜。

图腾崇拜：每个氏族都有自己崇拜的图腾，黎族的图腾有动物图和植物图。动物图腾崇拜主要有龙、鱼、鸟、狗、牛、猫等崇拜。植物图腾崇拜主要有葫芦瓜和竹子等。

说到祖先崇拜，黎族普遍认为祖先鬼最可怕。各家族的祖先鬼是指父氏家族男性正常死亡的远祖和祖先。在黎族村子门前或大榕树下，都有用几块石头筑成的小石屋，这是黎族祭拜的土地庙。庙里设有神位和香炉以及一块被称为“石祖”的石头。黎族把“石祖”当作灵魂的具体化身来祭祀。每当农历七月十四日和春节前后，村民便置酒摆肉，烧香祭拜祖灵，祈求氏族人丁兴旺、平安、健康长寿。

甘什黎村

五大图腾区

前面是黎族人所崇拜的图腾展示区，由于居住环境、生活习俗、服装服饰以及语言上的差异，黎族又分为“哈、杞、润、赛、美孚”五大方言区，其中不同的方言区所崇拜的图腾也是不一样的，在大家左手边的这五大图腾柱的高矮和图案就是根据五大方言区的占地面积、人口的多少及生活习俗制作而成的。比如，在黎族中“哈”方言区的人口最多（占总人口的58%），分布最广，所以它的图腾柱是最高的。而“美孚”方言区的人口最少，仅占总人口的4%，所以其图腾柱相对是最矮的。这一根大大的沉木上刻的这两个字叫作“晚犸”，意思就是很久很久以前的故事，前面这里大家还可以看到很多青蛙的雕塑，青蛙是黎族人崇拜的动物，它能保护庄稼不受害虫的侵害，同时，青蛙还是气象专家，因为“青蛙鸣叫，天可赐雨”。

朋友们，下面我们即将要参观的是黎族图腾艺术馆，在进入艺术馆之前大家请看一下前边这座建筑，它是以竹木为架、泥巴和稻草糊墙、茅草盖顶建造而成的。黎族房屋最大的特点就是冬暖夏凉，另外，大家可以看到这是一幢大楼房，所以在黎家也有“高楼大厦茅草盖”的说法。黎族文化源远流长，博大精深，是中华民族文化宝库中的一朵奇葩，也是全人类宝贵的文化遗产。这里所展示的彩塑艺术作品，描绘的是黎族风土人情、图腾崇拜、民间故事及非物质文化遗产等内容，是由海南民间艺术家陈玉湘女士利用几年的时间对黎族文化进行研究并用新型环保材料制作而成。在这里我将选择具有代表性的作品给大家介绍。

非物质文化遗产陈列馆一

朋友们，接下来我们要参观的是非物质文化遗产陈列馆一。黎族宗教具有浓厚的原始色彩，它主要包括自然崇拜、图腾崇拜、祖先崇拜等。究其原因是在原始社会时期，由于生产力极其低下，人类根本无法解释自然界中发生的事情，由此先民们认为人类社会生活中的所有一切，都是拜自然界的神灵所赐。因此，黎族的原始宗教就是在这样的基础上慢慢形成的，广大黎族群众普遍崇尚“万物有灵”，如“山有山神，石头有石头神，树有树神”，而黎族人崇拜石头，是因为他们认为石头神能促进人的生育，还能保护庄稼不被鸟兽吃掉。

黎族文身馆

黎族妇女的绣面文身是一种古老的传统习俗，也是一笔极其宝贵且正在逝去的文化遗产。他们将氏族的符号、崇拜的图腾纹于躯体上，包含着原住民对生命的祈求、对幸福的盼望、对灾难的回避以及对美的追求。因此，黎族是中国目前唯一的“以人类皮肤作为载体记录氏族符号的民族”，“绣面文身”也被人类学家称为“海南岛黎族的敦煌壁画”。在过去，黎族女子如果不文身的话，会被众人非议和歧视，成年以后也难以出嫁。此外，如果身上没有祖传的氏族标志，其死后将不被祖先认领，成为孤魂野鬼，因此，尽管文身的过程很痛苦，但是其对于黎族人来说是非常神圣的。黎族妇女文身，大多是从 12~16 岁开始，个别人从 8~10 岁开始，几乎都是在结婚前完成。因为社会审美观的发展和改变，使得文身形式发生很大变化，加之文身是个痛苦的过程，同时对妇女的生长发育有一定影响，中华人民共和国成立后严令禁止该项习俗。现在年轻的黎族阿妹都已不再文身了，而拥有文身的阿婆也所剩无几，因此，再过若干年，我们也就只能在历史的长河中去回味这种特有的文化了。

百年谷仓群

防火是茅草屋的关键。在村口有历史悠久的百年谷仓群。谷仓用于储存粮食，一般都建于村口外面。主要是为了防火、防盗。因为黎族民风淳朴，“夜不闭户，路不拾遗”。在这里您可以数一数，咱们村里有多少个谷仓，便可以知道村里有多少户人家了。而峒主的谷仓比普通人家要多些，有 3~5 个，它们分别用来储存水稻、旱稻、玉米等粮食，显示了峒主的财富和地位。谷仓一般分为三种：一是泥巴谷仓，二是竹片谷仓，三是建造材料最好的木板谷仓。木板谷仓坚固结实，防潮性能好，同时也显示了主人的勤劳、富有和地位。

温馨提示：禁止进入百年谷仓群内拍照；不要随意乱丢瓜皮纸屑；不要模仿爬树阿哥爬树，以免受伤；注意茅草屋和其他建筑的防火。

峒主石

位于村口中心的峒主石是这个黎族村寨的标志、同时也是权力的象征，石上的洞一般是自然形成的，大小则表示村落的大小。每逢村里有较大的庆典、祭祀等活动的时候。峒主便会敲响蛙锣，召集村民。如果举行盛大的祭祀活动，“奥雅”就会在峒主石前施作仪式。

石头上有个象形文字，远看就像一个戴头钗的妇女怀里抱个孩子，这就是中国人的汉字“孝”，百善孝为先，黎族人也是非常注重孝道，他们对家中老人也非常尊敬、孝顺，所以到村子里您可以看到很多生活幸福且长寿的老人。

黎族传统竹编工艺

黎族传统编制工艺始于唐代，一直兴盛至今。在古代它是进贡给朝廷的贡品，现已被列入海南非物质文化遗产名录。它的编制材料主要以红藤、白藤为主，其藤制产品如今已发展成了100多个花色品种，主要用以出口美国、意大利、西班牙等十几个国家。竹编是黎族传统的手工艺之一，几乎盛行于黎族民间家家户户。其竹编制品做工细致，造型独特，既实用，又不失为精美的工艺品，在黎族日常生活用品中占据了很重要的地位。

黎族竹木器乐

黎族竹木器乐是祖国民族器乐宝库中的瑰宝，入选第二批国家级非物质文化遗产名录。

鼻箫、口弓、唎咧、口拜、洞勺、哔哒等竹木乐器，有璀璨的民族特色，不但在国内堪称一绝，在国际的乐器上也是罕见的。而竹木器乐曲更为丰富，音乐色彩独具一格，鼻箫声轻委婉，口弓声细缠绵，唎咧音清高亢，口拜声悠扬嘹亮，洞勺声沉宽厚，哔哒声脆致远，配以声美音清的琴弦和声音厚重的独木鼓，演化出一首首美妙的乐曲。

竹木器乐曲蕴含着原生态的音乐特征，曲体结构灵活、自由，旋律顺畅，音调古朴清纯，它融汇了黎族的传统文化、审美意识、民俗风情等诸多元素，为黎族人民所喜闻乐见。

陶艺馆

在日常生产劳作中，黎族男女具有明显的分工，如打猎是男人的工种，并且有讲究，那就是男人的猎枪女人不能触碰（否则难打到猎物），而制陶则是女人的工种，讲究女人制陶，男人不得靠近（否则制作不成功或不耐用）。从母系社会开始原住民就已经掌握了制陶技艺，其制作工艺分为泥片贴筑法和泥条盘筑法，此外，制成陶坯后他们会采用露天烧制的方式，温度在 800℃左右，所以烧出的陶器硬度不高，也没有挂釉。可以说，汉族人制陶讲究美观，而黎族人制陶讲究实用。如今，黎族制陶技艺已被列为国家非物质文化遗产保护项目。

大型原生态黎苗文化实景演出——《槟榔·古韵》

亲爱的游客朋友们，接下来我们即将前往的是大型原生态黎苗文化实景演出《槟榔·古韵》大舞台，在这里您不仅可以欣赏到一台独具特色的原生态黎苗歌舞，还能领略到槟榔谷浓郁的风土人情。《槟榔·古韵》是由海南著名的作曲家莫柯作曲，黎族导演苏和荣执导的一场大型原生态黎苗族歌舞表演，演出的节目有《钻木取火》《织黎锦》《捏》《拜扣帕曼情歌对唱》《捨米》《黎族传统服饰》《打柴舞》。热情好客的黎家阿哥、阿妹已经给大家准备好了美味的文化大餐，相信会给您的心灵带来巨大的震撼以及视觉上的冲击和满足。

波隆人家

波隆人家是国内首家由景区经营的黎苗美食主题餐厅，不仅建筑风格独特、环境优美，还能在此感受到当地的风土人情。波隆人家推崇长寿健康的饮食理念，坚持原生态的绿色餐饮，并拥有五星级的服务团队，堪称黎苗美食的招牌餐厅。

波隆人家里原始神秘的黎族图腾错落有致，柔和的灯光与别具匠心的设计，使波隆人家弥漫在浓厚的文化气息之中。餐厅拥有 5 个风格别样的独立包间和可容纳上千人的大型宴会厅，坐在舒适高雅的环境里，大家可以品尝到精致难忘的菜肴，享受到高品质的个性化服务。为了能让客人获得更好的享受，餐厅还特地设置一条休闲长廊，顾客可以在半山腰吃饭、喝茶，俯瞰山下美景，感受微风拂面。

波隆人家的菜品也非常棒，五指山牛全席、东山羊全席、五脚猪全席等人气招牌全席，在厨师长精湛厨艺的料理下，菜品口味独特、令人回味无穷，除了这些经典的菜肴之外，波隆人家会不定期推出创新菜品，其中的簸箕餐和长桌宴是典型代表作，以不断追求美食的最高境界，旨在打造代表中国黎苗饮食文化的国际新品牌。

意见站

朋友们！整个槟榔谷将参观游览结束，希望您能够为景区留下宝贵的意见和建议。请把您的不满意告诉我们，您的满意就是我们服务的宗旨。

欢送词

亲爱的朋友们，快乐的时光总是短暂的，首先非常感谢大家在槟榔谷游览期间对我的信赖与配合，我们像朋友一样在这梦幻般的地方领略、体会海南原住民文化的奥妙，相信你们和我一样陶醉，也希望你们和我一样开心，在旅程结束之前，让我献上对你们最真诚的祝福，祝愿大家生活美满、工作顺利！也欢迎各位朋友今后再次走进我们美丽的槟榔谷，我也能再次为大家服务，祝大家旅途愉快。

6. 蜈支洲岛旅游区

亲爱的游客朋友们，大家好！欢迎大家来到美丽的蜈支洲岛，我是大家本次的导游，我叫张超，大家可以叫我小张。我们即将要参观的景点是蜈支洲岛。

蜈支洲岛位于中国海南省三亚市的国家海岸——海棠湾，又名情人岛，从上空俯瞰呈天然的心形，宛如绽放在南海之滨的璀璨之星，是国内首座集海上娱乐、特色潜水、高端酒店、美食餐饮与休闲观光于一体的海岛旅游度假胜地。

岛上有 2700 多种原生植物，植被覆盖率高达 90% 以上；海水能见度最高可达 27 米；周边海域珊瑚种类丰富，活珊瑚覆盖率高；该岛位于世界旅游胜地的黄金纬度——神奇的北纬 18°，宜人的热带海洋季风气候，让身心在此诗意地栖居。

蜈支洲岛拥有得天独厚的自然条件，其引进了国际先进的海上娱乐设备，打造一站式全方位的海岛旅游新标杆。其潜水、拖伞、摩托艇、动感飞艇、海天飞舞等系列高端产品将带您上天入海，欣赏缤纷珊瑚与群鱼环绕，纵览海天一色，释放速度与激情，开启一场肾上腺素飙升的海岛之旅！

接下来我们一起分享一下安全注意事项，只有两句，很重要，大家都要仔细听！首先，由于环岛路比较狭窄，所以车辆行驶过程中，请大家抓好扶手，身体的任何部位都不要突出车体，以免和路边的石头“碰撞出爱的火花”。其次，我们景区是无烟景区，请大家不要吸烟。文明旅游你我他，生态环保靠大家！

我们此次环岛行程为 5.7 千米，车上时间约为 30 分钟，下车游玩的时间由大家掌握。普通环岛游环岛一圈，各位请把车票保管好，站点下车不限时间游玩，凭票转车即可。环岛游全程不走回头路，终点站就在起点码头。

礁石游览区

我们现在进入的是封闭式管理的礁林游览区，一路美景，这条路线是不允许游客步行的，只允许我们游览车进来，其原因主要有两个：一是为了您各位的安全着想，因为如果大家都步行进来，肯定会爬上石头拍照或去礁石上抓鱼捕蟹，而这边的石头又是被浪冲刷了成百上千年，特别滑，非常危险；二是为了环保，只要有人进来，这边的自然风景就会遭到相应的破坏。

海陆空全方位讲解

亲爱的游客朋友们，想更好地了解蜈支洲岛的好玩的项目、好看的景点，我们可以从三个方面来深度了解，那就是“海，陆，空”，首先我们来了解一下海里的好玩项目，在我们右手边的就是珊瑚礁潜水区域，它属于国家级珊瑚礁保护区，水下景观非常丰富，可以由我们的专业教练带您下潜到水下 3~8 米的深度，价位是 580 元一位，旁边还有一些其他价位的潜水项目，详情可到游客中心咨询。蜈支洲岛作为一座热带海岛，其岛上人文资源也十分丰富。岛上的游览景点有观海长廊、观鱼平台、观日岩、妈祖庙、金龟探海、情人桥、生命井等，相信这些人文胜迹会让大家拥有更为原始、静谧、浪漫的休闲体验。接下来就要隆重介绍空中好玩的游览项目了，这就是“空中飞人”，空中飞人是在完全没有束缚的情况下体验像超人一样飞起来的感觉，也是一次挑战自我，超越自我的绝佳机会。“空中飞人”利用脚上喷水装置产生的反冲动力，让你可以在水面之上腾空而起。另外配备有手动控制的喷嘴，用于稳定空中飞行姿态。它能让你在水底潜行，并像海豚一般跃出水面，激起层层浪花！还有人说他的动作如钢铁侠一般！通过喷射装置产生的巨大推动力，可以产生 100 马力，并将您的上升高度提升至近 10 米，领略高于一切的海岸新视角！

野菠萝（时来运转）

大家请看左手边这种叶子带刺的植物，我们车上的朋友有没有认识它的呢？这个是菠萝的“大表哥”——野菠萝，它可以入药也可以吃，虽然口感没有菠萝好，但是它全身都是宝！在这里主要介绍三宝：第一宝，它的根清热解毒，可治疗感冒发烧；第二宝，它的叶子是旋转生长的，我们管它叫“时来运转”！用它做的粽子特别（用鼻子嗅）香；第三宝，它的籽可以做成“珍品滴血莲花菩提子”，有“菩提皇后”的美称！滴血莲花有养生保健、防病治病的功效，这也是我们岛上三大神奇植物之一！

跳跳鱼（水中人参）

各位游客朋友，请大家看礁石上黑色的像泥鳅一样的就是跳跳鱼，学名又叫弹涂鱼，大家知道《舌尖上的中国》这个节目吗？第二期的节目内容就是讲跳跳鱼的做法，它的做法多种多样，有清蒸、椒盐、爆辣以及白汤跳跳鱼等，节目一经播出，吸引了很多美食家的关注，也使得跳跳鱼的市场价格一路看涨，有的高档酒店跳跳鱼卖到了一斤 168 元！为什么这么贵呢？因为跳跳鱼有很高的营养价值和食疗功效！其营养成分超过了海参、龙虾等名贵水产品！被誉为“水中人参”，它有舒筋活血、滋阴壮阳的神奇功效，同时对女士来讲，吃跳跳鱼还有美容养颜的作用。

石头蟹

石头蟹在我们这里有非常多，其身体上有跟石头颜色相近的保护色，通常吃石头上的青苔长大，壳多肉少，一般是用来煲汤。在我们岛上目前有三种螃蟹：灵芝蟹、沙滩蟹和石头蟹。灵芝蟹生活在丛林里，全身呈棕红色，具有很高的药用价值，一般很少见；沙滩蟹平常在沙滩里都是晶莹剔透的，像块可爱的水晶，但只要出来晒到太阳立即会变色！

热带雨林（天然氧吧）

我们现在进入的是岛上热带雨林区，在岛上有2000多种植被，其中热带植被就高达1700多种，小岛森林覆盖率超过90%，空气中负氧离子的含量丰富，达到每立方米4000多个，负氧离子被誉为“空气维生素”，可改善心脏功能，有明显的降血压作用，还可以降低血脂和血糖的含量，增加钙的含量，有效防止骨质疏松。

观日岩

各位游客朋友，前面就是观日岩，站在观日岩上凭海临风，登高远眺，辽阔的南海可尽收眼底。这时我们可以用一首诗概括此情此景：万丈光芒染海风，波涛汹涌四时同，雄鹰展翅三千里，日月乾坤一线中！从观日岩看下去有一块大大的奇石，就像一只“巨龟”缓缓爬向大海，阳光洒在“巨龟”身上使其充满了灵性，所以又称“金龟探海”。

龙血树

请大家注意一下右手边这棵树，就是叶子尖尖朝天长的这棵，这就是龙血树，为什么叫龙血树呢？因为它受到损伤时，会流出深红色像血液一样的液体，如同传说中的“龙血”，因此称作“龙血树”。它堪称“植物界的大熊猫”，药用价值极高，有止血化瘀、止痛消肿的功效，也是云南白药里的主要成分。此外，龙血树的树龄越长，枝干就越空。

旺夫石（望夫石）

请大家看一下右手边上方半山腰上那块凸出来面朝山的正方形的奇石，它叫作“旺夫石”，就像一个孕妇，手托着大肚子，望着大海的方向，等待着她的丈夫归来……望夫石的“望”和兴旺发达的“旺”是谐音，所以在这里祝大家：福旺财旺事事旺。

“南海”石（剑劈石）

请大家看左手边有一块特别平整的石壁，上面刻有两个大字——南海，当然，大家也可以念海南，意思是站在海南看南海！那大家刚才也看见那块石壁特别光滑，就像被人用宝剑削过一样平整，所以它也被称为“剑劈石”。

飞来石

请大家抬头往上看一下这块挂在半山腰上的石头，它叫飞来石。我们海岛每年都要经历好几次台风，但是它都纹丝不动，如同一座守护神一样，保佑着这里的平安。地质学家认为，飞来石这一奇观是地质变化过程中形成的，可谓大自然的鬼斧神工。

云海别墅区

在我们左手边上方就是我们岛上的酒店客房区域——云海别墅区，这边的房型有单间和套房，门市价为每晚一千多元到四千多元。

临海木屋

在右手方的这条木廊就是岛上的观海长廊，这里拍照效果非常棒，特别是婚纱照。左上方就是岛上的酒店——临海木屋区。临海木屋一共有 6 套，每套设计都非常豪华，还配有一个淡水游泳池，它的门市价是每套每晚 2000 元左右。

岛主别墅

左边中间那一整套就是我们岛的岛主别墅，两边的是豪华别墅，岛主别墅就相当于酒店的总统套房。它也是对外开放的，每晚房价 18800 元。左右两旁各有两间豪华别墅，每晚房价 5000 元左右。

内环区

我们的外环游览就到此结束了，现在转入内环。内环主要是一些人工景观，像刚才那种壮观的自然风景在这边就没有了。这边也属于中部休闲度假区，有客房和餐厅。

右手方就是私人定制电影取景地，游泳池为淡水，都是免费对外开放。在泳池旁边有一个休闲酒吧，名为“海盗吧”，里面提供各种酒水、饮品、烧烤等。左手边前方是一个动物乐园，里面放养了一些孔雀、和平鸽、珍珠鸡等热带鸟类，还有几只活泼可爱的梅花鹿。右边山坡上星罗棋布地点缀着一些比较大的木屋，那是岛上的海韵木楼，一共有 16 栋，每栋分上下两层，里面采用榻榻米式设计，还配有一个淡水游泳池，每层每晚的门市价是1350元。前方下坡即将到达的是茶馆，茶馆是咱们豪华环岛游套票中盖碗茶的体验休息区域，咱们可以在茶馆中品茶香、听相声，在此处静心休息。另外，还有椰子、瓜子、爆米花等小零食，供各位游客自费尽情享用。好啦，咱们的茶馆到了，豪华环岛游的朋友下车请注意安全，一会儿凭票在此处转车即可。祝大家玩得开心！

大家请看咱们右手边下方这些叶子长得像心形的植物，它的学名叫海芋，北方的朋友管它叫滴水观音，它可以起到净化空气的作用。

右边就是我们岛上的一个夏季码头，大家今天上岛的那个码头是冬季码头，这两个码头就是根据季节、风向、浪的大小和潮汐关系来交替使用。右边这座桥是情人桥，是根据铁索链桥改建而成的，由于铁索链桥摇摇晃晃很不安全，后期为了安全起见我们把它改成了木制的。我们岛上的沙主要以珊瑚沙为主，大家请看，沙滩上的沙是不是特别白、特别细？这些沙子都是由海底珊瑚石上脱落下来的粉末形成的，所以看上去格外洁白细腻。右手边长势较翠绿的树叫草海桐，你们看它根茎比较粗大，可以起到防潮、固沙的作用，它们都是未经人工修剪自然形成盆景状态，而且一年四季都是绿油油的。右手边下方就是岛上唯一的海滨浴场了，其游泳区域仅限于那些浮球围起来的区域。此外，这边都有沙滩椅、太阳伞和泳圈出租，还有儿童乐园、更衣室等。前面就是环岛游终点站码头了，也就意味着我们本次的环岛游就要到此结束了。等会儿各位等车停稳之后再下车，千万不要着急，随身物品请检查好以免遗落在车上，在此希望美丽的蜈支洲能给您留下美好的印象，也期待着您的下次光临！

7. 天涯海角游览区

各位游客朋友们，欢迎来到天涯海角，愿大家好运情缘！

我是景区讲解员小王，今天非常高兴能有机会陪同各位一起欣赏、追寻、感悟这片充满中华情感、能给大家带来好运的神奇土地——天涯海角，希望我的讲解能给各位的天涯之旅带来美好享受，留下一段美好的回忆。

提起天涯海角，相信大家早已慕名已久，成语“天涯海角”源自中国历史上南北朝时期南朝的最后一个朝代陈朝梁武帝左仆射（相当于丞相）徐陵所作的《武皇帝作相时与岭南酋豪书》中的“天涯藐藐，地角悠悠，言面无由，但以情企”。三亚古称“崖州”，崖就是“地之角”的意思，而这里以南就是大家向往已久的天涯了。

现在我们的旅程正式开始，让我们一起揭开天涯海角神秘的面纱。在游览的过程中，大家如果有任何需要，可以随时找我，我将竭尽全力为大家提供最优质的服务。

在景区游客中心和五星级厕所里都提供了存包服务，如果有需要，大家可以把除贵重物品外的行李存放到那里，然后跟我一起轻松游天涯。

三亚是热带滨海城市，阳光和这里的人一样热情。在游玩的过程中，请大家做好防晒措施。另外，景区海边的礁石很多，礁石经过海水的长年冲刷，生长着各种贝壳，十分锋利，为了大家的安全考虑，请大家不要攀爬礁石。

天涯文化渊源

谁能够告诉我，大家是从哪里了解到天涯海角的呢？（内导与游客的互动，成语、自古流传的诗句、《请到天涯海角来》歌曲、媒体的宣传等）

大家了解天涯海角的方式不尽相同，那么，大家心目中的天涯海角又是怎样的呢？也许每个人一直追寻着心中的“天涯情结”，今天，我们有缘相聚在这里。现在，让我们走一走天涯路，感受这片土地的神奇。

天涯海角有着丰富而深厚的历史文化内涵和情感：这里有着“海内存知己，天涯若比邻”（唐代诗人王勃）的友情；这里有着“海上生明月，天涯共此时”（唐朝宰相张九龄）的亲情；这里有着“陪你到天涯海角，爱你到地老天荒，海枯石烂不变心”的永恒爱情；这里有着“同是天涯沦落人，相逢何必曾相识”（唐代诗人白居易）的漂泊兴叹；这里更有着“请到天涯海角来，这里四季春常在”的发自我们内心的热情邀请。千百年来，文人墨客的强烈情感，人们心中寄托的追思等，如此强烈、丰富的“天涯情结”，如此深远的文化渊源，让天涯海角游览区从一个边陲海滩，成为“天涯情结”的窗口和载体，如果说中国的万里长城是用砖头堆砌的，天涯海角则是用情感积淀的，被誉为中华民族“用情感堆砌的长城”。所以第四套人民币1元纸币的背面是万里长城，而2元纸币的背面是天涯海角的南天一柱。

好运天涯景观大道

这条道路叫“好运天涯景观大道”，面向大海，宽敞平坦，犹如大家今后一帆风顺的爱情和事业。正如之前所说，每个人心目中都有各自的“天涯情结”。随着时空变换，畅游今天的天涯海角已经是时尚的旅行，是幸福好运的象征，是释放心境情怀的好去处，更是好运情缘和表达浪漫爱情的圣地。往前方看，那里碧海蓝天，风景如画，预示着我们的人生充满美好愿景！

天涯海角火车站标

大家往左侧看，可以看到一块写有“桶井—马岭”的火车路牌，这里曾是中华人民共和国成立后改建的标轨铁路的乘降所，之前的窄轨铁路曾是日本侵略海南岛时遗留下来的。抗日战争时期，日本人在石碌（今昌江市）大量盗采富铁矿，利用这条铁路运输线从海南岛西部的昌江运至南部的三亚港后，利用轮船运回日本来冶炼钢铁，制造枪炮。这条铁路是日本占我河山、窃我资源的铁证。抗日战争胜利后，这条铁路成为海南岛南部唯一一条主要运输干线，为海南岛的建设立下了不可磨灭的功劳，至今已有近百年的历史。

天涯海角广场

我们现在所处的广场是天涯海角广场。广场左右两侧分别镇守着两位骑着骏马、神态威猛、手执金戈、傲立南海的将军，他们的背后还立着象征凯旋门的菱形记功铜柱。左为路博德，右为马援，他们都是汉朝著名的伏波将军。

路博德，西汉西河平周人，汉武帝元封元年（公元前110年）南越王叛乱，汉武帝授命路博德为伏波将军，领军平定南越王叛乱，南越人慑于其威名皆降，大获全胜。越地平定后，在岭南设置九郡。其中珠崖、儋耳两郡就在海南岛上，这是海南有文字记载的最早行政建制，海南自此正式纳入中国版图。后人建有伏波庙以示纪念。

马援雕像

马援，东汉扶风茂陵人，东汉著名的军事家。汉光武帝建武十七年（公元41年），交趾（今越南）征侧，征贰两姐妹因不满当地太守的暴政，反叛自立为王。光武帝任命马援为伏波将军，南征交趾（今越南），并铸立铜柱作为汉朝最南边界。其“老当益壮”“马革裹尸”的气概得到后人的崇敬。马伏波在海南留有许多历史遗址，其中儋州白马井相传就是因他的白马踢沙涌出泉水而闻名于世。海南历代建有伏波将军庙以示纪念。

两位将军都是稳定祖国南疆，开发海南岛的有功之臣。在他们身后的柱子顶上的动物就是中国《易经》中“南朱雀，北玄武，左青龙，右白虎”中的南朱雀，它代表了南方的守护神，和两位将军一起镇守我国的南大门，取稳定南疆，保护国土之意。

日月石

大家往前方的海面上看，在海天一色的海面上有两块交叉矗立的巨石，分别刻着“日”“月”两个字，它是原《人民日报》总编范敬宜所题写的，两石构成“心”形，相依相偎。围绕着这两块石头有很多美丽动人的爱情故事，所以也叫“爱情石”。1986年版的电视剧《西游记》中，孙悟空从石头缝里蹦出来的场景，就是在这儿取景拍摄的。

天涯海角星

请大家回头看，广场正中央的这尊雕塑叫作“天涯海角星”。1997年6月3日夜晚，国家天文台河北兴隆观测基地的天文学家们发现了一颗小行星，临时编号为1997LK。2002年7月14日，国际小行星中心正式授予永久正式编号第9668号。2006年11月，经国际天文学联合会小天体命名委员会批准，国家天文台将这颗国际永久编号为第9668号的小行星正式命名为“天涯海角星”。2008年在此树立了“天涯海角星”纪念雕塑。创作者是厦门大学教授蒋志强。雕塑运用古代天文仪器——浑仪、赤道经纬仪的形象特征，融入天文学元素，在它周围的24只蟾蜍代表中国民间的24个节气。

2008年11月6日，北京奥运会体操全能冠军杨威与杨云在这里举行了轰动全国、举世瞩目的浪漫婚礼。在广场的左右侧，矗立着两块石刻，左侧刻着“爱”字，右侧是杨威、杨云的爱情宣言“情定天涯海角，相爱白头到老”。这些爱情石刻围绕着广场中央的天涯海角星，与海面上的心形“爱情石”遥相呼应，是“情定天涯，白头到老”之意，也是“海上生明月，天涯共此时”之意。

每年一度的天涯海角国际婚礼节，吸引了无数有情人。为了一个崭新生活的开始，为了一个让爱永恒的承诺，为了一个永不变心的约定，他们携手相伴，来到美丽的天涯海角——中国最浪漫的地方举行婚礼，共同演绎着情定天涯海角，相爱白头到老的动人爱情故事。每年12月12日的天涯海角国际婚庆节，吸引了大批中外情侣、夫妻参加，从1996年至今已经成功举办了很多届。

在天涯海角广场也曾经举办过许多大型活动，比如，天涯海角中秋欢乐节、海南岛欢乐节闭幕式、首届世界太极拳健康大会，还有在国际上非常有影响力的第53届世界小姐总决赛和新丝路模特大赛，以及2008年北京奥运会火炬传递天涯海角站、2008年5月4日境内奥运火炬首传站《凤舞天涯》庆典晚会活动等。

“三亚人”浮雕

眼前这块人造浮雕表现的是11000多年前，“三亚人”渔猎、采集、农桑、宗教的原始生活场景。1992年和1993年，考古专家们在三亚落笔洞经过两次挖掘，发现了人类活动遗迹，这是迄今为止我国旧石器文化分布最南的一处遗址。中国科学院将这些三亚地区最早的先民命名为“三亚人”。为纪念“三亚人”这一重大考古发现，艺术家以“三亚人”为题，创作了这块浮雕。

天涯海角石景

天涯海角游览区有2千米长的海岸线，岸线较为平直，沿岸巨石叠累，沙白滩阔。这些巨石岩礁是在1亿多年前的地壳运动时形成的，与海南岛的生成大致在同一时期。景区依山傍海，这边下马岭山脉的余脉伸入海中，其花岗岩山体剥露后，受海浪、阳光、风力等外力侵蚀，加上本身垂直节理发育，迸裂散落成百余块巨岩散布于沙滩上，形态各异、巍峨壮观，石上有大大小小的凹坑，是典型的海蚀现象。大自然的鬼斧神工，让我们叹为观止，给予了我们丰富的想象空间。

热带雨林奇观

大家肯定对海南的阳光深有感触吧，从太阳的炙烤进入树荫马上就会感觉到凉爽舒适。我们现在所处的凉爽之地是热带雨林生态区。这是景区在野生热带植被的基础上，进行植物修整和移植营建而成的。通过修建人造溪流，营造了湿度和温度适中的小气候环境。成为海南热带雨林景观的小小缩影。其中，特别吊植了热带雨林中的特有寄生植物“鸟巢蕨”，更添热带雨林景观特色。古木参天，藤萝交织，小桥潺流，令人心旷神怡，乐而忘返。这条溪流取名“海纳百川”，热带雨林尽头还建有“平安桥”，预祝大家一路平平安安。沿路而下，阵阵清凉。沿途的景致或明或暗，曲径通幽，在这里观石、赏花、听溪，你能触摸最原始的野趣，呼吸最清新的空气，穿过雨林栈道，释放最真实的情感，体会“海角逢春，天涯为客”的美好意境。（另有龙须藤、龟背竹等植物，在经过时可以介绍一下）

滨海摩崖石刻群

看！这片海岸，沙软潮平，二百米开外的那几块巨石就是有名的南天一柱了，大家有没有熟悉的感觉，这里的景观就是第四套人民币两元背面的图案。远处的那块黑沉沉的大石头就是大家期待的“天涯”，“海角”在它的右后方，让我们脱下鞋子，踩着沙滩、海水向天涯海角进发吧！

这种海岸的术语叫“砂岩交替型海岸”，大家是不是有点奇怪这些花岗岩大石头怎么都圆滚滚的，那是因为它们存在这里亿万年，在阳光的暴晒、风雨的侵蚀和海浪的拍打冲击下，经过热胀冷缩的物理作用，一层层剥落，最后就形成了这种花岗岩石景观。不过亿万年间它们并不寂寞，有海浪给他们伴奏，还有植物陪伴它们，大家看到那里没有，一棵榕树竟然从石头当中长出来，让我们叹服它的顽强生命力。这也是我们海南人民乃至中国人民的象征：不管环境多么恶劣，只要有一线生机和空间，我们就能顽强地生存并发展。

海判南天石刻

首先我们看到的是“海判南天”，说到海判南天石刻，大家知道天涯海角游览区最早的摩崖石刻是哪一块吗？不是天涯石，不是海角石，也不是南天一柱石，就是我们面前的这块巨石“海判南天”石。海判南天石前面这块像屋顶的石头，大家仔细看看，它的棱角非常分明、光滑平整，有人工雕琢的痕迹，跟景区里的其他石头的自然天成不一样。

其实最早的天涯海角并不在这里，宋元时期，在当时属于广东管辖的钦州有“天涯亭”，合浦廉州有“海角亭”，那时古人认为中国的南海与中国的南天相对应，这个南天就是指太阳的行区，或者说就是北回归线以南。

清朝的康熙皇帝按照孔子儒经《尚书》重新划定了南天的界限，据考证发现，“海判南天”题刻是在清代康熙年间进行的中国历史上第一次全国《皇舆全览图》地图测绘活动中留下的测量纬度的标志。康熙五十三年（1714 年），康熙皇帝指派清朝大臣苗受、绰尔代以及法国路易十四皇帝的使者耶稣会士汤尚贤三位钦差于此主持测绘并剖石刻写“海判南天”四个大字。“海”指的是中国南海，“判”是划分的意思，“海判南天”就是把中国南海划分为南海和南天的意思，大家知道中国被称为赤县神州，而“海判南天”的意思正是中国版图的天地分界线，南为赤县，北为神州。

“天涯”指的是这里以南的南天，每年冬至正午 12 点时太阳就会与这半躺的石面重合。大家是否油然而生了天苍苍，海茫茫，任沧桑岁月变迁，我自岿然不动的感觉呢？这一石刻就是我们景区最早的石刻，至今已有 200 多年的历史，并于 2012 年被中国科学院国家天文台等三家单位确立为康熙时期中国天文大地测量遗迹，是这次天文大地测量的唯一遗迹。“海判南天”这四个大字经考证，很有可能是康熙亲笔所题。

沈鹏题字石刻

这块石壁上的行草书法刻字是 1996 年 5 月，我国著名书法家、中国书法家协会主席沈鹏先生在再次游览了天涯海角游览区后，为天涯之巍然大观所感，应邀即兴挥毫泼墨赋诗一首，并拓刻在此的，“巨石洪荒千叠浪，远洋遥看绝疑仙；南天一柱殷红字，顿觉人心似火燃”。这幅行草作品气韵生动，令人浮想联翩。沈鹏先生创作的书法作品达 15000 件以上，不仅被人民大会堂等重要场所收藏，而且刻于全国各地的风景名胜区以及在海外广为流传。

南天一柱石

大家看前面这尊高耸的圆锥形奇石，这便是“南天一柱”石，它高约 7 米，侧面看像一艘古船上升起的“双桅帆”。正面看犹如一根神柱矗立于此，坚韧不拔、顶天立地，任由惊涛骇浪冲刷，巍然屹立不倒。《史书》记载清代宣统年间（1911 年）崖州知州范云梯多次体察民情且经常往返于此地，看到此石如此浩瀚，刚正不阿，心里立下了“一日为官，终生为民”的誓言，后拟书“南天一柱”并命人在此石上刻上“南天一柱”四个大字，以祈求施政一帆风顺，有国泰民安、丰衣足食之意。所以“南天一柱”石由此而来，且至今已有上百年的历史了。

1909 年（宣统元年），范云梯调任崖州直隶州知州，据传那年春节，他在州城衙门张贴了自己撰写的一副春联：

在一日位，尽一日心，自我无私严执法，敢视机关为传舍；

让几分情，说几分理，大家有事好商量，莫因涉讼到公门。

在天涯文化苑收藏有宣统二年（1910 年）范云梯题刻在崖州州府的楹联。

一副为：“有如此锦绣江山恰称天南极地，看将来文明气象居然海上雄州。”题写时间为“宣统二年秋月”，落款是“权崖州直隶州事永安范云梯”。

另一副只有下联：“酷贪两不敢可将心事质神明。”2009 年元月，当代著名书法家、中国楹联学会顾问沈鹏先生重游天涯海角时，获悉此联，为其补撰上联，合起来就是：

得失皆无惊，何以世间施诡谲？

酷贪两不敢，可将心事质神明。

今天的“南天一柱”的景象其实早已经融入了我们国民生活的每一天。大家有没有发现分别于 1980 年和 1990 年发行的第四套贰元人民币，它的背面图案就是大家面前的“南天一柱”，大家知道这第四套的壹元人民币背画是“万里长城”，贰元人民币上是“南天一柱”，伍元人民币背面图案是“长江巫峡”，十元人民币背面为“珠穆朗玛峰”。人民币被称为“国家名片”，“南天一柱”石，可以与万里长城、长江巫峡、珠穆朗玛峰图相媲美，称为“国家名片”。今天我们所见到的“南天一柱”石是财大气粗和好运的象征。俗话说摸摸石丰衣足食、拍拍石投一进十，抱抱石财源滚滚如落石。大家抓紧时间与财富石合影或拥抱一下，希望能给大家带来“财运”。

天涯石

大家看看远处那块巨石，那就是著名的“天涯”石，是景区的标志和象征。高 10.8 米，周长约 66 米，依山傍海的“天涯石”圆中见方，方中呈圆，“面朝东方”“四平八稳”独占海湾一角，已有亿万年的历史，可谓“坚如磐石”，所指的就是这里。

雍正五年，崖州知州程哲不经意在一块巨石上写下了“天涯”二字。为“天涯”重新进行了界定。有趣的是钦州的天涯亭是北宋庆历年间（1041—1048 年）钦州知州陶弼建的。这“小小芝麻官”知州题写的“天涯”却把天涯海角永远定格在中国的历史上了。

智慧石

看完“天涯”石，“天涯不是终结”，大家请跟我来，看这块巨石，由于经过海浪长年冲刷而形成的天然巨石，石头上的纹理与人类大脑的纹理极其相似，石头上面还长着一棵小树，像头上的饰物，人们常常开玩笑说，热闹的大街不长草，聪明的脑袋不长毛。

大家注意了！进步石并非攀爬之后方能进步，这里没有任何安全设施，是不允许攀爬的。如果大家追求进步，就请与智慧石合影共勉吧！

海角石

海边矗立着巨大的花岗岩石，走到最里边可以看到一组高耸的岩石高峻雄奇，顶天立地。恰似天造地设的铜墙铁壁伫立在南海海边，正如时任总书记江泽民 2000 年 12 月 22 日，第三次来天涯海角时的题诗为“任他风起云涌，我自岿然不动”。最高尖石上题刻着“海角”二字，与“天涯”二字遥相呼应，构成了完整的天涯海角。

1938 年 10 月，广州陷落后，国民党将军王毅临危受命，任琼崖守备司令部司令，负责琼崖的防务。1939 年 1 月 8 日，他在马岭也就是现在的天涯镇举行六千黎民歃血会盟共赴国难动员大会，王毅对黎民致训，号召黎民百姓团结起来，共同抗日。之后来到下马岭海滨，刻“海角”于石上。1939 年 5 月 10 日，王毅将军带领部下来到琼中县和平镇乘坡河边层叠的巨石边上，为鼓励士气，将军饱含感情地写下“唯战能存”石刻。这两幅石刻的署名同为“王毅”。

在“海角”石背面的石丛中有一个碉堡，这碉堡便是日本军队占领海南岛后修建的，也是日本侵略中国的历史见证。

站在这里，大家往山上看，山上的建筑是 1990 年第十一届亚洲运动会的南端点火台。1990 年 8 月 23 日，亚运会火炬南端点火仪式在这里隆重举行。现在与我们景区爱情主题相呼应的中华烽火台（爱情殿堂）正在建设中，建成之后将成为情侣们山盟海誓的地点之一。

刚才我们在天涯路上欣赏了石树奇观的“绝处逢生”，现在换一个角度看这个景点，从海滩这边看是否更能感受到小树顽强的生命力呢？

结束语

20 世纪 80 年代初，一曲《请到天涯海角来》热情四射的邀请，让天涯海角成为亿万中华儿女心中的向往。如今，每年有数百万中外游人来到这片由中国人用才情、用情感堆砌起来的心灵圣地——天涯海角游览区。相信今天的游览，已经让大家真正领略到了天涯海角的独特魅力。今天的旅程已经结束，我也要和大家说再见了。

常言道“相见时难别亦难，送君千里终有别”。在此，非常感谢各位朋友对我工作的支持。短短几小时的时间，大家给我留下了非常深刻的印象，谢谢大家的合作！在游览过程中，若有不尽如人意之处，请各位批评指正，您的意见将是我努力的方向，您的建议将是我改进的目标。希望大家有机会能再聚天涯海角，欣赏“美丽三亚，浪漫天涯”的风景。

最后祝愿大家一路平安！阖家欢乐！身体健康！

4A 级旅游景区

1. 兴隆热带植物园

兴隆热带植物园为国家 4A 级旅游景区，创建于 1957 年，由中国热带农业科学院香料饮料研究所开发管理。园区占地面积 645 亩，主要承担我国香草兰、咖啡、可可、胡椒等热带香料饮料作物的产业化配套技术研发任务，收集保存热带、亚热带植物种质 3000 多种，是一座集科研、生产、加工、科普、观光和种质资源保护为一体、三产充分融合的综合性热带植物园。

美丽植物园

兴隆热带植物园依山傍水，风景秀丽，葱葱绿海，幽幽果香，喁喁鸟语，清新世界，令人心旷神怡，流连忘返。“到海南必到兴隆，来兴隆定去植物园”道出了兴隆侨乡这颗绿色明珠的奥秘。

奇特植物园

神奇的老茎生花，美丽的空中花园，独特的板根现象，妙趣横生的独木成林，在兴隆热带植物园里孕育着神奇的热带雨林奇观，处处给您留下惊喜；还有“巧克力之母”——可可、植物界的“大熊猫”——黑桫椤、随着音乐翩翩起舞的跳舞草、“沙漠甘泉”——旅人蕉、使人一招毙命的见血封喉、长在树上的铁西瓜等奇花异果，等待您来探索。

体验植物园

在兴隆热带植物园，您可以参与手工巧克力 DIY、兴隆咖啡研磨冲泡、东南亚糕点制作、天然植物香薰调配等精彩体验活动，还有独具东南亚风情的歌舞表演以及咖啡和香茗的免费品饮，为您提供集学习、休闲、娱乐于一体的热带植物体验之旅。

历史植物园

兴隆热带植物园创建于 1957 年，目前已经从当初的 9 名科研人员和 10 多名工人，发展到现在拥有强大研发能力的科研机构。在60年的发展历程中，得到了党和国家领导人、各级政府部门及各界人士的关怀与支持，先后有周恩来、朱德、邓小平、习近平等 20 多位党和国家领导人，以及何康、韩长赋等 80 多位省部级领导来园视察和指导。

科技植物园

兴隆热带植物园由中国热带农业科学院香料饮料研究所开发管理。主要从事香草兰、胡椒、咖啡、可可、苦丁茶、米香茶等热带香辛饮料作物的引种试种、丰产栽培、病虫害防治及产品加工。建所以来，已取得科研成果 100 多项，其中获国家级、省部级成果奖励 43 项；制定技术标准 45 项；发表论文 800 余篇、出版专著 55 部；申请并获授权发明专利 58 项、实用新型专利 10 项。

建所以来，先后研制出可可系列、咖啡系列、胡椒系列、香草兰系列等特色热带香料饮料作物产品（十大系列共 140 多种规格），实现年产值近 5000 万元。

科普植物园

您知道巧克力是怎么来的吗？您知道黑胡椒与白胡椒的区别吗？您知道什么是世界三大饮料吗？来到兴隆热带植物园，我们会为您一一揭开谜底。兴隆热带植物园兼具生物多样性保护、科普教育、科学研究和植物观赏的功能，多年来坚持向游客普及热带植物科学知识，并不定期举办科普讲解大赛、科普展、自然笔记、游园认植物、寻香之旅等科普活动，在开展公众科普教育方面得到了社会的广泛认同。此外，依托热科院香饮所科技优势，以兴隆热带植物园为窗口成立的海南省农业科技 110 香料饮料服务站也积极开展了一系列服务三农的科技咨询与推广活动。

2. 南湾猴岛生态旅游区

各位朋友，大家好！我是大家的讲解员，我叫小李，接下来由我来带领大家游玩。

日益发达的城市，带给我们的是拥挤的人潮和让我们喘不过气的压力。我们总希望有那么一处地方可以让我们放下手中的一切，回归大自然，重新找回人与自然和谐相处的乐趣。所以，我们今天将要前去游览的就是四季花果飘香，猕猴生息繁衍的理想之地——南湾猴岛。

南湾猴岛是世界唯一的一个热带岛屿型猕猴保护区，它位于陵水县的最南端，南非湾猴岛的猕猴，学名叫作恒河猴，属于灵长类动物。现在在我们的岛上一共有 2000 多只猕猴在自由自在地生活着。

在我们的猴岛上，猴子才是我们真正的“主人”，我们是拜访他们的“客人”，而我们的经营管理者却是“仆人”；这就是猴岛独特的经营理念——“三人原则”。

南湾猴岛由跨海观光索道、猴岛雕塑广场、花果山猕猴游览区、猴杂技表演区及猴演艺场等几个部分所组成。

跨海观光索道

如果要进入我们的猴岛，你可以选择乘船或者是观光索道。不过，这条中国最长的跨海索道如果不去体验一番，确实会让我们有些许的遗憾。乘坐在索道上，神秘的南湾猴岛、迷人的热带海湾、浓郁的“疍家民俗风情”尽收眼底，带给你的将是不一样的感受。

猴岛雕塑广场

踏上南湾猴岛，大家首先看到的将会是猴岛雕塑广场。广场上有一只猴子正坐在达尔文的《物种起源》上捧着人的头盖骨在思考。这个雕塑可是美国著名的红色资本家哈默博士送给苏联领导人列宁的礼品雕塑的复制品。他也在告诉着我们：人类要学会遵守自然法则，学会尊敬自然。

花果山猕猴游览区

观赏完雕塑，大家就会来到花果山猕猴游览区与可爱的猕猴来次亲密接触。在这里你可以看到由猴队长的带领下高举旗帜的可爱猕猴，这是他们欢迎远道而来的客人的一种特别的方式，是不是很有趣呢？而在猕猴的水上乐园——“浴圣池”里你可以看到或潜水或游泳或高楼跳水的猕猴们正在向游客们展示他们的能耐。如果你想和可爱的猴子们亲密无间地合上一张影，不妨买上一包食粮，这些富有灵性的猴子便会批准你和它们合影了。

猴杂技表演区

如果说我们在花果山猕猴游览区看到的是充满“野性”的猕猴，那么在我们的猴杂技表演区你就可以看到充满“人性”的猕猴。在这里，你能看到有很高模仿力的猕猴为你奉上精彩的表演，它们在驯化师的带领下，表演各种高难度的杂技，绝对会让大家为之震惊。

猴演艺场

如果这些还不能使你心情舒畅、捧腹大笑，那就让我们一起来到会带给我们更多欢乐的猴演艺场吧。这些经过挑选的极具表演天赋、相貌俊俏、身材一流的猕猴会与人共演一出情景喜剧——《毛毛的一家》，看过之后保证你烦恼全无。

南湾猴岛醉游人

南湾猴岛有素有“海上街市”之称的风情渔排、古陵水八景之一的“桐楼渔火”等景观。从新村渔港港口乘坐索道，跨过大海，越过群山便到达风情万种的猴岛，你就会陶醉于此。它们会热情地向你致意，多情备至地与你合影。还能将猴子的天性本领一一展现出来，以此博得你的掌声，大家可以送上一把糖果、小食品，它们就会十分满足。

游完猴山，沿索道而下，乘上一叶小舟，便可直达海上渔排酒家。一座座星罗棋布的渔排构成了水乡特有的风情。无论你踏上哪家渔排海鲜排档，热情好客的黎苗姑娘就会笑脸相迎，热情款待您，只要您有胃口，您可尽管放开手脚，放心品尝，包你尝到无数种你在海口、三亚，或者其他地方从来没有听说过的海鲜，其中有一种螺叫鸡腿螺，也叫“美人腿”，味道鲜美无比，营养丰富有余。

好了，各位游客朋友，我们的旅游车已经驶入我们的景区，大家是不是已经心驰神往，想要与我们的可爱猕猴们一起玩耍了呢，那就让我们带上好心情，一同去体味人与自然和谐共处的乐趣吧！

3. 中国雷琼海口火山群世界地质公园

尊敬的各位嘉宾，真诚欢迎莅临海口火山群世界地质公园，我是本次为您服务的全程讲解员小何，很荣幸能为各位进行讲解。中国雷琼海口火山群世界地质公园海口园区位于海口市秀英区石山镇，园内火山最高海拔 222.8 米，是琼北最高峰，面积 108 平方千米。其拥有的海口火山群是世界罕见的第四纪火山群，距今约 1 万年，火山锥多达 40 座，岩溶隧道 30 多条，是我国唯一的热带城市火山群世界地质公园。

海口火山口地质公园标志碑

园内共有三个具有意义的标志碑，为雷琼世界地质公园主碑、园区标志碑、国家地质公园主碑，分别位于售票口处、游客中心处及主园区入口处，十分抢眼且有特色。

仙人掌园

仙人掌原产于墨西哥，是一种生命力顽强的植物，其分支曲折，茎节扁平多刺，花多黄色，耐旱畏劳，扦插繁殖，形态千姿百态，有球状、掌状、圆柱状、四棱形状等，品种多样。火山地区由于玄武岩石多孔，渗水性强，很适合仙人掌的生长。

“仙人掌园”里建有四个小花坛:（1）火山魂，花坛里有名贵的金刚纂、仙人掌;（2）火山情，花坛里有全年常青的无刺仙人掌，其浆果可食;（3）火山缘，花坛里有霸王树、刺黄果;（4）火山恋，花坛里有一块玄武岩呈葡萄状形态，它是由熔浆从已经冷却的岩石空隙或小洞中挤出而形成的，其纹理清晰可见，地质学上称为结壳熔岩，并称为观赏石。仙人掌园里最高的仙人掌已经生长了 20 多年，而这么高大的仙人掌是比较少见的。

火山口休闲广场公园

火山口休闲广场公园是游客休闲、娱乐的最佳场所。内设有玄武岩石桌，百年荔枝木茶台、多张椅子、小型舞台、火山小吃等，游客们爬完山后可以在此品味美味的火山小吃以及观看精彩的火山风情演出。火山小吃种类丰富，有粉、面、杂粮等各式地道的火山小吃，游客在品美食的同时，广场的舞台中心也会为游客上演精彩的节目，有竹竿舞、树叶吹奏、民俗歌曲等，让游客既饱了口福的同时还饱了眼福。

根雕艺术园

根雕艺术园建于 2009 年，展示有荔枝、龙眼、刈嘴罗等火山区珍贵树种的根雕。由于火山地区土层薄、石头多，根部会沿岩石裂缝延伸，形成盘根错节、千姿百态的树根。数百年后树木枯死，树身当用材，树根经清理成根雕，成为一种艺术品。

火山地区的根雕形状奇特，很具有观赏性，远近闻名。游客可进到火山根雕园内参观，选择自己喜欢的根雕留影，感受来自火山的大自然灵气。其中的“山殿”根雕像是一座龙椅，吸引了不少游客前来拍照留念。而“天地之根”和“生命之源”是经过人工雕刻而成的根雕，中间“繁衍”是由七个树根叠成的，它的寓意是“多子多孙，繁荣昌盛”。

火山生态景观道

火山生态景观道，又称火山神道，以景区主碑为起点，一路延伸至风炉岭火山口。

其景观路美丽而具特色，充分展示了火山口的生态，路面用含气孔且凸凹不平的玄武岩石铺设，光脚走在上面有按摩足底的功效，可以促进血液循环，人们也称之为健康之道。火山生态景观道两旁都种上了榕树，茂密的榕树林相互交错，形成了别致的景观，夏季到来，游客不用打伞就可以享受到阴凉。此外，您还可以一路观赏到独具特色的天然火山象形石、热带植物等，当地的火山岩与热带植物的融合，构建了这条独具魅力的景观大道。

玄武岩石柱

玄武岩石柱是火山口独特的景观。那一条条像是切割的象形石矗立在火山生态景观道内，其实它是天然形成的，是均质的岩浆在冷却过程中，由于均匀冷却收缩裂开形成的多边形柱状体，有四变形、五边形、六边形，但以六边形居多，十分奇特。地质学上称为“柱状节理”，它与干涸的稻田和泥塘被太阳暴晒后形成泥块的现象是相似的，世界上比较著名的“柱状节理”有美国的“魔塔”和北爱尔兰的“巨人堤”，火山口的玄武岩石柱与之形成的原理是一样的。

翠趣园区

园区最大的特色是热带生态与火山的融合，翠趣园就是一个热带生态缩影，一条木栈道穿过盆景园，是当地艺人对本土生态文化的喜好，精心培育出来的各种盆景，造型考究、典雅神韵，奉献给游客观赏，再绕过几百年的高山榕树群，千姿百态、根如盘龙、枝条繁茂，栈道让人们感受到了原始的趣味，还有那直冲云天的重阳树、清新素雅的鸡蛋花、没有头绪的野菠萝群、盘根错节的爬藤植物，仿佛让人进入了雨林世界，之后经过一片果园，享受菠萝蜜、阳桃、石榴、莲雾等热带瓜果飘香，会令您流连忘返。然而翠绿有趣的生态园却生长在玄武岩风化的土壤上，这就是 8000 多年前火山爆发，生物灭绝，生物演替所带来的令人震撼的景象，前面便是风炉岭火山喷发溢出的一片熔岩流遗迹，它可以直观地向您展示当时熔岩流动的过程。

火山季雨林栈道

与翠趣园区对应的是火山季雨林栈道，同样是木栈道但却有着不同的风格，火山季雨林栈道更偏于雨林风，既展现了海南的热带雨林风景，又将火山口独有的山林风景体现得淋漓尽致。由一条石头路，一堵石头墙，一条木栈道穿越原生的百年爬藤、火山竹、榕树群、黄花梨、菠萝蜜树、野荔枝树、滴水观音等热带火山季雨林植被，展现了具有海岛特色的热带火山季雨林的优美性，让游客可以在天然的大氧吧中休闲漫步，呼吸新鲜空气，享受惬意阴凉，感受火山自然生态之美。

由于火山季雨林栈道处于公园内相对于游客活动点较偏的山林中，很多游客很容易错过，但这里绝对是您可以近距离感受到火山魅力的地方，也是不能错过的绝佳休闲、养生之处。

石门与龙湫

“石门”是仿造以前火山地区的村门建造的，以前火山地区每个村落都用火山石垒起一个村门，主要是用于防御外来入侵和野兽袭击，传说古时候火山地区有一种野人，它们身材高大，四肢发达，且形象古怪，指甲很长，但是不能下蹲，经常到村里伤害小孩和偷窃财物，村民为了防止野人入侵，便用火山石垒起矮小的村门，以防止野人进入村庄。石门也叫“龙门”，跨石门有“一跃成龙，飞黄腾达”之意，火山地区跨门槛是有讲究的，一般“男跨左脚，女跨右脚”。

龙在火山地区是人们崇拜的瑞兽和图腾，火山地区有一个传统，每到端午节的时候，当地民众都会过来排队摸龙湫，洗“龙水”，以讨好兆头。水是从玄武岩层中涌出的地下矿泉水。

火山石文化展示区

据传，秦汉时期，火山地区的人们就开始用火山石垒墙筑屋，距今已有1500多年，房屋为石木结构，屋顶铺瓦，房梁上都雕刻有图腾，屋前放有多个水缸。石屋左右展示了许多用火山石制成生活或生产的器具。这就集中再现了生活在火山岩的人们在生产生活过程中创造的文化。

走进石屋，我们可以看到木质榨油机、竹磨、耙钩、木犁、铁锹、躺柜。躺柜一般是富有家庭的生活用具。其上可以当床用，其下分成几格，可以存储重要物品。躺柜设有暗格，可放置贵重物品，这就是最早的保险柜了。

石屋的周边展示有石盆、石缸、石磨、石臼、石舂、石制榨汁器。其中石制榨汁器颇有意义，因当地种有甘蔗，人们会用牛拉着木杆转，把甘蔗放在两个石制的圆柱形齿轮中，挤出生蔗汁，经煮蒸、烘干后做成糖块、糖条。这些物品充分展示了先人的智慧。

风炉岭火山口

风炉岭火山口最后一次喷发是8000多年前，是一座活火山或休眠火山口，它是世界上保存最完整的火山之一，海拔222.8米，为海口市制高点，火山口直径130米，深度69米。

风炉岭火山口有两大特点：第一，不积水，这对于很多火山口景观而言是非常少见的，特别是风炉岭火口在海南多雨的天气下依然不积水更显得神奇；第二，植物覆盖率高，植物的覆盖率高达85%以上，为海口市的“绿肺”，这也是十分奇特的一点，而且洞口的植物长得很有层次，从上至下依次是乔木、灌木、蕨类和苔藓。此洞口在夏季到来时更像是天然的空调房。火山周边方圆108平方千米分布有40多座火山口，目前只开发了风炉岭火山口，它的开发也让更多游客近距离感受到了火山的魅力。

各位朋友，我们此次旅行到此全部结束，火山口的美景永远在这里等待您的下次光临，祝大家旅途愉快！

4. 博鳌亚洲论坛永久会址

尊敬的各位来宾，真诚欢迎您光临博鳌亚洲论坛国际会议中心，我是本次为您服务的全程讲解员小陈，很荣幸能为各位进行讲解。

博鳌亚洲论坛永久会址景区是国家4A级旅游景区，地处万泉河入海口，濒临南海。每年4月，这里会成为举世瞩目的焦点，全世界政商领袖汇聚于此，共商发展大计。这里自建成以来已成功举办了数十届博鳌亚洲论坛年会，是世界著名的论坛会址。

景区坐落在神奇美丽的东屿岛上，占地面积2670亩，建设有国际会议中心、论坛大酒店、论坛高尔夫球会及论坛景区。从空中俯瞰，整个东屿岛就像一只缓缓游向南海的巨鳌，鳌头独立，三江入海，风景十分独特，是神奇博鳌的核心所在，也因此被确定为博鳌亚洲论坛永久会址。

景区内的主要景点有喷泉广场、会议中心、祈台阆苑、鳌石广场、三江交汇（玉带滩）、乐美风光、一带一路、新闻中心等。

喷泉广场

喷泉广场是一处由一个涌泉托起的镂空金属地球仪和一个椭圆形的喷泉池组成的景观区。地球仪上亚洲所在的位置正好伸向进岛公路的主干道，它寓意着亚洲论坛是一个开放、发展的论坛，同时代表着博鳌亚洲论坛国际会议中心欢迎来自四面八方的朋友们。喷水池四周成梯形瀑布，水流向花坛绿丛弥漫，象征着博鳌亚洲论坛的意义向四海传播。椭圆形的喷泉池结合“鳌”

身形状做了个抽象化的设计，池内喷管分为三层，从内而外，分别由 14 根、96 根、62 根不同粗细的喷管组成，喷泉喷涌的规律错落有致，层次分明。

国际会议中心

（1）酒店大堂至北门路段。

尊敬的各位游客，前方就是国际会议中心主会场的入口了。主会场就是每届年会召开开幕式和闭幕式的地方，2002—2023 年，博鳌亚洲论坛永久会址已成功举办了 21 届年会。

现在我们到达的是国际会议中心的北门，年会期间，参会嘉宾就是从北门踏着红地毯经过安检进入主会场参加会议，这里两侧也是媒体记者们集中的区域，很多媒体就是在这里抓住嘉宾安检等待的机会，对想采访的对象进行采访。

（2）主会场（引导进主会场）。

尊敬的各位游客，我们现在就进入主会场了，这里就是博鳌亚洲论坛的核心所在，主会场的总面积为 2592 平方米，高 11 米，东西走向 50 米，南北走向 55 米，可同时容纳约 2000 名代表开会，周边配套 2 个国宾接待室。

习近平总书记分别于 2010 年、2013 年、2015 年、2018 年、2021 年、2022 年出席了年会，是我们国家出席博鳌亚洲论坛次数最多的领导人，这充分代表着我们国家对博鳌亚洲论坛的重视。

各位游客，每年的开幕式演讲，是中国对参会嘉宾的欢迎，更是我们国家对世界的发声。主席台上悬挂的国旗，代表博鳌亚洲论坛 29 个成员国。2018 年 4 月 10 日，习近平主席就是在这个台上，在那个白色的单人演讲台前，主持了开幕式并发表了题为《开放共创繁荣　创新引领未来》的主旨演讲，一句“久久不见久久见，久久见过还想见”成为经典。

祈台阆苑

相传观音大士伏鳌于此，上设阴阳水池，循五行之位，通函其中。人立穴上，昂首朗声可得上苍回音绕顶，久鸣不散，也得天地日月光华辅佐，堪称一绝。但凡诚者临台祈愿，福、禄、寿、喜、财皆有灵验。

鳌石广场

传说中的鳌，是长着龙头、龟背、麒麟尾的通灵动物，景区鳌石广场内安放有一尊采用整块黑龙骨石雕刻而成的鳌石灵像，重 8 吨，高 2 米。2006 年 9 月 16 日，由著名的道玄之士主持开光。

三江交汇（玉带滩）

现在大家正前方就是三江水交汇的地方了，对面那个沙滩就是玉带滩。玉带滩是一条自然形成的地形狭长的沙滩半岛，外侧南海烟波浩渺，一望无际，内侧万泉河、沙美内海内外相映，构成了奇异的景观。其南北走向全长 8.3 千米；东西最宽处约 300 米，最窄处涨潮时仅 10 余米，为世界上分隔河海最狭窄的沙滩半岛。其地形地貌酷似澳大利亚的黄金海岸、美国的迈阿密和墨西哥的坎昆，在亚洲地区可谓绝无仅有。玉带滩于 1999 年 6 月被国际吉尼斯总部在中国的权威代理机构上海大世界吉尼斯总部以“自然分隔海、河最狭窄的沙滩半岛”载入“吉尼斯世界之最”。玉带滩的尾部就是三江入海口，它也是世界上江河入海口保存最完美的处女地。这条沙滩原本是连在一起的，由于 2013 年被台风“海燕”横腰冲断，所以中间大大的缺口不是真正的三江入海口，大家要分辨清楚。大家可以回头看我手指的方向，那就是鳌头。所谓博览天下，独占鳌头，就是起源于那里。

乐美风光

一径通幽凉夏至，日光星点叶隙间。风送鸣蝉回声杳，涤荡温柔似呢喃。这里是乐美风光区，2019 年当地修建了长约 618 米、宽 3 米的乐美路，走在这清幽的小路上，呼吸畅然，感受宁静，回归自然。东屿岛距离江河入海口处较近，其含盐分的水域围绕着东屿岛，这片水域和淤泥浅滩非常利于红树林的生长，因此为了更好地保护东屿岛上的红树林自然生态及景观，当地建成了乐美湖红树林保护片区。在乐美湖岸，大家可近距离观赏稀有的木本胎生植物——红树林。一株株红树纵横交错，褐红色的树干弯弯曲曲，盘根错节，形成一座座立体栅栏，支撑着硕大的树冠，犹如幽静而神奇的仙境。在乐美风光区的外侧有一条全长 2.5 千米的环岛路，它东起鳌身池，西至培兰大桥，沿途河、海、青草、绿树构成一条美丽的休闲走廊。其中全长 888 米的星光路，每当夜晚的时候，耀眼夺目，闪闪发光。在夜幕中，抬眼满天星光，脚下银河闪烁，周围水面上银光闪闪，好似星星与月亮的陪伴，如同走在神秘的童话世界里。

新闻中心

我们现在看到的这个形似海鸥的建筑就是新闻中心，整个新闻中心是一个钢结构建筑，它的设计是按照亚洲最先进最标准化的新闻中心来建设的。此建筑名为“海鸥展翅”，寓意着博鳌亚洲论坛的腾飞，中国的腾飞，亚洲的腾飞。新闻中心总建筑面积 5358 平方米，能够接待近 2500 名记者。该设施总投资达 1.1 亿元，里面的设施设备先进，拥有 6 间独立的同声传译室可同时实现 6 种语言的同声翻译，能为媒体工作人员提供科技便捷的服务。该设施已于 2016 年博鳌亚洲论坛年会期间正式投入使用。

各位朋友，我们的亚洲论坛永久会址之旅到此全部结束，景区的美景永远在这里等待您的下次光临，祝愿大家旅途愉快！

5. 三亚西岛海洋文化旅游区

亲爱的游客朋友们，今天我们将参观的是世界稀岛——西岛，它是海南最大的原住民旅游海岛，坐落在中国唯一的热带滨海城市——三亚，位于三亚湾向南的八海里处。这里尘嚣隔海，风情浓郁，碧礁环绕，风光旖旎。由于周边海域的海水澄澈湛蓝，海底深邃迷人，这里现已成为公认的潜水胜地之一。这里不仅有动感刺激的海上运动，还有古朴的百年渔村以及原始的海岛风光，人们称其为“海上桃源，动感天堂。”

潜水胜地

西岛海水澄澈湛蓝，海底深邃迷人，海底生物种类繁多，在这里您可以纵身海底，盘桓于珊瑚丛中，感受被珊瑚礁簇拥、与鱼群共舞的乐趣。

海上游乐世界

西岛是一个汇集了海底、海面、空中娱乐项目为一体的海上娱乐乐园，被三亚湾环抱着的西岛，湛蓝萦绕、水阔潮平，是开展海上运动的天堂。在这里您可以尽情体验海上速度与激情的较量，将自己置身于蔚蓝的大海中，感受动感刺激的独特魅力，尽情享受纵身海洋的欢乐时光。

牛王岛

在西岛的最南端有一座毗邻的袖珍小岛，名为牛王岛，由两座风景秀美的小山丘组成，整座小岛被澄碧的海水所环绕，岛上峰峦雄峙、礁石嶙峋、和风鼓浪，宛如海上仙境。

站在牛王岛的听涛轩，可以闭目倾听大海的心声；登上牛王岛的北峰，可以遇见那头蓄力奔海的大金牛；踏过那座凌空飞渡的情人桥，在古树情缘前的观海台上，可以与这片大海留下360°无死角的唯美合影；而南中国海的秘密，藏在海风徐行的海誓山盟亭里；在这里，您可以赏岩听涛，一睹诗情画意的中国南海风光。

滨海景观大道

西岛滨海景观大道是独具浪漫特色的海岛婚纱摄影基地，其拥有诗情画意的海岸风光，蓝天碧海，绿草如茵，树影婆娑。诗意的小木牌、心形的观海亭、树林间的鸟巢屋、浪漫的花拱门以及百年古井、古船等文艺浪漫的网红打卡点也都齐聚在这里，整条路都洋溢着爱情的温馨和甜蜜。

您可以追着海风的尾巴，穿过稀松的椰林，听着海浪的声音，在安静的临海栈道上踩出欢乐的节奏；或是正逢日落，晚霞落在退潮后的珊瑚滩里，您的眼眸里，必将又是一番不可方物的美景。

400年最美渔村

在这座尘嚣隔海的小岛上，藏着一座古老的小渔村——西岛渔村。西岛渔村已经在大海的怀抱里隐居了400多年，风情古朴，恬静心安，被评为“全国最美渔村”。

信步游走在海风轻拂的临海路上，海的彼岸是迷人的三亚湾城市风光，沿路的珊瑚矮墙上缀着小巧玲珑的艺术品。你会遇见市场路转角的“大爱心”，遇见渔村码头上那只样子古怪但无比霸气的“重生鱼”，还有悬着漂流瓶的艺术船，港口里还停泊着渔民捕鱼的船只。

在海上书房，你可以感受风吹哪页读哪页，心随海阔、读书品茗的风雅；或到女民兵展览馆里，听民兵老奶奶讲一段她们传奇故事；或是走进安静的巷子，看看那古韵犹存的珊瑚老屋，品味西岛400多年的人文历史；抑或在某条小巷的转角，你会遇见那些静卧在渔村院子里的温馨民宿。那两间名为“文创馆”和“奇思妙想屋”的庭院里，藏着许多稀奇古怪的手工艺品。人来人往的渔村市集，无不洋溢着这世外桃源的烟火气。

西岛女民兵

西岛渔村里有这样一群可爱的“渔家铁姑娘”，她们曾是名扬全国的模范女民兵，被誉为“八姐妹炮班”。

这段传奇的红色历史要从1959年说起。

1959年8月1日，为加强南海国防前哨的防御力量，西岛组建了民兵营。生活在岛上的8位渔家姑娘，陈粦梅、陈发妹、苏兰亲、王福花、王乃莲、陈洪柳、陈香兰、苏日农，怀着对祖国的一腔热爱，加入了女民兵炮班的行列。当时的她们正值青春芳华，其中年龄最大的19岁，最小的只有16岁。这群可爱的人，在那个火红的时代，在党的光辉旗帜引领下，燃烧青春，为祖国南海国防作出了巨大的贡献，取得了一个又一个荣誉，塑造了一个又一个辉煌。20世纪70年代，电影《海霞》闻名全国，故事就是以这群可爱的人为原型创作的，它记录了那段光辉的红色历史，由此，也让海岛女民兵这个群体名扬大江南北。

时光冉冉，当年意气风发的“渔家铁姑娘”，如今已变成了白发苍苍的老奶奶，有的甚至已经永远地刻入了历史的丰碑，但西岛女民兵的红色精神一直在西岛上传承至今。而在西岛女民兵展览馆里，那些承载着西岛红色记忆的物品，依然以另一种方式，为全国各地的游客讲述着西岛女民兵的传奇故事。

西岛院子

游弋在百年渔村里，您可以品味淳朴文艺的渔家风情，而在渔村临海路隔海远眺三亚城市风景的不经意间转身，便可遇见西岛院子。精致的海岛生活从西岛院子开始，在这里您可以逃离城市的拥挤和喧嚣，畅享尘嚣隔海的清心宁静。

好了，各位游客朋友，我们的旅游车已经驶入景区，大家是不是已经心驰神往，想要即刻体验一番呢，那就让我们带上好心情，去体味西岛的乐趣吧！

6. 鹿回头风景区

鹿回头风景区是一个集黎族文化、情爱文化和生态文化的主题景区，素有“南海情山”的美誉。景区坐落在三亚西南端鹿回头半岛内，总面积 88.89 公顷，共有五座山峰，最高海拔 181 米，景区三面环海，一面毗邻三亚市区，是登高望海和观看日出日落的制高点，也是观看三亚全景的最佳去处。请大家记住鹿回头的三个 IP，分别是：牵你的手去鹿回头，一见钟情鹿回头，鹿回头上望鹿城。

提及鹿回头风景区，不禁让我们想起了马万祺先生一首有感而发的抒情诗：

人生莫负海南游，五指山高景物优。

最爱凤凰临宝地，三亚难舍鹿回头。

它描述了鹿回头风景区在海南旅游中的地位。作为一个生态文明山，我们尽了自己最大的努力来维持自然赋予我们的一切。也请各位在游览的过程中不要乱扔垃圾，不要随地吐痰，听从工作人员的安排，有序地排队。让我们一起维护自然的和谐。

现在，由我来向各位游客朋友们讲解分享鹿回头风景区的各个景点。

凤凰岛

映入我们眼帘的这五栋大楼的所在地就是凤凰岛。该岛全长 1250 米，宽 350 米，由一条 395 米长的海上观光大桥连通三亚市的中心城区。这 5 栋高 100 米共 28 层的曲面建筑是三亚湾最豪华的全海景建筑群。

这五栋楼里的房间均是 360° 海景房，它的外形是 5 个环形。这 5 个环象征着奥运五环的精神。同时，2008 年奥运会火炬传递的点火台就是在凤凰岛。火炬经过沿途的各个市县一直传递到北京的鸟巢体育馆，寓意着凤凰归巢。

该岛三面依托山景，四面临海，拥有得天独厚的山海天旅游风光，当地计划新建 4 个邮轮码头，其中 10 万吨泊位 1 个、15 万吨泊位 2 个和 22.5 万吨泊位 1 个。届时，凤凰岛可同时停靠 6~8 艘邮轮，年接待游客数达到 200 万人次，将成为全球最大的国际邮轮母港之一。

三亚湾

三亚湾位于凤凰岛北侧，延绵 20 多千米的海岸线椰树成林，因此也有“椰梦长廊”之称。三亚湾也是三亚市最繁华的地段，长长的海湾分为三段，一段是游乐观光漫游区，稍微远一点是公共海边泳场和海上活动区域，再远一段是拥有一批度假村的海坡休闲度假区域。三亚湾的尽头就是我们驰名中外的天涯海角景区了。

东西玳瑁岛

在凤凰岛西侧的海面上伫立着两座小岛，左边的叫东岛。东岛是我国军事基地，戒备森严，一般人是不让进去的。右边的是西岛，西岛是一个旅游景区，面积 2.8 平方千米，岛上有居民 3000 多人，世代打鱼为生，景区开放之后很多热衷于海上项目的年轻人都喜欢去那边玩。

这两座岛并称为东西玳瑁岛。玳瑁不是咱们俗称“戴帽子”的“带帽”。玳瑁是一种生活在热带深海里海龟科爬行动物，属国家 2 级保护动物，寿命长达 1500 年。其外形很像乌龟，但是它的甲壳上有十三枚鳞片，又称“十三鳞”，也叫长寿龟。南海渔民都视之为海里的吉祥物，认为“十三鳞”是龙的第九个儿子，所以会用玳瑁背上的鳞片制成手镯、吊坠及戒指随身佩戴，以起到驱灾避邪、逢凶化吉的作用。

吉祥平安树

这棵树就是海南十八怪之一的小叶榕了，其树根长在树皮外。大家看，这就是它的树根，学名为气生根，它能吸收空气中的营养和水分，向下生长，根落地以后，伸入土壤里久而久之就像这个枝干一样，而这个枝干又会慢慢地形成一棵新的树。就这样枝生根，根生枝地繁衍下去，一棵树就会形成一片深林，“独木成林”指的就是这种榕树。

当地黎族人给这棵小叶榕取了个很好听的名字，叫作吉祥平安树。因为在海南的原住民是黎族人（目前黎族人口占整个海南省人口的 17%）。黎族人认为榕树是有灵性的，它是人类善良的朋友。大叶榕是“雨仙”，种得越多，这一地区的水量越丰富；小叶榕则被认为是村寨的庇护神仙，它能保护全村人丁兴旺、丰产丰收和大吉大利。因此也叫作吉祥平安树。

注意事项

第一，在咱们鹿回头山上有野生猕猴，是国家二级保护动物。这种猴子生性凶残，野性十足。如果咱们在游览过程中遇到这种猴子，一定不要逗猴，耍猴，也不要和猴子对视和喂食。

第二，鹿回头是一座生态之山，环境优美，森林覆盖率很高。咱们团友要注意森林防火，请勿吸烟。

现在我们继续沿途而上，欣赏俗称“一半是天堂，一半是海水”的半山半岛旅游度假区。

在右上角的海域有一片白色围墙围起来的正方体（发着紫色光芒的）的地方就是半山半岛帆船港了，半山半岛帆船港也是世界沃尔沃帆船赛的竞赛点和停泊点，也是国际帆船比赛经停港之一。最远处的那座山就是我们的鹿回头山，从高空俯瞰它就像是一只奔跑的坡鹿。靠右边有一片房屋比较密集的地方，那就是鹿回头村了。眼前这一片红色房顶的别墅群就是鹿回头国宾馆，鹿回头国宾馆是专门接待各国政要的一个宾馆。它的前身是鹿回头招待所，于 1959 年开始动工，1961 年正式营业。最后，我们看最左边的那片海，这片海就是享有“南海珍珠”之称的小东海，是国家珊瑚保护基地，因为小东海的海水温度常年在 25~26℃，特别适合珊瑚的生长。

我们现在进入的是鹿回头的核心景点——情爱文化景点群，爱的美丽传说，凝固成隽永的风景从这一刻开始：

在我们的左前方，有一块心形石刻，就是爱心永恒石。它因外形像颗爱心得名，大自然就是有这么神奇的力量，把这个石头巧夺天工地雕琢成一个爱心的形状。底下蓝色的图案，就是黎族人的图腾。黎族是一个只有语言没有文字的民族，平时他们记载事情会依靠图腾。这个图腾上面表示的也是爱心永恒的意思。

海枯不烂石

往上看就是鹿回头的一大特色石头——海枯不烂石。它不是花岗岩，也不是大理石，而是亿万年前的海底火山岩化石，由于地壳运动，这一片海底山逐渐上升成山脉，这些石头也随之浮出水面。我们通常用海枯石烂来形容历时久远，比喻对爱情坚定的意志永远不变。那么海枯石不烂就更能体现对爱情的忠贞和永恒了。人们都说，鹿回头，一花一木无不含情，一草一石处处有爱，到了鹿回头的情侣，他们的爱与情就会像山上的石头一样，即便海枯了，石头也不会烂。正因为鹿回头山上遍布了这种海枯不烂石，再加上美丽的爱情传说，便有了“南海情山”之称。

山盟碑

亭子里的这块碑就是“海誓山盟”的山盟碑了，而“海誓”则在天涯海角。每年 11 月的天涯海角国际婚庆节，来自国内外的情侣们，会先到天涯海角“海誓”，然后到鹿回头山上“山盟”，海誓山盟永结同心，祈求百年好合，美满幸福。

这块碑上面有一颗红太阳，太阳的左边是一条龙，右边是凤，正所谓龙凤呈祥。

那么咱们男左女右，所有的情侣都可以在这里起誓。起誓一定是得手牵着手的，因为“执子之手与子偕老”。我们看这个“盟”字，是由一个月字和一个日字组成的，日代表阳月代表阴。这个碑已经矗立在这有百年的历史了，它不断吸收日月的精华所以已经带有一些灵性了。我们男生摸日女生摸月，摸完有什么效果，我们一摸便知。

陶醉在情爱文化的景点之中，我们也不要忘了观赏鹿回头的森林植被和珍稀动物。在游览过程中，我们要爱护大自然，保护环境，不要攀爬、刻名留字，做到文明旅游。

现在我们顺着台阶走到观海亭。这个拥有 270° 视野的观海亭就是整个鹿回头景区俯瞰三亚市风景的最佳处。右手边就是整个三亚市，其三面环山，一面临海，所以整个三亚市区是沿着三亚湾这条海岸线一直延伸，到尽头就是天涯海角、南山寺和大小洞天了。

游客朋友们，在我们前方就是鹿回头核心景点——鹿回头雕塑，让我们揭开她美丽动人的面纱。她会给我们诠释着一个美丽动人的爱情传说：

相传在很久很久以前，在海南中部山区住着一对勤劳善良的黎族母子，儿子阿黑哥是当地有名的猎手，但他只猎毒蛇猛兽，对一些小动物却是爱护有加。有一次，他们的部落族长想要拿森林中的坡鹿给他滋补身体，族长知道只有阿黑哥才有这样的本事，所以族长将阿黑哥的母亲关了起来逼迫他进山，阿黑哥只好被迫去寻找坡鹿。

当他进入一座森林，在一条小溪边，忽然看到一只美丽的坡鹿在低头饮水，阿黑哥实在不忍心伤害，但想起自己的母亲还被关押着，只好狠一狠心搭起弓箭，正要发射，坡鹿忽然一跳，跃过小溪开始逃跑。一路上你追，它就逃，你停它就回头望，就这样一直追逐着，翻过了九十九座山，蹚过了九十九条河，追了九天九夜，一直跑到三亚湾边上的这一座珊瑚崖上来，前面是茫茫的大海，后面是紧追的猎手。坡鹿再也无路可逃了，它在山顶上回过头来，鸣叫一声，回头之处出现一片五彩云霞，彩云散尽后，鹿已不见了，出现在阿黑哥面前的是一位含情脉脉回头凝视他的美丽少女。她穿的五色筒裙像天上的彩霞一样美丽，她的双眸像黑夜中的星星一样闪亮。阿黑哥当时惊呆了。回过神后，阿黑哥过去一问，原来这位是天上的仙女，她看中了阿黑哥的勤劳善良，所以才用这种方式将他引到这水草丰美的地方来。

后来，阿黑哥在仙女的帮助之下，回到老家，打败罪恶的族长，救出母亲，一起来到三亚。在此过着幸福甜美的爱情生活。因为这个美丽的爱情传说，从此，这个村就叫“鹿回头村”，这座山就叫“鹿回头山”，这个半岛就叫“鹿回头半岛”。

这个传说告诉我们，人生在世，无论是对爱情、光明还是真理，都要有一种锲而不舍的追求精神，哪怕追到天涯海角也不要放弃，也许胜利就在不远处。

在鹿回头的山顶上远眺起伏的山峦，景色极为壮观，白天，放眼望去，山、河、城、海浑然一体，大海长空一色。入夜，山下万家灯火，山上玉树琼花，夜空五彩斑斓，水面波光粼粼，如诗般醉人。

游客朋友们，我们现在看到的游步道两侧画着各种不同图案的摩崖石刻就是景区的黎族文化图腾。

丰收图

黎族信奉万物有灵的原始宗教。其盛行图腾崇拜、自然崇拜。最初的原始宗教与古代的生产和生活有密切关系。当时人们对变幻莫测的自然现象存在着畏惧，在万物有灵的思想影响下，认为自然界与人类一样具有动机、情欲和好恶，因此，他们会通过祭祀祈求自然的喜悦、宽恕和恩赐。黎族有稻谷精灵崇拜的习俗，这实际上是万物有灵观念的体现。为了祈求丰收，黎族人从播种到收割都需要举行一系列祭奠仪式，在丰收时，主人要备酒到田地里拜祭“地鬼”，表示酬谢，这种自然崇拜，无疑是中国古代从事农业的民族对自然崇拜的遗风。

祭奠图

这个石头上的图案就是黎族人的图腾了。这幅祭奠图主要是祭奠黎族人崇拜的两种动物，上面的是青蛙，黎族人认为青蛙是一种吉祥的动物，是稻田里的守护者。下面这个是牛，牛日出而作，日落而息，在日常生活中黎族人是离不开它的。

黎族人对动物的崇拜产生于“万物有灵”的观念，而图腾崇拜、祖先崇拜和自然崇拜一道构成了海南黎族先民的原始意识形态，并在漫长的征服自然、改造自然的历史发展过程中产生积极良性的影响。

“鹿回头山崖的前方有‘天涯海角’，再前方就是茫茫的大海。人们知道，尽管南方海域中还有一些零星的岛屿，就整块大陆地而言那儿恰恰是中华大地的南端，于是那儿也便成了中华民族真正的天涯海角。中国的帝王面南而坐，中国的民居朝南而筑，中国发明的指南针永远神奇地指向南方，中国大地上无数石狮、铁牛、铜马、陶俑也都面对南方站立着或匍匐着，这种目光穿越群山、越过江湖，全都迷迷茫茫地探询着碧天南海，探询着一种宏大的社会心理走向的终点，一种绵延千年的争斗和向往的极限，而那头美丽的鹿一回头，就把这所有的目光都兜住了……”余秋雨先生在《天涯故事》中的这一段精彩描述，道出了鹿回头的文化和精神境界。

美丽的鹿回头，畅享着人间真爱，歌颂着美好爱情，传递着生活真谛，召唤着人们回归爱的港湾！

7. 三亚水稻国家公园

亲爱的游客朋友们，今天我们即将参观的是水稻国家公园。它是三亚市最大的农旅融合主题旅游区，集农业生态、农业观光、农耕文化、稻作文化、科学研究、科普教育、动感体验、民俗风情、休闲度假等为一体，是演绎大地、田野、稻作在人类生存繁衍中的文明与精彩，诠释生态、生命、生活的文化主题景区。

目前景区涵盖：稻作文化广场、中国水稻—农耕文化博物馆、袁隆平国家水稻研发中心、中国恐龙明星园区、百龙大道、大地之夜高科技声光秀、低空飞行体验区、中国农耕文化大型实景演出、亲子乐园、白鹭湿地保护区、稻作文化观光体验功能区、花卉文化观光体验功能区、热带蔬果观光采摘体验区、稻田温泉康体养生体验区、稻田盛宴特色餐饮、稻田房车营地、水稻风情小镇、稻田休闲七星级酒店等。下面我将通过游、娱、食、住、行等方面给大家做介绍：

游

水稻奇迹——袁隆平水稻科研基地

水稻的起源由水稻的科属禾本科分化演变而来，其历史可上溯到白垩纪时代。经过科学的历史考证，最早将野生稻驯化为栽培稻的是中国，已有一万多年的历史（浙江河姆渡距今 7000 年前，江西万年距今 14000—12000 年前，湖南道县玉蟾岩距今 18000—14000 年前）。

首届国家最高科学技术奖得主、中国工程院院士、中国研究与发展杂交水稻的开创者袁隆平，以三亚作为种子繁殖基地，先后成功研发出“三系法”杂交水稻、“两系法”杂交水稻、超级杂交稻一期、二期，演绎了水稻“驯化”的现代史诗。在将近半个多世纪里，袁隆平院士的研究成果推动了中国农业科学的复兴，解决了国人温饱问题，为国家粮食安全做出了重要贡献，被誉为“世界杂交水稻之父”“当代神农”，他还将“五谷苍生”的梦想传播五洲，为社会进步、世界和平树立了丰碑。

稻田寻梦——千亩稻海

在这里，你可以贴近大地，走近泥土，体验天人合一的意境，感受千亩稻浪的视觉震撼，认知水稻从种植到收获的全过程，了解几千年华夏水稻文化文明史，体验田间地头农耕的乐趣。徜徉稻田，穿行在“二十四节气文化长廊”中，登临富有传统农耕文化和五行文化的五色土休闲阁（红土阁、黄土阁、黑土阁、白土阁、青土阁），可以让您充分领略中华稻作文化的博大精深。

稻田地热温泉

水稻国家公园拥有热泉带，其多处热泉眼终年潺潺流淌，平均水温59℃，水中氟、偏硅酸均达到命名矿水浓度标准，氡的含量达到医疗价值浓度标准，同时水中还富含锶、锂等有益微量元素，除观赏价值外，这里还可开发稻田温泉疗养。

浪漫花海

这里千亩花海，姹紫嫣红，群芳争艳，有美人蕉园、龙船花园、三角梅园、紫薇花园、九品香水莲园……缤纷绚丽、浪漫唯美！让您感受“请到天涯海角来、这里四季花常开”的真实意境。水稻国家公园也是热带雨林区和水生花卉培育基地，可供您赏花、观花、学花、悟花。

果蔬原乡

这里是亲子体验、家庭户外活动、团队户外拓展的好去处！这里的热带瓜果、蔬菜种植观赏体验区不仅有火龙果、番石榴、阳桃、莲雾、杧果、百香果、人心果、草莓等，还有各种热带蔬菜，它们均采用生态化种植栽培，您可走进蔬果园，亲自动手采摘绿色、有机、生态的健康果蔬，体验不一样的“农夫”乐趣，享用健康安全的有机食品。

中国明星恐龙园

中国是恐龙大国，世界上已知的1000多种恐龙中，中国已发现的就有280余种。以1:1复原的来自黑龙江、新疆、四川、云南等20余省区的277种共323只中国恐龙穿越亿万年时空汇聚三亚水稻国家公园，成为全球规模最大的恐龙户外博览基地和科普基地。这些数字化设计的仿真恐龙不但能灵活转动身躯还能模拟发声，小的不到1米，大的高达38米。夜幕降临、繁星闪烁，苍穹之下，这些来自远古的生命身披绚烂的灯光，或昂然长啸或慨然低鸣，给人带来视觉、听觉的绝对震撼！

百龙大道

长达1.5千米的百龙大道横陈在稻田之上，数百只仿真动感恐龙带您走进远古，探寻生态、生命的意义。

亲子乐园

这里是稻田里的儿童梦幻世界，有恐龙小火车、恐龙拉稻草车、时空邮局、恐龙电动车、科普中心等，可以满足孩子们的奇思妙想，让孩子在成长中获得知识和体验乐趣。

娱

田野狂欢

这是三亚首个大型山水实景演出，由国内著名山水实景演出创始人梅帅元担任编剧、艺术总监，著名实景演出导演严文龙导演，以中华农耕文明、稻作文明、太阳风车等图腾文明，以及当地黎族民俗风情为文化脉络，讲述春夏秋冬、二十四节气；讲述乡村、水稻、劳作、梦想；讲述太阳、月亮、土地、风车、稻草人；讲述姑娘与小伙，劳动与爱情；讲述吃饭这件看似很小其实很大的事……演出内容为《序》；第一幕《春耕和插秧》；第二幕《太阳和月亮》；第三幕《水妹与春仔》；第四幕《稻草人和云彩》；第五幕《秋收和太阳》。

演出剧场占地面积40余亩，超大型山水舞台，漫天繁星的山幕，会生长的层层稻田，全景式的黎族村寨，300位艺员的精湛表演，震撼感官的声光音效，将为您带来一场精神、文化、艺术的饕餮盛宴。

大地之夜

这是一场融多媒体、声光电、大型纱幕和全息影像技术一体的“大地之夜”大型声光秀，其以再现恐龙生命奇迹、呼唤生态文明、呼唤人与自然的和谐为主题，让您可以完全融入交互式体验和沉浸式体验场景，给您带来震撼的体验。

食

稻田盛宴

它是水稻国家公园原创开发的原生态餐饮体系，是稻田边“长出来”的餐厅，占地面积2.3万平方米，建筑古朴沉雄、大气通透，可同时容纳2800人就餐。独具特色的海鲜广场拥有72个海鲜档口，配备有超大型的中央可视加工厨房。这里还特邀国内顶级烹饪大师围绕中国“稻文化”主题，开辟“米文化”长廊，让您在椰树下、稻田旁、鸭塘边，满足对“吃”的美妙想象！

住

稻乡归隐　房车营地

稻田房车营地坐落在千亩稻田花海旁，占地1万平方米，拥有房车20辆，配备五星级内设，有一房一厅、两房一厅、KTV、茶歇酒吧、儿童泳池、接待中心、篝火晚会、烧烤自助、风情表演等，为家庭式自驾游群体及团队提供独特的休闲住宿体验，为各类亲子、交友、聚会、研学游学、夏令营、冬令营提供私人定制。

行

景区内设置有6千米长的游览车彩色通道，稻田木栈道九曲回廊，设计了各种亲近稻田花海的生态游步道。景区内还拥有50多部环保游览电瓶车，为游客提供乘车观光和漫步体验相结合的游览方式。电瓶车一票通达整个园区，各个景点随处上落。个性化定制的VIP包车服务，是家庭、情侣、好友聚会的最佳选择。

好了，各位游客朋友，我们的旅游车已经驶入我们的景区，大家是不是已经心驰神往，想要即刻体验一番呢？那就让我们带上好心情，一同去感受人与自然和谐共处的乐趣吧！

8. 海南儋州石花水洞地质公园

各位游客大家好，我是本次带领你们的导游许丹，你们可以叫我小许。该景区占地面积 29 万平方米，地处北纬 18°，是目前我国成功开发的纬度最低的天然溶洞，素有“海南第一洞”之称。其总长约 5 千米，其中旱洞长约 2 千米，已开发 650 米；水洞长约 3 千米，已开发 350 米，这是一个 140 万年前天然形成的一个溶洞，历经演变，造就了独特的溶洞奇观。

本景区由地上石林景点、地下溶洞、地下河景点和热带水果园景点组成。石花水洞不是一个普通的山洞，洞内景区由旱洞和水洞两部分组成，洞道系统复杂，总长约 5000 米，分有迎宾区、石花长廊区、宝玉明珠区、南海龙宫区等。旱洞内的“一石二花”卷曲石、文石花、方解石晶体花及其组合堪称国家级珍品和世界一绝。石花水洞地质公园被誉为“南国奇洞”“神奇的地下艺术宫殿”。

旱洞内还有石钟乳、石笋、石柱、石旗、石瀑布、石舌、辉锑矿晶簇、水晶石晶簇等。水洞已开发 350 米，水最深处达 17 米。其曲折蜿蜒的地下河水光怪陆离，五彩斑斓，轻舟漫游，宛若遨游龙宫，让人遐想万千。

景区外围是“八一”总场重点建设的万亩橡胶林，多年来产胶量名列海南垦区前茅。橡胶林与热带水果林以及景区的石林，共同构成了自然和谐的优美风景。

石花水洞山灵、水秀、石奇、洞幽。上善若水，止水清丽，洞中有洞，景中有景，是集探险科考、旅游观光、科普教育与环保教育于一体的综合性园林景观，是一部活的地质景观教科书，更是休闲度假的好去处。

地质条件

石花水洞所处的英岛山上有多种类型的地质遗迹，最重要的是洞穴、洞穴次生化学沉积物、石林和溶蚀形态，原为石灰岩矿（变质大理岩），品位较高，氧化钙含量高达 52%。主要由喀斯特（岩溶）景观构成，岩溶景观是由在广泛分布的碳酸盐岩之上发育出的形态特殊的多种地貌形态组成，地表石峰挺拔，地下洞穴绮丽多姿，不仅钟乳石琳琅满目，而且洞内有奔流不息的地下河。

在石花水洞景区我们可以观赏到地球表面的三大岩类——沉积岩、火成岩和变质岩。石灰岩属于沉积岩；辉绿岩岩脉是地幔岩浆沿断裂及构造带上升侵入到石灰岩中，所以岩脉属于火成岩；岩脉上升侵入到石灰石中，石灰石受热后变质为大理岩，因此大理岩属于变质岩类。这为石花的形成奠定了基础。

特色

石花水洞的洞道总长虽然不长，但其组成要素齐全，反映出洞穴通道多种成因特点。从洞穴的发育史看，有正在发育中的地下河，有已经脱离地下水位的旱洞洞道；从洞道的发育方向看，有水平延伸的通道，也有垂向发展的竖井；从洞穴成因类型看，有在渗流带（包气带）发育的竖井，有在潜流带发育的洞穴环，还有在地下水位附近生成的地下河洞道；从洞道组成看，有主洞，也有小的支洞，共同组成复杂的立体洞穴网络系统。石花水洞的洞道系统、竖井和裂隙、地下河河道和下游的岩溶泉共同构成有序的岩溶洞穴——水文地质系统，它们之间有组织的空间分布规律和时间上的先后生成以及发展序列为热带岩溶洞穴和热带岩溶水文地质研究提供了一处天然实验场所。

奇景

洞穴石花主要有三种矿物成分，即方解石、石膏和岩盐，故又可分别叫作方解石石花、石膏石花和岩盐石花。

石花水洞的石花的形成与石笋、石柱、石钟乳、石幔、石瀑布等有所不同，后者多为滴水、流水和停滞水沉积而成，而石花则由渗透水、飞溅水、毛细水沉积而成。其化学成分是碳酸钙，人们经过碳十四的测定，推断石花开始形成于十多万年前，同时石花的形成条件需要几种条件很巧合地相存。在至少 40 万年前，儋州应该位于海底贝壳类富集的位置，这才致使石花水洞内外都是富含碳酸钙的岩石，从而成为石花形成条件的一大前提。因为海水的运动会冲刷带走部分的碳酸钙，时间长了就形成了如石花水洞这样的石洞。

由于地球的内力作用使地形变形，石花水洞完整的岩层顶部产生了或多或少的裂缝，每逢下雨就有雨水渗入。同时，由于空气和微生物等各种原因，使有的雨水含有了二氧化碳，水和二氧化碳合成碳酸钙并渗入裂缝中去。有的洞裂缝较多令雨水流动的速度较快，难以形成钟乳石，却在温度和湿度比较稳定的条件下逐步结晶，从而形成了一些白色晶体，这就是石花了。

溶洞内的石花是一簇簇、一丛丛地附着在岩壁上，其形状若银针，或状若玉笛，或貌状秋菊，或貌状珊瑚，无不晶莹剔透，皓如白雪，坚硬如玉。在灯光的反射下，簇簇石花怒放，熠熠生辉，令游客倾倒。几乎所有石花都是历经千百万年沉积而成，而且还在不断生长中，为国内外罕见。

石花水洞内的石花有三大特点：

（1）剔透凝球，晶莹如玉，洁白无瑕。

（2）千姿百态，奇特瑰丽，集世界石花之大成，有针状、球状、塔状、卷曲状、放射状、灵芝状。

（3）附着于岩壁之上，不受重力影响生长而向四面节节开花，见气成石，持续生长，变幻无穷。并且石花 100 年才长 1 厘米。

在洞里还有国宝级珍品——卷曲石。这里的卷曲石是地质专家在洞内探测时意外发现的，位于旱路中部的顶部，卷曲石主要由方解石组成，分布在卷曲石通道的侧壁及洞顶。其多沿某一岩层露头、裂隙呈条状产出，在窝穴中呈密集状，在岩壁上呈零散状。石花水洞中的卷曲石数量甚多，形态也很优美，是旅游洞穴非常引人入胜的一种沉积物。卷曲石的生长方向不受重力作用限制，他们往往是向上、向侧方生长。其色泽纯白，直径一般在 5~6 厘米，目前只有在美国、罗马尼亚、中国等少数几个国家发现过。

大家眼前的这些树木是大王棕，它上下两头比较小、中间比较大，像一枚快要发射的导弹，所以它也叫作“导弹树”。它是棕榈科的常绿乔木同时也是古巴的国树，它上面的果实富含油料可以制作成鸽子的饲料。

迎面走过的这条是时来运转大道，也是景区一道亮丽的风景线。走过大道，清风徐徐迎面吹来，可以给您带来好运气。我们来看一下前方的一棵百年老榕树，可以说儋州地区百年以上的榕树随处可见，树下挂的祈福带就是客人为自己家人和亲戚朋友送上祝福、祈求平安的。

各位游客，我们现在走的这条林荫小道两边种植的这种植物叫扶桑花，一般我们叫它大红花，其夏季和秋季最为旺盛，据说土著女郎会带着这种花在海边跳草裙舞，如果她把花插在左耳上就表示她已经成年，希望有个爱人，如果她把花插在右耳上，表示她已经有爱人。

我们来看一下右手边这棵榕树，它的特点就是这些垂落下来的毛细根吸收空气中水分和养分后落地生根，最终能够形成独木成林的景象。

我们继续来看一下右手边的这棵大榕树，它的特点就是其根部像一个巨大的爪子。下面我们要走过的这条长廊就是我们景区极具特色的情廊了，它是由扶桑花和榕树交错形成的，两边的树枝垂下来就像个弯弯的拱门，好似结婚时的殿堂，这也是一条延续亲情、爱情和友情的长廊。不知道大家有没有听说过海南八大怪：三条杀虫一碗菜；三个老鼠一麻袋；一条蚂蟥当腰带；树根长在树皮外；老太太爬树比猴快；牛头下雨牛尾晒；头上斗笠当锅盖；青石板上煎鸡蛋。

我们大家再来看一下右手边有两棵树叫作绞杀树，这是热带雨林常见的一种现象，这棵绞杀树里面包裹的是一棵油棕树，外面是榕树，我们常吃的棕榈油就是由这个油棕提炼出来的。它们是一些小鸟、松鼠或者蝙蝠吃了榕树的果实后产生的粪便里有榕树的种子在油棕树上生根发芽形成的，它们现在还是一个寄生的现象，慢慢地，榕树会吸收油棕树的养分和水分，把它绞杀掉。这就是绞杀树的由来。

我们大家走到凉亭可以看到那里有一只神龟。关于这只神龟有个顺口溜。摸摸乌龟的头，万事不用愁。摸摸乌龟背，一辈子不受累。从头摸到尾，顺风顺水。

朋友们，欣赏了一路美景，对石林、溶洞以及地下河的形成、发展也有了一定的了解，我的讲解到此就圆满结束了，俗话说："两山不能相遇，两人总能相逢！"我期待能再次见到大家，再次为大家服务！祝各位在新的一年里事事顺心、平平安安、旅途愉快、一路顺风！

9. 东坡书院

各位朋友大家好，我是你们此次游览的导游小史，很高兴为大家服务，希望我的服务能给各位带来温馨和快乐！东坡书院是苏东坡在儋州留下的重要遗迹之一。它的前身是“载酒堂”，始建于北宋元符元年（1098 年）。元代泰定三年（1326 年）重建，并设立东坡祠。明代嘉靖廿七年（1548 年）重修后更名为东坡书院。1996 年，东坡书院被列为国家重点文物保护单位，是海南著名的文化旅游胜地。

载酒亭

载酒亭建于明万历二十三年（1595 年）。载酒亭为重檐结构，上檐四角，下檐八角，十二根圆柱支撑起翠顶，典雅古朴。亭内镶嵌有 8 幅木刻画，描绘着东坡居儋生活、交友、授徒、离别等情景。

“春梦婆”的故事

版画里那个头戴斗笠的是苏东坡，旁边是一位农妇。据传有一天，苏东坡遇到这个去田间给丈夫送饭的农妇，只见她头发蓬松，口嚼槟榔，嚼得嘴巴乌红乌红的，于是奚落道：“头发蓬松口乌乌，天天送饭予田夫！”这农妇听了当然不高兴，毫不客气地回应道：“是非皆因多开口，记得君王贬你乎？”其意思是说你知道朝廷为什么贬你到这里不，就因为你说话口无遮拦、信口开河！

苏东坡发现这位农妇不一般，很聪明，于是问她：“你能说说这世道如何吗？”农妇说：“这世间的荣华富贵，说白了全是一场春梦！”苏东坡一下被这个心直口快、深谙世故的农妇彻底折服了，于是送了她个外号“春梦婆”。这就是从北宋流传至今的“春梦婆的故事”。

载酒堂

“载酒堂”建于北宋元符元年（1098 年），也就是苏东坡到儋州的第二年。有一次，苏东坡受昌化军军使张中（当时儋州的地方长官）之邀，一起去拜访黎子云。交谈中，大家提议在黎子云住宅旁边建一座房屋，作为东坡设帐讲学、文友聚会的地方，苏东坡非常赞同这个倡议，并带头凑钱，还借用“载酒问字”的典故为房屋取名“载酒堂”。苏东坡在载酒堂设帐讲学，培养出了海南历史上第一个举人姜唐佐和第一个进士符确，形成了“人知教子，家习儒风，青衿之士，日以增盛”的局面，对未来产生了深远影响。

这里还有一个“载酒问字”的典故：相传西汉著名的辞赋家扬雄，博学多才，但这人比较贪杯，于是找他拜师求学的人就投其所好，带着酒肴到他家来求学。这就是“载酒问字”典故的由来。

大殿塑像

塑像的中间是苏东坡，左侧是黎子云。他既是苏东坡的学生，又是苏东坡在儋州交往最深的朋友。当年，军使张中因为关照苏东坡被罢黜，苏东坡被逐出官舍，失去栖身之所，就是黎子云等人伸出援手，帮他在桄榔林中建起三间庵舍。也是黎子云献地出资又出力，才有了如今的载酒堂。

右侧的英俊的小生名叫苏过，是苏东坡的小儿子。1097 年，苏东坡被贬儋州时，苏过只有 25 岁，正值争取功名的大好年华，但是，为了照料苏东坡的生活起居，苏过独自随父渡海，与苏东坡相依为命，度过了三年的艰难岁月。因为苏过是个大孝子，所以儋州人要建祠立像纪念他。

坡仙笠屐图

《坡仙笠屐图》的作者为南宋画家钱选。据记载，有一天，苏东坡去看望黎子云，路上遇到下雨，于是向农家借用竹笠和木屐，穿戴后怪模怪样，惹得妇女儿童相随争笑，农家的狗也对着他吠叫。苏东坡也乐了，说：“笑所怪也，吠所怪也！”从宋至今，《东坡笠屐图》的版本很多，流传很广，但东坡笠屐的故事的实际发生地是儋州。

东坡祠

东坡祠俗称“大殿”，始建于元朝延祐四年（1317 年），地点在城南的桄榔庵，于 1326 年迁至现址。

东坡祠还有一尊东坡闲适铜像，它是儋州市政府 2015 年立于大殿的，由雕塑家、清华大学教授何宝森设计。东坡悠闲自在地坐在木椅上，手握书卷，目光沉静地凝视远方，表现出苏东坡面对苦难泰然处之的精神世界。

苏轼《寒食帖》

《寒食帖》被称为“天下第三行书”，在我国书法史上影响很大。此帖真迹现收藏于中国台北故宫博物院。

西庑廊

苏轼《别海南黎民表》，是苏东坡获赦北归、离开儋州时写给黎子云的赠别诗：

我本儋耳人，寄生西蜀州。忽然跨海去，譬如事远游。平生生死梦，三者无劣优。知君不再见，欲去且少留。

苏轼《自题金山画像》

1101 年 5 月，东坡北归途经镇江，在金山寺看到李公麟 10 年前给他画的肖像还在寺里，抚今追昔，百感交集，写下了《自题金山画像》：心似已灰之木，身如不系之舟。问汝平生功业，黄州惠州儋州。苏轼用这首诗对自己的一生做了总结，两个月后，苏东坡就在常州病逝，因此这首诗也是苏东坡的绝笔诗。

东庑廊

中华人民共和国成立以来，先后有数十位党和国家领导人到访过东坡书院，这些都是他们参观东坡书院时的珍贵照片。

杧果树

这棵杧果树植于清乾隆三年（1738 年），枝繁叶茂，使整个庭院平添幽静和清爽。每年夏季，树上还会结满金灿烂的杧果，是非常珍贵的馈赠礼品。

钦帅泉

这口古井名叫“钦帅泉”，据说是苏东坡当年与学子煮茶用的水井，明代经过疏浚，正式命名“钦帅泉”。这口古井一年四季从不干涸，泉水清澈甘甜。大家可以打上一桶“文化圣水”，饮上一口，洗一洗手，沾一沾“苏学士”的才气，是学生，来年定能“金榜题名”，是公务员，定能才如泉涌，前程似锦！

“钦帅泉”也叫“酒井”，还流传着一个有趣的故事。相传，附近有一位妇人，家里很穷。一天，她来“钦帅泉”挑水，唉声叹气地说：“要是井水能变成酒水该多好啊！”夜里，苏东坡托梦给她：“从明天起，井水就会变成酒，你挑去换钱度日吧。”第二天，妇人将信将疑来到井边，果然井水变成了香醇扑鼻的美酒，她也从此富裕起来。可是她还嫌不够，埋怨说：“井水变酒好是好，要是再来些酒糟让我喂猪就更好了。”于是，苏东坡再次托梦给她，说道：“天高不为高，人心比天高，井水当酒卖，还嫌酒无糟。”从此，井水便再无酒味儿。此则故事告诫人们，做人切忌贪心。

春牛雕塑

北宋时期，当地的黎人思想落后，盛行迷信，他们用珍贵的沉香从内陆换取耕牛，常常是“一牛博香一担”，换来的牛却不用于农耕，而是搭起祭坛，杀牛祭神，导致农业生产一直停留在刀耕火种的原始状态。苏东坡对此十分痛心，专门写了《书柳子厚〈牛赋〉后》等文章，劝导黎族同胞革除陋俗，珍惜耕牛。在他不遗余力的教化和启迪下，这种“杀牛祭神”的陋俗才得以杜绝。雕塑上的《减字木兰花》是苏东坡为儋州人民创作的一首咏春词，他用欢快的笔触描写了儋州绚丽的春光，也寄托了他对儋州人民的美好祝福：

春牛春杖，无限春风来海上。便丐春工，染得桃红似肉红。

春幡春胜，一阵春风吹酒醒。不似天涯，卷起杨花似雪花。

习近平总书记就曾引用苏东坡“不似天涯，卷起杨花似雪花”的诗句，称赞海南的青山绿水、碧海蓝天，并且指出：“海南生态环境是大自然赐予的宝贵财富，必须倍加珍惜、精心呵护，使海南真正成为中华民族的四季花园。”

东坡私塾

苏东坡在载酒堂设帐讲学，向儋州子弟传播中原文化，并且吸引了许多内陆学子纷纷前来求学，使儋州成为当时全岛的文化教育中心。

大家现在看到的东坡私塾，最大限度地还原了苏东坡先生当年所使用的文房用品、教材典籍以及北宋时期的各种礼乐器具。2018 年，东坡书院先后被确定为“海南省中小学生研学实践教育基地”和“国家中小学生研学旅游教育基地”，东坡私塾开设有研学课堂，学生可以穿宋服，进私塾，学礼仪，拜孔子，吟诵东坡诗词，来一次时空穿越，真实体验古代儒生的学习场景。

狗仔花

狗仔花是一种很特别的花卉，这种花只有在东坡书院才可以见得到，不但名贵稀少，而且花也开得奇妙。关于狗仔花，有一个有趣儿的故事。相传王安石曾写过这么两句诗“明月当空叫，五犬卧花心。”苏东坡看见了，认为写得不符合现实，于是便给改成了“明月当空照，五犬卧花阴”。后来苏东坡被贬儋州，在载酒堂亲眼看到了狗仔花，并且见到了在皓月当空的夜晚凌空而叫的明月鸟（一种山麻雀），这才恍然大悟，自己当年原来是错改了王安石的诗。“狗仔花”也因这段逸事而名扬天下。

狗仔花开花的时候，绽开的花瓣内有 5 个小花蕊，形似 5 只小犬头顶头卧坐一团，因此叫作“狗仔花”。

陈列馆

“陈列馆”三字由著名的书法家商承祚用金文题写。陈列馆主要介绍了苏东坡的生平事迹、年谱和行踪示意图，重点介绍了苏东坡的居儋功绩。

东坡笠屐铜像

东坡铜像取材于《东坡笠屐图》，他头戴斗笠、脚穿木屐、旷达乐观、入乡随俗、与民相亲的形象，永远活在儋州人民的心中。东坡笠屐铜像的创作者是我国著名雕塑家李汉仪先生。其汉白玉基座正面的“东坡居士”四个字，是郭沫若的手迹。

休闲驿站

大家可以在休闲驿站休息一下，品一品香莲茶，尝一尝儋州风味小吃，选购一些特色纪念品。有兴致的朋友，可以穿上宋代服饰，拍照留念。驿站的这棵古榕树，在当地被视作“神树”，有“神树祈福”习俗。游客在上面系满了祈福带，表达对古树的敬意和对家人、朋友的祝福。

周末的时候，大家可以在这里欣赏到“东坡乐坊”的歌舞表演，还可以欣赏到誉为“南国奇葩”、列入国家非物遗产的儋州调声，感受火热的黎乡风情。

各位朋友，我们的东坡书院之旅到此全部结束，东坡书院的美景永远在这里等待您的下次光临，祝大家旅途愉快！

10. 母瑞山革命根据地纪念园

尊敬的各位游客朋友，大家好！欢迎各位莅临海南革命的摇篮——母瑞山。我是今天的讲解员小唐。

母瑞山是五指山向东北延伸的一条山脉，是海南革命的摇篮，在琼崖两次革命低潮时期，母瑞山两度保存了革命火种，为海南人民坚持武装斗争作出了重大的贡献。

保存革命火种

1928 年年底，海南第一次低潮时期，王文明同志带领琼崖特委、琼苏政府机关、红军战士、赤卫队员、红军医院、交通处等 600 多人，从乐会四区冲破敌人的重重封锁，渡过万泉河，上了母瑞山，开辟革命根据地。

刚上山时，条件相当艰苦，住无房，吃无粮，穿无衣，病无医。为了解决这些问题，王文明同志亲自深入到山村苗寨，发动苗胞，在苗胞的支持下，建起了 40 多栋茅草房，安营扎寨，解决了住的问题。

吃的怎么办？王文明同志再度动员军民，发扬自力更生、艰苦奋斗的精神，砍山开荒，办起了三个红军农场，有 300 多亩地，种下了水稻，山兰、玉米、木薯、番薯、瓜菜等作物。过了半年多时间，也就是这些作物收获了，红军的供给慢慢地得到好转，生活逐渐得到改善，解决了吃的问题。

穿的怎么办？他们偷偷派人下山，到翰林、领口、石壁等附近乡镇购买那些粗布，组织缝衣组缝制成衣服，解决了穿的问题。群众发动起来了，解决了吃、穿、住的问题，红军就在母瑞山上站稳了脚跟。

随着革命形势的发展，在母瑞山腹地和周边 40 多个村庄先后成立了两个红色政权，也就是两个乡政府，一个叫大山乡，一个叫母瑞乡，开展了轰轰烈烈的土地革命斗争。

1929 年 6 月，红军独立团在母瑞山诞生。在此基础上，他们还办起了红军医院、红军军械厂、红军军政学校、红军消费合作社，建起了粮食加工厂，组织红军剧团排练山歌、海南戏等一些节目来活跃红军的精神生活。尽管当时生活那么艰苦，但红军战士仍然保持着高度的乐观主义精神，他们对革命的前途充满着胜利的信心。至此，母瑞山变成了一个小社会，样样俱全。

经过一年多的艰苦奋斗，在王文明同志的领导下，母瑞山革命根据地建立起来了。母瑞山革命根据地的建立，保存了革命的火种，也标志着海南的武装斗争发展到一个崭新的阶段。

二次保存革命火种

1932年秋，海南第二次低潮时期，冯白驹同志带领特委机关、琼苏政府机关一个警卫连100多人在母瑞山上坚持8个多月艰苦卓绝的斗争，克服了种种难以想象的困难，渡过一个又一个难关。

首先是粮食困难。国民党采取了并村移民政策，企图把母瑞山变成无人区，隔绝红军与老百姓的来往，把红军饿死在这个革命摇篮里。冯白驹同志带领100多人在母瑞山上几个月来没吃过一餐饱饭。刚开始时，每餐每人还可以分到一个拳头大小的饭团，后来粮食越来越少，饭团变成一个椰壳稀饭，最后只能喝用锅巴煮的饭汤。粮食没有了，连饭汤也喝不上了，怎么办？只好上山找野菜，摘野果，下河沟抓鱼摸虾，上树掏鸟巢、找鸟蛋、抓小鸟。凡是山上找得到的东西，只要没有毒的，嚼得烂的吞得下去的都找回来充饥。当时山上有一种野菜，叶嫩、茎脆、有一点苦味，红军把这种野菜当作“主食”，用来维持生命，但大家都不知道这种野菜叫什么名字。为了给这种野菜命名，冯白驹同志主持召开了一个命名会，会上有的同志说，这种野菜能够吃饱肚子，就叫它“饱肚子菜”吧！也有的同志讲，这种野菜是山中的宝，那么就叫“山中宝”吧！冯白驹同志最后吸纳了大家的意见，语重心长地说：“这种野菜在革命最困难的时候救了我们的命，我们就把它叫作‘革命’菜吧！”但这种菜属性很凉，红军天天吃，餐餐吃这种没有油，没有盐煮的革命菜，时间长了很多同志也得了水肿病、夜盲症、痢疾等各种疾病。

其次是没有房子住。1932年秋，国民党陈汉光部队1000多人在飞机的掩护下，攻进了母瑞山，占领了母瑞山革命根据地，把红军住的茅房全部烧掉，把红军留下来的物资全部抢光，把红军农场的作物全部毁坏，每个红军身上仅剩下一件衣服。他们只好住在低矮潮湿的山洞里。今天住这个山洞，明天要换另一个山洞，今天住在这个山头，明天又要搬到另一个山头。为了躲避敌人的追查，有时一个晚上要换几个地方睡。到了秋冬季节，风雨交加，寒风刺骨，晚上红军在山洞里冷得睡不着，只好烧火取暖，到山上割芭蕉叶放在火上烤热，一张铺在地上当席子睡，一张盖在身上当被子用。红军在深山老林里、在山洞里度过了一个又一个漫漫长夜。

再次是没有衣服穿。红军身上仅剩下一件衣服，几个月下来，风吹、雨淋、太阳晒、树枝刮，这件衣服穿在身上没有换的，湿了又干，干了又湿，时间一长全部烂掉，变成挂在身上的布条和布块，最后烂的没办法再穿了，只好穿树叶、树皮。就是到山上找那些叶子比较大、比较厚的树叶和那种比较柔软的树皮，用麻绳连起来做成“衣服”穿，不管是男同志还是女同志，只要能够用树叶、树皮把自己身体上那些关键部位包起来就行了。头发长没有剪刀怎么办？只好躺在地上，将头发放在树头、树根上用砍刀砍短。冯白驹同志带着这 100 多人在母瑞山上度过了 8 个多月原始人般的生活。

最后是在山上不仅要跟敌人斗，还要跟恶劣的自然环境作斗争。当时母瑞山死的人很多，战死、饿死、病死、冻死、被毒蛇咬死的人不计其数。母瑞山北面棺材沟一带仅病死、饿死就有 100 多人。马鞍岭东北面有一棵大榕树，在树荫底下，一天就饿死了 9 位同志。红军战士来到树荫底下坐下休息的时候就再也没有力气站起来，最后活活地饿死在大树底下。

冯白驹同志带领的这 100 多人最后只剩下 26 个人，其中有 4 名干部 22 名战士。这 22 名战士中有 2 名是女同志，一名是冯白驹夫人王惠周，一名是炊事员李月凤。这时，冯白驹考虑到，如果继续在山上，东躲西闪，难于接触群众，不能打开局面，对革命的生存和发展不利，所以特委研究决定，一定要突围下山，寻求一条革命的活路。他们也组织过四批人突围下山，但没有一批成功。不是半路上被敌人发现杀害，就是由于环境恶劣，下了山没有办法再回来。一直坚持到 1933 年春节，趁着春节敌人放松警惕的时机，冯白驹同志亲自组织这 26 人并由李月凤同志带路，向澄迈新兴方向突围。

当队伍突围来到李月凤同志的家乡，冯白驹先派李月凤同志进村探听情况，想办法找点水喝，弄一点吃的，其余的同志就埋伏在村子附近的树林里等待着李月凤同志带回消息。不料李月凤同志进村不久，就被坏人告密，被敌人抓住并杀害了。这时，冯白驹等 25 位同志只好怀着悲愤的心情，迈着沉重的脚步，默默地离开了这个村子，经过两天两夜的艰苦跋涉，重返了母瑞山。

这时山上的日子就更加难熬了。山洞里的火种已经熄灭，山上的野菜、河沟里的鱼虾也很少了，加上敌人天天放狗搜山，红军已经失去了基本的生存条件，这段日子也是琼崖革命最艰难的时期。但这 25 人团结一致，在特委的领导下，凭着理想信念、顽强意志苦苦地支撑着，一直坚持到 1933 年 4 月。

母瑞山精神

王文明、冯白驹同志在母瑞山参与了两次保存革命火种的斗争历程，也铸就了母瑞山精神，这就是：崇高理想，坚定信念；不怕牺牲，勇于献身；相信群众，依靠群众；自力更生，艰苦奋斗。

各位游客，过去革命战争年代，革命老前辈闹革命，打江山，求解放，谋幸福，迎来了中华人民共和国的诞生，靠的就是母瑞山精神。但愿母瑞山精神光辉照千秋！

11. 椰子大观园

大家好，欢迎来到椰子大观园游览，我是你们的导游李丹，大家可以叫我小李，希望我的讲解能给您带来愉悦的心情。

椰子大观园是中国热带农业科学院椰子研究所在原有椰子种质资源库的基础上改建而成，位于我国“椰子之乡”——海南省文昌市，毗邻海南著名风景区东郊椰林。园区始建于 1980 年，占地面积 54.4 公顷，是以椰林为主体背景，集科学研究、科普教育、旅游观光、休闲娱乐为一体的具有浓郁椰子文化特色的生态景区。

园区汇集了 217 种棕榈植物、130 种海南特色珍稀树种，是我国目前棕榈植物品种保存最多、最为完整的植物园区，品种繁多、造型奇异的植物让人惊奇感叹。依托椰子研究所的科研力量，椰子大观园向世界各地采集和交换椰子种质，现已收集椰子种质 17 份，列全国椰子种质收集的第一位，被誉为“世界椰子博览，中国椰子之窗”。

2021年，由中国热带农业科学院椰子研究所携手海南爱也文旅发展有限公司共同打造了以“推进椰子产业与旅游融合发展”为核心的椰子主题综合旅游景区。椰子大观园以弘扬椰树精神，打造国内一流棕榈种质资源科普研学基地，整合椰子研究所农业科技力量，延伸椰子产业链，开发椰子产业发展平台为使命，打造了集椰树精神、椰子文化、科普、文旅、产业升级等功能为一体综合性主题景区。项目建成后将成为琼北旅游的主打旅游产品，其中包括椰子侠勇士营、椰子文化科普研学、星空露营地、萌宠乐园、爱椰广场、椰林迷宫、奇异椰子、椰树精神等特色主题景点。

椰子侠勇士营

椰子侠勇士营是椰子大观园景区为椰子侠IP量身打造的拓展活动组织中心，旨在传播椰树精神，践行少年强则中国强的发展理念。营内拥有拓展器械、拓展场地等相关配套设施，满足企业团建、破冰拓展、亲子拓展、家庭运动休闲等综合功能。让家长与孩子们跟随着椰子侠的步伐，参与勇士营内丛林魔网、攀岩走壁、环环相扣等项目，投身于艰苦的训练环境下，在勇士营中得到锻炼，培养吃苦耐劳、艰苦奋斗、积极向上的优良品质。通过亲子游戏等多种互动交流方式让父母学会与孩子沟通，不断提升沟通的能力，使亲子关系更加和谐。

椰林迷宫

穿越“时空椰墙”，唤醒沉睡的“宝藏”，紧跟椰子侠的步伐，探索未知的迷宫世界，寻觅隐藏于深处的“珍品”。

萌宠乐园

萌宠乐园位于奇异椰子区旁，以萌宠互动为主题，集萌宠亲密接触、游乐休闲、亲子互动、科普教育、萌宠表演等为一体，打造萌宠主题乐园度假新体验。在这里游客可以看到憨态可掬的小松鼠，触摸呆萌淘气的小兔子，喂食聪明伶俐的鹦鹉，与活泼可爱的豚鼠互动拍照，激发人们热爱大自然的情怀和敢于探索的互动精神，将萌宠乐园置身于椰林之中，旨在为游客打造贴近自然沉浸式的萌宠互动方式。

奇异椰子

“鬼斧神工”的雕刻艺术是大自然留给人类的惊喜，在奇异椰子区游客可以观赏到“Y”形结构的分叉椰子树，椰子树通常是“树干笔直，无枝无蔓”，一般不会分支分叉，民间常用“椰子树分叉”来比喻不可能发生的事情。这里有“三阳开泰”“五福临门”的多胚椰子树，还有不开花不结果的“椰仙”，其中“椰仙”为世界罕见、国内独有，具有极高的研究价值。这些奇异的椰子树皆是自然形成，人工无法干预。

椰树精神

椰树精神区是椰子大观园景区的主要游览区域，也是海南椰树精神集中展示的核心区域。区域内皆是被台风吹倒却依然顽强生长的椰子树，这些椰子树依然热爱这片土壤，千丝万缕的气根支撑起生命的桥梁，继续守护一方土地，反哺大自然。其大风刮不倒代表着扎根守土的精神；倒下的身躯依旧笔直地向着阳光生长代表着坚韧不拔的精神；终其一生将一切奉献给人们代表着无私奉献的精神。这些精神激励着海南人民顽强拼搏，共筑美好家园！

椰子科普馆

椰子大观园以开发椰子产业发展平台为使命，打造集椰树精神、椰子文化、科普研学、文化旅游、产业升级等功能为一体的综合性主题景区。现形成以“九区一馆”——国家热带棕榈种质资源圃、椰子侠勇士营、椰林迷宫、椰树精神、奇异椰子、椰林婆娑、椰林湖光、游客驿站、星空露营地和椰子科普馆为核心资源的研学基地，并于2022年11月被中国科协认定为“2021—2025年第一批全国科普教育基地”。

游客驿站

独具匠心的设计风格，秉承着人与自然和谐相处的理念，既体现了绿色环保，同时也凸显出椰子主题特色。精心打造的空中花园以文心兰、猪笼草、鸟巢蕨等多种热带珍稀植物为主，假山塑石、水域水系为辅，分布于驿站各处，形成热带南方特色园林及室外生态公园。驿站集茶歇休憩、观赏美景、品尝景区特有椰子水等功能为一体，为游客带来优质的观景体验。

各位朋友，我们的椰子大观园之旅到此全部结束，椰子大观园的美景永远在这里等待您的下次光临，祝大家旅途愉快！

12. 七仙岭温泉国家森林公园

各位游客朋友，欢迎大家到美丽的七仙岭温泉国家森林公园来观光游览。七仙岭温泉国家森林公园位于保亭黎族苗族自治县的东北边，包括温泉区和森林区两部分，其魅力在于温泉、奇峰、民族风情和热带田园风光。1998 年经国务院和国家林业局联合批准为国家级森林公园，于 2016 年 12 月 29 日被正式批准为国家 4A 级旅游景区。

七仙岭温泉国家森林公园是海南岛内仅有的几片保存较为完好的热带雨林之一。森林公园内古树参天、藤萝交织。目前已探明的各类珍奇植物有 500 多种，野生动物有 500 多种。在登山石板栈道约 700 米处有一片集中分布的桫椤群落，杆高 9 米多，桫椤被誉为“植物活化石”，是国家重点保护的古老孑遗植物，其古老可上溯到恐龙时代。漫步七仙岭原始热带雨林，可尽情欣赏动植物景观，饱吸原始热带雨林中高浓度的氧气和负氧离子，可起到保健作用。

景区旅游资源十分丰富，地貌景观壮观生动，水文、植物、气候旅游资源俱全，还有众多的社会人文旅游资源等，是一处集奇峰、温泉、风情、田园、气候、森林为一体的大型生态旅游区。

自然环境

七仙岭地区气候温润，这里常年平均气温 23℃左右，最高月平均气温 27℃，最低月平均气温 18℃，年降雨量 1900 毫米。全山密布原始热带雨林，是天然的动植物王国。其中包括海南黄花梨、蝴蝶木、桫椤、见血封喉、眼镜王蛇等国家珍稀保护的动植物。在海南，七仙岭温泉国家森林公园是唯一一个温泉与热带雨林相结合的森林公园，公园负氧离子浓度高达 8200 个 / 立方厘米，十分有益于人体健康。

七仙岭的七座山峰似人的掌指竖立，直指苍穹，又如仙女亭立，岭名由此而得。七仙岭的前峰高大，海拔 1126 米，后六峰相依而小。在七仙岭的三、四峰之间有一小石峰与第四峰相对而立，小石峰形若童子，四峰远观神似观音，人们称此景为“童子拜观音”。登上七仙岭峰顶，可尽有“与仙同游、与人同乐、与景同醉、与山同寿”的无穷乐趣。

当晨雾弥漫时，远眺中的七仙岭，酷似七位姐妹披着薄纱直立，端庄窈窕。时近中午，云雾消散，此时的七仙岭又像七把利剑直指云天，气势十分雄伟。

神话传说

传说古时候，海南岛的保亭地区遍布温泉，黎民百姓劳作之余，用橘叶泡温泉沐浴能消除疲劳，医治百病。在温泉中嬉水游戏，更使人容颜美丽，精神焕发。这事传到天宫，王母娘娘就派了七仙女下凡，落实这块地方是否可以与天宫的瑶池相媲美。

七仙女来到保亭，只见满目绿水青山，祥云缭绕，温泉升腾，鸟语花香，好一派人间仙境。七仙女陶醉了，天天游玩于这片山水之间，住了好久才回到天庭。这件美差被海上一位魔力高强的风神知道了，也想占有此处作为栖身之地，但是他每次来这里玩耍，都要带来狂风暴雨，淹没大片的土地，损毁大片美丽的田园。

七仙女看在眼里，气在心上，奏请玉帝，与风神进行了一番殊死的争斗，最后打败了风神，将风神赶到海洋深处。为了不让风神再来破坏此地，七仙女决心守护着这块美丽的土地，永驻人间，后来竟化作七座秀丽的山峰，这就是如今神奇的七仙岭。

九大奇观

热带雨林里遍布九大奇观，分别是高板根、根抱石、古藤缠树、老茎生花、空中花园、植物绞杀、猛龙过江、腐木生芝和通天树。

高大的树木一心向上争抢阳光，为了避免头重脚轻，重心不稳，它们有的就自己设法解决，长出如墙体似的宽厚粗壮的板根，不断向两边延伸来帮助自己加固根基，热带雨林中潮湿的空气，肥沃的土壤为它们的生长提供了充足的条件。有的树种没有长板根的本领，它们就伸展自己粗大的树根，紧紧拥抱住身旁的巨石，它的根基也就稳如磐石了，这就形成了高板根和根抱石奇观。

老茎生花奇观则发生在聚果榕树身上，其开花结果不在树枝上面而在树的茎干上，也算是树中一绝了。

空中花篮起因于禽鸟的杰作，是它们在不经意中把兰花和蕨草的种子或幼苗，带到了高大的乔木树冠上或垂挂于空中的藤蔓上，并使它们在那里生根、开花，于是便形成了空中花篮奇观，为热带原始森林增色不少。如"一树穿花"就十分典型。但如果禽鸟无意中将高山榕的种子带到一棵树上，那它就扮演了森林杀手的帮凶，这棵树最终将会慢慢被高山榕的支持根扼住它赖以供应水分和营养的全部通道而被绞杀。

由此可见，森林中不仅动物会为生存而互相残杀（"螳螂捕蝉，黄雀在后"就是一例），树木中的高山榕同样是热带原始森林中可怕的植物杀手，因此貌似安宁的森林也并不和平，其中却是暗藏杀机。真可谓物竞天择，适者生存。

景点一览

传说天生神力的黎族英雄猎哥出征抗击风魔，与心爱的部落首领女儿婀甘，在此石下挥泪告别。日复一日的等待，婀甘没能盼来猎哥，却被觊觎已久的外族首领峒主，乘机掳回了山寨。

思念情郎的婀甘，泪水汇成了湖泊，对爱的忠贞不渝终于换来了山神的帮助，婀甘以银钗化作羽翼，变身飞鸟冲破云霄，向着家园飞去。打败风魔的猎哥身受重伤，终日在当年分手的石下守望。一天从远处飞来了一只鸟，其羽毛上的图腾让猎哥明白，这就是心爱的婀甘，于是一跃化身为鸟，跟随婀甘而去，守望石从此成为黎族、苗族青年男女爱情守护之地。

各种奇形怪状的巨石散落在山间，构成了雨林仙境独特的奇观妙景。对自然神力的崇拜，让黎族世代，形成了以巨石为图腾的山神祭拜仪式。

相传很久以前，七仙岭因盛产奇珍异草而被南海风魔觊觎。曾经一片富饶的黎族家园变得生灵涂炭。在族长'迪'的号召下，年轻的英雄猎哥与部落勇士们，开始了一场抵抗风魔的保卫战。守护一方的山神也闻讯而来，赋予巨石神奇的灵性，一个个硕大无比的"巨灵石"攀上了山顶，又让"树精灵”用坚韧的藤条将它们牢牢捆绑在一起。高大的石墙暂时堵住了风口，黎族的勇士终于有了喘息的机会，失散的人们得以团聚，万物生灵得以恢复。

巨大的榕树已有上百年历史，由于太过高大遭雷击而被拦腰折断，但是由于七仙岭得天独厚的气候，榕树在断裂处发出新芽，长出五个粗壮的侧枝，古藤缠绕享日月精华。七仙岭周边的山民之后便形成了一种习俗，就是有什么心愿都会来在这棵榕树前祈愿，许下的愿望常常都能够实现，此处也是七仙岭居民们心中的一块圣地。

瀑布在中国传说中便是连接凡间与仙界的纽带，古人对天上的向往，赋予了瀑布美好的想象。相传天潭瀑布的源头来自南海仙界的“不老泉”，长久沐浴与饮用，可使容颜不老，青春永驻。

在七仙岭还生长着这样两棵参天大树，它们同根双茎，合抱相生，在黎族人眼里，被称为守护爱情的“情人树”又称“夫妻树”。关于它的形成，黎族至今还流传着一个美丽动人的故事。

传说黎族英雄猎哥和族长女儿婀甘，自小便青梅竹马，一个英勇无比，一个能歌善舞，无论到哪里，猎哥总是守护在婀甘身边，他们将寓意爱的种子埋进了山间，随着日月更替，曾经山盟海誓的信物，如今已是遮天蔽日的大榕树，两枝苍劲的根脉努力地汲取着养分，相依相拥缠绕不分，如同相爱的恋人。神奇的情人树传遍了部落，人们认为这一定是神的安排，纷纷向他们送去真诚的祝福。

各位旅客朋友，攀登通往顶峰的天梯要做好防寒准备，这里山势险峻，天梯也非常陡峭，在攀登过程中要踩稳抓实，尽量扶着旁边的栏杆，避免拥挤。天梯越往上越陡，越上越险，至高处犹如行于浩渺的云海之间，甚至会有摇摇欲坠之感。

登仙台位于七仙岭第二峰峰顶之上，也是传说中七仙女脱胎化石，得道飞升的灵秀之地。登仙台上，气象万千，四时景象变幻奇特，非寻常之境，然有得道者曰“一日七仙岭，胜似千日间”。登仙台，作为黎族人民心中的神山圣境，守卫一方祥宁，不仅是精神信仰的图腾，更是祈愿美好未来的寄托之地。

景区规划

七仙岭景区规划面积约22平方千米，包括温泉区和森林区两部分。七仙岭温泉国家森林公园主要分三个游览区域，第一区域是七仙岭国家公园体验之旅，另外两个区域分别为热带雨林猎奇之旅、探险登峰之旅。

七仙岭景区服务区面积占地70亩，设施包括建筑面积为3000平方米的景区游客中心、长4500米、宽13米的穿梭车道、7800平方米的停车场、1300米的木栈道、2300米的石栈道、10个连体商铺建筑、沿途有10个景观服务平台、6个环保生态厕所、1个游客中心厕所，1000平方米的中餐厅、700平方米的咖啡厅以及700平方米的大型商场。

各位朋友，我们的七仙岭温泉国家森林公园之旅到此全部结束，七仙岭温泉国家森林公园的美景永远在这里等待您的下次光临，祝大家旅途愉快！

13. 海南文笔峰盘古文化旅游区

各位游客朋友，大家好！欢迎大家来到海南文笔峰盘古文化旅游区参观游览。我是大家此次游览的导游小吴，很高兴为大家服务，希望我的服务能给大家愉快的旅程增添光彩。下面将由我来为大家介绍海南文笔峰盘古文化旅游区。

海南文笔峰盘古文化旅游区，位于海南省定安县龙湖镇丁湖路6号文笔峰山麓，地处定安县境内东南约20千米处，它平地拔起，山色秀美，为定安八大名景之一。这里自古被视为“龙首龟背”的风水宝地。清幽恬静的原生态自然环境中，远古时代的造化遗迹熠熠生辉。天人合一的山水意境融合了盘古文化、道教文化和历史文化等优秀文化理念，使这里成了一座集旅游观光、休闲娱乐、道教养生、宗教朝圣和文化研究为一体的国家级大型文化旅游区，2012年10月，该景区被评为国家4A级旅游景区。

海南文笔峰盘古文化旅游区面积仅3平方千米，主峰海拔188米，像一座飞来峰突兀于海南东北部平原之上，因外形得名尖岭，其东西南北等距离处分别有一小山岭，像四个保护神。唐朝末期，李将军率兵途经此峰，发现该峰气势非凡，登峰极目，赞叹不已，于是上奏皇帝命名此峰为李家岭，以此为中心纵横三十里划为李家都，据为皇家宝地。1488年，两广总督按察司副使陈英得知李家岭诸多神奇，改李家岭为文笔峰，以振文运。此后，文笔峰所在的定安文人辈出，国史公认的“海南四大名人”丘浚、海瑞、王弘诲、张岳崧，后二人均出生于定安，其中张岳崧为一甲进士及第探花。全岛中举、中进士者，定安均居第一。文笔峰成为定安文化的象征，许多举人进士都将自己的成功托付于该峰。

道教南宗五祖、南宗内丹派创始人白玉蟾生于海南琼山。他年少聪慧，精通诗书。12 岁时以特荐身份到广州参加“神童科”考试，考官以“织机”为题令其赋诗。白玉蟾脱口吟道：“山河大地作织机，百花如锦柳如丝。虚空白处做一匹，日月双梭天外飞。”少年胸襟如此豪迈，理应中选。然而考官认为他骄狂而不取。白玉蟾考场失败，从此潜心向道。1231 年，白玉蟾在盛名时突然隐遁，传说文笔峰顶的巨石台地就是他羽化升天之处，巨石之侧至今留有其脚印和手掌印。人至此处，回首俯瞰，确有凌虚御风之感。

文笔峰从山腰至山顶主要由玄武岩和片理岩组成，山上植被茂盛，山顶常有云雾缭绕。文笔峰，又名文豪岭。明朝礼部尚书王弘诲就出生雷鸣镇龙梅村，著有《南溟奇句录》《尚友堂稿》等。至今，龙梅村还有一座为纪念王弘诲所建的富有海南建筑特色的明代牌坊，建筑设计造型古朴雄伟、坚固大方，叫作“太史坊”。

文笔峰相传为盘古的鼻梁所化，是盘古开天辟地之后，世间最早出现的一座山峰。盘古是宇宙万物之初始，是世界文化之根源，盘古的鼻子自然是吸纳天地精气的地方，被当地黎民百姓视为祥瑞之地，受世代海南人民的顶礼膜拜。峰峦云海之间是南宗圣境玉蟾宫，其供奉祭祀的中国古代先祖有数百位，上有沧海桑田盘古蟾，内有神仙修行真洞天，东有北斗七星守苍翠，西有九宫八卦护乾坤。烟云浩瀚，殿阁缥缈，宛若蓬莱仙境落人间。

据司马迁《天官书》记载，文笔峰盘古文化旅游区与天上的南极星相对应，南极仙翁即南极星，因南极仙翁主寿，是古代神话传说中的老寿星，文笔峰的人杰地灵便缘于此。

文笔峰道家文化苑于 2006 年举行开光大典，建有目前海南规模最大的、宋代风格的建筑群。苑内玉蟾宫、文笔书院、慈航殿、七星亭、转运殿、钟鼓楼、养生堂等，均是特色景观。该苑以“大道和谐”为文化核心，开展了多种特色旅游活动。

各位游客请看，这就是玉蟾宫，它是道教在海南唯一的合法庙宇，被道教奉为“南宗宗坛”。玉蟾宫拥有世界上最大的道教建筑群，由祈求平安的慈航殿、和合姻缘的月老殿、嘱照本命的元辰殿、开启智慧的文昌阁、健康长寿的药王殿、发家致富的财神殿等近20座殿堂组成。建筑结构完整、风格鲜明，系统地展现了道家主题文化特色。殿宇美轮美奂、雕刻精妙绝伦，体现了古代劳动人民的卓越才能和艺术创造力。

玉蟾宫诸殿，环绕在文笔峰潮周围。文笔峰南坡的自然走势，大致在子午线玉蟾宫诸殿上。以南坡自然走势为中轴线，以峰顶巨石及制高点为背景依托，以东西两侧为双翼，以园林艺术点缀、绵延于中国古建筑群之间，整体布局生动、和谐。生动是整体有腾飞之意，站在峰顶俯瞰，会让人产生驾雾腾云之感；和谐是古建筑群疏密合度，庄严与亲和相互映衬，建筑与园林互为补充能拓展游览的观赏空间和想象空间，无重沓之感，展现了天人合一的文化内涵。

各位游客朋友，关于海南文笔峰盘古文化旅游区的介绍就为大家讲到这里，现在大家可以自由参观一下，按照计划的时间回到这里，祝大家玩得愉快。

14. 海口观澜湖旅游度假区

各位游客朋友，大家好！欢迎大家来到海口观澜湖旅游度假区参观游览。我是大家此次游览的导游小杨，很荣幸陪同大家一起参观游览，希望我的服务能给大家带来愉快的心情。下面将由我来为大家介绍海口观澜湖旅游度假区。

大约1万年前，位于海南的琼北火山群爆发，熔岩奔腾，一泻千里。历经大自然的浩瀚神工，这里形成了广袤神奇的黑色岩石地质遗迹。羊山，距海口市市中心咫尺之遥，却是万年火山岩形成的石漠地区的腹地，海口观澜湖旅游度假区就建在这里，位于海南省海口市龙华区龙桥镇观澜湖大道1号，是集运动、商务、养生、旅游、会议、文化、美食、购物、居住等为一体的国际休闲旅游度假区。度假区内各种设施一应俱全，有高尔夫球场、海口会所、海口高尔夫学院、海口观澜湖度假酒店、矿温泉水疗中心、观澜湖国际会议中心、兰桂坊娱乐街、海口观澜湖华谊冯小刚电影公社、专卖店等。这里为世界各地的游客提供了一个绝佳的旅游目的地，2014年被评为国家4A级旅游景区。

高尔夫球会

海口观澜湖高尔夫球会拥有全世界最多的球洞数，10个国际高尔夫球场形成全球最大规模的公众火山岩高尔夫球场群；这里所有的球场都坐落于一万年前火山喷发形成的火山岩之上，最大限度保留了火山地区的自然和人文原始风貌，这里既有火山岩地貌特征的球场，也有貌似墨尔本沙丘地带的沙地球场。这里有一望无垠的天际线、辽阔的黑色裸岩、苍郁的古荔枝、低矮的老石墙、由采石坑改造成的水景湿地，置身其中，犹如置身月球之上，“失重”的放松感油然而生。观澜湖世界明星赛、观澜湖高尔夫世界杯、世界女子高尔夫锦标赛、泰格伍兹VS麦克罗伊观澜湖世界第一挑战赛等在此精彩上演，全球各地的顶尖球手、文体巨星纷至沓来，海口观澜湖已经成为海南运动休闲旅游的新地标。

休闲疗养胜地

海口观澜湖，也是全球休闲旅客向往的身心疗养之地。观澜湖温泉酒店是集旅游度假、高球运动、精致美食和温泉水疗于一身的理想下榻之地。最值得一提的是酒店拥有的天然火山资源。它有蕴含丰富养生矿物元素的168个冷热泉池，是汇集五大洲风格的被吉尼斯世界纪录认证的世界第一大温泉度假区。这里大量运用竹子、火山石为材料作为装饰，营造出古朴自然的气息，一条500米长的竹廊迤逦前行，将层叠青石掩映，水雾蒸腾的汤池环抱其中，点染着温泉世界的声色韵影。在这里您可体验源自全球五大洲的不同温泉风俗，同时还可以一览别样风情。

电影旅游的新天地

这里也是电影旅游的新天地。观澜湖集团携手华谊兄弟公司、著名导演冯小刚，打造了中国独具特色的电影主题旅游商业项目——海口观澜湖华谊冯小刚电影公社，是集建筑旅游、电影旅游、商业旅游于一体的电影主题旅游胜地。电影公社包括 1942 街、南洋街、芳华军区大院、老北京街、教堂广场区、冯氏贺岁电影园林景观区、影人星光大道、大型摄影棚拍摄区八个主题区，其中包含全球最大的 8000 平方米大型室内摄影棚，是中国星光绽放的影人聚集地。

运动休闲特色小镇

海口观澜湖，正着力打造观澜湖体育健康特色小镇，并成为全国首批运动休闲特色小镇示范项目。观澜湖体育健康特色小镇，依托海南“生态立省、国际旅游岛、最大经济特区”三大优势，以“足球、高尔夫、篮球”三大体育运动为核心，以体育健康为主题和特色，打造集综合旅游产业聚合功能、体育运动训练和体验功能、健康养生休闲功能、体育赛事和体育活动功能、体育文化交流等功能于一体的中国最大规模的体育健康特色小镇。

海口观澜湖体育健康特色小镇三大体育运动核心包括：（1）高尔夫运动，这里拥有全球最大规模的公众高尔夫球场群、高尔夫学院及赛事会所等相关设施；（2）足球运动，这里拥有包含 30 片足球训练场、办公、住宿、游泳馆、健身房、医疗中心、更衣室、媒体中心等设施的中国足球（南方）训练基地，还有巴塞罗那足球学校及巴塞罗那足球博物馆；（3）篮球运动，这里拥有海口观澜湖 NBA 训练中心、NBA 博物馆以及体验中心。三十项适合全民参与的运动项目包含乒乓球、羽毛球、网球、游泳等。此外，小镇还创建了足球、高尔夫、滑板、攀岩等项目的国家级体育训练基地，为奥运选手培训、专业运动员培训、体育后备人才培养搭建基地。

海口观澜湖体育健康特色小镇建成后，将成为体育产业链完整、体育项目丰富、职业体育训练与家庭体育兼顾、体育文化鲜明、空间布局合理，集全民健身基地、体育培训基地、体育文化基地、奥运冠军摇篮四位一体的健康运动休闲特色小镇，成为“旅游＋体育”的典范。

文旅商休闲目的地

这里也是值得游历的文旅商休闲目的地。观澜湖集团斥资百亿元打造海口观澜湖新城，包括观澜湖兰桂坊时尚娱乐街区、国际免税购物中心、狂野水世界主题公园、海南华侨中学观澜湖学校、万丽酒店、丽思卡尔顿酒店和硬石酒店等，成为真正的海南新时尚城市中心。

观澜湖兰桂坊酒吧街是由观澜湖集团和兰桂坊携手打造的全新时尚娱乐地标，融娱乐、购物、休闲、餐饮于一体，让游客尽享时尚潮流乐趣。

海免观澜湖国际购物中心由观澜湖集团与海南省免税品有限公司联手倾力打造，一期运营面积达 5 万平方米。国际购物中心不仅引入一线国际品牌，还有丰富的时尚潮流品牌，运营理念上着力于线上渠道与线下渠道并举，成为海南一站式购物之旅的高品质标杆之作。

观澜湖集团还建造了世界顶级水上乐园项目——海口狂野水世界。这是国内首个集“户外 + 室内”于一体的水上乐园，其中占地 8000 平方米的室内水上乐园可以突破季节、天气限制，提供与室外同质的娱乐体验。狂野水世界的娱乐项目既能满足家庭娱乐，又带有极限刺激，为游客带来不同风格的水上游乐体验。

国际教育是海口观澜湖新城的另一亮点。观澜湖集团与海南华侨中学携手合作，共同打造国内一流、具有国际化特色的优质学校——海南华侨中学观澜湖学校。学校将为海南省海口市提供优质学位，还将引入国际教育方法。借助观澜湖集团丰富的海外名校资源，海南华侨中学观澜湖学校将构建起中外教育合作的平台，促进国际交流与合作，为拓宽国际视野和培养国际型人才起到积极作用。

各位游客朋友，关于海口观澜湖旅游度假区的介绍就为大家讲解到这里，现在大家可以自由参观一下，按照计划的时间回到这里，祝大家玩得愉快。

3A 级旅游景区

1. 五公祠

各位游客，大家好！我是景区讲解员小杨，希望我的讲解能给各位的五公祠之旅增添美好享受，留下一段美好回忆。

五公祠是海南思古抒怀之地。该祠由五公祠、苏公祠、观稼堂、学圃堂、五公精舍、琼园等一组古建筑群构成，人们习惯以五公祠统称。这片古建筑群始建于明代万历年间（1573—1619 年），陆续建至 21 世纪初。五公祠游览区占地约 7 公顷。这里奇花异木掩映楼阁，地近闹市，独有清幽，自古有“琼台胜景”之美称。

五公祠为该建筑群的主体建筑，两层木结构，单斗拱，面积 560 平方米，楼高 9 米，人称“海南第一楼”。该祠为纪念唐宋两代被贬谪来海南的李德裕、李纲、李光、赵鼎、胡铨五位历史名臣而建，至今已有百余年。祠内五公石雕栩栩如生，满面思绪。楼上高悬“海南第一楼”金字横匾。祠内柱上，清人长联落地有声，评价了五名臣，颇为“第一楼”增辉。

五公祠右侧是学圃堂，乃清代浙江名士郭晚香来琼讲学旧址，现陈列汉代以来铜钟、铜鼓等古文物。学圃堂再右是五公精舍，是晚清海南学子研习经史之处，今陈列历代书画。五公祠左侧是观稼堂，观稼指观赏“粟井浮金”和“金穗千亩”景色，堂取此名为纪念苏东坡指凿井泉。

苏公祠与五公祠毗邻。祠内陈列了一批苏东坡的诗词碑刻，祠前有牌坊、拱桥、荷池、风亭。祠东有琼园，占地 10 亩，园内有浮粟泉、粟泉亭、洗心轩、仙游洞等景观。

浮粟泉有“海南第一泉”的美称。相传 1097 年苏东坡被贬儋州，途经此地投宿，见居民饮城河之浊水，于是察地形而指地曰：“依地开凿，当得两泉。”当地居民凿之，果然得清浊二泉，俱甘甜。清为浮粟泉，浊为洗心泉。后人在两泉周围陆续建了苏公祠等建筑。洗心泉在明初湮没。现存浮粟泉，由清代（1793 年）知府叶汝兰改建成方形古井。

粟泉亭距今已有 300 多年，由明代（1614 年）郡守翁汝遇始建。此亭后因翁郡守升迁而停建，由继任知府谢继科续建完成。

洗心轩为一长形平屋，原名“食源亭”，因苏东坡的一首诗而兴建，经历代重修保存至今。

仙游洞是民国五年（1916 年）到海南任观察使的朱为潮所建。相传他修琼园时，梦见和宋代海南历史上第一名诗人、道士刘遁在粟泉亭饮酒。刘遁指着亭外说此地是他的出生遗址，便飞升而去。朱醒后，颇为感慨，在刘遁所指处建了一个假山石洞，并依刘遁诗句“仙游洞里杳无人”为假山石洞命名。现假山石洞口“仙游洞”乃朱为潮题。

五公祠内常年展出许多珍贵文物。其中有宋徽宗赵佶手书《神霄玉清万寿宫诏》碑，其瘦金体书法刚劲清秀，对研究道家学说和书法都有重要参考价值。还有著名清官海瑞的古唐诗书法，也很受人喜爱。以上诸多名胜景致和五公祠连成一片，组成海南置人文古迹的第一胜境。与五公祠等古建筑群隔桥相望的是建筑面积 4200 平方米、有 8 个展厅的五公祠陈列馆，这里经常举行海南历史、摄影和美术作品等展览。

五公生平简介

李德裕（787—850 年），今河北省人，曾在唐代文宗大和七年（833 年）和武宗开成五年（840 年）两度为相，是一位较有才能的政治家。因遭奸党陷害，一贬再贬，于 848 年贬为崖州司户，849 年到达海南，次年逝。逝后被封太尉，赠卫国公。

李纲（1083—1140 年），福建人，是我国历史上一位民族英雄，也是宋代一位有才华、有魄力的宰相。因被谗言所害而被贬，于 1129 年到达海南。逝后朝廷追赠李纲为陇西郡开国公，谥号“忠定”。

赵鼎（1085—1147 年），今山西省人，宋代名臣，曾任右司谏侍御史、参知政事。支持岳飞抗金，并荐其为统帅。因反对秦桧投降而数遭贬谪，最后于 1145 年被贬到海南。死后被宋孝宗封为丰国公，赠太傅，谥忠简。

李光（1073—1157 年），今浙江省人，宋代名臣，曾任参知政事、资政学士，因反对秦桧投降的和议而一再被贬。1131年被贬海南，居海南10余年，逝后宋孝宗赐谥号为“庄简”。

胡铨（1102—1180年），今江西省人，曾任秘书少监、起居郎。因上书请斩主降派秦桧等而被贬，后因秦桧私党诬告被充军到海南，居海南10年，卒后宋孝宗追赐谥号为“忠简”。

2. 三亚凤凰岭海誓山盟景区

各位朋友们，大家好，首先欢迎大家来到三亚凤凰岭海誓山盟景区，我是大家的讲解员，我叫小王，接下来由我来带领大家游玩。

三亚凤凰岭海誓山盟景区是中国第一个以爱文化为主题的热带雨林山海景观景区。景区宣扬“爱”的主题，我们有个打招呼的手势——“哇爱噜”手势，大家一起来做这个手势（互动教游客做手势），并向我们的朋友、家人、爱人大声说出“哇爱噜！”“哇爱噜”什么意思呢？就是海南话“我爱你”的意思，在这里表示欢迎与祝福，各位来到我们景区的朋友一定要学会这句话，向我们最爱的人大声说“哇爱噜！”

四大特色

各位朋友来我们景区看什么呢？第一，凤凰岭是三亚的最高山，上到山顶上可以一览三亚全景——四湾八景。第二，我们坐索道上山，缆车是来自奥地利原装进口，全长1624米，先进、安全、平稳，被称为“索道中的劳斯莱斯”。第三，这里是三亚市中心最茂密的一片热带雨林，是三亚负氧离子含量最高的地方，被称为“三亚之肺”“天然氧吧”，大家上去可以好好呼吸纯净空气。第四，我们景区最大的特色是山顶上有一座山海景观水晶圣殿，通体透明，圣洁漂亮。请注意，山上景区禁止烟火，各位朋友上去后就不能吸烟了。现在我们团队就准备去坐缆车，我们团队是包含来回缆车票的，为防止大家在山上走失掉队，全程一定要跟紧我，现在大家就跟着我开始我们的凤凰岭之旅！

索道站集合团队

现在我们看到的就是我们亚洲第一观海索道缆车，奥地利原装进口，非常先进和安全，一辆缆车坐 8 位，大约 10 分钟可以登上山上，请注意，坐在缆车内可以观赏三亚风景，但请不要随意站立晃动，更不要把头或身体伸出窗外。现在我带前面的朋友坐第一辆缆车上山，后面的朋友请有秩序地按照我们工作人员安排依次乘坐缆车。

第一观赏区——四湾八景观赏区

海誓山盟广场

各位朋友，现在我们到达的是我们景区的观景广场——海誓山盟广场，也是我们三亚四湾八景的第一景——海誓山盟，后面就是我们壮丽的山海景观。大家可以看到眼前这座石碑，上面刻着“海誓山盟”四个大字，气势磅礴！旁边有个落款大家看得出写的是什么吗？是应辉书，应辉是谁呢？他就是中国书法协会副会长何应辉先生！何应辉先生曾携夫人一起登上我们凤凰岭，在这里被眼前的山海景观所震撼，大笔一挥写下“海誓山盟”四个金字赠予我们景区作纪念。石碑后面我们看到刻的是“北纬 18 度”，这就是三亚所处的纬度线，而北纬 18° 又被旅游界称为“爱的纬度”，为什么要叫“爱的纬度”？因为同在北纬 18° 这条纬度线上，世界上有很多知名的旅游胜地，除了三亚之外，还有夏威夷等，而这些都是结婚度蜜月的最佳胜地，所以人们认为这条纬度线充满爱的文化，因此称为“爱的纬度”。

榆林湾锦母角

在石碑的底下蔚蓝的海湾就是我们三亚四湾八景的第一个海湾——榆林湾，榆林湾是我们传统的一个海军基地，下面有我们英勇的海军舰队驻扎，现在南海问题时局敏感，我们不便多作介绍，但请我们的游客朋友即使拍了照片也不要轻易上传网络，以免招来麻烦。目光放远望去海面上有两条八字形长线，这是我们三亚的拦海大坝，主要起的是防洪护堤的作用，而它更是被称作我们中国的南大门，因为从这里出去就是我们美丽的南海了。再看左边那条长线连着那座山头，那里就是我们三亚四湾八景的另一景——锦母入海。它叫锦母角，因为它就是中国大陆架版图的最南端，前面就是南海，所以那里就是我们南海将士驻扎的地方，山尖上有座灯塔，那里有我们的军人巡视、为船只导航。曾经我们团队中有一个白发苍苍的老爷爷，拄着拐杖登上我们凤凰岭，站在这个地方凝望许久后热泪盈眶，他很激动地告诉我们年轻时候他就在这底下当兵，时隔 50 年后重新回到这里，物是人非。50 年对这片大海来说弹指而过，而对于这位老人来说却是整个青春年华。多少位南海将士像这位老人一样在这锦母角下挥洒青春，抛头颅洒热血为我们保家卫国，守护南海平安，他们是伟大的，让我们向这群可爱的人致敬吧！

四湾八景导览图

这是我们即将游览的四湾八景观赏区导览图，这里就是三亚的最高点，三亚电视塔也在这边，因为这里信号覆盖范围最广。这里能 360° 看到三亚全景，刚才我们已经看了一湾两景，更美的风景还在上面。我们现在所在的位置就在海誓山盟广场，待会经过九曲同心桥后会依次来到来仪台，舞凤台和望鹿台，这三个平台是我们风景视野最宽阔的地方，同时也是我们三亚文化的发源处。一圈游览下来大概是一个小时时间，同时山上是茂密的热带雨林，大家一定要跟好我，以免迷失，现在我们登上台阶向前出发。

登高望远，来到凤凰岭，我们就要看三亚充满魅力的四湾八景，大家看完一定要知道有哪四湾，哪八景。同时，我们出来旅游，目的是开阔视野，但开阔视野的同时，更重要的是增长见识，见识从哪来，就从导游这里来，所以我们不仅要看美景，还要知道美景后面的故事，因为那才是最动人的。

高山榕

这种树叫作高山榕，高山榕被称为海南十八怪之一，怪在哪里呢？怪就怪在树根长在树皮外，这种树根非常奇特，长在树皮外面，当它扎根到土壤里随着时间推移就会长成粗壮的树干，再干旱再恶劣的环境下它都能扎根生存，而海南经常发生强台风，但再大的台风都从没吹倒过高山榕，这种坚韧不拔的毅力让当地黎族人非常崇拜，黎族人崇拜自然，石头、大树都是他们崇拜的对象。所以高山榕被黎族人奉为神树，于是每当过年过节的时候，黎族人都会在高山榕下祈福祭拜，在树上绑上红带子，写上家人爱人的名字，祈求平安，祈求幸福。而这里是三亚最高点，又是南海边上，风水极佳，意义非凡，所以很多当地人和游客更热衷于在这里祈福祝愿，祈求家人平安，祈求父母康健，祈求夫妻和睦，祈求孩子有成，祈求恋人同心，祈求友谊长存。前面就是我们的九曲同心桥，很多情侣夫妻喜欢在我们桥上挂上一把同心锁，同心同德，幸福美满。人生路上起起伏伏历经波折，而在我们身边却一直有家人、恋人陪伴，携手一起走过艰难路途，就像这把同心锁，刻上两人名字，就锁住了我们彼此情谊，即便有再多曲折都不害怕。

落笔生花

现在我们走的是九曲同心桥，桥依山势而建，蜿蜒曲折，恰好形成九个弯，象征着我们所讲的九曲同心。右边连绵的青山苍翠欲滴，而前方所在的位置（两山中间凹口处）就是我们三亚四湾八景中的一景——落笔生花。落笔洞是个巨大的溶洞，山洞里有块巨大的钟乳石，形状就像毛笔一样倒挂下来，因此得名落笔洞。而那里就是远古海南人猿生活的地方，据考古学家发掘，山洞里挖出了 7000 年前海南人猿的头盖骨，也就是说，早在 7000 年前，这里就已经有了远古人猿活动的踪迹，现在被认定为最早海南人生活的地方，也是海南远古人猿历史保护遗址。落笔洞附近古木参天，人迹罕至，环境优美，许多疗养院建造在里面，三亚众多高等院校坐落在附近，人文气息也十分浓厚。有个问题不知道大家有没有想过，三亚临海而居，那为何海南的远古人猿不选择在海边生活，而选择生活在山洞里呢？原因其实很简单，生活在海边的人其实能了解，海边通常湿气、潮气较重，生活久了其实对身体不好，而且海边多灾害，风灾水灾频繁，人身安全难以保障。而生活在山里就不一样了，空气好，海拔高，重要的是山里有山洞能够抵御灾害，防御野兽，山里还能狩猎采摘果实，所以说，我们海南的远古人猿还是具有很大的智慧的。

美丽之冠

前面的小山岭叫虎豹岭，虎豹岭后面有九幢像大树一样的建筑物，那个地方叫大树公馆，是个豪华酒店群。大树公馆底下有个白色的像皇冠一样的建筑，那就是我们三亚四湾八景中的一景——美丽之冠。“美丽之冠”像盛开的凤凰木，也像一顶水晶皇冠，因为它就是世界小姐选美决赛的场馆。我们都知道，从 2003 年开始，三亚就连续多届被选中为世界小姐选美大赛的决赛场地，而让三亚声名大噪，至今为止三亚总共举办了六届世界小姐选美决赛，而在 2007 年那一届，同样是在三亚举行，中国小姐张梓琳就在里面夺得了桂冠，成为第一个获得世界小姐选美决赛冠军的中国人，同时也让三亚有了美丽之都的名号。而去年 2015 年的世界小姐选美决赛同样在三亚举行，来自世界各地的 30 多位佳丽登上了我们凤凰岭观赏三亚美景。而现在三亚的城市口号就叫作“美丽三亚，浪漫天涯”，美丽三亚指的就是美丽之冠，浪漫天涯指的是哪里呢？答案是天涯海角。

月老泉

现在我们所看到的是月老泉，左手姻缘簿，右手红线的就是我们的月下老人了。我们这边有没有单身的青年男女呢？有的话可以拜拜月老，祈求桃花运哦！而我们的情侣、爱人也可以拜拜月老，感谢月老给您带来了今生挚爱！

在月老泉旁边有棵青梅树，黄梅时节家家雨，四五月份就是我们的黄梅季节。黄梅果子富含果酸和维生素 C，有开胃健脾的功效。而在这里想给大家介绍的是我们青梅树底下生长着一片竹子，有青梅树的地方一定会长竹子，这就是我们常说的“青梅竹马”，以此来寓指青年男女间的深厚情谊。

现在我们即将走进 360° 环形木栈道，栈道两旁都是翠绿的热带雨林，旁边的植物品种繁多，小动物也时常跑出来透透空气晒晒太阳，因此导游提醒大家，尽量往栈道中间行走，不要去触碰两旁的植物，也不要去打扰小动物。

龙凤门

前面是我们的龙凤门，人们认为龙与凤摆放到一起有着吉祥的寓意，这边我们的龙凤门也自然象征着吉祥之门，幸福之门。在这里有个传统，就是我们到这边的家人、朋友、爱人都要一起手牵着手，一起走过我们的龙凤门，象征着一起走向幸福之路。而注意了，我们常说幸福不回头，一直走到头，我们一起走过龙凤门之后千万注意不要回头！

在山下时导游反复强调了上来时最重要的一件事就是要多做深呼吸，凤凰岭是三亚制高点，同时拥有三亚最茂盛的热带雨林，负氧离子含量全三亚最高，被称为“三亚之肺”“天然氧吧”。特别是我们吸烟的朋友，要好好地做下深呼吸，清洗清洗自己的肺。海南山好水好空气好，被称为最长寿的省份。而其中的长寿秘诀就是这里的生态环境。

来仪台

现在我们来到的就是我们三亚凤凰岭视野最宽广的观景平台——来仪台。“箫韶九成，有凤来仪”表示这里是太平祥瑞之地，有贵人驾临。今天迎来各位贵人们，来看一看三亚市中心最壮丽的视野风景。前面我们看到的海湾就是我们三亚最长的海湾，四湾八景中的第二湾——三亚湾。三亚湾全长 22 千米，是三亚市内最长的一道海湾，以沙滩平缓，日落唯美著称，海滩上布满了一排椰子树，属典型的热带滨海风光，椰风海韵，非常漂亮，时任总书记江泽民曾在那里提了四个大字“椰梦长廊”，所以很多人喜欢到三亚湾去看日落、乘船夜游，非常唯美。顺着三亚湾右边尽头望过去，那边是天涯海角、南山佛教旅游区所在地。最远处的那座山叫鳌山，底下坐落的白色雕塑就是三亚著名的南海观音像。三亚南海观音像，是目前亚洲最大的观音塑像，108 米高，一体三身像，分别代表智慧、慈悲、清净，2005 年落成，当时来自国内外 108 位高僧大德集体为南海观音像开光，据说开光仪式开始时天上的云都聚拢过来形成一朵莲花的形状，成为中国佛教史上一件盛事。

远处看海面上有两个小岛，这也是我们三亚四湾八景中的一景——浮波双玳，也叫东西玳瑁洲。左边是东岛，右边是西岛，以前那边盛产玳瑁。现在西岛是著名的旅游海岛，东岛是个驻军地，以前是民兵驻扎，而且是女民兵，东岛女民兵在海南非常出名，留下许多英勇传奇故事，毛主席有一首诗赞扬我们东岛女民兵，赞扬了我们女民兵挥洒热血，保家卫国，守卫南海的大无畏精神。

而在三亚湾正前面有五根手指一样的建筑物，这是我们三亚的地标性建筑——凤凰岛。凤凰岛，是耗时十年填海造陆建成的人工岛，其拇指所在的位置是一栋国际七星级酒店，仿造迪拜帆船酒店建成的被称为“东方迪拜”。右边四栋是酒店公寓，就是三亚房价最高的地方，最底层 8 万元一平方米起步，楼层越高房价越贵，最贵在 2012 年曾炒到十多万元一平方米，360° 都是海景房。更有意义的是凤凰岛是 2008 年火炬传递的第一站。奥运圣火从希腊传到中国最先就是在这边点燃后开始向祖国四面八方传递，最终传到鸟巢，因此称它为凤凰还巢。

我们现在看到的这种树就是海南最毒的箭毒木，俗称“见血封喉”，其树皮非常厚非常坚韧，没有毒，但里面白色的树浆却有剧毒，身上如果有伤口碰到这种汁液的话不出 30 分钟就会导致全身血液凝固而死，所以本地人称它为“见血封喉”。但刚才讲到它的树皮非常厚而且没有毒，中华人民共和国成立前本地人用这种树皮来干什么呢？用来做衣服。据说这种树皮做出来的衣服非常耐用，有句话说一件树皮穿三代，毕竟以前可没有人人都有好衣服穿啊，但可见以前辛勤的劳动人民非常具有智慧的。可惜的是现在树皮衣这门制作手艺失传已久，现在只能在博物馆或是一些景区看到这种树皮衣的存在了。

舞凤台

现在我们来到了舞凤台，这里的视野跟刚才的来仪台是差不多的，但在这里导游主要想给大家讲的是三亚的凤凰文化。刚才给大家讲了三亚的地标性建筑叫凤凰岛，三亚的机场大家都知道叫凤凰机场，三亚最高山也就是我们景区叫凤凰岭，三亚还有凤凰路、凤凰镇等。大家会发现三亚非常喜欢凤凰乃至整个三亚的城市图标都设计成凤凰的图案。为什么三亚这么喜欢凤凰呢？因为凤凰在我们中华传统文化里是吉祥的象征，在阴阳五行中凤凰属火，火的位置在南方，三亚是中国最南端的城市，所以三亚也被称为“凤凰城”。

望鹿台

刚才讲到三亚被称为“凤凰城”，但其实早在 20 世纪 80 年代初，三亚更普遍地被称为“鹿城”，鹿文化也一直是三亚文化的重要组成部分，鹿文化就起源于前面这片鹿回头半岛。鹿回头半岛是我们凤凰岭的余脉延伸到海里组成的一段山海间盆地，也是我们三亚四湾八景中的一景——半岛传奇。为什么说是传奇？就是在 2009 年随着国际旅游岛政策出台，半山半岛集团在上面建成一批观海公寓，据说当天销售额突破 3 个亿，三天狂销 15 个亿，打破了海南乃至全国房地产界有史以来的销售记录，因此那边被称为半岛传奇。

在整个游览过程中，我已经给大家讲解了三亚的“四湾八景”，大家还记得是哪四湾，哪八景吗？站在三亚的制高点上，山海做证，许下人生的庄重诺言。这里的前方就是真正的天涯海角，爱字就是一个承诺，苍天在上，日月为誓，两个人在一起相守相望就是一种最大的幸福。面对最南端许下一个爱的誓言，我们会带着这个盟约走完自己的一生！

第二观赏区——水晶圣殿观赏区

现在我们来到的是第二观赏区——水晶圣殿观赏区，这一路我们依次会经过鹿心亭、如影阁和执手台，最终到达目前国内首个山海景观水晶圣殿，也象征着从相知，相守，相爱，最终步入婚姻的殿堂，为了让大家更好地亲近自然，感受自然，全程行走在环行木栈道上，第一站取名叫鹿心亭，缘由就如青年男女初次相见，一见倾心，怦然心动，也许我们都有过这样的心动时刻，那是一种无以言表的心情，也是一种难以抑制的幸福甜蜜感觉。

我们现在看到的石碑是仿造简牍的形式，上面记载的正是汉乐府《诗经》第一篇，也是我国第一首情诗《关雎》，关关是象声词，形容水鸟在水面上发出欢快愉悦的声音，而雎鸠是一种水鸟。实际上，《诗经》在古代并不是像我们现在这样逐字地朗读出来，而是需要有韵律地唱出来。大家都听过邓丽君那首《在水一方》吧？其歌词就是来自《诗经》。

石碑的下面刻满了爱字，有不同的颜色，代表爱是五彩缤纷的。我们来看下面这个大大的爱字。我把中间的心字遮住，我们能看出这是什么字吗？“受”字，爱是需要用心去感受的，爱也是需要彼此相互接受的，同样爱还是需要包容和忍受的。

大家请跟我往前走，蓦然回首，我们可以看到路边这棵树犹如一只梅花鹿亭亭玉立，深情回眸。这就是大自然赋予我们的神奇，因此成就了“心如撞鹿”这句成语佳话。

我们所走的这条路，就是爱的旅途，两边的植物也是大自然赠予的产物。我们看，这种植物叫红桑，象征着红红火火，而爱情就像一把火，燃烧了我们所有人的心窝。这个植物叫变叶木，又称“老来俏”，它嫩芽时是青色的，象征着青涩的初恋，等到叶子变得五彩缤纷，也象征着爱的果实已经成熟了。

我们今天的爱情之旅即将结束，从轰轰烈烈的恋爱到开开心心走进婚姻圣殿再到相互包容过着平淡的生活，这就是一辈子。所以每个人都要像呵护信仰一样去呵护你的婚姻，不然你就会知道——世界上最遥远的距离不是路途遥远，而是两颗相爱的心却不能在一起，请记住，当我们还能牵手时就请不要只是并肩，当我们还能拥抱时就请不要只是牵牵手，既然拥抱了，就请不要轻易分开。在这里真诚地祝福大家：真爱永恒，真情永远，家庭幸福，事业有成，天长地久，永远幸福。

各位朋友，我们的凤凰岭之旅到此全部结束，现在我们坐缆车下山，同样八人一组，凤凰岭的美景永远在这里等待您的下次光临，祝大家旅途愉快。

3. 海口骑楼建筑历史文化街区

亲爱的游客朋友们，今天我们将参观的是“中国历史文化名街”——海口骑楼建筑历史文化街区。海口骑楼建筑历史文化街区，俗称海口骑楼老街，距今已有 100 多年历史，现有骑楼历史建筑约 600 栋，其中 331 栋被认定为历史建筑挂牌保护，是国内现今保留规模最大、保存基本完好的骑楼建筑群。现存骑楼建筑主要集中在 12 条街道上，总长 3919 米，总占地面积 121.3 公顷。

骑楼建筑将一层部分做成柱廊或人行道，用以避雨、遮阳、通行，二楼及以上层部分骑跨在人行道上。这种建筑十分符合我国南方沿海地区日照强、降雨多的气候特点，同时其“前店后厂、下店上宅”的建筑形式非常便于经商贸易。近现代以来，骑楼这种建筑在我国东南沿海的港、澳、闽、粤、琼等地多有分布。

骑楼建筑最早由英国传入西班牙，再传入东南亚。近代，活跃于东南亚的琼籍华侨将欧亚混交文艺复兴式、欧亚混交巴洛克式和南洋式等建筑风格和样式带到海口，并与琼北传统民居相结合。单栋骑楼建筑彼此相互连接，道路两侧的单个骑廊连接形成长廊，将整条商业街连成一片，形成了独特的、中西合璧的商住两用建筑形式。近代海口也因此形成独特的欧亚混交的城市风貌，以及“开放、包容”的精神和气质，并成为近代中国对外开放交流的窗口。20 世纪初，海口骑楼老街曾设有美、日、英、德、法、挪威等十国领事馆（领事）。

海口骑楼老街作为在漫长的历史发展进程中积累起来的文化精髓，浓缩了海口的市井文化、建筑艺术文化、南洋文化、儒教文化、佛教文化、红色文化、海洋文化等诸多文化内涵，各种传统美食、民间艺术等都在此扎根成长。这里曾发生了很多动人的革命故事、南洋故事等。海口骑楼老街同时也是海外琼籍华侨的“乡愁”所在，是返乡探亲时必到之处。

海口的骑楼老街建筑群初步形成于 19 世纪 20~40 年代，距今有 100 多年历史，其中最古老的建筑四牌楼建于南宋，至今有 600 多年历史。海口骑楼大多是 19 世纪初，一批批从南洋回来的华侨借鉴当时的南洋建筑风格所建。那时，出海闯南洋的海南人“叶落归根”，携带着毕生血汗钱回乡建屋，海南由此出现不少南洋风格的欧式骑楼建筑。

朋友们，中山路到了，2010 年海口骑楼老街区保护与综合整治正式开始，中山路连同得胜沙路、博爱路、新华路、解放路五大道老街区得到修缮，五大道老街区面貌自此焕然一新。

在中山路上我推荐几处地点大家可去重点游览：

一是泰昌隆。据说，当年到海口来的南洋客，一上岸就马上被“接客”的本地人拉到他们认为你应该到的旅店去，如你操琼海口音，他们二话不说，就将你连同行李带到大亚旅店，因为大亚的老板是琼海人；而你如果是文昌口音，那肯定会带你去泰昌隆，因为泰昌隆的老板是文昌人。

二是地处中山路 87 号的“700 年妈祖古庙”。海口天后宫俗称“妈祖庙”“大庙”，始建于元代，至今七百多年历史，不论是建筑还是妈祖信仰，您一定会有所收获。每逢妈祖诞辰（农历三月二十三），老街居民便会举办妈祖大巡游活动。

三是地处中山路 35 号的海口南洋骑楼老街文化展示馆。展馆分两层：一楼有海南省海上丝绸之路中转站示意图；二楼由两部分组成，第一部分是通过图片、实物、音像资料等展示了海口百年的历史人文。第二部分是海口骑楼老街修缮工艺展示厅，展示了著名的工艺匠人，修缮工程中的材料采集与操作工艺流程。让传统工艺爱好者传承学习，使源远流长的中华文化传统工艺发扬光大。

2009 年 6 月 10 日，海口骑楼老街以其悠久的历史文化和浓郁的南洋骑楼风格，在首届中国历史文化名街评选中荣获“中国十大历史文化名街”的称号。同年8月，海口骑楼建筑历史文化街区保护与综合整治项目立项批复。2010年9月，海口市政府启动海口骑楼历史建筑保护工作。2014年4月，海口骑楼老街被文化部评为“2014年度特色文化产业重点项目”。至今，海口骑楼老街仍然发挥着海口市旧城老街的主要商业功能，形象地记录了海口市从无到有，发展成为一个繁荣的沿海大都市的历史，体现了海口城市区位与东南亚一体的热带地方特色。

骑楼老街是老海口的神韵，它见证了海口的百年沧桑，保存和延续着一段珍贵的城市记忆。现在就让我们走进骑楼、回味历史，感受文化、传承海纳百川的精神。

4. 尖峰岭国家森林公园

各位朋友大家好！我是你们此次游览的导游王丽，大家可以叫我小王，很高兴为大家服务，希望我的服务能给各位带来温馨和快乐！尖峰岭是中国现存面积最大、保存最完好的热带原始雨林。位于海南岛西南部，地跨乐东、东方两个黎族自治市、县，总面积600平方千米，主林区面积260多平方千米，主峰海拔1412米，从中国最南的滨海城市三亚向西北行50千米便可抵达。

尖峰岭地区自然生态环境条件独特，从沿海至林区腹地的最高海拔处约15千米的水平距离内，年平均气温从滨海的25℃降低至高海拔区域的17~19℃，年平均降雨量则从1300毫米增加至3500毫米。

走进尖峰岭，眼前古木参天，良材济济。林海中奇形怪状的树根、盘根错节的藤蔓互相缠绕，构成一道道天然屏障。就连那些枯死的大树上，也有附生植物巧妙地繁殖着，千姿百态，美不胜收。雨林的底层，是不计其数的真菌，以及各式各样的花草。在海拔六七百米的河谷地带，则密集地生长着坚硬如铁、千年不腐的石梓、黄檀等优质乔木。这里还有与恐龙同时代的“植物活化石”——树蕨，几米或十几米高的主干从山涧中昂然挺出。这片热带原始雨林也是一个动物世界。这里有四大类人猿之一的黑冠长臂猿，以及云豹等动物16种，有鸟类近150种，昆虫4000多种。这里仅蝴蝶就有300余种，可与号称“蝴蝶王国”的中国台湾相媲美。蓝天白云、峡谷溪流、参天古树、飞禽走兽、奇花异草、珍稀物种，尖峰岭无处不体现出“回归自然”的主题。在当今世界的旅游热潮中，以“回归自然”为主题的森林旅游业前景十分被看好。美国阿拉斯加的寒带丛林，印度尼西亚群岛上的热带森林，西班牙的“乡村之旅”，泰国北部的“森林骑象之旅”，菲律宾苏比克湾的“热带雨林野营之旅”，无不令游客们赞叹不已。中国的张家界国家森林公园，年接待游客达60万人次以上。而总面积10倍于张家界的海南尖峰岭热带原始雨林，近年来也越来越引起中国乃至世界的瞩目和重视。

尖峰岭1992年成立国家森林公园，2000年海南省政府批准保护区扩大到20000公顷，尖峰岭森林覆盖率为96%，几乎浓缩了世界热带地区所有的植被类型，区内物种资源非常丰富，其生物多样性指数与南美、非洲、亚洲的热带雨林相近似，全区有维管植物2800多种，约占全国植物种类的8%，被国内外专家学者誉为“热带北缘丰富的物种基因库”，是中国现存面积最大，保存最完好的热带原始森林，具有重要的科研、科普、教学和森林生态旅游价值。由于热带雨林得到严格的保护，林区内几乎所有溪流的水质都达到国家一类水质标准，可以直接饮用。公园内有丰富的景观资源，如千年睡佛、将军岩、虎啸龙吟、凤鸣谷、雨林沟谷等生态旅游景点。雨林深处有大板根、空中花园、绞杀等雨林特征，诠释着雨林的奥秘、自然的法则。

尖峰岭四周有18座奇峰环抱的天池，碧波荡漾，宛若仙境，这里四季如春，年平均温度19℃，空气纯净，负氧离子浓度高达50000~100000个/立方厘米，有显著的森林保健功能，公园有游客中心、各式宾馆、水庄、雨林别墅，完善的设备设施，能满足您旅途中的各种需要。是开展热带森林休闲度假、探险猎奇、避暑避寒、科研科普、会议培训、医疗保健的理想场所。

景区特色

森林公园内共有热带雨林树种300多个，其中以坡垒、子京、花梨、油丹等70种最为珍贵。坡垒、青梅树干挺拔笔直，材质坚韧，材色鲜艳，百年不朽。子京树坚硬如铁，钉子打不进，有“绿色钢铁”之誉。粗榧树含有21种单体生物碱，其中4种具有抗癌作用，可用来制药。尖峰岭还有沉香木、肖桧、高山蒲葵、陆均松、母生等热带珍贵林木，这里还有一种形态奇特的树——高山榕，其树龄可达百年以上，一棵树能生有几十条大小不一的树干，互相交叉重叠，构成一组野鹿的群雕图案——或跳跃，或散步，或蹲伏，或低头饮水，形态逼真，因此这种高山榕也被称为“海南鹿树”。

尖峰岭的自然奇景除森林外，还有云雾、大海奇观。进入尖峰岭，就如同置身于雾海，云雾蒸腾，一片苍茫。深山里、高峰上、森林稠密处，雾气越加浓重。山风吹时，身边的云雾随风翻滚，会出现瀑布云，仿佛大海的波涛，气势磅礴。在尖峰岭的黑岭东边，有一个群山环抱的盆地，由于终日被云雾笼罩，云雾在其中翻卷飘荡，因此得“天池”美称。

避暑胜地——天池

天池海拔810米，是尖峰岭国家森林公园的主要景区。清华大学作的《尖峰岭国家森林公园总体规划》和海南省旅游发展研究院作的《尖峰岭热带雨林旅游区旅游发展规划纲要》中，都把天池作为公园建设的启动区。

森林旅游、探险

公园内有全国面积最大、保护最完整的热带雨林区，蕴藏着丰富的生物资源，被誉为“热带北缘的生物物种基因库”。在园内2800多种维管植物中，有与恐龙同时代的活化石桫椤、见血封喉等78种珍稀濒危植物和近百种珍贵用材树种。

这里还是动物的乐园。黑长臂猿、云豹、狗熊、孔雀雉等54种国家级保护动物和24种省级保护动物，400多种蝴蝶，215种鸟类在此生息和繁衍。尖峰岭国家森林公园古木参天，藤缠蔓绕，珍禽异兽嬉闹林间，尽显热带雨林的古朴、悠远、神奇的魅力。“空中花园”是热带雨林的一大奇观，几十种花、草、蕨等观赏植物附生在同一棵千年古树上，群芳荟萃。园内还有千米以上高峰18座，登峰远眺，云雾弥漫，气象万千。此外，景区还有“千年睡佛”“将军岩”“猴峰”“龙洞”等景观，令游客叹为观止。

主峰下为河的发源地，古木遮天蔽日，溪水潺潺、清澈见底。这里石水相映成趣，且有“玉女池”“龙殿”“森林浴场”“鸳鸯瀑布”“九龙溪”等景点。

热带海滩

尖峰岭海滨旅游区与岭头港相邻，拥有 16 千米长的金沙海岸，这里长夏无冬，阳光充足，年平均气温 25℃，年平均水温 24.5℃，沙滩平缓空旷，沙粒洁白细腻，海水清澈湛蓝，海湾和风细浪，海边林木茂密，是天然的海滨浴场和进行帆船等水上运动的理想地。

浓郁的民族风情

尖峰岭地区是海南黎族集中居住的地方。因遵循历史和文化传统，至今还保留着淳朴的民风和独特的民俗。黎族“三月三”等节庆活动，具有浓郁黎族色彩的舞蹈、对歌以及精彩的传统体育竞赛，每年都吸引了众多的中外游客前来观光。

朋友们，欣赏了一路美景，大家对尖峰岭有了一定的了解，我的讲解到此就圆满结束了。俗话说：“两山不能相遇，两人总能相逢！”我期待能再次见到大家，再次为大家服务！祝各位在新的一年里事事顺心、平平安安、旅途愉快、一路顺风！

5. 霸王岭国家森林公园

各位游客朋友，大家好！欢迎大家来到霸王岭国家森林公园参观游览。我是大家此次游览的导游小杨，很荣幸陪同大家一起参观游览，希望我的服务能给大家带来愉快的心情。下面将由我来为大家介绍霸王岭国家森林公园。

海南霸王岭国家森林公园位于海南岛西南部山区，地跨昌江黎族自治县和白沙黎族自治县，地理位置坐标介于东经 109°03′~109°17′，北纬 18°57′~19°11′，总面积 8444.30 公顷，是中国唯一保护长颈猿及其生存环境的国家级自然保护区。保护区内群峰叠翠，林海浩渺，古木参天，自然生态系统保存完整，热带生物资源极其丰富。有珍贵的巨、云豹、黑熊等 60 多种珍稀动物，以及热带兰花、馒头果、山石榴、山竹子、乌墨、青果榕、山橄榄、毛牡丹和野荔枝等珍贵植物。

海南霸王岭国家森林公园地形复杂，以山地为主，海拔在 100~1654 米。土壤以花岗岩、砂岩为母质发育而成的砖红壤为代表类型，随海拔的增加逐渐过渡为山地红壤。

海南霸王岭国家森林公园属热带季风气候，四季不明显，受季风影响大，年均温度21.3℃，最热月均温度22.8℃，最冷月均温度13.5℃。平均年降雨量1657毫米，雨量主要集中在7—10月份，随海拔升高降雨量逐渐增加，相对湿度加大，年平均湿度84.2%，园内土壤终年湿润。

植物资源

截至2011年，海南霸王岭国家森林公园内复杂的生存条件成为野生动植物栖息繁衍的理想场所，内有维管束植物2213种，属于国家一级保护植物的有海南苏铁、坡垒2种，国家二级保护植物的有油丹、海南风吹楠、海南梧桐、蝴蝶树、海南紫荆木等17种。

动物资源

截至2011年，海南霸王岭国家森林公园内有陆生野生脊椎动物有365种，其中被列为国家一级重点保护动物有海南长臂猿、云豹、海南山鹧鸪、孔雀雉、蟒蛇、巨蜥6种；被列为国家二级保护动物有海南水鹿、海南大灵猫、猕猴、海南青鼬、海南兔、巨松鼠等46种。

海南长臂猿过去广泛分布于海南岛的五指山、鹦哥岭、吊罗山、黎母山、东方和白沙，目前仅分布于海南省霸王岭自然保护区。海南长臂猿为中型猿类，体矫健，体重7~10千克，体长40~50厘米，前肢明显长于后肢，无尾。毛被短而蓬松，胸腹部浅灰黄色，常染有黑褐色。“海南黑冠长臂猿”的命名，还因为它们头上长有一顶“黑帽”。公猿通体黑色，体形比母猿略小，头顶有短而直立冠状簇毛，如怒发冲冠；母猿全身金黄，体背为灰黄、棕黄或橙黄色，头顶有菱形或多角形黑色的冠斑，恰似戴了顶女式黑帽。雌雄均无尾，也无颊囊。

海南长臂猿是世界四大类人猿之一，栖息在海南岛霸王岭国家级自然保护区的热带雨林中，属于国家一级保护濒危物种。它们天性机警、行动敏捷，而且居无定所，野外观测十分困难。它不仅是一个濒临灭绝的珍稀物种，还是研究人类起源和进化过程的重要对象，其珍稀程度不亚于“国宝”大熊猫。

雅加景区

游客朋友们请看，这里是雅加景区，景区主要分布着“情道”“霸道”“天道”三条游览栈道，并建有别具生态特色的雅加度假（会议）中心。“情道”是霸王岭雅加景区山、水、林、石结合得较好的景点所在地，在“情道”可以观赏到落差达 150 米，岩面宽 30 米的雅加情侣瀑布，有“不观雅加瀑，枉来霸王游”之说；“霸道”是领略霸王岭的霸气的佳处；“天道”是“追求成功”之道，集长、高、陡于一身。

白石潭景区

游客朋友们，这里是白石潭景区，它位于离霸王岭林业局 11 千米处的热带低山雨林中。白石潭景区内部景观各异、特色鲜明、一步一景。白石潭景区已建成了一条游览观光栈道——“钱道”。“钱道”是人生财富之道。“钱道”两旁有藤树争艳、聚宝峰、元宝石、步步高等景点。

雅加瀑布

游客朋友们，现在映入大家眼帘的是雅加大瀑布，它位于霸王岭林业局公路中线 8 千米处，地处雅加河中游，落差 150 米，瀑面宽约 30 米。瀑布顶是一个梯级瀑布群，共有 5 级，落差为 2~20 米，宽度为 15~20 米，且为同一石脉，长度约 400 米，雨季时的水景就像传说中的“望娘滩”，旱季时像一个个天然大石床。另外，瀑布入口处有一深水塘，深约 5 米，长约 30 米，宽约 20 米。

霸王岭国家森林公园有很多美景，同时，也有一个传说，下面我给大家讲一讲。很久以前，有一个恶毒伯父，他为了争夺皇位，带着一帮人来到皇帝洞，将自己的亲侄子杀害了。当伯父把侄子的头一刀砍下来的时候，只见地动山摇。霎时，从侄子的头上冲出三股血柱，直射出皇帝洞口落到很远的地方。当时，吓得伯父脸色苍白，全身直打哆嗦。他马上令自己的手下把他抬离皇帝洞，来到霸王岭一带的一个坝子上居住下来。恶毒伯父退居到霸王岭一带后，自封为大王。由于他居住在坝子上，当地人们称他为坝王。恶毒伯父当上大王之后，整天好吃懒做，无恶不作。甚至有一年，天气大旱，粮食歉收，当地的老百姓实在过不下去了，于是纷纷上山采食霸王岭上的野荔枝。但是，恶毒伯父知道后，就把荔枝树给霸占起来，不仅不让当地的百姓摘，还殴打百姓。后来，当地百姓都不叫他“坝王”，而改称他为“霸王”，其中的“霸”是霸主的意思。而原来的“坝王岭”，也改为“霸王岭”了。

好了，看完这么多美景和听了传说之后，我给大家介绍一下景区实行的管理体制。海南霸王岭国家森林公园实行“管理局—管理站—管护（监测、检查）站点”的三级管理体系：第一，保护区的日常工作由行政办公室、保护宣传科、科研教育科、社区事务科、计划财务科及派出所 6 个部门组成；第二，这里分别建立了雅加、东一、东六和青松 4 个管理站；第三，这里设立了高峰和二号桥 2 个管护点，葵叶岗和十字路 2 个海南长臂猿监测点，二号桥和南雅 2 个检查站。这些管理制度的实行为景区的环境保护及可持续发展提供了保障。

各位游客朋友，关于霸王岭国家森林公园的介绍就为大家讲到这里，现在大家可以自由参观一下，按照计划的时间回到这里，祝大家玩得愉快。

2A 级旅游景区

1. 海瑞墓

各位游客朋友，大家好！我们今天要前往的是海瑞纪念园，去拜见刚正不阿、一身正气的明代政治家、思想家海瑞。海瑞纪念园位于海口市滨涯村。海瑞纪念园也被称为“海瑞墓”。

在到达海瑞纪念园之前，我们先了解一下海瑞的生平。海瑞，海南琼山（今海口市）人，字汝贤，一字国开，号刚峰。一生经历嘉靖、隆庆、万历三朝，大部分时间在福建、浙江、南京为官。他以刚正不阿、清正廉明被世人称为“海青天”“南包公”，深受老百姓的爱戴。1589 年，许子伟奉皇命专程来到海南监督修建海瑞墓。相传在海瑞灵柩运至今墓址时，棺绳突然断开，人们以为是海瑞自选风水宝地，于是就地下葬。

整个海瑞纪念园呈长方形结构，布局五层构架。第一层是石牌坊，第二层是海瑞墓，第三层是海瑞石塑和扇形扬廉轩，第四层是三层圆楼，叫“清风阁”，第五层是假山屏障和八方亭。纪念园整体给人一目了然的感觉。

好了，朋友们，现在我们已经到达了海瑞纪念园了，我们所看到的这座石牌坊就是海瑞纪念园的正门，上面横书凹刻着“粤东正气”四个朱红大字，这是明万历皇帝御笔所赐，正是对海瑞生前为官的真实写照。

进了石牌坊正门，是一条用花岗石条铺砌的长长的甬道直通海瑞墓。树道的中间置放着一只石龟，它表达了人们对海瑞的无比爱戴。可惜这只石寿龟在“文革”中被砸毁了，现在看到的是复制品。每年农历二月二十二至二十五日的祭海公节，海瑞墓前都是人山人海，众多民众前来叩拜，400 年来从不间断。

在墓道的尽头就是海瑞墓了，海瑞墓前竖立着一块墓碑，上面刻着“皇明敕葬资善大夫南京都察院右都御史赠太子少保谥忠介海公之墓”，这是海瑞生前的官衔及死后的荣誉封号。海瑞墓后面部分是 20 世纪 90 年代扩建的。

塑有一尊海瑞塑像，以表示海瑞精神熠熠生辉，激励后人。

好了，各位朋友，海瑞纪念园就为大家介绍到这里，剩下的时间大家可以自由参观，去了解海瑞清廉的一生。我的讲解完毕，谢谢大家！

2. 红色娘子军纪念园

各位朋友大家好，我是你们此次游览的导游，很高兴为大家服务，希望我的服务能给各位带来快乐！红色娘子军纪念园是融热带风情园林、大型主题雕像、娘子军珍贵图片文物资料、歌舞表演及休闲购物为一体，集升旗广场、和平广场、纪念广场、纪念馆、歌舞广场、娘子军连部、人工湖、椰林寨、南霸天旧居等景点于一园的大型红色旅游景区。首先，让我们走向和平广场。

和平广场

各位朋友，这里是和平广场。这座是解放雕像，高 8 米，长 12 米，宽 4 米，由锁链、斗笠、号角以及和平鸽组成。锁链，象征旧社会人民的苦难。追求解放的号角，象征我们的党，以及共产主义理想。斗笠，象征当年红色娘子军浴血奋战。和平鸽象征今天我们的美好生活。战争与和平是人类历史的一个永恒的主题，和平也是人类世代奋斗的目标。

浮雕

现在咱们来观看这座浮雕，它长 60 米，高 3 米，记载着红色娘子军不平凡的战斗历程。

第一幅：真理的召唤。在过去，广大妇女备受政权、族权、神权和夫权的重重压迫，被剥夺了种种做人的权利，生活在万泉河畔的妇女，更是处在水深火热之中，是中国共产党用真理的声音唤起广大妇女的觉醒，她们纷纷投身到反帝反封建的斗争中去。

第二幅：扛枪求解放。1931 年 5 月 1 日，中共琼崖特委决定成立“中国工农红军第二独立师女子军连”。那天，一百多位青年妇女参加了女子军，扛起枪杆，闹革命求解放，开始奏响了中国革命和妇女解放运动中最光彩的乐章。

第三幅：沙帽岭战斗。红色娘子军成立不久，就配合红军主力诱敌深入，把敌人引进红军主力的伏击圈，战斗不到一个小时，歼敌100多人，俘敌70多人，缴获大批枪支弹药，俘虏了国民党乐会县剿共总指挥陈贵苑。浮雕生动地再现娘子军凯旋的喜悦情景。

第四幅：火烧文市炮楼。沙帽岭战斗后，女子军又配合主力攻打文市炮楼。女子军战士们一边进行政治攻心喊话，一边佯作进攻，主力部队挖掘地道。经过三天三夜的艰苦奋战，地道挖通，红军用火攻下文市炮楼。

第五幅：活捉冯朝天。冯朝天是文市炮楼中的一个民团中队长，气焰十分嚣张，女子军和红军主力火攻文市炮楼后，一举将他活捉。

"常青树"

榕树，不管在崇山峻岭，还是树前地角都能生长，根深叶茂，四季常青。大家都看过电影或芭蕾舞剧《红色娘子军》吧？党的代表洪常青在战斗中负伤后，落入南霸天的魔掌，就是被绑在大榕树上，用火活活烧死的。这位党代表的艺术形象让人感动，人们便把榕树称为"英雄树""常青树"。2001年，中国芭蕾舞剧团《红色娘子军》剧组来我们纪念园演出，四位洪常青的扮演者就一起在这棵"常青树"下拍过照。大家也可以在这里拍个照，不枉我们此次参观纪念园。

红色娘子军雕像

红色娘子军雕像是用花岗岩石雕刻的，高10米，宽4.5米，雕像上头戴红军八角帽，背斗笠、肩扛钢枪，脚穿着草鞋，两眼炯炯向前，形象逼真。看着雕像我们会回想起娘子军当年战斗的峥嵘岁月。底座上的"红色娘子军"这五个金光闪闪的大字，是胡耀邦同志的题词。雕像背面的碑文记载着红色娘子军的诞生和英勇战斗的光辉历程。

纪念馆

这是中宣部拨款300万元，一共投资600多万元建起来的红色娘子军纪念馆。其由"八一"五星组成，外观非常雄伟、壮观。门口的这座群雕再现了当年红色娘子军战士英勇杀敌的飒爽英姿，红色娘子军成立于1931年5月

1日，最早是一个连，有100名女战士，后来发展为两个连共140多名女战士。这后面有红色娘子军140名指战员的名录。

娘子军连成立时，连长是庞琼花，指导员是王时香。发展为两个连后，第一连连长是冯增敏，指导员是王时香，第二连连长是黄墩英，指导员是庞学连。

在海南岛，在琼海市，为什么会诞生红色娘子军呢？红色娘子军是怎样诞生的呢？请大家参观图片展览。

1919年“五四运动”后，琼乐、乐会的一批进步青年宣传新文化、新思想，从事妇女解放运动。1926年6月，共产党员鲁易、吴明等人到琼乐、乐会开展革命活动，创办学校，培养妇女骨干。广大妇女走出家门积极参加农会，进入学校读书，琼东、乐会妇女运动蓬勃兴起，不少妇女参加了中国共产党。

这是琼东、乐会的第一个女共产党员林一人。过去，妇女连起名字的权利都没有，她丈夫杨善集于是给她起了“林一人”这个名字，意思是说，妇女也要做一个真真正正的人。

1927年秋，杨善集、王文明、陈永芹等领导琼崖人民进行武装斗争，在琼海万泉河畔的椰子寨打响琼崖武装革命第一枪，宣告中国共产党领导下的琼崖人民武装诞生了。在椰子寨战斗中，琼崖革命武装创始人杨善集、陈永芹光荣牺牲，1930年8月，琼崖红军第二独立师成立。

1931年3月26日，琼崖特委批准成立乐会县赤色娘子军连，1931年5月1日，红色娘子军在乐会县第四区内园村宣告成立。在万人庆祝大会上，100名英姿焕发的红军女战士全副武装列队红色操场上，连长庞琼花从师长王文宇手中接过“中国工农红军第二独立师第三团女子军特务连”的连旗，全连指战员在军旗下庄严宣誓。从这一天起，红色娘子军开始了在中国革命史上最富有传奇色彩的战斗生活。

这支女子部队在异常艰苦的环境中进行军事训练，站岗放哨，看守犯人。她们一面学习文化知识，宣传和发动群众，一面打击敌人的进攻围剿。在两年间，女子军作战50余次，重大的战斗主要有：

沙帽岭伏击战。1931年6月，女子军在沙帽岭配合红三团诱敌深入，一举击毙敌军 100 余人，俘敌 70 余人，缴获枪支 146 支，子弹 1000 余发。活捉国民党乐会县剿共总指挥陈贵苑，而女子军无一伤亡。从此，女子军的英名威震琼岛。

火烧文市炮楼。沙帽岭战斗后不久，女子军配合红三团主力攻打文市炮楼。她们和主力部队一起用挖地道的方式火攻文市炮楼，活捉民团中队长冯朝天。她们还配合红军主力先后攻打阳江、学道、中败、分界等 18 个地方的敌炮楼。女子军还独自进行文魁岭保卫战和大肆打援等战斗。

最著名的战斗是马鞍岭阻击战。1932 年 8 月，国民党派重兵对琼崖根据地进行围剿，为了掩护领导机关安全转移，女子军一连和红军一营在马鞍岭顽强阻击敌人三天三夜。子弹打光了，战士们用石头、木棍当武器和敌人进行战斗，直到第四天接到特委命令才向母瑞山转移。女子军二班为了掩护全连撤退，全班 10 位女战士在弹药断绝的情况下，同敌人开展激烈的肉搏战，全部壮烈牺牲在阵地上。她们遗体的周围是被摔断和砸碎的枪，她们身上沾满血迹。身体仍然保留着与敌人搏斗的姿势，衣服撕得稀烂，可见，她们牺牲之前与敌人进行过一场十分激烈的战斗。

1933 年春，为了保存革命力量，琼崖特委决定红二师所属各团化整为零，疏散到各地转入秘密斗争。女子军短短两年的革命斗争可歌可泣，她们中有 17 位女战士在战斗中倒在敌人枪口下，包括连长、指导员在内的 8 名指战员被捕入狱，受尽严刑拷打，威逼利诱，但没有一个人变节自首。1937 年抗日战争爆发后，国共第二次合作，她们才获释出狱，仍然以各种方式进行革命斗争。

1956 年，海南省军区政治部宣传干部刘文韶第一个发掘和宣传女子军革命事迹，第一个将女子军称为“红色娘子军”。毛主席、周总理高度评价红色娘子军。为了表彰女子军的革命精神，1960 年毛主席在北京接见了女子军连连长冯增敏，并赠给她一支半自动步枪。

反映女子军战斗历程的电影、芭蕾舞剧、京剧、琼剧的《红色娘子军》，把这一红色传奇唱红神州大地，唱响五洲四海。红色娘子军已成为我们这个时代极其宝贵的精神财富。

歌舞广场

各位朋友，我们现在可以到歌舞广场观看展现红色娘子军战斗与生活片段的歌舞表演。那“向前进！向前进……”的激越歌声，是永远的战歌，永远激荡万泉河畔，永远激荡在椰林间，永远鼓舞着我们为实现美好的明天而努力奋斗。

南府

电影《红色娘子军》中，有一个狡诈奸险、无恶不作的大地主恶霸南霸天，他生活过的南府究竟是个什么样子呢？让我们到椰林寨看看吧！

这南府有2间正屋，9间侧房，总面积1000多平方米。南霸天就是在这里过着花天酒地的糜烂生活。左侧房是会客厅，当年化装成南洋客商的洪常青就是在这里与南霸天周旋的。当然，这座南府是仿造的，里头的右侧有红色娘子军陈列馆，陈列了大量的实物和图片，生动地反映出红色娘子军不平凡的战斗足迹。那里还有2001年中国芭蕾舞剧团到我们纪念园演出的剧照等，大家参观之后，一定会有新的感受。

各位朋友，参观完红色娘子军纪念馆，相信大家对红色娘子军英勇壮烈的战斗历程已经有了深刻的了解。让我们一起弘扬红色娘子军精神，为我国全面建成小康社会，推进我们的现代化建设事业而贡献出自己的力量。

第三篇

其他旅游景区

1. 三亚千古情

各位贵宾，大家好！欢迎光临三亚千古情景区，我是大家的讲解员杨阳，非常荣幸可以带领大家参观这座充满魅力的园区。三亚千古情景区由中国文化企业 30 强、中国文化演艺第一股宋城演艺自行设计，并投资 10 亿元建成。独特的造园手法和艺术表现形式结合了三亚当地独有的黎苗文化特色，将三亚在万年历史长河中的转变浓缩在其中，向我们展现了落笔洞遗址到国际旅游岛的历史文化变迁。

图腾大道

我们现在所在的位置是图腾大道，四周树立着八根讲述着黎族起源故事的图腾柱，上方是甘工鸟，下方是蛇与蛙神。相传黎族人的女始祖——黎母，是由雷击蛇卵而生，因而蛇是黎族的民族图腾之一。而蛙神是黎族的吉祥兽，寓意着风调雨顺，人丁兴旺。

广场地面上的花纹，同样与黎族文化有关，它取自于黎族的传统手工艺品——黎锦。黎锦制作精美，多姿多彩，富有特色，有海南“双面绣”之美称。

南海女神像

这座高大伟岸的雕像就是我们的南海女神像了，这里是进入景区的第一扇大门。她高 28 米，宽 60 米，作为妈祖娘娘林默的化身，不仅是三亚的精神图腾，也是海南女性的化身，更是海南的守护神。在景区内还有一座妈祖庙，香火不断。

大厅王者之城

四位象神分别代表了我们海南的四位女英雄：妈祖、冼夫人、黎母、黄道婆。在这里着重向大家介绍下黎母。

黎母：黎族民间信仰存在山神崇拜和石祖崇拜。黎族的石祖崇拜是与黎族人民的生殖崇拜联系在一起的，体现了黎族人民希望人与自然和睦相处的朴素自然观。历史上，黎族所处的母系氏族社会时间比较长，所以最先获得崇拜的是女性祖先。直至今天，黎族女性的社会地位依然非常之高，这是许多民族所无法比拟的。千百年来，黎族人民崇祀黎母神，就是在这样的社会状况和民间信仰基础上产生的。

（1）保护神。黎母神是黎母山和生活在这里的黎族民众的保护神，她不仅统管着这里的山山水水，使黎母山区山清水秀，同时用她健美的臂膀，保佑着生活在这方水土上的黎族人民。

（2）生育神。黎母神是黎族人民尊奉的始祖，掌管着黎族人民的婚姻与生育。在她的荫佑之下，黎族人民在这片土地上，世代繁衍，生生不息。黎族人民在绵延不已的历史进程中，生儿育女、传宗接代，让血脉延续、香火不断的理想充分地体现在对黎母神的祭祀和崇拜中，因此，黎母神的地位不亚于观音菩萨。

（3）长寿神。黎母山地区山清水秀，人杰地灵，黎族人民在这里安居乐业，世代繁衍。这里盛产灵芝，山水清澈，人民普遍长寿。对此，历代文献都有记载。宋代周去非《岭外代答》在介绍黎母山时写道："其上之人，寿考逸乐。"《乾隆琼州府志》亦载："黎母山下有一村，代生寿妇，山下有泉极甘，傍皆果壳鸟羽。"在黎母神的保佑之下，这里良好的自然环境、优质的水资源、原生态的食物来源，加上黎族人民豁达乐观的性格，使得这里的人民生活安逸，长寿健康。可见，黎母神是名副其实的长寿之神。

（4）丰收神。黎母定居黎母山后，"子孙众多"，因此必须"开山种粮"，以满足子孙生活的需要。黎族社会长期以来以农耕和狩猎为主，种植庄稼对于一个民族的生存来说，尤为重要。五指山合亩地区过去有祭祀"稻公""稻母"的耕作仪式，黎族人民希望通过祭祀"稻公""稻母"，以祈获得庄稼丰收。通过黎母神"开山种粮"的事情可以看到，黎母神是最早率领黎族子孙开辟山地，种植庄稼的人。就是在她的庇佑之下，庄稼才连年丰收，黎族人民才得以过上好日子。

（5）纺织神。黎族妇女的纺染织绣技艺举世闻名。一个黎族妇女若不掌握织布技术，她在黎族社会中是没有地位的。这种技艺的传授特点是母传女，是世代传承下来的。黎族妇女在纺织过程中，忌讳男人触摸到纺织工具，否则将无法织出像五指山上的云彩那样美丽的花纹。黎母是黎族的祖先神，她的后代至今还传承的纺染织绣技艺也是由黎母发明，而且经由她手把手地教授给子孙的。这样看来，黎母神就是黎族人民的纺织神了。

（6）财神。如上所述，黎母神统辖着黎母山的山山水水，以及山上的各种动物。黎母山有着无尽的宝藏，为当地的黎族人民提供了赖以生活的物质条件。所以黎母神就是黎母山区的财神，也是黎族人民心中的财神。

爱情谷

爱是人类永恒的主题，您面前的爱情广场正是为此而建，月老祠坐落于爱情广场之上，它的右前方是风铃廊，正前方是天香炉。从 2013 年 9 月 25 日景区开园那天起，天香炉里的火就从未熄灭，祝愿每一位到三亚千古情景区的游客，未来的生活红红火火。如果您愿意，也可以亲自加一把火，祝福您的家人、朋友身体安康，事业蒸蒸日上。

月老祠

“夜入北国装成白，万物尽隐玉情怀。月老无约暗庆喜，天女翩翩含笑来。”这一首诗形容的是月老，我们现在所来到的地方便是月老祠，月老祠是为纪念黎族美丽的爱情传说《鹿回头》而修建。传说很久很久以前，有一个残暴的洞主，想取一副名贵的鹿茸，便强迫黎族青年阿黑上山打鹿。有一次阿黑上山打猎时，看见了一只美丽的花鹿，正被一只斑豹紧追，阿黑用箭射死了斑豹，然后对花鹿穷追不舍，一直追了九天九夜，翻过了九十九座山追到三亚湾南边的珊瑚崖上，花鹿面对烟波浩渺的南海，前面已无去路。此时，青年猎手正欲搭箭射击，花鹿突然回头含情凝望而却步，变成一位美丽的少女向他走来，于是他们结为夫妻。这就是流传于民间的鹿回头的故事。后来，他们二人被奉为黎族的爱情之神。走进祠堂，祠堂内供奉着中国人的爱情之神——月老，一位慈眉善目的老人。月老在中国民间具有非常重要的地位，他是中国民间传说中主管婚姻的红喜神。他在冥冥之中以红绳系男女之足，以促成姻缘。传说中的月老形象正如我们眼前所看到的这位老人，端坐在堂中看着来祈求姻缘的善男信女。

风铃廊

在三亚，风铃是具有召唤爱情魔力的信物。古时，黎苗的少女成年后就会在自家的门前或走廊悬挂一串风铃，代表着自己可以正式和男孩子谈恋爱了，久而久之这风铃也就成为三亚祈福的信物。在这里挂上一串许愿风铃，也寓意着无论您走到天涯海角，您亲人和爱人的祝福都会与您相伴一生。

共生树（夫妻树）

这看似一棵树，实则为菩提树环抱棕树，两树亲密相拥共生，故名为共生树（或夫妻树）。该树植于月老祠旁，寓意着有情人终成眷属。而菩提树与佛教渊源颇深，被誉为“佛教圣树”，在佛教信徒眼中它是神圣、吉祥和高尚的象征。民间更有在菩提树树干上缠绕一圈圈线绳以祈愿祝福的习俗。

“缘缘石”

在这个爱情谷里，有一块吸收了亿万年天地灵气的石头叫作“缘缘石”，在唐代的时候曾被雕琢成著名寺院佛塔的塔顶，后来被皇家所收藏，历经沧桑变化，一直传承至今。关于“缘缘石”一直流传有这样的说法：一摸，福如东海水长流；二摸，禄厚爵高展宏图；三摸，寿比南山不老松；四摸，喜乐盈门家和睦；五摸，财源茂盛达三江。福禄寿喜财，可谓五福临门。“缘缘石”后面刻的是山盟海誓几个大字，也象征着海枯石烂心不变，天荒地老情不移的爱情信念。

陶笛

陶笛是一种世界性的乐器，多数地域都有过使用陶笛的记录。制作陶笛的材料非常多，可以用陶土、紫砂等。这是一种非常轻盈的乐器，别看它个子小小的，却能吹出非常美妙的声音，有极强的音乐表现力。并且陶笛的吹法也很简单，经过短时间的练习，也能吹出令人满意的曲子。

手工陶艺

陶艺是中国的传统文化。中国是陶瓷古国，说起陶瓷，外国人就会想到中国。制作陶瓷的基本材料是土、水、火。制作者只有掌握了水土糅合的可塑性，流变性，以及成型方法和烧结规律，才能促成陶艺形态的产生和演化，使陶瓷器物产生美的形式。同时注重造型与装饰的有机结合，通过人们敏锐的灵感和创新意识，捕捉并揭示泥土的塑性美、柔韧美以及表现活力，这样就出现了全新陶艺形态。随着陶艺热的逐步升温，陶艺制品获得越来越多人的青睐，亲手做陶艺成为人们工作学习之余放松精神释放自我的又一休闲方式。在近几年的发展过程中，相关教育部门从素质教育出发，把陶艺列入了教学课程，这样孩子从小就可以受到艺术的熏陶，从中锻炼了动手能力，非常好地体现了素质教育的成果。在陶艺馆里，您可以亲自动手做一件属于自己的陶器，看它在你手中慢慢有了生命和形状。

黎锦

黎锦是海南岛黎族民间的织锦，堪称中国史上的活化石，其历史已经超过 3000 年了，是中国最早的棉纺织品。黎锦制作精巧，富有夸张的浪漫主义色彩。现在我们看到黎族阿婆在织黎锦，其织法非常精细、复杂，黎锦以棉线为主，麻线、丝线为辅交织而成，阿婆所用的工具用海南话念作“qiong”和“cai”，黎锦是国家级非物质文化遗产，但是很少有年轻人会织黎锦了。您可以看到我们传统的黎锦服饰，有各色的图案，都是黎族人民信仰的图腾。

花生糕

在京城有一种非常著名的小吃，就是我们眼前所看到的花生糕，花生糕是古代宫廷膳食，源于宋朝，经过元、明、清三个朝代 600 余年流传至今，是古代开封的特产。据说清朝时，八国联军入侵，慈禧太后到西安避难，在她回銮途中品尝了开封官员赠送的花生糕，品尝后赞不绝口，此后便将花生糕定为宫廷的贡品。花生糕以精选的花生仁为主料，辅以白糖饴糖等经过熬汤、拨糖、垫花生等几道工序制作而成，成品呈片状，多层次，疏松度强，食之口味桦脆，香甜可口，发展至今不仅做工讲究而且包装精美，是馈赠亲友之佳品。

草编

草编是利用各种柔韧草本植物为原料加工编制的工艺品。2008 年入选第二批国家级非物质文化遗产名录。目前可见中国最早的草编遗物是由河姆渡人所制作，距今已有 7000 年之久。古人的智慧是我们无法想象的，他们会利用随处可见的植物，编织一些日常生活用品以及工艺品。在海南天气炎热，人们出门时通常会戴一顶帽子遮阳。除此之外，也可以用帽子进行摆拍，因此，草编在海南是非常受欢迎的。

牛角梳

牛角梳是以牛角为原料，采用传统的手工工艺精心制作而成。牛角梳质地坚实、不易弯裂、不伤皮肤，不伤头发，有很好的护发效果。据《本草纲目》记载："牛角，酸咸、清凉、无毒。"用牛角梳梳头的时候，它的药理作用能在按摩头皮和头部神经时充分发挥，促进血液循环。

非洲鼓

大家有没有听到一首欢快的乐曲呢，没错，这就是从爱乐坊传出来的。这就是非洲手鼓。非洲手鼓是在 2010 年世界杯的时候传入我国，它的鼓面由山羊的脊背皮制成，鼓座由桃花木制成，分为高中低音，用手拍打鼓面的不同地方，就会传出不同的声音。手鼓的打法有 3 种：第一种是坐在椅子上，鼓身微微向前倾斜，双脚夹住鼓，背部挺直。第二种是用背带把鼓绑在身上，站立并把鼓夹在双腿之间，身体微微向下倾斜。第三种是把鼓横放在地上，坐在上面击打。这里需要特别留意的是，在打手鼓之前，请先把手上的饰物取下，以避免伤及手部和鼓面。

慢递生活

想过五年十年后的你过着什么样的生活，看着什么样的风景吗？想和十年后的自己谈谈吗？"时间胶囊"与"传统书信"的创意结合——慢递生活就能帮你完成这个心愿，书信上熟悉的文字是现代电话短信等即时通信所无法传递的。让我们置身在千年前的崖州古城，提笔给未来的自己写下一段话，在收到信件的刹那发生时空的错位，让现在和过去重新连接。在快节奏的生活方式里千万不要遗忘最宝贵的回忆和憧憬。

糖画

在宋代的千年市井街上有一家制造甜品的小摊位，摊位虽小却常常吸引了许多人驻足观看，还不时还传出啧啧赞叹声，这就是大家眼前的糖画了。

糖画是一种汉族民间手工艺，起源于明代的“糖丞相”。那大家会不会好奇为什么叫“糖丞相”，而不叫“糖百姓”呢，这是因为在明朝每逢新年祭祀神仙的时候，就把糖融化铸成各种动物及人物作为祭品，所铸造的人物个个都“袍笏轩昂”俨然文臣武将，所以当时戏称为“糖丞相”。到了清代，此物更加流行，制作技艺也日益精妙，题材也更加广泛，多为龙、凤和大众所喜闻乐见的吉祥图案。

糖画以勺为笔，以糖为墨。用来制作造型所用的工具仅一勺一铲，汤料一般是红白糖，加上少许饴糖，放在炉子上用温火熬制，熬到可以牵丝时即可用来浇铸造型了。在绘制造型时，由艺人用小汤勺舀起融化了的糖汁，在大理石板上飞快地来回浇铸。因为大理石板温凉的性质，易作画不易粘连。当造型完成后随机用小铲刀将糖画铲起，粘上竹签便可完成。民间俗称“倒糖饼”“倒糖人”。

糖画造型生动、色彩鲜艳，深受广大群众，尤其是孩子们的喜爱。在糖画小摊位前各位贵宾可以边看边回忆小时候看糖画、吃糖画的甜蜜时光，这是童年的记忆。

吹糖人

景区的吹糖人深受游客朋友的喜爱，因为游客不仅可以尝到它的美味，同时还可以亲自和手工艺人合作一起吹一个自己喜欢的造型，是不是特别有趣。这里还有两张“吃货”的照片，大家应该都不陌生了，奔跑吧兄弟在三亚千古情景区拍摄时，陈赫和王祖蓝都品尝了吹糖人哦。

黎村

这里是景区最热闹的街区之一，不仅有科技游乐馆，戏水区等游乐项目可以免费体验游玩，还有精彩绝伦的外景演出，如程知府招婿、黎家婚礼巡游、怕椰子等表演，让您仿佛置身千年前的古城中，感受一把穿越之旅。

科技游乐馆

现在我们来到了“科技游乐馆”。游乐馆运用高科技的手段再现了暴风眼、海角沉船、怪街、苏东坡“居士府”等。

暴风眼

位于我们左手边的便是暴风眼。三亚多台风，2014 年第 9 号台风“威马逊”登陆时风力达到 17 级，导致海南 131.1 万人受灾，同时造成很严重的经济损失。暴风眼采用仿真模拟道具，配合声效、风、雨、雾、光、电系统，再现飓风来袭时天昏地暗、树倒屋塌的逼真场景。

听音室

在暴风眼的对面就是深受游客喜爱的“海角沉船”听音室。胆大的游客，不妨进去听一听，一千年前的这艘古船，是如何在古代海上丝绸之路沉入海底的，在那期间，又发生了怎样诡异的事件呢。室内运用多声道环绕立体声效和氛围互动场景，能带给参与者一种身临其境的刺激感。

斜屋

斜屋内一切设施都是斜的，中间的立柱却是垂直正常地面的，此屋利用参照物产生错觉原理，人进去以后有失重的感觉，一定要小心！如果感觉到头晕目眩的话，可以盯着地板试一试。

倒屋

这里是一个颠倒世界，房顶变成地板，所有的家具都倒挂在房顶，举起双指拍张照片，你将惊奇地发现，你竟然倒吊在天花板上了。

镜子迷宫

这是镜子迷宫，游客在迷宫中摸索前行，各种镜光倒影让道路真假难辨，眼花缭乱。据说迄今为止没有人从这里顺利地穿行，要走出这个迷宫需要的不仅仅是勇气了。

偷窥墙

从古至今，好奇心总会诱使人捅破那层窗户纸。大家瞧！窗户上已被人捅破了好多洞，里面会有什么令人惊喜的事情呢？

居士府

很多游客朋友会问为什么要在景区里建一个居士府呢？这居士又是指谁呢？这居士指的就是苏东坡先生，他跟海南有着很深的渊源。我们都知道，古代海南是作为官员的流放之地，据说在宋朝，放逐海南是仅比满门抄斩罪轻一等的处罚。但苏东坡先生流放至此地时并没有郁郁寡欢，他把儋州当成了自己的第二故乡，还说道："我本儋耳氏，寄生西蜀州。"他在这里办学堂，介学风，以致许多人不远千里，追至儋州，向他学习。在宋代100多年里，海南从没有人进士及第。但苏轼北归不久，这里的姜唐佐就举乡贡。为此苏轼题诗："沧海何曾断地脉，珠崖从此破天荒。"人们一直把苏轼看作儋州文化的开拓者、播种人，对他怀有深深的崇敬。在儋州流传至今的东坡村、东坡井、东坡田、东坡路、东坡桥、东坡帽等，均表达了人们的缅怀之情，连语言都有一种"东坡话"，正所谓"东坡不幸海南幸"，所以苏东坡先生是非常受我们当地人尊敬和感谢的。上天无疑是偏爱海南岛的，温润灵动的自然美景已属不易，还要锦上添花地赐予它令人仰视的人文渊源。

神奇祖先像

正堂上挂着一幅先祖的画像，看似很寻常，仔细观察您会发现，他的眼睛一直在盯着我们，无论您移动到哪里，他的目光总会跟随着您。时而他还会向我们微笑、点头，像是在欢迎我们。

卧房

很多游客都会好奇，为什么苏东坡先生的床铺是像婚床一样的大红色呢？其实这是为了纪念他的结发之妻王弗所特意修建的。苏东坡先生深爱着他的妻子，可惜他的妻子很早就离开了人世，他十分怀念他的妻子，也曾写下"十年生死两茫茫，不思量，自难忘"的诗句。所以这个婚床也见证了他们坚贞的爱情。

书房

这间是居士的书房，您想体验古人泼墨挥毫的感觉吗，只要站在地面的脚印处，对着书法卷轴轻轻挥笔，就可以题诗写词了。

琴房

谈笑有鸿儒，往来无白丁。居士府里进出的莫不是文人雅客样样精通？这里是苏东坡先生平常演奏的琴，将手放在琴弦上，只要稍稍一拨，一首天籁之曲就会飘然而出。

戏水区

现在我们可以看到的是我们的戏水区，也是游客朋友们最喜爱的水上游玩项目，这里涵盖“秋千桥”“水上漂”“独木桥”等项目。炎炎夏日，有兴趣的游客朋友可以尽情地去感受一把清凉之夏。

程府招婿

位于正前方这雕梁画栋、喜气洋洋的二层楼房就是程知府家，程知府有一独女，到了年方二八还未出阁，二八就是十六岁，大家别误以为是二十八岁哦。今天程知府便会在此搭彩楼抛绣球招婿，各位在场的未婚男士就有福利了，趁着现在赶紧去找个有利的位置去争抢绣球，抢中的人就可以登上彩楼和小姐拜堂成亲成为我们程知府的女婿喽。

崖州古城

向左转，我们即将步入的是崖州古城，三亚古称崖州，历史悠久，人文璀璨。早在秦始皇设立南方三郡时崖州便是其中之一。古崖州也是古代海上丝绸之路的重要中转地区，往来商客如云，天下珍宝皆汇聚于此。“弦诵声黎民物庶，宦游都道小苏杭”说的便是古崖州，将我们的古崖州比作“小苏杭”，可以见得当时崖州的繁荣昌盛。大家看到，街道的角角落落都是我们从民间收集而来的石器，几经沧桑，无论朝代如何更迭，那些承载着历史符号的石头仿佛一直在诉说王朝的故事。

小吃广场

在小吃广场我们可以品尝到具有海南特色的文昌鸡、椰子饭、海鲜烧烤、竹筒饭等传统小吃，还可以喝到海南特色的椰奶清补凉，解渴又美味，您游玩累了，可以坐在这里，慵懒地体验海南下午和夜晚的休闲时光。

在古城街道上，除有让您垂涎欲滴的特色小吃外，还有穿梭于此的各色路人——黎家阿妹、达官贵人、侠客、乞丐、醉汉、西域波斯美女、士兵、更夫、和尚等在此发生的一幕幕前所未闻的故事足以让人大开眼界。

六间房广场

在我们的六间房广场上每天会上演我们的外景演出，有“草裙锅庄”“冼夫人练兵”等，在这里，您可以尽情地释放您的热情，跟我们的阿哥阿姐一起尽情地跳舞和歌唱。

锅庄火把节

锅庄火把节也被称为“东方的狂欢节”。在古代，每进入秋月，禾黄稻熟，椰果丰美，黎苗的祖先会聚集在空旷的广场跳舞。明月之下，围着篝火，女人们会顶着陶罐，男人们会举着火把，唱起丰收歌，以此表达消灭害虫，祈求风调雨顺，确保五谷丰登、六畜兴旺、人丁平安。

上巳节

每年的三月三日是海南省黎族人民最盛大的民间传统节日，也是黎族青年的美好日子，又称爱情节、谈爱日。它是海南黎族人民悼念勤劳勇敢的祖先、表达对爱情幸福向往之情的传统节日。

泼水节

泼水节，来源于黎苗的朴素民俗。传说很久很久以前，中原大地发大水，一批黎苗的祖先涉海过洋，一直漂流到三亚。但见这里绿树成林、鸟语花香，先民们于是在此地定居下来。但令他们苦恼的是，这里唯独缺少生活必要的淡水。没有了水源，就不能生火造饭，先民食不果腹，艰难度日。眼看日子再也过不下去了，忽然有一天，部落的首领在昏迷熟睡中梦到了七位美丽的仙女，她们托梦告诉他水源所在。醒来后，首领根据梦的提示，终于在不远的山林里发现波光粼粼的河溪。族人们大喜过望，一起在溪中泼水嬉闹。为了感恩送来圣水的七仙女，先民保留下了泼水节这一民风习俗，并作为一项重大节庆世代流传至今。

新禾节

每逢农历六月初六，在禾黄稻熟，椰果丰美之时，苗族同胞，都要欢度民族传统佳节——新禾节，它是苗族庆祝丰收的节日，其隆重程度仅次于苗年节和清明节。明月之下，大家围着篝火唱起丰收歌，以此表达消灭害虫，祈福风调雨顺，五谷丰登，人丁平安。

爱牛节

每年农历的十月初五，是苗族同胞欢度爱牛节的日子，这一天人不下地，牛不拉犁，用四方篾箩拾来香喷喷的糯米饭和一些肉，让大牛尽情饱餐，妇女们把用山花编织成的花环围在牛脖子上，男人用红彤彤的枫叶装饰牛角，分享着一年辛勤劳动换来的丰收喜悦。

新春大庙会

新春庙会是三亚每年一度的文化大餐。庙会源于古代的集市。黎、苗等少数民族载歌载舞，并把日常用品沿街贩卖吆喝，场面热闹喜庆，年味十足。

鬼蜮惊魂

大家刚刚听了冼夫人的故事后有没有感到热血沸腾，仿佛自己就是一个充满了力量的战士呢？那大家不妨借着这股胆量，去感受一下鬼蜮惊魂。这座超大规模的鬼屋，利用各种高科技手段以及逼真的投影技术，营造出风、雨、雷、电、瘴气、毒蛇猛兽、诈尸、累累白骨等惊悚场景。青面獠牙的僵尸，兀然坐起的尸体，叮当作响的铁链桥下忽然抓住你的白骨，众多逼真的体验绝对让您难以忘怀！

千古情大剧院

任何的相遇都是一种缘分，是多么值得让人珍惜。就在今天，在你与我之间，在情与景之间，缓缓地向您诉说着这一段绵延千古的佳话。一路走过，我们仿佛感受到穿越了几个世纪的人文风貌，也许千年前的这一刻，我们就这样相遇，而千年后的此时，我们又在此重聚，这就是那冥冥中缘分的延续。为了这一场浪漫的邂逅能让您刻骨铭心，我们的艺术创作团队、景区设计团队在总导演、总设计师黄巧灵先生的带领下，深入到三亚的角角落落调研采风，这也是我们的主创人员接受三亚文化洗礼的过程。从人头攒动的海滨沙滩到人迹罕至的历史遗存，从遮天蔽日的热带雨林到大山深处的黎苗人家，都留下了宋城人“沙海淘金”的身影，我们要拨开历史的迷雾，把三亚尘封的文明通过宋城对历史文化的独特表述方式展示在每一位游客面前。

《三亚千古情》演出中不仅有鹿回头美丽的爱情传说，能听到落笔洞的万年回声，能看到鉴真东渡时的惊涛骇浪，更能领略到巾帼英雄冼夫人收复失地征战沙场的荡气回肠。剧院为三亚千古情量身定制世界最先进的灯光、音响、舞美、特效以及 390 多套舞台机械共同演绎了这些精美绝伦的场面。三亚灿烂的文化，动人的传说，淳朴的民风在此得到了最完美的诠释。相信这场一生必看的演出，一定会为您带来一场宏大的视觉盛宴与来自心灵的震撼。

热场《一沙一世界》

我们三亚千古情演出的开场选择用“沙”作为介质，沙是海洋的重要组成部分，有鲜明的地域感以及历史的沧桑感。沙也代表时间的流逝，一天就是一颗沙，千年就是千古情的历史。

序《落笔洞》

一万年前的三亚是怎样的？远古人类是怎样漂洋过海来到这里，又是如何在这里繁衍生息的？ 1992 年 3 月考古学家曾在落笔洞发现一万年前的三亚遗址，发掘出人类牙化石、石制品、蚌壳化石等，还有大量的用火遗迹。古人类在那里生活、渔猎，铭刻下中国最南端人类生存的印记。在序幕中，蹦极抓鱼的表演真实地还原了当时古人类的生活。

第一场《鹿回头》

“最爱凤凰临宝地，三亚难舍鹿回头。”三亚不仅有着悠久的历史，也流传着许多动人的爱情故事，鹿回头就是其中最美的传说。在《三亚千古情》演出采用电影叙事手法，将鹿回头的爱情故事通过高科技的声光电技术，融化在空灵的仙境、茂密的热带雨林、唯美的黎村之中。

第二场《冼夫人》

历史有着惊人的相似，在我们今天这块剧院的土地上，就是当年冼夫人的封地。558 年，隋文帝开始了统一中国的步伐，此时，岭南地区发生战乱，冼夫人在战争中强忍丧夫之痛，巾帼不让须眉，带领将士征服百越部落，让孤悬海外 600 多年的海南岛重归中央政权，隋文帝为了表彰她的功绩，将古崖州划归她管理。

第三场《海上丝路》

三亚港在宋代已经成为“海上丝绸之路”的中转站，中国的瓷器从这里运往海外，来自印度洋、波斯湾的香料也在这里汇集。八月十五这天，崖州知府会举办中秋赏月会、款待各国宾朋，场面恢宏盛大，壮观至极。

第四场《鉴真东渡》

唐天宝年间，高僧鉴真为了弘扬佛教文化第六次东渡扶桑，在他第五次东渡时遭遇飓风，漂流至三亚，受到了当地官员的热情款待。在《三亚千古情》演出中用高难度的空中飞人杂技表演，来表现鉴真大师东渡扶桑过程中与风浪搏击、险象环生的惊险过程。

尾声《美丽三亚》

美丽三亚、浪漫天涯。阳光、海水、沙滩、椰林让三亚拥有“东方夏威夷”之称；悠久的历史，浪漫的传说，带给人们无尽的遐想。在椰风、海韵、沙滩、比基尼美女的陪伴中，邀您来感受这里美丽的夜晚。

各位贵宾，今天我为大家的讲解就到此结束了，但愿后会有期，能有机会再次为您服务，愿三亚千古情一行可以留在您美好的回忆中。接下来是大家自由活动的时间，在自由活动的期间，请保管好您的随身物品并注意安全，欢迎您的再次光临，谢谢，再见！

2. 亚龙湾国家旅游度假区

大家好，欢迎光临亚龙湾国家旅游度假区，我是您的导游陈丹，您可以叫我小陈。我希望我的讲解能给你带来愉快的心情。

亚龙湾原名琊琅湾，后称牙龙湾。由于在古代地处荒僻，远离州城县治，历代史志对它的记述很少。据说“琊琅湾”出自本地黎语，这与这里海湾的沙子有关，琊或琅意为白玉、洁白，形容沙子洁白如玉。因为这里的海湾呈月牙形，后来才被人们称为“牙龙湾”。中华人民共和国成立之后，这里设置军事基地，长期对外封闭，因此鲜为人知。

1992 年 10 月 13 日，海南省人民政府主持召开了“关于牙龙湾风景名胜区总体规划评议会”，经过讨论，一致通过将牙龙湾更名为亚龙湾。从文字上看，只是一字之差，但其含义却有天壤之别。牙字和亚字谐音，但其含义则差别极大：第一，从狭义来讲，“亚龙”是三亚之龙；第二，从广义来讲，“亚龙”是亚洲之龙；第三，中华民族都是炎黄子孙，是龙的传人，而“龙”又是中华民族最崇拜的吉祥物。寓意着这块沉睡千年的美丽海湾，将像巨龙一样腾飞而起，光照亚洲。

名字的来历及演变，反映了它由原始落后至现代文明的沧桑巨变。度假区近 30 年的发展，使亚龙湾成为人们心中的度假天堂，是家庭、情侣度假休闲游的选择地，同时重大国事活动、国内外各类顶级赛事、文体活动等的成功举办，使亚龙湾同样成为各类会议的目的地。

如今，亚龙湾已经美名远扬，并成为国内外知名的旅游品牌。在国内，选择亚龙湾度假已是一种时尚，这里如诗如画的自然风光、舒适完善的旅游度假设施和独具特色的旅游项目已成为旅游者向往的度假天堂！

亲爱的朋友们，我们的亚龙湾国家旅游度假区之旅到此结束。我们将一直在这里等待您下一次的到来。祝您旅途愉快！

参考文献

［1］纪俊超．英语海南导游［M］．北京：中国旅游出版社，2009.

［2］万华，陈武现．海南导游手册［M］．上海：复旦出版社，2007.

［3］王兰春，王硕．海南旅游景区导游词精选［M］．北京：中国人民大学出版社，2013.

［4］姚宝荣．模拟导游教程［M］．北京：中国旅游出版社，国家旅游局人事劳动教育司，1999.

［5］王浪．中国著名旅游景区导游词精选［M］．北京：旅游教育出版社，2010.

［6］李幼伍，杨卫平．模拟导游［M］．海口：南海出版公司，2006.

［7］陈大坚．模拟导游［M］．海口：南海出版公司，2012.

［8］黄学坚．海南［M］．广州：广东旅游出版社，2001.

［9］陈栋康．海南大观［M］．海口：海南人民出版社，1988.

［10］常辅棠．海之南［M］．海口：南方出版社，2006.

［11］陈耀．海南旅游概览［M］．海口：南海出版公司，2004.

［12］彭庆海．海南好［M］．海口：南海出版公司，2001.

［13］沈之称．海南三百景游［M］．上海：中华出版社，2002.

［14］王建成．海南民族风情［M］．北京：民族出版社，2004.

［15］朱玉书．海南传说［M］．广州：广东旅游出版社，1986.

［16］邢益森．新编海南岛旅游［M］．上海：中华出版社，2000.

［17］杨昭宽．海南旅游导趣［M］．海口：海南出版社，2001.

［18］方鹏．海南岛历史，民族与文化［M］．海口：南方出版社，2003.

［19］https://ar.explorehainan.com/en/about/jqjd.shtml.

［20］https://www.hnftp.gov.cn/mlhn/hngl/hnjj/.

［21］https://baike.baidu.com/.

［22］https://en.hainan.gov.cn/hainan/zrzy/201706/f275306f8835415c9f9a693d83f7beac.shtml.

Part I

Hainan Tourism Information

1. An Overview of Hainan Province

Hainan Province is located at the southernmost point of China. To the north, it borders Guangdong Province through the Qiongzhou Strait, faces Vietnam across the Beibu Gulf to the west, and borders the Philippines, Brunei, Indonesia, and Malaysia to the east and south in the South China Sea. The administrative regions of Hainan Province include the islands, reefs and sea areas of Hainan Island, the Xisha Islands, the Zhongsha Islands, the Nansha Islands, and it is the largest province in China. The total land area of the province (mainly including Hainan Island, Xisha Islands, Zhongsha Islands and the Nansha Islands) is 35,400 square kilometers, and the sea area is about 2 million square kilometers. The total length of the coastline is 1,944 kilometers, with 68 harbors of various sizes.

As of December 2022, there are 4 municipal level administrative divisions (prefecture level cities), 25 county-level administrative divisions (10 municipal districts, 5 county-level cities, 4 counties, and 6 ethnic autonomous counties), and 218 township level administrative divisions (22 streets, 175 towns, and 21 townships) in Hainan Province. Among them, prefecture level cities include Haikou, Sanya, Sansha, and Danzhou; County level cities include Wuzhishan City, Wenchang City, Qionghai City, Wanning City, and Dongfang City; Counties include Ding'an County, Tunchang County, Chengmai County, and Lingao County; Autonomous counties include Baisha Li Autonomous County, Changjiang Li Autonomous County, Ledong Li Autonomous County, Lingshui Li Autonomous County, Baoting Li and Miao Autonomous County, and Qiongzhong Li and Miao Autonomous County.

As of the end of 2022, the permanent population of Hainan Province was 10.2702 million, an increase of 65,600 people compared to the end of the previous year. The urbanization rate of the permanent population is 61.49%, an increase of 0.52 percentage points. The Han, Li, Miao, and Hui ethnic groups are the hereditary ethnic groups in Hainan Province, while the other ethnic groups are cadres, workers, and immigrants who migrated after the establishment of the People's Republic of China, scattered throughout the province. The Li ethnic group was the earliest inhabitants of Hainan Island. The Li, Miao, and Hui ethnic groups, who have lived for generations, mostly reside in autonomous counties such as Qiongzhong, Baoting, Baisha, Lingshui, Changjiang, and Ledong in the central and southern regions, as well as in Sanya City, Dongfang City, and Wuzhishan City; The Han population is mainly concentrated in the northeast, north, and coastal areas.

Hainan residents have a wide variety of languages, mainly using 10 dialects, including: Hainan dialect, Li dialect, Lingao dialect, Danzhou dialect, Jun dialect, Miao dialect, Village dialect, Huihui dialect, Mai dialect, and Danjia dialect. Hainan dialect is the most widely used and widely spoken, with over 5 million residents in the province. It is mainly distributed in most areas of cities and counties such as Haikou, Wenchang, Qionghai, Wanning, Ding'an, Tunchang, and Chengmai, as well as coastal areas of cities and counties such as Lingshui, Ledong, Dongfang, Changjiang, and Sanya. In different places, the pronunciation and tone of Hainan dialect vary, and the standard accent is generally based on the pronunciation of the Wenchang people.

Hainan Province is rich in natural resources. It is the largest "tropical treasure land" in the country, with a total land area of 3.5187 million hectares, accounting for 42.5% of the country's tropical land area, and a per capita land area of about 0.44 hectares. Due to superior conditions such as light, heat, and water, farmland can be planted year-round, and many crops are harvested 2-3 times a year. Grain crops are the largest, most widely distributed, and most valuable crops in Hainan's planting industry, mainly including rice, upland rice, and shanlan rice, followed by sweet potatoes, cassava, taro, corn, millet, beans, etc. Economic crops mainly include sugarcane, hemp, peanuts, sesame, tea, etc. There are many kinds of fruits, mainly pineapple, litchi, longan, banana, citrus, mango, watermelon, carambola, jackfruit, rambutan, pitaya, etc. There are over 120 types of vegetables. Tropical crop resources are abundant, among which tropical crops with large cultivation areas and high economic value mainly include rubber, coconut, betel nut, coffee, pepper, oil palm, sisal, lemongrass, cashew, cocoa, etc. Hainan has fast vegetation growth and a wide variety of plants, making it the birthplace of tropical rainforests and seasonal rainforests. Hainan Island has over 4,600 types of vascular plants, accounting for about 1/7 of the total number in the country, of which more than 490 are unique to Hainan. There are 660 species of terrestrial vertebrates in Hainan, including 43 species of amphibians, 113 species of reptiles, 426 species of birds, and 78 species of mammals. Among terrestrial vertebrates, 23 species are unique to Hainan. Rare and precious animals in the world include black crowned gibbons and deer, water deer, macaques, black bears, clouded leopards, etc.

Hainan's marine aquatic resources are characterized by a wide range of marine fishing grounds, a variety of species, fast growth, and a long fishing season, making it an ideal place for the development of tropical marine fisheries in China. More than 800 kinds of fish have been recorded in the offshore waters of Hainan Island, more than 1,000 kinds of fish have been recorded in the northern continental shelf of the South China Sea, and more than 500 kinds of fish have been recorded in the waters of South China Sea Islands. At the same time, Hainan Island is an ideal natural saltern. In the arc area hundreds of miles from Sanya to the eastern coast, many harbors and mudflat can be used for drying salt. Large salt farms such as Yinggehai, Dongfang, and Yuya have been established, among which Yinggehai Salt Farm is the most famous. Hainan has a wide variety of mineral resources. A total of 88 mineral resources have been discovered in the province, of which 70 kinds have been evaluated as having industrial reserves. Among them, 59 kinds have been identified and included in the statistics of mineral resource reserves, with 487 production areas. Hainan's mineral resources mainly include oil, natural gas, ferrous metals, non-ferrous metals, precious metals, rare metals, metallurgical auxiliary materials, chemical raw materials, building materials, other non-metallic minerals, groundwater, hot mineral water, and drinking natural mineral water.

Hainan has abundant tourism resources and distinctive features, mainly in the following aspects:

Coastal landscape

On the 1,823 kilometer long coastline of Hainan Island, the sand bank accounts for about 50% to 60%, and the width of the beach can be as short as 100 meters, and as long as over 1,000 meters. The slope towards the sea surface is generally 5 degrees, slowly extending; In most places, the wind and waves are calm, the seawater is clear, the sand is as white as fluff, and it is clean and soft; The shore is shaded by green trees, and the air is fresh; The temperature of seawater is generally between 18℃ and 30℃ , with abundant and bright sunlight. Most of the year, one can take sea bathing, sunbathing, sand bathing, and wind bathing. The five elements that international tourists love today, including sunshine, seawater, beaches, greenery, and air, are all present along the coast of Hainan Island. From Haikou to the east coast of Sanya, there are over 60 places that can be converted into seaside baths. There are different types of coastal scenic spots along the roundabout coast. On the east coast, the special tropical coastal forest landscape — mangroves, and the unique tropical coastal landform landscape — coral reefs, all have high ornamental value. Mangrove conservation areas have been established in Dongzhai Port in Haikou, Qinglan Port in Wenchang, and other areas.

Islands

There are over 100 islands around Hainan Island, mainly distributed along the eastern and southern coasts. There are 22 islands in the Xisha Islands, with a land area of 8 square kilometers, of which Yongxing Island is the largest. These islands are located in the tropics, with long sunshine, abundant light energy, clear seawater around them, and abundant aquatic resources, making them highly valuable for tourism. The islands that have carried out tourism projects include Wuzhizhou Island, West Island, Fenjiezhou Island, the Xisha Islands, etc.

Mountains and tropical primitive forests

Hainan Island has 81 peaks with an altitude of over 1,000 meters, stretching and undulating, with unique mountain shapes and majestic momentum. Famous attractions include the serrated and five finger shaped Wuzhi Mountain at the top of the mountain, the majestic Yingge Ridge, the Dongshan Ridge with strange stone peaks, the Taiping Mountain with cascading waterfalls, as well as the Qixian Ridge, Jianfeng Ridge, Diaoluo Mountain, and Bawang Ridge, all of which are popular destinations for mountaineering tourism and summer vacation. The most distinctive feature of Hainan's mountains is the dense tropical primitive forest, which includes four tropical primitive forest areas: Ledong Jianfeng Ridge, Changjiang Bawang Ridge, Lingshui Diaoluo Mountain, and Qiongzhong Wuzhi Mountain. Among them, Ledong Jianfeng Ridge is the most typical.

Rare birds and exotic beasts

In order to protect species and facilitate viewing, Hainan has established multiple wildlife nature reserves and domestication sites, including the Changjiang Bawangling Black Crown Gibbon Nature Reserve, the Dongfang Datianpo Deer Nature Reserve, the Wanning Dazhou Island Golden Swallow Nature Reserve, the Lingshui Nanwan Peninsula Macaque Nature Reserve, and the Tunchang Deer Farm.

Scenery of rivers, waterfalls, and reservoirs

Rivers such as Nandu River, Changhua River, and Wanquan River are intertwined with beaches and ponds, winding and flowing with clear water. They are excellent places for tourism and sightseeing, especially famous for the scenery of Wanquan River throughout the country. Deep in the mountains, there are numerous small rivers or streams, and numerous waterfalls. Among them, Wuzhishan Taiping Mountain Waterfall and Qiongzhong Baihualing Waterfall have long been famous. There are many reservoirs on Hainan Island, especially those such as Songtao, Nanfu, Changmao, and Shilu, which have the beauty of lakes and mountains, and are not lakes but lakes.

Volcanoes, caves, hot springs

Historical volcanic eruptions have left many dead volcanic craters on Hainan Island. The most typical example is Shishan located in Haikou, which has a double ridge with an altitude of over 200 meters. There are two volcanic craters on the ridge, with a concave ridge in the middle, resembling a saddle, also known as Ma'anling. The Leihuling and Luojingpan volcanic craters near Shishan are also well preserved. There are many diverse karst caves, among which famous ones include the Luobi Cave in Sanya, the Qianlong Cave in Baoting, and the Emperor Cave in Changjiang. The hot springs on the island are widely distributed, with most of them having low mineralization, high temperature, large water volume, and good water quality. They are therapeutic hot springs, and the area where the hot springs are located has pleasant scenery. Xinglong Hot Springs, Guantang Hot Springs, Nanping Hot Springs, Lanyang Hot Springs, etc. are suitable for developing tourism that integrates sightseeing, recuperation, scientific research, etc.

Historical sites and scenic spots

The historical sites with significant historical significance in Hainan mainly include the Wugong Temple built to commemorate five famous historical officials, including Li Deyu, who were exiled to Hainan Island during the Tang and Song dynasties. The Dongpo Academy, also known as the Juqiong Site of the Northern Song Dynasty literary giant Su Dongpo, and the Su Gong Temple built to commemorate Su Shi, the Qiongtai Academy built by the Qing Dynasty's Lei Qiong Bing Bei Dao Jiao Yinghan, the tomb of the Ming Dynasty famous minister Qiu Jun, and the tomb of the Ming Dynasty's honest and upright official Hai Rui, According to legend, General Ma Yuan, who was sent by Emperor Wu of Han to lead troops into Hainan, ordered the excavation of the Han Ma Fubo Well to save troops, as well as the ancient city of Yazhou, the Wei Family Temple, and the Confucian Temple in Wenchang.

Revolutionary Memorial Site

The revolutionary memorial sites in Hainan include the former site of the First National Congress of the Communist Party of China in Qiongya, the former headquarters of the Qiongya Column, the Red Women's Army Memorial Park, the Jinniuling Martyrs Cemetery, the Baisha Uprising Memorial Hall, the former site of the Soviet Government in Lingshui County, as well as the ancestral residence and exhibition hall of Song Qingling, and the General Zhang Yunyi Memorial Hall.

Ethnic customs

The traditional ethnic minorities in Hainan Island include the Li, Miao, and Hui ethnic groups, which still retain many simple and honest folk customs and living habits, making Hainan's social landscape unique and colorful. Hainan is the only Li ethnic group settlement area in China, with distinctive ethnic culture and customs, and unique tourism and sightseeing value.

Tropical crops and pastoral scenery

Hainan Island is home to a large number of tropical crops, greatly enriching the natural landscape. Tourists can enjoy the tropical countryside scenery and broaden their horizons on the island, as well as taste tropical fruits for a satisfying feast.

2. An Overview of Haikou City

Haikou, also known as "Coconut City", is a prefecture level city and provincial capital under the jurisdiction of Hainan Province, a national strategic pivot city of the "the Belt and Road Initiative", and a core city of Hainan Free Trade Port. Located in the northern part of Hainan Island, adjacent to Wenchang City to the east, Ding'an County to the south, Chengmai County to the west, and Qiongzhou Strait to the north, facing Guangdong Province across the sea. Starting from Laocun in Roughly Slope Town in the east and ending at Banan Village in Xixiu Town in the west, with a distance of 60.6 kilometers between the two ends; Starting from Wucheshang Village in Dapo Town in the south and ending at Dahai in the north, the two ends are 62.5 kilometers apart. The land area is 2,296.82 square kilometers and the sea area is 791 square kilometers.

Haikou City is located in the tropics and is a southern coastal city rich in coastal natural scenery. Located on the northern edge of the low latitude tropics, it belongs to a tropical monsoon climate. Since the opening of the port in the Northern Song Dynasty, it has a history of over a thousand years. It is the political, economic, technological, and cultural center of Hainan Province, as well as the largest transportation hub. Haikou is a southern coastal city rich in natural and beautiful coastal scenery. On December 9th, 1926, Guangdong Province approved the establishment of the Haikou City Hall, which was traditionally referred to as Haikou City. In August 1929, the City Hall was renamed the Municipal Bureau, and Haikou was liberated on April 23rd, 1950. On April 13th, 1988, Hainan Province established an economic special zone and Haikou City became the capital of Hainan Province. In 2002, the merger of Haikou and Qiongshan opened a new chapter in the development of Haikou.

Administrative divisions

Haikou City has jurisdiction over four districts (county-level), Xiuying, Longhua, Qiongshan, and Meilan; It consists of 21 streets, 22 towns, 208 communities, 248 administrative villages, and 3 farmhouses. As of the end of 2021, the city has a permanent population of 2.98 million, consisting of 49 ethnic groups including Han, Li, Miao, Hui, Manchu, Yao, Mongolian, Korean, Tujia, Buyi, Dai, Dong, Zhuang, etc. Among them, the Han population accounts for 98.61%, and the minority population accounts for 1.39%. The languages used in Haikou include Hainan dialect, Mandarin, vernacular, military dialect, Hakka dialect, Minnan dialect, Sichuan, Henan, Hunan and other local dialects, as well as various ethnic minority languages.

Ecological environment

Haikou has a beautiful ecological environment, and the air pollution index is better than the national standard. It has a comfortable and pleasant climate and a first-class ecological environment, ranking the first in the air quality list of 168 cities at and above the prefectural level released by the ministry of ecology and environment of the People's Republic of China all the year round, with a green coverage rate of 43.5%. It has been selected by the world health organization as China's first "world healthy city" pilot site.

Haikou has "the Chinese charm city", "China's happiest cities", "China's most investment potential city", "China excellent tourism city", "national environmental protection model city", "national health city", "national garden city", "national famous historical and cultural city", "national civilized city", "national model city" and other honorary title, and won issued by the ministry of the annual "China habitat environment prize". In 2018, Haikou was rated as one of the world's first "international wetland cities" by the United Nations international convention on wetlands.

Natural scenery

Haikou city faces the sea to the north. Its sea area is 830 square kilometers, and its coastline is 131 kilometers long. The seafloor of the ocean is mostly flat, dominated by ooze, followed by silt. Near the beach, the sea bottom is dominated by fine sand. Most of the coast slope is gentle, and the coastline is open and continuous. The sandy shore has fine and white sand. There are tropical ocean world, holiday beach, Baishamen beach, Xixiu beach, Guangdong railway channel south station dock beach, Dongzhai port beach, Guilin ocean beach and other seaside scenic areas and recreation areas. There are a few reefs and tidal flats in the harbor and offshore. The offshore water is clear and the wind is light and the waves are flat all the year round. Blue sky, blue sea, sunshine, beach, coconut trees constitute a charming coastal scenery, which make visitors linger.

Historical sites

Haikou has an ancient military site built during the Hongwu period (1368-1398) — the Fucheng Drum Tower in the Chengmen Tower of the Ming dynasty. The West Temple was built in 1567 to commemorate Wang Zuo, a famous Hainan scholar in the Ming dynasty. The temple of lady Xian was built in 1583 in memory of Xian Ying, a famous historical figure who safeguarded the reunification of the motherland and promoted national unity. The tomb garden of Hai Rui was built in 1589 to commemorate Hai Rui, an honest official of Ming dynasty. Qiongtai academy was founded in 1710 to spread culture and train Hainan's children. The temple called Wugong Temple, which was built in 1889 to commemorate Li deyu, a tang dynasty official and Li Gang, Li Guang, Hu Quan and Zhao Ding, famous officials of the song dynasty who were relegated to Hainan but has spread culture and promoted cultural development and exchanges in the island.

Xiuying fort was built in 1891 to defend against foreign aggression. Xiuying fort, together with Tianjin Dagu fort, Shanghai Wu songkou and Guangzhou Humen fort, are known as the four major forts in the late qing dynasty. The former residence founded in 1919 of Feng baiju, who was is the main leader of Qiongya party, government and military. Here is the site of the first Qiongya congress of the communist party of China held in June 1926. Here is the Zhongshan memorial hall built in 1926 to commemorate sun yat-sen, the forerunner of the Chinese democratic revolution. Here is a monument to Hainan revolutionary martyrs built in 1951 to commemorate the more than 20,000 martyrs who died in the long standing Hainan Island revolutionary struggle and the heroic crossing of the sea to liberate Hainan. Here is to commemorate the second period of cooperation between the communist party of China and the Qiongya red army for the anti-Japanese independence team and built in 1952 Yunlong adaptation site; Here is to commemorate the liberation of Hainan sea crossing heroes martyrs and built in 1957 Jinniu ling martyrs cemetery; Here are some revolutionary scenic spots, such as the Li suoxun memorial pavilion, built in 1986 to commemorate Li suoxun, secretary of the Guangdong military commission of the communist party of China, who went to Qiong to guide the armed struggle.

Festival

In recent years, various folk festival activities have gradually become a major highlight of Haikou. It attracted many enthusiasts to come and observe or participate, further integrating culture and tourism. The large-scale traditional folk activities in Haikou include the Yuanxiao Lantern Festival on the 15th day of the first month, the Flower Change Festival, dragon and lion dances, and the Junpo Festival in memory of Madam Xian. Large scale festival activities include Happy Festivals, Spring Festival Galas, etc.

Folk customs

After nearly a thousand years of development, Haikou has gradually formed its own folk customs and traditions under the cultural influence of different historical periods and the joint catalysis of specific social environments. After the establishment of Hainan Province as an economic special zone in 1988, Haikou City developed rapidly with an increasing number of immigrants. Traditional cultural customs and foreign cultures in Haikou permeated and integrated with each other, and forming a folk customs that is mainly based on Chinese national culture, compatible with Eastern and Western cultures, and combining traditional culture with modern culture. Qiongzhou is the main local opera genre in Haikou, and coconut carving and shell carving are the main traditional handicrafts in Haikou. The indigenous people of Haikou have a simple and honest folk style, and have preserved many folk customs. For example, eating a fireplace on New Year's Eve and fasting on the first day of the Lunar New Year. On the 15th day of the first lunar month, the Yuanxiao Festival, commonly known as the Little New Year in Haikou, is a festival where citizens gather in Fucheng, Evergreen Park and other places to send and exchange flowers, pass on friendship and wish each other good luck. It has gradually become the Yuanxiao Festival. On the ninth to twelfth day of the second lunar month, there is a tradition of "disturbing military slopes" and rushing to temple fairs to worship the southern heroine Xian Taifu Xian Ying during the Northern and Southern Dynasties period. The traditional worship has gradually evolved into the Hainan Xian Taifu Cultural Festival held annually at the main venue of Xinpo Town, Longhua District. In addition, Haikou people have the custom of drinking "father tea" (also known as public tea). This kind of public tea can be seen everywhere in Haikou City, which costs about 20 yuan to brew a pot of tea, add some small Dim sum, and chat about friendship, family habits, and exchange information and business while drinking tea.

3. An Overview of Sanya City

Sanya, also known as deer city, is located at the south of Hainan island, adjacent to Lingshui county in the east and adjacent to Ledong county in the west, Baoting county in the north and the south China sea in the south. In May 1984, with the approval of the state council, Ya county was abolished to establish a county-level Sanya city. In 1987, Sanya was upgraded to a prefecture-level city. In February 2014, the state council approved Sanya city to abolish six old towns and established four new districts. In January 2015, the four new districts in Sanya city were formally established.

Administrative divisions

Sanya City is governed by four administrative regions: Haitang, Jiyang, Tianya, and Yazhou, with a total land area of 1,921.40 square kilometers and a sea area of 3,226 square kilometers. There are a total of 57 neighborhood committees, 92 village committees, and 491 natural villages. The coastline is 264.42 kilometers long, with 19 harbors of various sizes and 66 main islands. The total land area is 192,151 hectares. Among them, 64,074 hectares was mountainous areas, 48,343 hectares was hills, 34,722 hectares was plateau, 44,936 hectares was plain, 75.71 hectares was other place. By the end of 2022, the registered residence population of the city will be 731,090, an increase of 20,191 over the end of the previous year. Among them, there are 366,967 males and 364,123 females. According to ethnicity, there are 457,971 Han people, accounting for 62.6% of the total population; The Li ethnic group has 244,640 people, accounting for 33.5% of the total population; The Hui ethnic group has 11,697 people, accounting for 1.6% of the total population; The Miao ethnic group has 4,370 people, accounting for 0.6% of the total population; The Zhuang ethnic group has 2,804 people, accounting for 0.4% of the total population; The other ethnic groups have 9,608 people, accounting for 1.3% of the total population. At the end of the year, the permanent population of the city was 1.0659 million. Among them, the urban population is 76.52, the rural population is

300,700, and the urbanization rate is 71.8%.

History and humanity

Sanya is called Yizhou in ancient times. It has a long history and a long history. There are many outstanding people born here. In October 1992 and November 1993, in the Luobi cave within the territory of Sanya, archaeologists found the Sanya man site 10,000 years ago, which is the earliest known human settlement site on Hainan island and the site with the southernmost distribution of paleolithic culture in China so far. It has advanced the human history of Hainan by two to three thousand years. As early as 110 BC in the western Han dynasty, Sanya was in the territory of China. Since ancient times, Sanya has been called "Tianya Haijao" because it is far away from the capital of the country and in the sea alone. However, since the Sui and Tang dynasties, it has been connected with the central plains in politics, economy, culture and other aspects. It was the "Tang mu yi" (lodging place) of lady Xintai in the Sui dynasty. It was once the land of Tang dynasty monk Jianzhen's floating landing and preaching. In the Tang and Song dynasties, seven prominent officials were banished to Sanya. To the south of the central plains people dressed in clothes, objectively played the role of educating people to transfer knowledge in the local, leaving a lot of historical cultural sites, laid the splendid historical and cultural foundation of Sanya. According to the history, in the Song, Yuan and Ming dynasties, Sanya had initial economic development and the cotton industry in the leading position in the country. The story of Huang Daopo learning textile technology from Li women in her early years is the witness of history. During the Ming dynasty, the great Confucian scholar Zhongfang, one of the "three stars of Qiongzhou", also emerged. Intangible cultural heritage resources in Sanya are abundant and widely distributed. The dance of the Li people beating the wood and the Ya City's folk songs was recorded in the national intangible cultural heritage protection project in 2006. In 2007 and 2009, 7 items of original pottery of Li nationality were listed on the list of provincial intangible cultural heritage protection projects, and 11 items of drilling for wood and fire were listed on the list of municipal intangible cultural heritage protection projects.

Ecological environment

In 2022, the air quality of Sanya reached the standard (AQI ≤ 100) for 365 days, with a 100% air quality compliance rate. The average concentration of fine particulate matter (PM2.5) is 11 micrograms per cubic meter, and the average concentration of inhalable particulate matter (PM10) is 21 micrograms per cubic meter. There are 7 nature reserves in the city, including 1 national level and 1 provincial-level. The total area of the nature reserve is 12,354.74 hectares, including 8,500 hectares of national level reserves and 1,844.60 hectares of provincial level reserves. The afforestation area is 133.72 hectares. Among them, artificial afforestation covers 36.98 hectares; Renew afforestation of 96.74 hectares. The forest area is 134,700 hectares, with a forest coverage rate of 70.1%, an increase of 1.2 percentage points from the previous year. It has won many honors such as "national ecological demonstration zone", "national garden city", "national health city", "China human settlement environment award" and "beautiful landscape city".

Natural scenery

The geographical environment of Sanya is very unique. It is the only city in China that can have both tropical rainforest and ocean scenery. Sanya is surrounded on three sides by mountains. Mountains, seas, and rivers merge naturally, and many hilltops offer commanding views of the sea, river bays, and urban landscapes. The clear water, high visibility, and moderate water temperature make it suitable for swimming throughout the year. Sanya urban area has two rivers, Sanya east river and Sanya west river. The natural mangrove forests on both sides are very lush and evergreen, which is the habitat of the famous egrets. Beautiful natural scenery and excellent ecological environment makes Sanya a beautiful paradise for living, traveling and vacationing.

Revolutionary tradition

During the agrarian revolutionary war from 1927 to 1937, Zhongtian ridge was the first revolutionary base in Ya county, which laid a solid foundation for the establishment of the red revolutionary armed forces and the strengthening of the Soviet regime. During the anti-Japanese war, under the extremely cruel fighting environment, according to the instructions of the Qiongya party committee, the party committee of the cliff county moved to Meishan, established the anti-Japanese guerrilla base area, launched and organized the people to fight with the enemy, and became a strong anti-Japanese fort. Zhongtianling monument to revolutionary martyrs and Meishan revolutionary history hall is valuable spiritual wealth of Sanya.

Part II

A-rated Tourist Attractions

5A-rated Tourist Attractions

1. Daxiao Dongtian Tourism Zone

Hello everyone, I am Yang Jie, your tour guide for this trip. You can call me Xiao Yang. The driver who drove for us is surnamed Li. It's my pleasure to serve you and I hope our service can bring warmth and happiness to you all! Welcome everyone to our country's first batch of 5A level scenic spots — Dongtian Park! Relying on the rich cultural landscape and beautiful natural scenery, Dongtian Park has become the first listed comprehensive tourism wedding photography and shooting base in Sanya, as well as the first batch of comprehensive tourism research, learning, and practical education bases in Sanya. Before starting, please allow me to remind you of six small tips: First, there are many roads in the scenic spot and there are a lot of tourists, please keep close to me in case you get lost. Second, because the sea rocks smooth, we are not allowed to climb the reef in the tour process in case of falls and scratches. Third, the scenic area for the ecological smoke-free scenic area, in order to prevent forest fires, please do not smoke. Fourth, Sanya city is vigorously carrying out the work of civilized tourism cities in the country now. So, we should observe the public order during the tour, pay attention to public health. Fifth, pay attention to the traffic, do not cross the road, walk please walk on the sidewalk. Sixth, it is forbidden to swim in the sea, pick coral and protect our Marine environment.

Our current location is in the Coconut Forest Bar. The Coconut Forest Bar is the place with the most coconut trees in this scenic area. The coconut breeze and the sound of waves best reflect the characteristics of Hainan Island. This is the largest leisure venue in the entire scenic area, with not only pavilions and rocking chairs, but also coconut (coconut juice and coconut meat contain a large amount of protein, fructose, glucose, sucrose, fat, vitamin E, potassium, calcium, magnesium, etc., which are delicious fruits suitable for all ages) and various local snacks in Hainan. Welcome to taste them.

Dongtian Park adheres to the development concept of Taoism, which follows the principle of nature and the unity of man and nature. During the development process of the scenic spots, there has been no excessive human intervention in the natural environment. Every plant, tree, flower and stone here have its value. For example, the pumpkins you see now also have a name called wild pineapple. Although its fruit looks like pineapple, it can't be eaten. Many people think that it is a worthless tree. Careful observation shows that its developed roots can prevent wind, dike and soil erosion. This is "Every man has his price".

Dear friends, do you know? Our Hainan province has the laudatory name of "The two most provinces". One is the largest ocean area (over 2 million square kilometers) and another is the smallest land area (35,000 square kilometers).

Everyone loves the blue sea, but how much do you know about the sea? Now Let's take a look at the sea. First, Let's talk about the sea water. Do you know why the sea water is blue? In fact, the sea water is colorless and transparent. Sunlight is a kind of compound light, which is composed of red, orange, yellow, green, blue, indigo and purple. When the sun shines on the sea, the longer light waves of red light and orange light can bypass all obstacles. They are constantly absorbed by the sea water and creatures in the sea as they move forward. While some of the shorter wavelengths of light such as blue light and violet light are absorbed by seawater and algae, most of them scatter to the surroundings or are simply reflected back as soon as they encounter the obstruction of seawater. What we see is this part of the scattered or reflected light. The deeper the sea water is, the more blue light is scattered and reflected, and the bluer the sea water we see.

The sea is the cradle of life, which provides the conditions for the birth and reproduction of life and has a great impact on the development and progress of human civilization. With the deterioration of the global ecological environment, the Marine environment is also facing severe challenges. With the support of the government of Sanya city and many other units and enterprises, the scenic spot initiated the establishment of the "blue ribbon" Marine protection association. Through various public welfare activities, the concept of Marine protection is transmitted, and the knowledge of Marine protection is publicized, so that the Marine protection plan starts from you and me. Here, I propose to you: do not throw rubbish into the sea, do not pick coral, let us act together to protect the ocean, love the ocean and care for our common home!

There is a tower on the right sea called the base point lighthouse of the territorial sea. From this base point tower, China's territorial sea extends 12 nautical miles outward and 200 nautical miles outward as the exclusive economic zone (1 nautical mile =1.852 kilometers). The base tower of the territorial sea not only has the function of navigation, but also is the symbol of China's declaration of sovereignty. It has long-term strategic and practical significance for safeguarding China's marine rights and interests, protecting the marine environment, and strengthening marine management.

The coast of Hainan Island can be divided into four types: sandy coast, bedrock coast, plant (mangrove) coast and coral reef coast. You can see that there are many coastal rocks in the scenic spot, which is a typical bedrock coast. It is mainly a rare stone landscape formed by granite weathering and is a famous scenic spot in Hainan. There is a reef on the shore shaped like a dragon head and called "dragon head stone". Especially when the tide is rising, the waves are rippling like the body of a dragon, with the dragon head looming in the blue sea.

Please look at here, This is the "Jian Zhen landing group sculpture". We know that master Jian Zhen five east crossing Japan failed and his fifth east crossing is here. In the seventh year of Tianbao (AD 748) of emperor Tang Xuanzong, master Jian Zhen took his disciples, Japanese monk Rong Rui, Pu Zhao and other 17 people, plus 18 sailors, set out from Shaoxing, Zhejiang province, on their fifth east crossing to Japan. Jian Zhen line drifting in the sea for 14 days and nights because of a typhoon destroyed the sailboat and blew them from the East China Sea to the South China Sea. Last escaped from the cliff state bay landing. The tang dynasty Yashu area is called Linzhen. A Zhishi from Linzhen learned that the famous Jian Zhen governor to this place at that time. Immediately Feng was ordered to take 400 people out of the city to meet them. After master Jian Zhen landed, he actively spread the culture of the central plains and repair the Dayun temple. He made a great contribution to the development of Hainan local culture. Next to the Dongtian Park, there is a port called Dadan Port, where there is a place called "sun slope", which was the place where Master Jianzhen landed to dry scriptures in the past. Master Jianzhen rested here for a year and a half, then went north to return to Yangzhou, Tianbao 12 years (753), the sixth east crossing to Japan was successful.

"Jianzhen landing group sculpture" was completed by renowned sculptor Lin Yuhao, who is from Yaxian County, Hainan. His famous works include "Nanjing Yuhuatai Revolutionary Martyrs Memorial" and "Luhuitou Park". After the completion of the "Jianzhen landing group sculpture" in the Dongtian Park in 1994, local residents and even international friends came to pay their respects and pay their respects. An 80 year old Japanese couple named Takashi and his wife came to pay their respects and brought a bag of soil and stones back to Japan as a souvenir. When the late President of the Chinese Buddhist Association, Zhao Puchu, came specifically to pay his respects, he left three words: "Unexpectedly", "remarkable", and "immeasurable merit".

"Jianzhen landing group sculpture" square is opposite by nine lovely big turtle and a small turtle constitute "when all was said and done". The nine big tortoises symbolize the old things and the little one represents the new and the flourishing. It also indicates that everything is cyclical, old and new, and so is human life. The end of all things is a new starting point, do not cling to the past, to hope for the future.

The next place we are about to arrive is the Nanhai dragon king courtyard, which houses the original image of the Nanhai dragon king — king Guang Li. The dragon king of the South China Sea originated from the dragon worship in ancient

China. In the Chinese classical culture, the dragon not only represents the masculine and enterprising spirit, but also embodies the moral character of nourishing and enriching things. The origin of the dragon in China is from the new time period of 7,000 to 8,000 years ago. It was a sacred object formed by ancient people who were in awe of various animals and the changes of the weather and gathered their vague impressions. According to legend, Fu Xi, one of the three emperors, gathered the most dominant features of several favorite animals at that time, and created the complex of horse head, antler, snake body, fish phosphorus, tiger paw, eagle claw and other animals — the dragon, and took the dragon as the emblem of the Chinese nation. From then on, we were called descendants of the dragon.

Dear Friends, we are at the Nanhai dragon king courtyard square now.

The Nanhai dragon king courtyard is composed of auxiliary hall and main hall, inside into three doors. There is a pair of couplets on both sides of the auxiliary temple gate. The couplet praises the dragon king for his virtues in bringing good weather and prosperity to the nation and security to the people. In the center of the courtyard auxiliary hall there is a Xuan Zhu Tai, Xuan Zhu Tai shape for the double dragon play beads and two white jade dragons holding a black xuanzhu, the xuanzhu symbol of the broad and profound "dao".

As the steps ascended, there was a word "dragon" on the wall, which was the imperial pen of emperor Kangxi. During the reign of emperor Kangxi, the people lived and worked in peace and prosperity. He thought that he was blessed by the dragon king and sent his ministers to pay homage to the dragon king of the South China Sea 11 times. We are located in the South China Sea dragon king courtyard main hall now.

Go forward, we are about to see one of the core scenic spots of this scenic area — Xiaodongtian. A lot of friends ask why there is only a Xiaodongtian, where is Dadongtian? To answer this question, we first need to know what a cave is.

The Taoist term "Dongtian" refers to the mountain resort where monks live in Taoist culture. The cave is not the cave, all called "insight into the world". It consists of ten cave days, thirty-six Xiaodongtian and seventy-two blessed places. The five sacred mountains of China are included in the cave days.

From the perspective of origin, the emergence and formation of Taoist theory of heaven and earth should be closely related to the mountain-dwelling habits of ancient Chinese ancestors in early history and early civilization. Therefore, we only need to consider that "stone chambers" and "caves" served as the basic residence places for monks in the pre-Taoist period and the early period of Taoism and we can understand. From the perspective of cosmology and existentialism, the Taoist theory of heaven and earth reflects the monastics' unique perspective of observing heaven, earth, people and things. The view of heaven, the view of earth, the view of man and the view of things in its are all meaningful and thought-provoking. It is different from our usual view of existence, non-existence, nihility and entity, but explains the existence form of heaven, earth, man and thing against the background of a kind of circumwinded and circumwinded universe constitution. This is consistent with the fundamental Dao theory of Taoism.

In the early years of the Southern Song Dynasty, the governor of Guya Prefecture Mao Kui advocated the art of Huang Lao, he discovered the "Xiaodongtian" when climbing the Nanshan Mountain. He decided that this was a "happy place with a cave sky" and inscribed the word "Xiaodongtian" on the cave mouth. Since then, the "cave sky" has become famous all over the world. This is also the only land directly named after the "cave sky".

According to the records of *Yazhouzhi*, there is also a "Dadongtian" near Xiaodongtian. The original text reads as follows: "There are few stone boats to the south, and there are pavilions. The plaque reads 'Dadongtian Heaven'. Pavilion four pillars, carved on two characters. Chen Jitong, a Hong Kong native. During Yongzheng's reign, he went to Nanshan Ridge to gather firewood, took a rest at the foot of the ox cart, stepped into the Dadongtian, and saw two old men playing chess on a stone."

Therefore, "Dadongtian" refers to the big environment of Nanshan.

"Xiaodongtian" refers to the place where monks practice.

Climbing up the steps along the trail, we enter the Dongtianhai scenic spot, whose coastline is about 3 kilometers long and is covered with stones of various sizes and shapes. This kind of coast belongs to granite mudflat in geology. The rocks here are very strange and uncanny. It is also a unique scenery line in our scenic spot.

When we come here, we can see the mountains and seas of Aoshan Mountain meet each other. The scenery is magnificent, with peaks overlapping green and blue waves flowing in all directions, just like a beautiful and incomparable long scroll painting. According to research, there are 99 stone scenes in the scenic spot. Facing the strange stone scenes, friends can use your imagination and feel them attentively to see what is similar to our daily life.

The landscape blends here is a good place for benevolent and wise people. According to records of *Yazhou County*, when Mao Kui left office, he came to Xiaodongtian and did not know where he was going. However, according to local people's legend, Mao Kui did not go nowhere but became an immortal. On the day Mao Kui became a fairy, when flying away from the top of Xiaodongtian, his aides saw him and rushed up one by one to hold his feet and hoping to take them to the fairyland together. However, there were many people and many hands. They only tore off one of Mao Kui's shoes and turned the beach behind Xiaodongtian into a stone. This stone is still alive today, which is a huge stone like a shoe not far in front of us and is called "fairy foot".

On the way forward, there is a "Lingying Spring". There was originally a pool here. The spring water in the pool is very special. It is salty water at high tide and fresh water at low tide. It is said that when Jian Zhen drifted ashore, he drank the spring water to quench his thirst. The pool has dried up due to its age, but it is still a historic site. Next to "Lingying Spring", there is a big stone that looks like fuels, like praying to heaven. We call it the "blessing stone".

The big rock in front of us is the famous stone scene "Jian Zhen Bathing the Sea". Look! The whole rock looks like a monk from Jian Zhen lying peacefully on the beach, listening to the sound of the waves and meditating. This reminds people of the legendary experience of monk Jian Zhen and his disciples who boarded Hainan Island more than 1,200 years ago.

There are buttonwood trees at home, attracting golden phoenix. There is an Erythrina tree here, attracting peacocks to roost. Going forward from "Jian Zhen Bathing the Sea", there is a group of landscapes formed by a huge rock and a sour bean tree. It looks like peacocks have been facing southeast and staring at the sea. It reminds people of the poignant love story between Jiao Zhongqing and Liu Lanzhi in "Peacock Flying Southeast". However, malachite here is a sign of good luck. Peacock yearns for the beautiful scenery here and turns it into stone.

In front of the boulder was Jiang Zemin's inscription: "The sea is clear and the sky is far away, and the cliffs are full of spring."

Looking ahead, next to Jiang's inscription, there is a huge stone shaped like a peach. It floats in the sea at high tide and connects with land at low tide. This is our "peach stone". There is a huge rock not far away, whose shape resembles a bull's head floating on the water. It looks thoughtful towards the peach.

On the bank not far from Xiantao Stone, the rock groups are contiguous, grotesque, and all-encompassing. There is a huge rock with a round head and a heavy tail, which is inclined. There are only three small supporting points under it. It looks wobbly, but in fact it does not move at all, and it is distinctive. This is also a sea erosion phenomenon, which we call stromatolite. The most distant place is the charming "Xiaoyue Bay", which extends forward in the shape of a crescent moon, just like a crescent moon inlaid between the sea and the sky. Xiaoyue Bay is also the last "virgin bay" in Hainan. The grass, wood, stone and even every grain of sand here have maintained their original appearance. The water here is so clear, the sand is so soft, the trees are so green, the air is so pure, the clouds are so light.

The scenic spot we are visiting now is the statue of the Antarctic fairy weng. The Antarctic fairy weng is also called "longevity" or "senior star".

The oldest old man is a white-haired man, and he has a gentle face and holds longevity peaches in his hand, which is a symbol of good luck and longevity. The prominent forehead of the longevity star is also closely related to the longevity image created by ancient health preserving techniques. For example, the crane's head is high. Therefore, in order to highlight the longevity culture of Nanshan, the scenic spot has carved the largest Antarctic immortal statue so far with natural boulders to embody the longevity culture of the scenic spot. And according to the fifth national census, Nanshan has the highest number of centenarians in the country. Nanshan also has a good reputation as a land of longevity.

Halfway up the mountain in Xiaoyue Bay, there is a Lao Zi Wang Chart carved by a famous Chinese sculptor, Master He Baosen. The statue only shows the face and takes the mountain as its body, which embodies the Taoist elephant's invisible and empty-hearted meaning. Overlooking the sea also shows Lao Zi's perception of the essence of water.

A natural stone with a length of 4.5 meters and a tail width of 1.9 meters can be seen not far up. People call it a "stone boat" because its shape resembles a wooden boat with a sharp head and a wide tail. This "stone boat" is one of the oldest stone scenes in our scenic area. It has been developed for more than 800 years, and can be said to be a historical witness of large and small caves. Legend has it that when Zhijun Zhou Kang visited the mountains and rivers here, he thought it was a fairy boat and a magic object. He sent a special person to take care of it. Later, due to its age, it disappeared into Shan Ye for hundreds of years. Until 1992, when we opened up the scenic spot, we searched carefully according to historical records and finally brought it back to light.

The stone tablet in front is the "longevity" tablet written by Empress Dowager Cixi. It is a key protected cultural relic in Sanya. It is 2.76 meters high, 1.1 meters wide and 0.3 meters thick. The word "shou" is inscribed in the center of the stone tablet. it is 1.45m tall and 0.68m wide. In the middle of the top forehead of the word "shou" was carved a five inch square seal of the empress dowager cixi. The right side of the word "shou" bears the inscription: "on September 28, 29th, Guangxu reign, empress dowager cixi duan you kangyi presented the royal pen of 60 years of life to empress dowager according to Yu Zhuang cheng shou gong Qin". There is a word "ci" on the right, the full text of the inscription in the shadow below the word "shou", and the inscription in the shadow below the word "shou" reads: "minister Wang gen".

The boulder next to it is called "Shishi". The inscription "Nanshan" was inscribed by Zhao Puchu, president of China's famous Buddhist Association. Nanshan is distributed along the mountain because of its many strange stones. It is strewn at random and looks like a collection of cottages from afar. When Chief Zhou Kang was touring Nanshan by boat along the coastal waters, he looked out into the mountains. In a trance, he thought there were people living on the mountains. When he came ashore to visit, he found it was a big stone. The stone was later called the Stone Chamber. The stone wall now bears the inscription "Zhou Kangqiyi of Hailing, burning with Wang Yan, the county's chief of staff, is adjacent to Zhou Pi in martial arts. Chun Xi came to watch the stone boat on the 9th of the third day of the third day of the fifth lunar month. Because of the strange scenery, it is the best of Haibang". This was written by Zhou Kang and inscribed in the 13th year of Chunxi in the Southern Song Dynasty (AD 1186). This is the earliest cliff stone carving in the scenic spot and a historical milestone in the scenic spot.

Going up, then we will enter the south mountain old pine park. Old pine is also known as dragon blood tree because of its stem color gray green, mottled as dragon scales, and also can secrete a bright red juice, so it got a good name. Native of the Canary Islands of west Africa, it lives in tropical forests. There are more than 150 kinds in the world and there are 5 kinds in the tropical forests in south China. Dragon blood tree is an evergreen tree, generally about 10-20 meters high, the trunk is unusually thick, often up to 1 meter in diameter. The tree is much branched, the tree is Y - shaped. The leaves were white, like long sharp swords, thrust tightly into the tops of the branches. White and green flowers blooms, yellow and orange berries bears.

The beautiful scenery of the scenic spot has attracted numerous literati to visit here, we can see many famous cliff carvings in the old pine park. The word “song” you see is the word of the famous calligrapher of the Qing dynasty. Cha Shibiao (1615-1698) was from xiuning, Anhui, who was the scholar in the late Ming dynasty and the famous calligrapher in the early Qing dynasty. His landscape painting which is brushwork sparse and extraordinary. This word “song” showed his abundant cursive writing foundation, brushwork handsome and unrestrained, let a person feel continuous, and deep verve.

The word “live as long as the southern mountain” on the old pine, which is said that the Su Dongpo was exiled to Hainan and authentic paintings left behind when visiting here. When you take a picture here, you can put “live as long as the southern mountain” four words and a thousand years of old pine shot down, just can confirm the old saying “live as long as the southern mountain old pine”, I hope everyone can be like the “not old pine”, youthful and full of vitality.

Ok, friends, after enjoying the beautiful scenery along the way, I think you may have a certain understanding of Taoist culture and folk dragon culture and longevity culture, my explanation has come to a successful end, as the saying goes: “Two mountains cannot meet, two people can always meet!” I look forward to seeing you and serving you again! I wish you all the best in the New Year, safe and happy journey!

2. Nanshan Cultural Tourism Zone

Hello everyone! I am your guide named Xiaoliu, and I will lead and company with you for the following visit. When you visit Nanshan Cultural Tourism Zone, you will naturally think of the auspicious saying “Blessings are like the East China Sea, and longevity is like Nanshan”, which has been passed down for thousands of years and is widely known. Although there are many mountains called Nanshan in China, it belongs to the southernmost part of Sanya Nanshan, which is truly a land of blessings and longevity. If you don’t believe it, let’s come into Nanshan Cultural

Tourism Zone to experience the marvelous and stunning Nanshan.

The Nanshan Cultural Tourism Zone in Sanya is located 20 kilometers southwest of Sanya City. It was completed and opened to the public in April 1998. Currently, it consists of seven major parts: "Three Gardens, One Temple, One Bay, One Valley, and One District". Two parks refer to "Ruyi Auspicious Garden", "Cihang Pudu Garden", and "Nanshan Sea Guanyin Cultural Park". One temple is "Nanshan Temple", one bay is "Nanshan Bay", one valley is "Changshou Valley", and the other district is the main scenic area. The location of the park we are currently in is the first scenic spot of Nanshan Buddhist Culture Park — the Gate Landscape Area.

The granite boulder you see is the Nanshan natural boulder which has been baptized for thousands of years in the South China Sea. And the seven words which means "Nanshan Buddhim Cultural Zone" engraved on it are written by Zhao Puchu, the former director of the Chinese Buddhist Association. Zhao Puchu is an important memeber in the development and construction of Nanshan. The geographical location of Nanshan Sea Guanyin and Nanshan Temple was selected by him. The zone we come to is Buddhist shrines. So what is Buddhism? The central thought of Buddhism is summed up in twelve words (it can be translated as): all evil should not be good enough to achieve its own intention. We can understand as: the thing can not be considered depend on the size. Therefore, as long as it is beneficial to all sentient beings, we must strive to do it while it is harmful to all sentient beings, we must avoid doing it. Because the society is complex, we need to purify our hearts. In conclusion, Buddhism is a kind of good education. All right, please turn your attention to the rear of the boulder. There are nine stone lamps standing behind the boulders which called the long life stone lanterns of Xumi lotus flower. It is a representative work of Mahayana Buddhism and also a great piece of Buddhist art in Nanshan. For the lamp, it is mainly composed of three parts. From the bottom to the top, Mount Xumi below is the central mountain of the Buddhist world. Then there are nine mountains and eight seas on the mountain, mountains outside the mountains, and seas overseas. That is the place where the gods live. The 33 lotus flowers in the middle indicate 33 kinds of avatars to survive all sentient beings by Guanyin Purdue.

Next, it is an open doorway which is the gate of the scenic spot. And it is called "Doctrine of non-duality". The whole architectural styles of doorway imitate the style of the Wei, Jin, Southern and Northern dynasties. In ancient times, it was called "que Lou". Also, "que" reprensents a palace which belongs to a royal building at that time, and it is a place for royal aristocrats to ascend to the high view and broaden their horizons. In a complex of buildings, it is gate etiquette architecture. Obviously, it means welcome you to our Sanya Nanshan Buddhism cultural zone. The four words of "bu er" in the front and "yi shi" on the back are all written by Gu Tinglong, a famous calligrapher, when he was 94. "bu er" represents a very high level of understanding in Buddhism. Here, uh, I will have a simple introduction to everyone. According to Buddhist understanding, the content "bu er" is equal to "yi shi", "bu er" refers to all things are equal and there is no difference among them. For example, on the surface, all sentient beings have the difference like rich and poor while, in the deep, everyone has Buddhist nature which is also called Bodhi and nature in Buddhism. In Confucianism, whatever called conscience means the same meaning. The so-called justice lies in the hearts of the people. Everyone has a spiritual mountain tower and everyone has Buddhist nature. It is Buddhist nature that is equal. Therefore, there is no difference among them and call "bu er". It is worth mentioning that "fa" means methods and "men" represent ways.

After visiting the "Doctrine of non-duality", you will notice a large garden landscape—peacock open screen. Peacock opening screen means welcome visitors from everywhere, no matter where you come from and whatever religious beliefs you have, it is karma to meet here. It shows the warm and hospitable custom of Chinese, Hainan and Nanshan people. And it is also the embodiment of Chinese garden art simultaneously using the conventional way to reach result of moving around and changing the scene. In the right, there is a fan-shaped leaky window and behind it, it is a triangular plum with full flowers. This is the frame view in Chinese garden art, that is, to frame the distant scene with a frame. Though this way, the aesthetic feeling can be better reflected. Also, peacocks represent auspicious. The "peacock" here seems like a screen in the layout of Chinese and it can prevent evil from entering the house and the outflow of blessing.

Maritime Guanyin

In China, Japan and South Korea, Guanyin is a famous Buddhist figure. Also, people worship in the city, the countryside or on board. Guanyin is the most widely known Buddhist characters, worshiping not only in all Buddhist temples, but also in thousands of home. In the field of literature, painting, music, sculpture and other arts, Guanyin is recorded. Guanyin Bodhisattva listens to the voice made by those who suffer in the world. In fact, the Guanyin Bodhisattva has become a Buddha earlier with "zhengfaming rulai" as its Dharma. Due to everyone living in pain, the Guanyin Bodhisattva came to our "posuo" world to help Sakyamuni Buddha carry out enlightenment in order to survive people. The days, every year of February 19th, June 19th, and September 19th, are commonly known as "the Guanyin Festical". And in those days, all temples will hold the Quanyin Dharma meeting that many people will go to the monasteries to worship in order to appreciate the great kindness and compassion of Bodhisattva.

At present, we all arrive at the scenic spot of Guanyin at sea. The scenic spots are composed of Phumen Jingzhuang, Guanyin Fu, shan Guanqiao, Hongyuan Avenue, Bazheng dao Hall, wishing platform, Guanyin Statue, and so on.

The first building we see is the gate of the square—the Pumen jinzhuang which is a construction of the Buddhist Taoist. The Buddhist Taoist buildings include monasteries, grottoes, pagodas, lanterns and scriptures. In Nanshan Park, except grottoes, the wisdom of symbolizing Buddha can subdue all troubles and in Buddhism it can be exorcism and demons. Jingzhuang is built by a number of stone carvings as octagonal.

Then, we can see three bridges side by side which is called "shanguan bridge" building by stone. The middle is "Huiguan Bridge" corresponding to the chiqie Quan Yin, the left is the jingguan Bridge corresponding to the lotus Guanyin, the right is the zhenguan Bridge corresponding to the chizhu Guanyin. The six words are engraved on the bridge that it is called "Daming mantra" as well. Many of the music you heard and many architectural decorations you saw are this sentence spelling "an ba ni ba ni hong" and it is also spelled as "an ma ni bei mei hong". The Guanyin Bodhisattva holds this spell and becomes a Buddha, so it is also called as zhengfaming Dharma.

The central avenue leading to Baifo Square is called Hongyuan Avenue. There are many kapok trees planted on bilateral roads. Because Kapok can be used as pillow bedding, Kapok cassock is also made by it. Also, Li people use kapok cotton to make Li Jin.

Visiting along the main road, you can see Buddha platform and the wishing platform which is the core area in the square. In this area, it is the best place for going sightseeing, Buddha praying, photography and other activities. If you want to worship Guanyin, the best place is Buddha Square with an area of 6,500 square meters and can holding thousands of visitors to worship the Buddha at the same time. Then, what is on the stone steps of Baifo Square is a relief sculpture of Rui Beast. And on the left from top to bottom, they are elephants, cattle and Kirin which is the auspicious representative of Buddhism, Taoism and Confucianism. Among that, elephant is the Rui beast of Buddhism. Because it is said that the mother of Sakyamuni, the Buddha, had dreamed that the six-toothed white elephant had come into her stomach and then gave birth to the Buddha. Cattle are a symbol of Taoism. Because it existed as feet of Laojun. And Laozi rides the cyan cattle to hanguguan leaving behind more than 5,000 words of the "moral Sutra" and then nobody knows his track. Kirin shows the characteristics of Confucianism symbolizing the best wishes that people yearn for peace and contentment. On the right from top to bottom, they are dragons, Phoenix and lions which are the mascots of Chinese traditional folk culture. Lion is the "king of beasts" and is a symbol of power. Then,

Dragon and Phoenix are the unique traditional cultural totem of China carrying hope for auspiciousness. These six beasts show that Buddhism is tolerant of all Dharma and everything.

Next, we can see the panoramic view of the Guanyin statue at sea. The design of the Guanyin statue at sea in Nanshan not only conforms to the Buddhist doctrine, but also embodies the great merciful image of the compassion and compassion of the same body. At the same time, it combines change of information and has the epoch characteristics of the modern aesthetics, architecture, sculpture, Buddhist statues art, science and technology.

The Guanyin statue began to construct in 1999 and was completed in 2005. It spent six years with a total investment of 800 million RMB. The Guanyin statue is 108 meters high, which is the largest open-air sea Guanyin statue in the world, and it is 14.4 meters higher than the American Statue of Liberty. The material of Guanyin statue is used titanium alloy in order to enhance the corrosion and wind resistance and seismic resistance of the statue. Because the statue is built in the island, using "white" is used to make the statue contrast with the blue sea water and enhance the visual effect. Zhao Puchu personally wrote "Nanshan maritime Guanyin" for the statue.

In terms of design, it adopts a three in one design, which is currently the most innovative three faced Guanyin statue in the world. From each side, there is a Guanyin statue, and the full view of the three Guanyin statues can only be seen by surrounding them. The gestures of the three Guanyin statues are different, namely holding a suitcase, holding a lotus, and holding a pearl.

The three Guanyin statues represent different images of Guanyin Bodhisattva, and are a comprehensive embodiment of Guanyin incarnation and Guanyin teachings. They express the image of Guanyin great compassion, which is that "great kindness can bring joy to all sentient beings, and great compassion can alleviate the suffering of all sentient beings".

Why is it necessary to position the height of the Guanyin statue at a height of

108 meters? The rule of 108 is related to "nine", because in ancient China, "nine" was believed to have a very high and auspicious meaning. And the twelve times of "nine" is exactly "108", pushing the artistic conception of "nine" to the extreme; The 108 chimes of the bell correspond to the number of twelve months, twenty-four solar terms, and seventy-two waiting periods (five days being one waiting period), symbolizing one year of reincarnation and eternity; Buddhism believes that people have 108 types of troubles, and tapping 108 times can relieve them.

Nanshan Temple

The genesis of the name of Nanshan Temple is from two aspects. One is named according to the location, another is to commemorate Jianzhen monk revered to the "lvzong", also known as the "Nanshan zong" who is same as the place name coincidentally. In order to spread the Buddhist culture, the monk in the Tang Dynasty led his disciples to Japan five times, but failed. The fifth they drifted to the surrounding area of Nanshan because of the typhoon. And then they constructed Dayun Temple spending Dharma for a year and a half. At that time, his sixth eastward journey to Japan was finally successful. At that time, although his eyes had been blind, he still had sturdy willing. And he was respected by the Japanese as "Master of Crossing the Sea" and "Tang monk". Later, Jianzhen taught in Nailiangdong temple in Japan and became the original ancestor of Japanese law. Therefore, he made great contributions to the cultural exchange between China and Japan.

Nanshan Temple is divided into four parts including Renwang Gate, Doushuai inner courtyard, Jintang and sea viewing platform.

Next, please follow me into the gate of Nanshan Temple — Renwang gate. In ancient time, many temples were built in the mountains and forests. So the first temple of the temple is called the mountain gate, also known as the "Sanmen" because the gate generally has three doors in rows. According to Buddhism, all sentient beings live in pain. So, in order to get rid of the pain, they can only learn Buddhism. Also, the only way to cut off all troubles completely and release themselves is learn Buddhism. Finally they can realize freedom and elevate the highest realm — nirvana. However, in the process of achieving the highest goal, people must go through three doors of liberation. And the three doors symbolize these three relief doors. The middle door is called "Kongmen", commonly known as empty door. Then, the left door called "Wuxiangmen" while the right door is called "Wuzuomen". But it is worth mentioning that some temples have only a door hole, not three. At this time, this door still represents three relief doors, so it is still called "Sanmen".

After entering the Sanmen Temple, we can see that the two bilateral Dharma gods on the left and right. They are the Miji King Kong and Naluo Yan King Kong who were sealed as Ren king by the Buddha for protecting the Dharma in order to protect the country and the people. Therefore, the gate of Nanshan Temple is called "Renwang Gate".

On both sides of the Sanmen Temple there are many statues who are the Buddhist gods protecting the Dharma. Buddhism calls that "Tianlong Babu" also known as the "Longshen Babu" or "Babuzhong" which refers to the eight ghosts and gods headed by the Tianlong.

Out of the Shanmen Temple, we continue to go ahead. And this is the second temple of Nanshan Temple — Doushuai inner courtyard. Doushuai is a boundary name and a heavenly name. Also, it means the Doushuai day (equal to a local name), is the fourth of the six days of the Buddhist desire realm which is divided into the inner courtyard and the outer courtyard. The outer court is the happy place of the gods while the inner courtyard is the pure land of Maitreya Bodhisattva. The first we can see the statue of the Buddha in the middle is the "Tianguan" Maitreya following with "Damiao xiang" Bodhisattva and "Fayuan Lin" Bodhisattva on the left and right, and are surrounded by the Dragon Squad.

The following you will see is the image of the Dragon Squad. Dragon Squad is the gods who protect the world in Indian Buddhism. They live on the hillside of Mount Xumi holding one side each one. The east is "Chiguo Tianwang", the south is “Zengzhang Tianwang”, the west is “Guangmu Tianwang” and the north is “Duowen Tianwang”. The images of them are different according to the times and hold different instruments. Most of the images of the Dragon Squad in modern times are the images of the Ming and Qing dynasties. So, the statues are tall and powerful, and most of them are sitting posture. Out of the Doushuai inner courtyard, suspended between the two buildings is the clock tower and Zhuanlun zang.

Standing in front of us in the main hall of Nanshan Temple is “Jin Tang”. The three images enshrined in the Jin Tang you see now, represent the “Hengsan Shi buddha” in space. And in the middle is the whirling world, that is, Sakyamuni, the founder of Buddhism in our real world. Sakyamuni is transliterated in Sanskrit which translates to “nengren” “nengru” “nengji” and so on, that is, to have mercy on all living beings with benevolence and also known as “Sakyamuni saints”. This is the honorable name of Buddhist disciples for Buddha. There are three Buddhist statues in Sakyamuni’s backlight symbolizing Sakyamuni Buddha. Sakyamuni Buddha is in the middle. On his left is Wenshu Bodhisattva, and on his right is Puxian Bodhisattva. And on both sides of Sakyamuni stood two great disciples. The older disciple, Kasyapa malanga, called the Toutuo Diyi, and the handsome young one was the second disciple, Anan, called Wenduo Diyi.

This statue on the left is the master pharmacist Buddha of the Bhasajya guru. There are three Buddha statues on his back of the backlight which symbolizes that the masters of Baisajyagurvai duryaprabhasa are pharmacist Buddhas. On his left is surya-prabha, and on his right is Candra-prabha. In the past, the pharmacist Buddha made twelve great wishes in the Bodhisattva way. He promises to satisfy all the wishes and to release all the pain of sentient beings. You might look at his handprint. The left hand is for fearless printing to encourage all sentient beings not to be afraid, and help them relieve pain. The right hand holds the medicine bowl, in order to relieve the suffering of all sentient beings. The whole statue of the Buddha shows does not be afraid of death. And Buddha’s wisdom can help all beings overcome the fear of life and death of worry and pain.

The statue on the right is the leader of the Western Pure Land sect, Amitabha Buddha. On the backlight of Amitabha Buddha, there are three Buddha statues, symbolizing that the Western Three Saints are Amitabha Buddha, with Avalokitesvara Bodhisattva on the left side and Mahayana Bodhisattva on the right side.

On both sides of the JinTang are Ocean's sixteen, and it is the earliest Luo Han group spread in China.

Now, everyone is free to watch or worship Buddha. Then we go to the sea viewing platform to enjoy the different characteristics of Nanshan Temple as the southernmost temple in China from other temples.

Next, please follow me to the sea viewing platform. We will enjoy the Nanshan Temple closing to the mountains and facing to seas and listen to the billowy waves.

Turning around then overlook the South China Sea and Guanyin Statue at sea. You can have imagery that the wide sea is higher than the wide sky with the same color. It is not only visual enjoyment but also a spiritual shock. Everyone will feel relaxed and happy.

Ladies and gentlemen, that's the end of Xiao Liu's guidance today, and then it is time for everyone's free activities. Please take good care of your personal belongings and pay attention to safety during the free activity, welcome to visit again, goodbye!

3. Yanoda Rainforest Cultural Tourism Zone

Dear distinguished guests, today we are going to visit the Yanoda Rainforest Cultural Tourism Area. Do you know Yanoda? Yanoda is the original dialect of Hainan on behalf of the number one, two, three. It says the "Yanoda" belongs to Hainan and aims to promote the local culture rooted in the thick soil of Hainan island, as well as the long-standing and profound traditional Chinese culture that gave birth to the local culture. Here, we give it a new and unique meaning: "Ya" means innovation, "No" means commitment and "Da" means practice. We will base on practice, fulfill our commitment, create an unprecedented green theme cultural tourism park through continuous innovation, and promote Hainan tourism to a new realm, "Yanoda" has another meaning, to welcome and bless, wish everyone a lifetime of peace, the best of both worlds, and three ways of harmony! Next, we affectionately greet each guest who comes here with a "Ya – No — Da"! Now, let us begin the magical, mysterious, and sacred Yanoda rainforest journey!

Dear guests, while you enjoy the surrounding scenery, let me introduce the tropical rain forest to you.

What is a rainforest? Around the equator of the earth, there is a special biological belt. Although it covers only about 8 percent of the earth's land area, it is home to more than half of the planet's biological diversity; The climate here is humid, high temperature throughout the year, there is no obvious seasonal change, and the temperate and cold zones are very different; It also pumps oxygen into the atmosphere. It's called "the lungs of the earth", this is the rainforest. The rainforest is mainly distributed in the amazon basin of South America, Southeast Asia and Congo basin of Africa. Among them, South America has the largest area of rainforest, Africa has the smallest rainforest, and most of the Asian rainforest is on some large islands. However, no matter where the rainforest is, the plant and animal species are somewhat different, but their internal structure is very similar. We know that trilobites and early gaint reptiles are very old, but the forests in the rainforests are much older.

China's tropical rainforests are mainly distributed in Taiwan, Yunnan, and Hainan. Hainan has China's lowest latitude and the largest area of the tropical rainforest. The plant species are abundant, and there has over 4,200 kinds of woody plants, among those there are more than 630 kinds of woody plants that are unique to Hainan. There are over 2,500 kinds of medical plants all over the island, it's also one of the important producing areas of Chinese southern medicine and known as the "natural pharmacy". That's the reason why we say that Yanuona rainforest is the real tropical rainforest which is as the garden of Sanya and located at 18 degrees north latitude. It is also the concentration of the five high-quality rainforest of Hainan and the most valuable natural exhibition of tropical rainforest. It can be considered as the diamond level rainforest in China.

Now, let's listen to this song (lyric: There is a beautiful place that people yearn for... It is evergreen all year round, where birds sing and flowers fragrance... Its name is Shambhala, and it is said to be the place where immortals reside...), this song is called "shambhala is not far away", when you hear this beautiful song, did you have any thoughts about "shambhala"? "Shambhala", also called "shangri-la", where there are valleys, forests, meadows, lakes, Snow Mountains and pure air. It is a place that people pursue and aspire to. Yanoda is known as the tropical shambhala of Hainan island. Is yanoda really as beautiful as shambhala? After you have enjoyed your stay here, you will certainly have your own feelings.

Speaking of which, I'm sure you can't wait to learn more about the mysterious and sacred rain forest of Yanoda. Don't be impatient, in order to ensure your safety during your tour, here are a few warm tips:

(1) Cherish rainforest vegetation, love grass, do not climb trees to pick flowers;

(2) Cherish the fresh air in the rain forest, do not smoke, do not use open flame;

(3) Cherish the rainforest environment, take away the garbage;

(4) Cherish the rainforest personality, mean what you say and do, and be a high-quality civilized tourist. Well, I'm sure you can do all of the above. Thank you very much for your support and cooperation!

Distinguished guests, please go directly to the service area after getting off the bus, do not stay in the parking lot, and thank you for your cooperation.

The Logo of the scenic spot

Dear guests, now please look at the stone on the right side, the carved pattern on the stone is the Logo of Yanoda. The English word "Yanoda" is depicted by vines, wood, birds, snakes and other rainforest biological forms as the main body of the composition, which reflects its unique rainforest culture. The Chinese word "Yanuoda" imitates the technological characteristics of Lijin in Hainan, and reflects the scene of celebrating life of Li people with song and dance. The colors of the logo include leaf green, sky blue, bright yellow and vermilion, which respectively symbolize ecology, island, culture and happiness. The logo design and color represent for harmony, bright and cheerful. It combines the ecology of the rain forest with folk customs and tourism properties. The logo is very special, and in line with the unique charm and cultural connotation of Yanoda rainforest, highlighting the innovation, commitment and practice of Yanoda striding towards the world. This is the introduction of the logo of the scenic spot, let us continue.

Millennial root hanging stone

Dear distinguished guests, now we have arrived at the Auspicious Terrace. Looking around, there is a picturesque scenery with clear mountains and clear waters. Climbing up the auspicious ladder, the most eye-catching one is this big banyan tree, which looks like a giant umbrella. Let's take a look at it. It is about 40 meters tall, over a thousand years old, and its huge root system has lifted the giant rock mass in the middle. Under the tree grew numerous sunflowers and sea taros, all held in the arms of the strong branches of the big banyan tree, thus supporting a piece of their own sky. After thousands of years of wind, rain, and wind, the entire tree and boulder almost merged into one. The intricate roots of the tree and the lush branches and leaves of the trunk are all miracles of natural life.

Locals call this tree as the "Dongzhu magic tree", Dongzhu is the mountain god of the Li people, in their eyes, each piece of the land is controlled by the mountain god. All of the mountains, rivers, lakes, trees, animals and birds are charged by the mountain god and nature is ruled by the god. Wanton intrusion into the land of the mountain god to cut down and hunt will be punished by the mountain god. The reason why the ecology of Yanoda remains so intact is inseparable from the worship of the mountain gods by the Li people.

Li people believe that the mountain god is the oldest and most magical tree in the mountain. When they wish, they write their wishes on a red cloth or carve them on a wooden board, and then throw them on a sacred tree to pray for their fulfillment, which is said to be very effective. Below the sacred tree is also the place where young men and women pledge their love, every year on the third of march, the girls and boys of the Li family will be in pairs under the sacred tree to pray for blessings, oath, and will be engraved on the names of the two small wooden plate thrown on the tree to hang up, that's also a symbol of two people's vows of eternal love, loyalty to love. Ok, let us continue.

The rainforest shooting gallery

Dear guests, along the way, the beautiful scenery and the ancient sacred trees are fascinating. In this green zone where is filled with mysterious, do you remember once in the jungle field warfare behind enemy guerrilla warfare, they shuttled in this dense and quiet mountains secretly and quickly, played their own armed forces. Now, we have arrived at the shooting range rainforest, across the Great Wall, through the long march of 25 thousand Li publicity board, rows of high imitation guns, shotguns, high-speed machine guns, sniper rifles, and, of course, the jungle hunting cannot little bow greeted, we seem to be returning to the battlefield, now you can visit the battlefield, feel the pleasure of high imitation guns firing, relive the bullet pop-up thrill of the moment.

Rubber trees

Dear guests, here is a strange forest, we call it "a thousand cuts by a thousand cuts", it is the rubber tree, as you can see it belongs to the big tree plant, the native place is in Brazil, introduced in China in the early 20th century.

It usually takes about six years from planting to harvesting. After 5~8 years of careful management and protection, the uncut garden begins the cutting period. Do you know when the workers cut the rubber trees? Glue workers generally began to cut at 4 o'clock in the morning, the lower the temperature, the more conducive to the flow of glue, glue output will be more, the sun came out, they called it a day, it is conceivable that the cutting work is very hard.

Natural rubber is one of the world's bulk industrial raw materials, is also a strategic material, the position is very important, because of its strong elasticity and good insulation, plasticity, water and air insulation, tensile and wear resistance and other characteristics, is widely used. China is the world's second largest rubber consumer, its natural rubber and synthetic rubber cannot meet the consumer demand, so China's public rubber is mostly imported from abroad. Ok, please go ahead.

Orchid creek

Dear guests, you have come to orchid creek, a paradise in the rainforest. There are a variety of wild orchids, you do not prevent a careful look for orchids small and exquisite, diverse forms, some sequence, like a string of crystal green pearls; some stretch like the golden wings of a swallow. One of the most attractive flowers is white jade, and two identical flowers on the handle, like a pair of born beautiful twin sisters. Did you see that? There are about 20,000 species of orchids in the world, which can be classified as terrestrial, epiphytic or saprophytic according to their habitats. And here common orchids are Dendrobium, blood leaves and tall orchid and the other nearly 30 types of flowers.

Here, you can also see some miniature tropical sceneries, some strange flowers and herbs that you even do not know the name, very characteristic thatched hut, long vine under the tree table tree chair. You must be extremely surprised to see such a unique scene in this secluded rainforest. The flowers, the water, the Bridges and the trees here all have some familiar feeling, but some are not quite the same. The classic Chinese traditional gardening techniques and the rainforest culture are so skillfully combined, which adds to the unique charm of the rainforest. Ok, so that's orchid creek. Please continue your tour.

Gymnospermae

Distinguished guests, in front of us by the roadside there is a tree about a meter high, leaves like a peacock's tail, it is called gymnospermae, it is not a tree, but a fern. About 180 million years ago, tree-ferns were the most abundant plants on the planet, as much a sign of the reptilian era as dinosaurs. However, after a long period of change, the majority of the earth's tree-ferns died, now only a few places in the world can see it, mainly growing in the wet slopes of mountain gullies and streams in the sunny place, known as the "living fossil", is listed as the first protected plants in China. Dear guest, it is not easy for us to see the gymnospermae in Yanoda today. So, we should pay attention to the life of every tree, every grass, they create a harmonious living space for us, we only have one home, lost will not be, the protection of the environment is our responsibility! Ok, please continue your tour.

Python gallery

Dear distinguished guests, in order to protect wild animals and reflect the harmonious coexistence between human with nature and animals, we specially built a home for the "rainforest elves" in the scenic area. Now please look to your right hand, in front of this oval like a giant egg is the home of the "rainforest elves". Among the "rainforest elves", the most feared is the python. Speaking of the python, a lot of friends will feel fear. In fact, they are not as ruthless as we imagine, here by me in detail for you to introduce it. Python is the most primitive and largest snake species. It often lives in the virgin forest with abundant water and dense vegetation, and some of them live in the desert area. In China, it is only found in the south, especially in parts of Hainan, where it lives in tropical rain forests and subtropical moist forests.

Observation platform

Dear guests, this is the best viewing platform in the whole rainforest valley. Standing here, you can look up and see the whole landscape of the rainforest valley, with mountains and trees in the distance, surrounded by mountains and water, the areca trees are straight, pavilions, Bridges, water dotted among them. When it rains, standing under the hut and looking out, the whole rainforest valley is bathed in the rain and fog, forming a unique picture of the tropical rainforest in the clouds. Looking at the geographical form here, the whole rainforest valley sits in the northeast to the southwest, the front view is open, there are green mountains in the distance, there is a water area, green mountains and green water, mountains and water around, the air is fresh, pleasant climate. It is the so-called "dragon mortar" in

Feng Shui. Therefore, it is very suitable for living here. Renowned Hong Kong Feng Shui master Juming Li called the Yanoda rainforest a "natural oxygen-rich treasure chest". Ok, please continue your tour.

Tong ting

Dear distinguished guests, do you know the poem "Missing" written by the Tang dynasty poet Wei Wang? "Red beans living in the south, how many branches can grow in spring? Wish you gather as much as you can, for this is what I miss most." Around the pavilion are some Hainan red beans. Have you seen them? Red beans, also known as the missing beans, have always been regarded as a symbol and token of love. People string red beans into necklaces, bracelets and other jewelry and give them to friends and relatives to express love and friendship. It is said that in ancient times, a man went to a war, and his wife stood on a high mountain every day to pray for him. One day, she missed her husband so much that she could not help crying, but what came out of her eyes were not tears, but drops of bright red blood. The drops of blood turned into red beans, took root, and grew into trees. When autumn came and her husband came back to her, the tree was covered with beautiful red beans. Hainan red beans are as red as gems, and some of them have a black spot, just like a lover's acacia tears. Some of them are in heart shapes, which resemble the lovers' hot hearts! Exquisite red beans as if to tell us, missing is both bitter and sweet, and cherish the feelings between people, is the most beautiful! Ok, please continue your tour.

The wishing bell

Dear distinguished guests, what come into our sight now are the wishing bells. The ancient Chinese people hang the bell, the practicability is higher than the decoration, is the sound of wind blowing jade vibration, to achieve the purpose of warning, meditation, blessing. Hanging a string of wind bells in the home now, is to use wind bell "good rhyme", change environmental space magnetic field, attract "good luck", because this wind bell symbolizes auspicious, also be the common adornment in the family. The wind blows cool and refreshing, listen to its sound can make the heart peaceful and quiet, refreshing. Tourists can hang wishing bells on the happiness rode in Yanoda and personally write a prayer essay on it — you can pray for a safe and healthy of family, pray for a thriving and booming business, and pray for children's academic success, smooth work, good luck as well.

The happiness rode

Dear distinguished guests, we are about to arrive at the happy heaven road, which is composed of the longest suspension bridge in the scenic area. In this long way of happiness, there are four doors, the first is called the door of friendship, the people who comes with friends must walk side by side through the door of friendship, friendship will last forever; The second is called the door of love, the lovers who walk through the door, must remember to hold your hands, so that people in love can hand in hand to face the life together; The third door is called the family door, through the door of friendship, through the door of love, all the feelings here into the thick family; In the end, we will arrive at the last door of happiness, here, all our friends will receive from Li family's blessing. Li people welcome guests in a very special way. You can guess what it is. And at the moment you receive the blessing, there will be our photographer for you to leave the most beautiful and most moving moment, so everyone in the door of happiness must pose the most beautiful and the happiest smile. Ok, let's continue our tour.

Scindapsus aureus

Dear guests, are you familiar with this plant? Do you have one or more pots at home or on your desk? Yes, this is the green plant. Here is the wild scindapsus aureus viewing area of the scenic area.

Dear guests, do you know the nickname of the plant? Will you be surprised at even does the scindapsus aureus have the nickname? The answer is yes, scindapsus aureus also called Gold Ge, it is the evergreen lianas of araceae, like hot and humid, breed easily. Its strong entanglements, developed roots, can climb on the branches of other trees, we see a lot of "hanging gardens", and these gardens have the shadow of the green.

Scindapsus aureus can purify air, you can put them in the kitchen of the home, toilet door corner side puts a basin scindapsus aureus, they can effectively absorb the chemical substance inside the air, also can absorb the odour that the bride chamber remains after decorating, at the same time it can send out moisture to the air, compensatory humidity. Well, that's all for the scindapsus aureus. Please take your time.

Wild peony

Dear friends, there are many beautiful flowers around you. There are a few wild peonies among them that you can admire. Wild peonies and peonies are different. Wild peonies belong to shrubs and are known as wild peonies due to their large flowers. If peonies are the king of flowers, then wild peonies should be the king of wild flowers. There are two types of wild peonies here, one is called hairy peony and the other is called light peony. Wild peonies are common wild ornamental plants in southern China. Meanwhile, it is also a commonly used herb in China, which can treat indigestion, diarrhea, and dysentery. Leaves can also be used to stop bleeding after trauma. Ok, please take your time.

Lingzhi Nature Reserve

Dear friends, we all know that there is ginseng in the north and lingzhi in the south. The location you are currently in is the Wild Lingzhi Nature Reserve. Ganoderma lucidum, known as the "immortal herb", traditional Chinese medicine has long regarded it as a precious Chinese herbal medicine that nourishes and strengthens the body, strengthens the body, and strengthens the body. It has a huge effect on improving the body's resistance. It is different from general drugs that have a therapeutic effect on a certain disease, nor is it different from general nutritional and health foods that only supplement and strengthen deficiencies in a certain aspect of nutrients. Instead, it regulates the overall balance of human functions in both directions, mobilizes internal vitality, regulates metabolic function, improves autoimmune ability, and promotes the normalization of all visceral or organ functions. In other words, although Ganoderma lucidum cannot be used to treat diseases, it can regulate overall balance and make people less susceptible to illness. At present, real wild Ganoderma lucidum is becoming increasingly scarce, and many bacterial species are facing the crisis of extinction. Although there are many artificially cultivated Ganoderma lucidum in China, their medicinal effects are far from comparable to those of wild Ganoderma lucidum. Because nature has its own laws, Ganoderma lucidum, as a natural product, cannot be replicated by humans in its natural environment. Ok, please continue your journey.

Jade pavilion

Dear guests, there is a pavilion in front of you. It is called jasper pavilion. If you are tired, you can go there for a rest. Now let's take a look at the bamboo forest around us. In our impression, bamboo should be green, but you can see the bamboo is golden yellow, with green stripes in the middle, this kind of rare bamboo is called gold jade bamboo, symbolizing gold and jade full hall, happiness, longevity and well-being, here wish you a promotion and a fortune.

Blooming and fruiting of old stems

Dear guests, the plants we usually see are flowers on the branches, so as the fruit. When you enter the rainforest, do you find the clusters of flowers, clusters of fruit on thick tree trunks, and some are even at the base of the trunk? This unusual phenomenon is "old stem flowers and old stem fruit". Then why do flowers bloom on the trunk? The phenomenon has to do with the environment of the rainforest. Because the tropical forest tree, according to the canopy occupied by the vertical space, generally can be divided into upper, middle and lower three levels. The problem comes when there are too many layers. These trees need insect pollination to form seeds. Flowers in the more open tree trunk or base are easy to be insects to find and visit, pollination opportunities are more. Therefore, nature is always ruthlessly weeding out those species that cannot be adapted to the environment, the survival of the fittest is the constant law. Well, please take your time to enjoy these wonderful views.

Guanglang Forest

Dear guests, we have now entered the scenic area of the Guanglang Forest. Guanglang is a unique palm tree species in Hainan, with a tall tree shape and graceful leaves, making it a highly ornamental plant. The mature tree is about 20 meters tall, with a stem diameter of over 50 centimeters and nearly a hundred feather like branches and leaves. Gum nuts usually grow scattered in the jungle, but in our Gum nut forest area, there are tens of thousands of trees. Despite the small area, Gum nuts are so dense, which is rare at home and abroad.

Dear friends, look at the bundles of emerald green flower stalks on the tree. There are countless clusters of flowers on each stem, and each cluster has dozens of flowers tightly squeezed together. If we poke the inflorescence, juice will flow out. After collecting and evaporating this juice, it becomes sugar, so people also call it sugar coconut. A palm tree can produce about 20 kilograms of sugar per year. And these clusters, like large grapes, are the sweet nut fruits. Each young sweet nut plant has thousands of fruit particles, with a maximum bundle weighing half a ton. Some friends may ask, is such a beautiful fruit edible? Tell everyone that fresh fruits are poisonous and cannot be eaten. Eating them can cause dizziness, vomiting, and a feeling of drunkenness. But after boiling, soaking and other processing, it can be consumed after removing the poison completely. Ok, that's all for the introduction of Guanglang. Please continue your tour.

Xiangsi Cable Bridge

Dear guests, we have arrived at the lover's valley of Yanoda. The bridge in front of us is called "Xiangsi Cable Bridge", which is composed of three parts: "bridge of predestined love", "bridge of pledge love" and "bridge of love lock". Next, the lovers and couples can walk hand in hand together. When walking across the bridge of love, we can recall the fate of our first acquaintance. When you walk across the bridge, you can think about the scene when he proposed to you; when crossing the love lock bridge, be sure to hold each other's hand tightly and lock each other's heart. After walking through the acacia cable bridge, I wish you and your family happy, festive, and harmonious. And finally, I wish the lovers have a happy ending.

Ok, this is the Xiangsi Cable Bridge, please continue your tour.

Root Stone Rainforest

Dear guests, now we come to the root stone rainforest area, here is a riverbed site, in the mountain formation period, due to the crust compression, the seabed uplift to form a mountain, some original rivers were also gradually raised, formed into such riverbed site. Here the forest has the characteristics of the original forest and there are stone caves, such as the landscape. Since the geology here is composed of granite boulders, mountain springs flow into the depths below the rocks, and the Ming River turns into a dark river. The roar of the dark river could be heard here, but it was difficult to find water. The main tree species here are Chinese parasol tree, green hard miscellaneous tree and tall banyan tree, shrub is African jasmine, rattan bamboo, crossing the river dragon, red yellow vine, thorn vine and so on.

Dear guests, all the way we walked in the rainforest, looking up, can you often see that, in the ten meters high in the air, there will be the lush "hanging gardens"? The hanging gardens, also known as canopy gardens, are actually the bizarre parasitic and epiphytic phenomena of the rainforest. Tropical rainforest has a rich variety of trees, in the high temperature and humid environment, these trees are generally up to 30 or 40 meters, the highest is 70 or 80 meters, such a large vertical space, for different epiphytes, climbing plants to provide a variety of places to stay, colorful "hanging garden" is thus generated.

So, you might be wondering: hanging so high in the air, how do these plants survive? By absorbing the nutrients of its epiphytic tree? The answer is no. Epiphytes have aerial rooting. What is aerial rooting? The roots of plants generally grow underground, absorbing nutrients from the soil. But some roots can live in the air. This root has the function of breathing, like a string, some cling to the trunk or branches, some hang in the air, which can absorb water in the air, this is the air root. In addition to aerial rooting, epiphytic plants can store more water. Some have thick leaves, while others are covered in a layer of wax that helps reduce evaporation. At the same time, there are some trees, such as double ninth wood, banyan tree, the barks are rough, and they contain lots of tannic acid, suitable for epiphytic plant growth. Therefore, they are always full of friends, blooming. Well, that's all for the hanging garden. Please continue your tour.

Millennium ganoderma hole

Dear guests, the road ahead is an ancient cave, called the millennium ganoderma hole. There is a thousand year old wooden Ganoderma in the cave, which can only be seen when passing by. Don't miss it later. The hole is not high, please be careful to pass, do not hit your head. In China, ganoderma lucid is a symbol of auspiciousness and longevity and is often used in painting, embroidery and architecture. In traditional Chinese medicine, ganoderma lucid is a Chinese herb that nourishes and strengthens the body.

Dear friends, there are a lot of wild ganoderma, you will see from time to time on the way to the tour, however you can just see and take a picture, but do not touch them and do not pick them, thank you for your cooperation. Ok, please continue your tour.

Rainforest peak landscape area, wild banana forest

Dear guests, on both sides of the plank road, are covered with a kind of large leaf trees, called wild banana trees. In the ripe season, there will be large fields of golden wild bananas. Plantain is one of the foods of our ancient ancestors, and it has always followed the course of human life. Wild banana is also the main food of the monkey, if we are lucky, we will see the traces of the monkey here. In traditional texts, plantains are often associated with autumn rain and are used in poetry and paintings to represent parting and sorrow. Perhaps the most famous line is the "red cherry, green banana". Jiangnan sizhu "the rain beat banana" song, expressed the bleak mood. In fact, the banana is planted in a corner of the courtyard or by the wall of the window, creating a relaxed and cool environment. Listen to the rain beats on the banana in the night, our troubles will be drift away with the wind and rain. Ok, let's look at the right side of the plank road. There is a plant with leaves like the ears of an elephant. It is also called Guanyin taro or lotus flower. Sea taro is more common in rain forest area, like the dark place, some still parasitic in the thick big tree. Sea taro is as the medicinal materials, it has the function of detoxification, swelling and other effects. Look at the big leaves of the sea taro. Isn't that interesting? During the rainy season, local residents often stand below the shelter. Plantains have huge leaves, so what are the benefits of big leaves? It captures more light, which is good for growth. Ok, let's move on.

Banyan tree observation deck

Dear guests, we have come to the banyan tree observation deck, where there are eight huge banyan trees. It is said that once there was a typhoon here. Among the eight banyan trees, two thirds of their roots had been blown off the ground by the wind. At that time, the banyan tree next to them use its shoulders in the wind to carry the fallen body of the tree, until now, you can still find the mark left by time the intersection of these two trees. The banyan ancient trees image to deduce the true feelings of the world and we call this group of banyan trees as friendship tree. Here you can also see a very typical picture of the tropical rain forest, roots embrace the stones and ancient figs embrace each other. Sitting here, have you felt the mystery, magic and sacred of Yanoda rain forest?

Old vine

Dear guests, although there are vines in all kinds of forests, the tropical rain forest has the largest variety of vines and the largest individuals.Botanists believe that they are the most tenacious life in the rainforest, they occupy almost all of the spaces, using every possible opportunity to climb and grow, forming an "ancient vine wrapped tree" rainforest wonders. We see them interlaced, tangled and dense as a web, just like dragons play in the sea. Not far away here were several huge trees, stuck like needles in the forest. Have you ever seen the American movie "Tarzan the Ape Man", in which the master, Tarzan, uses ancient vines like ropes to fly between trees and canyons? Walking in the sea of rattan dragon, do you also have this kind of immersive feeling? Ok, please continue your tour.

Shuangting Valley

Dear guests, we look at the front of these two pavilions, one is called a pillar pavilion. It looks like a wild ganoderma in the forest. Another pavilion called Fenghou pavilion. You can have a rest in the pavilion, and I'll tell you why. It is often mentioned in martial arts novels that some hidden weapons are painted with deadly poison, which can poison people if they are hit by it. Is there such a thing in the world? Yes, there is a tree next to the pavilion called curare wood, also known as "see blood seal throat", its milky juice contains highly toxic, when the poison from the wound enters into the human body, will cause muscle relaxation, blood coagulation, slow heartbeat, and finally lead to death. Fenghou pavilion is named after this magical plant, and because the seal throat and the "hou" homophony, so named Fenghou pavilion. I am here to bless you after the leaders of the scenic spots to increase the ranks, step by step. Ok, so much for Shuangting valley. Please take your time.

Boat shaped house, millennium couple banyan tree

Dear guests, let's take a look at the building in front of us. Does it look like an upside-down ship? It is called "boat house", which is a traditional residence of Li people in Hainan. The big banyan tree not far from the boat-shaped house is a yellow banyan tree with thousands of years of age. There is a yellow banyan tree next to it. Do you see it? They hand in echo, so they are called "millennium banyan couple". Look at this banyan tree, the root is an eight-shaped, this kind of root is one of the characteristics of the rain forest, called the plate root, the shape is like a wall, also like wings of doc, extend to the surrounding, firmly support the huge body, it's a symbol of the love between husband and wife, never abandon, mutual support, good union. Have you ever noticed that under the banyan tree there is a tree door, because "banyan" and the "dragon" homonym, so called it "longmen"(dragon door), through this "longmen", indicating that we will be prosperous in the road of life in the future. Ok, please continue your tour.

Angiopteris

Dear guests, at the bottom of the plank road there is a national secondary protection of the plant, called Avalokitesvara Rosetta fern. Through the explanatory card, you should be able to find that the Avalokitesvara Rosetta fern is about 1.5 meters high, belongs to a large land fern. Because its root shapes like a lotus, so it is called Avalokitesvara Rosetta fern. Rosetta ferns can be used in medicine, have the effect of dredging wind and removing silt, clearing heat and detoxification, cooling blood and hemostasis, tranquilizing mind. Humans have a very close relationship with ferns, and the coal we burn is made up of ancient ferns which have gone through a long geological process underground. Modern ferns also have a high economic value, the rhizoma stem contains rich starch, we call it fern powder, nutritional value is no less than lotus root powder, not only edible, but also wine; The rhizome of a fern like this one can weigh as much as 20 to 30 kilograms. In addition, the tender leaves of ferns are soaked in swill or water for a few days. After removing toxic ingredients, they have a special fragrance. Many upscale restaurants in the United States often make superior food with tender ferns. Ok, the view sound lotus fern stop here, please continue to visit.

Five banyan welcome guests

Dear guests, there are five banyan trees in front of a unique landscape, you see their roots connected with roots, branches linked with branches, like a huge open umbrella to keep out wind and rain for your arrival. we call it “five banyan welcome guests”. Can you see carefully which branch belongs to which banyan tree? Is it hard to tell? They are not the same as each other, integration, support the same sky, build a small world, isn’t it the best model of a harmonious society?

Tianchan bridge

Dear guests, the bridge before us is composed of eight toad sculptures with different expressions. It is called “Tianchan Bridge”. Toad is one of the totem worship of the Li nationality in Hainan. It is said that when you walk across the Tiantoad Bridge, the exams will went well, the love was good, the study career will be good, and the business was endless. Ok, please continue your tour.

Styrax macrocarpus

Dear guests, now in front of us is a tree with large leaves, bearing small green fruit, called benzoin. Have you found it? This tree looks unremarkable, but it is one of the country's rare and endangered plants. There are many large fruity benzoin trees in Yanoda, which can be seen later on the tour. It can be used as medicine, can also be used to treat rheumatic joint pain. It can also extract spices. Distinguished guests, here, we have seen a lot of rare and endangered plants, in fact, the nature of a grass and a tree, whether rare or not, should be protected, do you think so? Ok, please continue your tour.

Betelnut garden

Dear guests, have you ever heard the folk song "picking areca nuts"? This song shows us a picture of elder brother and younger sister picking betel nuts with affection. Now we come to the betel nut garden, these tall and straight trees are betel nut trees. The name of the fruit is betel nut, betel nut can be used in medicine, and it is the first of the four southern medicine in China, it can drive roundworm, beat accumulation, stop dysentery and so on, and it is very widely used.

Butterfly tree

Dear distinguished guests, you must have seen a butterfly, but have you ever seen a butterfly tree? There is a very rare tree here, called the butterfly tree, also known as Jiabu. There is a butterfly tree in the scenic area of the Yanoda, you can look for it through the explanation board. The butterfly tree is suitable for the high temperature; and the butterfly tree likes the soil which is thick static wind moist environment growth. It is quite strict with the growing environment, that means that wherever it is, the ecological environment must be excellent. From this butterfly tree in our Yanoda scenic area, it shows that the natural environment here is the first-class, is almost unpolluted area, you can do more deep breathing here, feel the charm of Yanoda "Natural oxygen-rich cornucopia".

Butterfly tree materials are very good, compressive and tensile. They are the best among the Hainan timber species that we know, are valuable shipbuilding and first-class furniture materials. They also have very good medicinal value: can clear heat and benefit from dampness, DE tumescence and detoxification, cure infectious hepatitis, cystitis, sore throat, eczema and other diseases. Unfortunately, due to the narrow distribution area of the butterfly trees themselves and the excessive deforestation, the resources have been gradually exhausted. The tree in front of you has been illegally cut down, but without success. You can see that the top of the tree is broken and that's the reason. Here, I advocate you and me together: protect flowers and trees, do green ecological citizens. Ok, please continue your tour.

Dear guests, it takes about 15 minutes from here to the gate service area of the scenic spot. Please sit firmly and take care of yourself. Yanoda scenic area is about to open a new scenic spot called Sandaogu, where there is a strange geological structure and rich medicinal materials. The stones inside, some of them are as magical as the surface of the moon, some as flat as a hand-cut while some as colorful as a drawing board. The water is clear, the green is blue, strange flowers are blooming, and the three valleys are a shambhala hidden deep in the mountains. Then you can explore the mysterious world.

Ok, it is about to arrive at the gate service area, after the car stopping, please take your belongings, get off in turn. I'm glad to serve you today. Please return the guide machine after you getting off the bus. The machine is disposable and will not be explained repeatedly. This explanation is provided by Yanoda rainforest cultural and tourism area, we are looking forward to your next visit. Finally, I wish everyone a lifetime of peace, the best of both worlds, and three ways of harmony again. Yanoda!

4. Boundary Island Tourist Attraction of Hainan

Dear visitors, today we are going to visit Boundary Island Tourist Attraction of Hainan which lies to the southeast of Hainan island. It's the first national sea-island type 5A scenic spot in China. There are tropical pristine island features and rare marine biological resources. It's about 0.41 square kilometers in size and 100 meters in height. It's approximately 1.2 nautical miles far from the nearest seashore of Hainan island and the one-way ferry only takes around 10 minutes. With an average annual temperature of about 25℃ , it is one of the best islands in Hainan for diving and viewing the underwater world.

Boundary Culture

This beautiful island in the south China sea has formed a unique culture due to its geographical location. The island and the Niuling Mountain on the opposite side of it mark the boundary between Hainan's northern and southern climates. Therefore, the mountain which is a few hundred meters long often has different weather condition. In ancient times, it was the cultural dividing line between Miao and Han. Today, it is still the administrative demarcation line between Lingshui county and Wanning city. Of course, here is not only the boundary for climate and administration, but also is known as the mind boundary for changing moods and understanding life.

Ocean Culture

There is a large-scale and unique ornamental marine animal theater under pure natural conditions. Not only can you watch the wonderful performances of dolphins, sea lions and turtles, but also interact with them intimately. In addition, you can visit about 2,900 square meters coral areas built on reefs to view live corals and coral specimens. The tourists also carried out a meaningful marine science education activity while watching.

South China Sea Hailao porcelain culture

There are many kinds of porcelain that span the historical periods of the Northern Song, Yuan, Ming, and early Qing dynasties. The Porcelain District is an arrangement and display of the South China Sea civilization, and is also a showcase for the history of Chinese ceramic culture and the history of marine civilization.

Ecological diving island

After diving into the seafloor, you can see not only a large number of well-preserved living coral reefs, but also mysterious ancient shipwrecks, idols, underwater villages and rich marine life. Here, you can experience such popular experience programs as snorkeling, reef diving, and ocean diving and can also sign up for professional diving train course like PADI-OW and PADI-AOW. Of course, for certificated divers, they can also explore more mysterious and exciting free diving spots.

Happy dream island

You can turn into a floating dragon to feel the thrill of flying into the sea. You can also parasail like a seabird, sit on a banana boat jumping on the top of the waves, and experience the fast and furious dynamic yacht. There are a variety of maritime entertainment items such as competitive sports, race tracks, entertainment experiences, etc., which makes the tourism products of Boundary Island develop in many directions such as leisure sports and entertainment. This is perfect for tourists of all ages to have an immersive experience.

Rainbow Sans souci island

After experiencing lively and exciting marine entertainment, you can also stroll through the mountains and have coffee in the gazebo. You can also lie down on the balcony of the cabin. Here has the original natural scenery and the endless sea views. You can relax here, forget all the trivia and spend a good time free of bother and distraction.

Romantic wedding island

Come to Fenjiezhou Island to enjoy your beautiful encounter and find the other half. It's one of the top ten romantic scenic spots in Hainan Province, and is also the designated shooting base for wedding photography agencies in Sanya, Haikou and surrounding cities. The natural elements of mountains, seas and islands are a special part of the romantic interactive experience. Unique island-style wedding and warm honeymoon room make Fenjiezhou Island a characteristic romantic island in Hainan.

Delicacies Island

The food on Fenjiezhou Island is as evocative as the scenery here. There are thousands of specialties in Hainan. In addition to the local cuisine in Hainan, there are also local snacks throughout the world. The abundance of delicious dishes makes tourists enjoy the pleasure while visiting the scenery.

5. Binglanggu Hainan Li & Miao Cultural Heritage Park

It has been a long time since we last meet, and I hope it will be a long time before we have to part. Dear visitors and friends, our president Xi's greeting with this folk lyric of Hainan now made this song popular around China. Today I sing the same song to welcome you for visiting Betel Nut Valley. As a scenic spot to inherit Li and Miao culture in Hainan, Betel Nut Valley always upholds the mission to excavate, protect, inherit, and carry forward of Li and Miao culture, and keeps its vitality, now this spot becomes the living fossil of Hainan national culture.

On this cultural land, the Betel Nut Valley Scenic Area has been open since 1998. With its strong ethnic culture and the unremitting efforts of the people of the Betel Nut Valley, it has become China's first 5A level tourist attraction for ethnic culture, as well as a national demonstration base for the productive protection of intangible cultural heritage. It has also been awarded the title of National Ethnic Unity and Progress Model Collective by the State Council. Our large-scale live-action performance <Areca·Ancient·Rhyme> had acquired the important culture export project issued by six ministries and commissions of the state. There are a lot of honors belonging to Areca Valley. The aborigines in here cherishing and inheriting the skills. The Areca Valley has a long history of love! Today let us put our hearts into the visiting process and comprehend this extraordinary attraction. Having a real and close touch with the culture of this great ethnic minority, trying to make yourself integrate into Li nationality, and having a happy and memorable experience of this cultural travel.

Before we start our journey, let me tell you a colloquial greeting way in Li language, because a lot of seniors hardly ever went out of their mountainous abode, so they are unable to understand mandarin we speak, after a few minute when we meet LI natives how can we greet them? It is easy and simple, just thumbs up with your right hands, and say "boloon!". It means betelnut in Li's language, it is a necessary present in developing friendship, attending on a wedding and celebrating festivals. It also symbolizes the meaning of happiness, auspiciousness and beautifulness. When you thumb up to somebody, it means "Hello, you are nice, handsome and bright", at the same time transmit your best wishes of blessing such as safety, lucky and auspiciousness to the guests. Have you all learned it?

The Gate of the scenic area

The height of the gate is 16.9m, and the length is 30m. This totemic gate is consisted of three main elements: god cattle, boat house and one of the most typical totems called "The Great Power God". It is believed in many Li nationality residents that The Great Power God is Omnipotent, he has been sheltering and guarding the village, blessing the good weather and ensuring an adequate harvest in agriculture. Li nationality has their own faith and worship, the content for main types of worships are include nature, ancestors and totem, amid this mass of worships, The Great Gower God is adapted ubiquitously in Li nationality. There are plenty of tales about The Great Gower God, when we arrive at the village, I will give you an elaboration. Cattles are accompanied with Miao nationality residents from cradle to grave. In Miao nationality, cattle culture is widespread in their architecture, garment, dance, festival, sacrifice rite, drinking custom and village regulations, they have been deeming the buffalo is the most powerful animals in the world. According to above reasons, they use buffaloes to exorcise the evil spirits, this animal also symbolizes wealth and power. The main part of the gate erected by totem of The Great Power God, cattle and boat house, which means Great Power God, the majesty, who rode his magical cattle arrived in the mortal world and protected Li nationality. Please pay attention to the base structure of this gate, it's mainly composed by stones and firewood, representing the lucky will come in time and bring more wealth for you. Now I am sending bless to my friends who come through this gate, wish you have a lucky life and gain more wealth.

In front of us is a cactus living nearly a hundred years, it can still bloom and bear fruit. It implies the god have decent to the mortal world, which guided and supported Li nationality, and also symbolized the spirt of persevering in our nationality. On this side is a dragon boat stone, the stone was discovered in this place when the scenic spot started to build the gate in 2015, it was sculptured and polished by nature for thousands of years, and without any artificial carving. Form a long distance, it seems like a boat, it is our jewel boat. In the ancient time, our ancestors had navigated to Hainan Island by canoes, and became the earliest aborigines, so it emblematizes the canoes of li nationalities' ancestors and wisdom of life.

Intangible Cultural Heritage Village

The first district we visit is named Intangible cultural heritage village. Here we present thousands of years of culture inheritance of Li nationality, and it is the most gorgeous part of this civilization. Li nationality has hitherto owned 1 world-class, 9 national-class intangible culture heritage protection projects, which Includes Firewood Dance, Primitive Pottery Technique, Traditional Spinning, Dyeing, Weaving and Embroidering Skills(World-Class), the Technique of Making Tree Leather Garments, Drill Wood to Make Fire, the Festival in March 3th, Bamboo Instrument, Boat House Building Technique, Traditional Costume and Folk Songs, other provincial-class projects and so on.

Boat House

Dwelling is an indispensable component in human being tangible culture. The local selection of Li's village depends on terrain and topography — Plain villages are established on the hillside for preventing the floods, residents here usually drink from wells and rivers; Mountainous villages are built under the foot of the mountain, which help the natives to avoid damage caused by typhoon, aborigines drink springs water rising from the mountain. The cottage's roof made by thatch, and its skeleton framed by bamboo and wood. It has two main types of architecture are called boat cottage and pinnacle cottage. Traditional boat cottage making techniques are not only the wisdom of aborigines, but also the embodiment of special type of indigenous culture.

Longgui

Among the Li nationality society, teenagers at the age of 13 or 14 will no longer live with their parents together. They build their own house which called Longgui. Boys build their own house with the materials they prepared on the mountains; girls build the house with the help of their parents. Li ethnic minority boudoir is usually built nearby their parents' cottage or on the margin of the village. It is just a small cottage with merely 8-10 square meters. These boudoirs are separated by genders, it is the best place for teenagers to live, socialize, play instruments, sing in an antiphonal style, and promise for engagement.

History of Li Nationality

3000 years age, A nationality called "Luoyue" as a branch of "Baiyue" nationality in southeast minority groups, due to the tiredness and persecution caused by war, immigrated to Hainan island where was still a barren land by boat, and became the earliest indigenous residents in this island. We now call it Li nationality. The current population of Li nationality is more than 1.4 million. They gather and inhabit mainly in south-central mountainous areas of Hainan island. Due to the discrepancies in dwelling environments, garments and ornaments, living customs and languages, it can make a further classification contents five dialect areas named "Ha, Ji, Run, Sai and Meifu". For thousands of years, the conscientious and intelligent aborigines have been living and breeding in this land for generations, they created fantastic, various and unique characteristic of national material civilization and spiritual cultures. Areca Valley is a miniature of this resplendent culture.

Garments in Five Dialect Areas

If you want to understand a nationality, first, you should start from their garments and ornaments. At present, the exhibition in front of your eyes are the clothes derived from five dialect areas. Garments of a nationality can reflect the relevant culture of itself in production, lifestyle, religion and affluence. First of all, in order to adapt their own lifestyles and the diversity of labor and productive activity, we see radical differences in their garments in different dialect areas, the clothes in areas living by cultivating are more exquisite, on the contrary, the clothes in areas where hunting for their foods are relatively crude. In the entire process of Chinese culture development, some habits of us are also based on production and work. In Han nationality, there is manifest phenomenon that males were superior than females. According to a statistic, on this aspect both south and north areas in mainland of China do not have huge differences, it is derived from ancient china agricultural society system. In comparison, males have more important value in productivity and greater contributions to family and society, Gradually, paternal clan society was formed. Together with thousands of years governed by feudal society, made this males' superiority much more severe in Han society. But in this context Li nationality disapproved with Han's perspective, male and female are equal in Li society. On Family's status, females' status even much higher than males' in clans. This difference was caused by the contrast of contribution in production and works for males and females in Li nationality, males used to hunt and cultivate, females are responsible for Spinning, Dyeing, Weaving and Embroidering, and also making clothes. In addition, females are the main power of giving birth to offspring and ensuring the prosperity of the family, so in the relationship of Li society, males have great respect for females. Today, I welcome you to visit Li's family, you will witness the dragon quilt which combines spinning, dyeing, weaving and embroidering skills together, this is the greatest art treasure invented by females in Li's history.

Li nationality traditional garment is multicolored, delicate, graceful, it has various patterns and substantial contents. It mainly weaved by cotton in island, linen, kapok and bark fiber. Four traditional crafts in Li nationality, spinning, dyeing, weaving and embroidery, are the indispensable bases of forming Li nationality traditional clothes. Traditional clothes of Li nationality are shaped by gradual development, evolution and accumulation in a long history of Li nationality. It is rooted from the social life of the Li nationality, embodies the wisdom of Li people and has distinctive national characteristics, local characteristics and rich national cultural connotation. It is "the living fossil" of Li nationality and has an extremely importance of researching value in the aspects for discussing social developing history, culture and art, custom formed, religion, product and works of Li nationality in Hainan. In ancient China there is a phrase called if wearing gold and silver, you must be a man of wealth. There is a misunderstanding by descendants, the real meaning of this phrase is wearing brocade with silver decoration, owning to the two characters of pronunciation is the same in Chinese, in ancient China, a man who wear brocade reflects his high social status. So, there are some proverbs like wearing brocade and jade, wearing brocade when back to hometown, which means the extravagant life. Before skills of weaving brocade popularized, the populace clothes are made by linen, only the riches and bureaucrat can wear brocade, but our Li nationality is one of the earliest nationalities to wear brocade. Traditional clothes of different dialect areas in Li nationality uses black and dark blue as the main color of basic tone and regards various colors as auxiliary tone. Colors of it are matched harmoniously and the crafts are exquisite. Inside of these areas, Run areas' dress is especially unique with distinct ethnic styles and characteristic. Tight skirt is short and narrow, the length is only 20cm, it is the shortest skirt in designs among five dialect areas, so it is also called "mini skirt".

Cultural Corridors

Tattoo Custom

There is a long history of tattoo custom in Li nationality. Since Han dynasty, it had been recorded by words. It is a rare cultural phenomenon among ethnic groups all around the world.

As a kind of traditional culture, Tattoo is the legacy leaved by matrilineal clans and the product of matriarchy. It is the artistic crystal of ancient religion, natural worship, ancestral worship and totemic worship. It is the sign of Cohesion, appeal and vitality in Li's history. Today, a very few senior females in Li nationality still keep in their body the totem imprinted by history. These splendid pictures are printed by blood and flesh and add a brilliant shine on Li nationality's history.

Tattoo both on the face and body is the ancient custom of Li nationality, it is also a precious and wealthy culture which is dying now, it embodies the worship, awe and veneration to ancestors of Li nationality. There is an old saying in Han nationality, the person who forgets his or her ancestors is unworthy of being a human. Li is one of nationality in china that uses human skin as a carrier to record the clans' symbols, and inherits the inspiration from Li's antecedents generation by generation, imprints the clans' symbols and worship of totem on body, is full of the desiring of long lifespan, wish of happiness, avoiding disaster and pursuing aesthetics. Girl in Li nationality usually starts tattooing at 12 years old, the whole tattoo must be finished before wedding. During the process of tattooing, first, the plant colors are applied with medical herbs to print the pattern on body, then using thorn stab along the pattern, the tattoo will never fade when it finished. But why females of Li nationality in ancient time have to tattoo? Because in the view of Consanguineous clan, when females died and go to underworld, their predecessors will not recognize them without tattoo on face and body. Due to the discrepancies of patterns in different clans, tattoos are used practically to recognize each other, prevention of marriage between blood relatives, in order to ensure the safe and healthy reproduction of offspring. In addition, as for Li females in the past time, tattoo is a kind of aesthetic, the more tattoo you have, the more beautiful you are. Because of the change of aesthetics, living habit evaluation, the negative impact of physical development, this custom has already been abolished, so nowadays teenagers do not need tattoo anymore. After a few minutes, I will lead you to see the seniors' tattoo, they are the last generation called living fossils, maybe after a too few decades, we can only see the ancient custom in the history and pictures. As a kind of culture phenomenon, Li's tattoo embodies consciousness of ethnic origin, totemic worship and ancestral worship. Professor Zelin Wu a celebrated Sociologist, ethnologist and educator said: "tattoo is 'Dunhuang frescoes' for Li nationality in

Hainan, keeping for over 3,000 years, and until now we can still find the remains of it, it is a real miracle."

Eating Habits

Fish Tea

Put raw flesh or row fish, and rice noodles together, then stir-fried, sprinkle a little salt, finally sealed within clay pot. After fermentation for one month, it can be eaten directly. In Li's language it called "Xiang". It is a kind of sweet, sour and delicious pickle made by Li family.

Li nationality has a lot of experience of utilizing wild herbs to keep healthy, diet cure even plays a crucial role to fight against illness in Li nationality.

Biang Wine

In the daily life of Li families, wine is indispensable. Whether it's in important festivals, weddings and funerals or other activities, everyone will put on a banquet with alcohol drinks. In common life, if there is a guest, the host will show his hospitality, in this procedure drinking is necessary. Li nationality is not only cordial with guests, but also has its own drinking culture.

A thousand years of Li medicine and a hundred years of Miao medicine

Li is a nationality without characters, the method of inheriting the medical knowledge and experience is oral teaching that inspires true understanding, it depends on passing from mouth to mouth and maintain the knowledge and experience generation by generation. The "oral book" is a treasure house for several generations of Li doctors. In the eyes of average people, Li doctors' oral explanation of herbs and diagnosis is all Greek! Hainan island is adequate with nature treasures, and gives birth to many excellent geniuses, here, we have various kinds of tropical herbs and medical usage plants. Li is a nationality that very good at identifying and using natural herbs as medicine, as a kind of folk worship, the faith is also existent in herbs, so herbs are the main materials used when Li medical men curing the diseases, all the herbs are available and can be synthesized easily. Usually, rhizome, flower, leaves and pericarp of plants can be directly exploited in prescription.

In addition, Li nationality's doctors emphasizes the body, remarks, lust and spirit of a man must be restricted. As for healthy people, the gestures of walking, setting and lying also need to put into considerations. Don't wear red lines and coins as amulets. Everybody should respect the seniors, take a good care of children, have a cohesive atmosphere with neighbor, in their opinions only virtuous man can keep healthy, happy and have a long lifespan.

There was a 400 years history since Miao nationality came to Hainan island, in this developing process Miao medicine from South China have a combination with local tropical natures resource, which gradually formed a distinct Miao medical culture valuable for science research.

Female Seniors Weaving Brocade

We can see several Grandma here, they are the masters who have the most consummate skills in field of weaving brocades in Li nationality. Day by day, they keep the bodies at this 90 angels posture, setting on the ground using the power from feet and waist to weave, they work such a long time a day, working in all their lifespan, then the side-effect comes, in the evening, they will suffer from the pains of shoulders and waist, so now, there are hardly any young girls willing to study the skills, the result is these traditional weaving skills are now facing to be handled down from the past generations. The tool they used called waist loom, it is made by some bamboos and woods, which is one of the oldest textile tools in China, but this grandmas can use it to spin hundreds of laces and patterns, and do not need any blue prints and manuscript, all these laces and patterns are derived from their imaginary thoughts, so every Li brocade's existence in the world is unique. To weave only one Li brocade will take 6-8 months, but in busy farming season it will take 8-12 years to weave. Before the start of weaving process, taking cotton out of seed and twisting it into lines, then dying them to favorable colors, they weave on the ground, after finishing weave, it also needs artificial embroidery, this process is exceedingly sophisticated, it is also a challenge to both the physical condition and weaving skills, every brocade is the epitome of a woman's life, it is the inheritance of Li nationality. Until now, Li nationality people still keep this form of art to promote the development of national culture. So, in 2009, the traditional spinning, dying, weaving and embroidery technique was listed as a world-class intangible cultural heritage protection project by UNESCO (The United Nations Education Scientific and Cultural Organization). Now, Li brocades are valued highly in history, culture, art, appreciation and collection.

If you think the Li nationality seniors have a really hard work, and coincidentally you also prefer and are interested in Li brocade, you can buy a pure artificial brocade as a collection and also to commemorate today's experience.

Explanation of the four Museums

Non-Woven Museum

Bark (tree skin) garment, one of the earliest and greatest invention by human. The appearance of it makes human beings get rid of the embarrassment of being naked, covers their bodies and keeps warm and becomes the witness of early human civilization. It is the ancestor and living fossil of human clothes. In May 2006, weaving skills of bark in Li nationality were selected into the first batch of national intangible cultural heritage list.

Linen Spinning Museum

Linen textile technology, which is a milestone in the textile industry, it can be said that without original linen spinning technique, there will be no famous li brocades today. Ancestors of Li nationality collects the wild linen from the nature as original materials, then after peeling, boiling, drying, soaking, beating, twisting and other procedures, linen clothes are finally made.

Cotton Spinning Museum

Li nationality is one of the earliest minorities to plant and use cotton, the spinning history in Li nationality is long-standing which can be retrospected to 770-221 B.C. with the reports by written words. Li nationality know how to use the local wild kapok to make various kinds of clothes before many years ago, the original cottons are apart to two species, one xyloid climbing kapok called red kapok, the other is herbal kapok called Hainan cotton or Chinese cotton.

Dragon Quilt Hall

Dragon quilt is the most brilliant and exotic flower in the traditional spinning, dyeing, weaving, and embroidery techniques of the Li ethnic group in Hainan. It is the most difficult, culturally tasteful, and technologically advanced brocade art piece among the four major processes of spinning, dyeing, and embroidery. It is also one of the treasures that the Li ethnic group has presented to feudal dynasties throughout history.

The Dragon Quilt Museum houses dozens of precious dragon quilt works, including the Dragon Teng Xiangyun and Qilin Twin Phoenix Auspicious Dragon Quilt, which have been awarded the title of "the world's largest Li ethnic dragon quilt" by the World Records Association.

Li ethnic group's Spinning, Dying, Weaving and Embroidery Techniques

There is an idiom in Li nationality: if there is no Li nationality, there will be no cotton exploited, then there will be no cotton garments. Because li is a nationality only has oral language but any written words, it is facing a dilemma to adherent the existence of crafts inheritance, Therefore, the inheritance of Li brocade weaving skills are becoming exceedingly precious. According to history, over 3,000 years, in Shang and Zhou dynasties, females in Li nationality had already known how to spin cotton garments with the utilization of cotton, after thousands of years of promoting and creating, it has formed Spinning, Dying, Weaving and Embroidery four traditional procedures gradually, inside this four procedures, spinning is the most important one.

Daopo Huang

She is the most celebrated weaver in the period of late song and the beginning of yuan dynasties. She shares her eminent and advanced techniques of spinning and promotes to use progressive machine to weave, because of these contributions, Thus, she commands deep reverence among the people. In Qing dynasty she had been recognized as the co-founder of spinning and weaving industry. She has always lived among Li sisters, and learned how to use cotton making tools and weave cliff quilts with Li people. Huangdaopo's most primary contribution is advancing and reforming the spinning technique, she had transformed the pedal-powered spinning machine into three spindles pedal machine, which triple the efficiency of it, this new machine was rapidly spread in province. (nearby her hometown Zhejiang). It is said that her machine is the most advanced spinning tool in the world at that time. In that feudal time, Huang suffered the persecution by feudalism wedding, then she escaped to Hainan and has been living lived over 30 years, during this time she had learned how to use the cotton processing tools and the methods to make quilt, then she learned to improve and generalize Li nationality brocades weaving technique. In the later years after returned to her hometown Shanghai, she passed on the advanced technique of spinning with cotton in middle and lower reaches of Yangtze River, which raised a swift and rapid development in industry of cotton spinning, finally she became one of the most notable female weaver in China.

Miao villages in the rainforest

Introduction to Miao Nationality

Miao is the second largest ethnic group in Hainan Island with a population of about 80,000. In the same case as Li nationality, there is only language but handwriting, Miao language in Hainan belongs to "Yao" language, a branch of Miao and Yao language, in Chinese language family. The language of Miao nationality in Hainan island is unified, without any dialect differences, they call themselves "Jinmen" or "Jindimen", Miao is a nickname. The migration of Miao nationality to Hainan Island began from emperor Jiajing to Wanli of Ming Dynasty(1522 — 1620). As soldiers from Guangxi and other provinces, they were recruited to Hainan by Ming empire. After the withdrawal of defense, some of Miao nationality soldiers decided to settle in Hainan, and others moved to Hainan Island for making a living. So far, it has a history of more than 400 years. By generations, it gradually evolved into the Miao nationality in Hainan island today.

The people in Miao nationality are brave and skillful in battle, they are called warriors, braves, they have been living in mountains for generations and lived by hunting. The ancestor of Miao nationality is Chiyou who is a tribal leader as famous as Emperor Yan and Emperor Huang. In Hainan island, the nationality belongs to black "Miao", they think black is beautiful, fat is beautiful. Miao nationality is famous for medicine, venomous insects, batik, silver ornament and tricolor rice.

Now it is a period for Li and Miao minorities to live in harmony in the mountains and create an affluent and colorful cultural industry. Next, we will visit Miao family of Guyin, it expresses the harmonious atmosphere of solidarity in Li and Miao nationality. Along the way, you will see the gate of the Miao family of Guyin. The gates are printed into whole black, with two silver butterfly patterns on both sides. Butterfly is regard as the totem of Miao nationality, black embodies the inability to forget hardships, silver embodies happiness and beauty, the combination of silver and black means no matter how impoverish and abominable the nature environment is, they will be stable as silver, all poisons will be inviolable, keep healthy and happy all the time. Chiyou is the ancestor of Miao nationality, he is also one of the three main predecessors of Chinese nationality. The old sayings said that Chiyou is a brave and skillful fighter who can make many kinds of weapons, later generations regard Chiyou as the ancestor of weapons and God of war. Miao people travel all the year round on the high mountains in the central part of Hainan island. They live in the forest and grow rice on the hillside, continuing their slash-and-burn cultivation year by year, so they extremely worship cattle, regard it as totem, pray for peace, wealth and higher status, now in front of us is cattle spirit totem of Miao nationality. Along the way, there are sculptures covered with silver ornaments, which are the original coconut sculptures in Hainan, among these, you can feel the harmonious atmosphere and cohesive spirit in Li and Miao nationality, the countless silver ornaments cracking with a clear and melodious sound, like a song to eulogize solidarity of Chinese nationality. By the way, here is 18° north latitude, the fresh air with high oxygen percentage is good for our health, you can enjoy this memorable journey.

Sacrifice Customs of Li Nationality

The custom of sacrifice in Li nationality reflects the relation between human and nature, guided by the doctrine called "everything has its spirit", natural worship, totemic worship and ancestral worship are extremely prevalent in Li nationality society.

Natural worship refers to the direct worship of natural objects, the highest level of worship is stone worship, such as worship of stone ancestor, worship of stone spirit and so on. Others are the worships like sky, earth, wind, trees and thunder, mountains, water, fire, and etc.

Totemic worship, every clan has their own totemic worship, Li nationality have animal worship and plants worship, animal worship is referred to dragon, fish, birds, dogs, cattle, cats and so on, worship of plants are mainly to gourd and bamboo.

Ancestor worship, Li people generally think that ancestors are the most formidable ghosts. The ancestors' ghosts mean the forefathers normally die in the paternal family. In front of the entrance of Li village or under the big banyan tree, there are small stone houses made by several stones. This is the Earth temple that Li people worship their ancestors. The temple has shrines and censers, and a stone which Li people call it "Stone Ancestor". Li people sacrifice "Stone ancestor" as the embodiment of soul. On July 14th in lunar calendar and around the Spring Festival, villagers place wine and meat, burn incense and worship their ancestors' spirits, and pray for the prosperity, safety, health and longevity of their lifespans.

Ganzha Li village

Five Totem Areas

In front of us is the exhibition of Li nationality's totemic worships, due to the differences in living environment, customs, dress, personal adornments and languages, Li nationality is separated to five dialect areas called "Ha, Qi, Run, Sai and Meifu". The totemic worships in different areas are also different, on our left hand, these five totems sizes and patterns are based on the covered area, population and living customs. For instance, Ha area is the most biggest dialect area among the five, it also have the largest population, so the totem of Ha area is the highest, but Meifu areas has the minimum population, it only occupies 4%, so the totem of it is the shortest among these five. The two words engraved on this big log are called "Wanma", which means the story of a long time ago, throughout the journey we have already saw a lot of frog sculptures, frog is one of animals worshiped by Li nationality, they believe it will protect the crops from pest, also frog is a meteorologist, because the old saying is "when the frog croaking, it is the time for raining".

Dear my friends, the next activity is to visit totemic museum in Li nationality, before we enter the museum, please pay attention for this building, it was constructed by bamboo, wood, mud and straw, the roof was made by thatch. The main characteristic of Li nationality architect is warm in winter and brisk in summer, in addition, we can see the big building here, Li people believe even the thatch can build a mansion. The history of Li nationality is long and profound, with extensive knowledge it becomes a unique masterpiece in cultural treasure house of the Chinese nationality, it is also a precious cultural heritage of humankind. Here we see the colorful sculpture of art describes the folk customs, totemic worship and the content of Intangible cultural heritage. they were made by Yuxiang Chen, a folk artist in Hainan, who spent several years studying Li Culture and using new environmental protection materials to make these. Here I will choose representative compositions to introduce for you.

Intangible Cultural Heritage Exhibition Hall I

Dear friends, next we will visit one of the intangible cultural heritage exhibition halls, the religion of Li nationality has a dense primitive color, it mainly formed by natural worship, totemic worship and ancestral worship. The reason of worship can be traced back to the primitive society, because of extremely low productivity, people cannot explicate and understand the nature phenomenon, our ancestors thought everything happened in mortal world are arranged by the god of nature. Therefore, Li nationality's primitive religion was gradually formed, massive

Li nationality people generally advocate "everything has its spirit", for instance: "mountain has mountain gods, stone has stone gods and tree has tree gods.", in Li national religion, the stone gods are especially popular, because they think this god can promote human fertility, he can also protect the crops not be eaten by birds and beasts.

Tattoo Museum of Li Nationality

Tattoo both on the face and body of females in Li nationality is an ancient traditional custom, it is also a precious and wealthy culture which are dying now. Imprinting totem of the symbol of clan and worship on the body contents the pray for life of aborigines, the hope for happiness, the avoidance of disaster and the pursuit for aesthetic. Therefore, Li is the only nationality in China which use human skins as carriers to record clan's symbols, tattooing on face and body is called "Dunhuang frescoes of Li nationality in Hainan Island" by anthropologists. In the past, if females in Li nationality did not have tattoo, she would be reproached and discriminated by others, it is also difficult to marriage when she becomes an adult. In addition, if there are no signs of ancestral clan on her body, she will not be recognized by her ancestors after her death and will become a ghost. Therefore, the process of tattoo is very painful, but it still a holiness for the people in Li nationality. Usually, the females in Li nationality start to tattoo at the age about 12 to 16 years old, rare of them start from 8 to 10 years old, but whenever the time of starting, the whole pattern will have been finished before her marriage. Because of the changes and development of social aesthetic, nowadays, the young generation toward tattoo has changed so much, the process of tattooing is painful, and it will also impact females' physical development, after the founding of the PRC, this custom has been abolished strictly. Today, young generation in Li nationality do not have tattoo anymore, but the seniors who has tattoo will become the past, due to that, after several decades, we may only see this special culture in the history pictures and books.

Hundred Years of Old Granaries

Fire prevention is the key to thatched cottages' safety. At the entrance of the village, there are some granaries existed over hundred years. Granary is used to stored grains and cereals, it usually is built outside of the entrance. It is mainly for preventing conflagration, and also anti-thief, because Li nationality people are simple and honest, if you lived here, you lost your wallet and no one will take it, you do not need to lock the door when you fall asleep, because there are no thief at all. You can count how many granaries here, then you know the number of residents live in the village. In order to exhibit the wealth and high position of the leader. Village head has more granaries than ordinary villagers, he will possess about three to five granaries. They are respectively used to store rice, upland rice, corn and other grains. Granaries are used to separate in three types: mud granary, bamboo granary and most extravagant wooden granary. The wooden granary is the most stable one among these three types, and it is also good at moisture resistance, at the same time it expresses the conscientiousness, wealth and high social position.

Warm prompt: taking photos in the granaries are not allowed; please do not litter rubbish around; for the sake of your safety, do not imitate the actor to climb the trees, and one of the most important things is "Fire prevention".

Village head stone

The Village Head Stone in the center of the village entrance is the symbol of Li village and also the stand for power. The cave on the stone is generally formed naturally, and the size indicates the scale of the village. Every time when there is a huge celebration, sacrifice and other activities in the village, the leader will ring the frog Gong, convene villagers together. If holding huge sacrifice activity like 'AOYA', ceremony will be hold before this stone.

There is a hieroglyph character on the stone, it seems like a woman is holding a baby in her arms, it is the character called Xiao in China, it means filial piety, it is the largest kindness in Chinese culture, Li people also pay great attention to it, show respect and obedience to the seniors in family, so you can see in our village seniors have a long lifespan with a happy life.

Traditional Bamboo Weaving Technique in Li Nationality

The traditional bamboo weaving technique was originated in Tang dynasty, and thriving until today. In the feudal time it was regarded as tribute to the empire, now it has already listed in Hainan intangible culture heritage. The main ingredients to make it include red and white veins, its veins products have developed into more than 100 varieties, mainly for export to the United States, Italy, Spain and more than a dozen countries. Bamboo weaving is one of the traditional craft techniques in Li nationality, it is almost prevalent in Li people's families. Its bamboo products are delicate, unique, practical and exquisite crafts. It occupies a very crucial position in daily necessities of Li nationality.

Wooden and Bamboo Instruments in Li Nationality

Instruments made by wooden and bamboo in Li nationality are the treasure in China national music treasure-house, it was selected in one of the second batch of national intangible culture heritage projects list.

Bamboo and wood instruments, such as the nose flute, the mouth bow, beeda and so on, have bright national characteristics. They are not only unique in China, but also precious and rare among international instruments. The compositions of bamboo, wooden instruments are also adequate, but each instrument has its special characteristics, paired with beautiful and clear strings and heavy wooden drums, they evolve into wonderful pieces of music.

Music played by bamboo and wooden instruments contain the original music characteristics. The structure of the music is flexible and free, the melody is smooth, and the tone is simple and pure. It integrates the traditional culture, aesthetic awareness, folk customs with many other elements of the Li nationality which is favored by indigenous people.

Ceramic Museum

In daily labor and production, males and females in Li nationality have specific work division. For example, hunting is the job for male, and it also has a stereotype that females cannot touch the shotguns (if she touches, the men will not hunt successfully). And pottery makes are women's job, when women are working, males are prohibited to approach, (if he touches the tools, the pottery will face a failure, or the products are nondurable). Since the matriarchal society, indigenous people had already mastered the techniques of pottery making. The techniques are apart from: mud pasted method and mud disk method, after these procedures, the semi-manufactures will be burned in the open air, the temperature is about 800℃ , so the final hardness of pottery is not too tough, and also without colorful glaze. It can be said that potteries from Han nationality prone to aesthetic, while potteries made by Li nationality are more practical. Today, pottery making technique of Li nationality has been listed as one of the national intangible cultural heritage protection projects.

A Large-Scale Real-Life Performance of Li and Miao Culture — Areca Ancient Rhyme

Dear friends, in next activity we will arrive to the large-scale real-life performance of li and Miao culture — Areca Ancient Rhyme, in here you can not only appreciate an unique and distinguished feature of original Li and Miao song and dance, but also can feel the dense local customs and folk practices of Areca valley. Areca ancient rhyme was a large-scale real-life performance of Li Miao culture which composed by one of the most notable composers in Hainan called Moke, directed by Herong Su both from Li nationality. The program includes: Drill wood to make fire, weaving Li brocades, fabricating, baikoupani love duet, striking rice, Li traditional garments and firewood dance. Cordial and hospitable Li people has prepared for us an abundant culture banquet, I believe it will bring you a big shock both from visual and affection.

Boloog Family

Boloog family is a restaurant themed Li and Miao delicious food, operated by scenic spot in China first, not only with unique indigenous architectural styles and cozy environment, but also can let tourists experience the folk characteristics and customs. Boloog restaurant advocates the ideal of long lifespan and healthy diet, persists in green catering in original ecology, and has a 5 Stars service team, it can be called distinguished brand of Li and Miao ethnic restaurant.

Boloog family has original and mysterious totems of Li nationality in order, gentle light with ingenuity design make boloog family pervade in strong cultural atmosphere. The restaurant has 5 independent compartments with different decoration styles and equips a large banquet hell which can contain more than one thousand people, setting in this comfortable and graceful environment, we can taste exquisite and unforgettable dishes and enjoy high-quality personal customized services. In order to provide better enjoyment to our guests, restaurant settles a Leisure Corridor especially which you can have a feast, tea, then overlook the splendid scenes under the mountain and feel the cozy breeze in hillside, what a lovely and picturesque life we have!

The dishes of boloog family are also above the standard, Five-finger mountain cattle full cattle course dinner, Dongshan sheep full cattle course dinner, five-foot pig full cattle course dinner and other popular signs full cattle course dinner. With the excellent cooking skill of the chef, the dishes are unique and memorable, besides these classical dishes, boloog family will continually upgrade and innovate new creative dishes. Among these different set of meals, dustpan meal and long table banquet are their representative, the restaurant aims to constantly pursue delicacy in the realm of eating, create an international brand which represents Li and Miao food culture in China.

Your Suggestions

My friends! The whole journey of Betel nut valley will be finished soon, we hope you can give us some precious comments and suggestions. Please tell us your dissatisfaction, your satisfaction is the purpose of our service.

Farewell Speech

Ladies and gentlemen, my dear friends, the pleasant time elapse so fast. First of all, I am very appreciated for your trust and cooperation during the sightseeing in Betel nut Valley, We visited this dream-like place to experience the mystery of

Hainan aboriginal cultures, I believe you are as intoxicated as me, I wish you are as happy as I am, before we end this trip, let me bless you with my best wishes. I wish you have a happy life, and everything goes well in your work. I also welcome you to visit here again, and I can be your guide once more, wish you have a very pleasant journey.

6. Wuzhizhou Island

Dear visitors and friends, nice to meet you! Welcome to fantastic Wuzhizhou Island, I'm Zhang Chao, the guide of this tour, and you can call me Xiao Zhang. The scenic spot we are about to visit is Wuzhizhou Island.

Wuzhizhou Island is located on the national coast of Sanya City, Hainan Province, China — Haitang Bay, also known as Lover Island. When viewed from above, it forms a natural heart shape, Like a brilliant star blooming on the coast of the South China Sea, it is the first island tourism and vacation destination in China that combines sea entertainment, specialty diving, high-end hotels, food and beverage, and leisure sightseeing.

There are over 2,700 native plants on the island, with a vegetation coverage rate of over 90%; The maximum visibility of seawater can reach 27 meters; The surrounding waters are rich in coral species and have a high coverage of live corals; Located at the golden latitude of the world's tourist destination — the magical 18 degrees north latitude, with a pleasant tropical ocean monsoon climate, allowing the mind and body to reside poetically here.

Wuzhizhou Island has unique natural conditions and has introduced internationally advanced marine entertainment equipment, creating a new benchmark for one-stop and all-round island tourism. Its series of high-end products such as diving, parachuting, motorboats, dynamic airships, and sea and sky dancing take you up to the sky and into the sea, enjoying the colorful coral and fish surround, admiring the unity of the sea and sky, releasing your speed and passion, and embarking on an adrenaline filled island journey!

Next, let's share some safety precautions together. There are only two sentences, which are very important. Everyone should listen carefully! Due to the narrow roundabout road, please hold onto the handrails while driving, and do not protrude any part of your body from the vehicle to avoid sparks of love from colliding with rocks on the roadside. Our scenic area is non-smoking, please do not smoke. Civilized tourism relies on everyone, and ecological protection relies on everyone!

Our island tour this time is 5.7 kilometers, the onboard time is about 30 minutes, and the time for getting off and playing is controlled by everyone. For a regular island tour around the island, please keep your ticket safe. You can get off at the station for unlimited time and transfer with your ticket. The island tour does not take any turning back throughout, and the final destination is at the starting dock.

Reef Resort

Now we are entering the reef resort under the closed management. Beauty tours all the way, and the stones in the gallery, only tourist coaches are allowed to enter this route, tourists are not allowed to walk. There are two reasons for stopping walking, one is for your safety, if everyone walks to here, there must have some people who will climb the stones to take pictures or go to the reef to catch fish and crab. The stones here are very slippery and dangerous because they have been battered by waves for thousands of year. Another is for environmental protection, the natural scenery will be destroyed if there are people come in.

Air-sea-land all-round explanation

Dear visitors and friends, if you want to know more about interesting project and beautiful scenery in Wuzhizhou Island, we can have a deep understanding through three aspects " sea, land, air". First of all, let's look at the interesting project in the sea. The coral reef diving area is on our right-hand side, it is a national coral reserve. The scenery underwater is rich, and you will be guided by our professional coach to dive 3-8 meter depth underwater. It takes 580 yuan one person, and there also have diving projects at other prices, you can go to the tourist center to consult details. As a tropical island, Wuzhizhou Island is also very rich in cultural resources. For example, sea view corridor, fish view platform, rock-viewing, Mazu Temple, golden turtle sea-watching, lover's bridge, life well, etc., I believe these cultural relics will let you have a more primitive, quiet, romantic leisure experience. Then I will solemnly introduce the amusing activities in the air. This is also called "flying trapeze". It's an activity for you to experience the same feeling of flying as the hero, which has no bondage at all. It's also a super excellent opportunity for you to challenge and transcend yourself. "Flying Trapeze" uses the recoil power of the water jet on your feet to lift you to the air above the water. In addition, it's equipped with a manual control nozzle to stabilize the air flight attitude. It can let you dive under the bottom, and jump out of the water like a dolphin, arousing layers of spray! Others say that his movements are as exciting as Iron Man! The huge impetus generated by the jet device can generate 100 horsepower and lift your rise to nearly 10 meters for a new view of the coast above everything else!

Wild pineapple

Please look at the prickly plants on our left-hand side, is there anyone who know this? This is pineapple's cousin—wild pineapple. Although it taste worse than pineapple, all parts of the wild pineapple are valuable, it also can be used as medicine. I will mainly introduce three functions: firstly, its root can be medicinal, clearing and detoxifying effect, it can be used for the treatment of cold and fever. Secondly, its leaves grow in rotation so we call it Shi lai yun zhuan. It's especially fragrant to use its leaves to make Zongzi. Thirdly, its seed can be made into "Collection of blood lotus bodhi", it has a reputation of "Bodhi queen". Drop of the lotus have the function of health care and prevent and cure diseases. It is also one of three magical plants on our island.

Mudskipper

Dear visitors, please look at the jumping fish on the reef which are black and looked like loach, its scientific name is also called mudskipper. Do you know a TV program called A Bite of China? The second episode is about the recipe of making mudskipper. The recipe is various, steamed in clear soup and soon, spiced salt, fried with pepper and stew in clear soup and soon. Once the program was broadcast, it attracted a lot of gastronomes' attentions. It also caused the price of mudskipper rise continually. Some of the upscale hotels even sell the mudskipper at 168 yuan per catty. Why is it so expensive? The reason is that the mudskipper has high nutritional value of health care and therapeutic efficacy. It is more nutritious than sea cucumber, lobster and other valuable aquatic products. It is also known as the "ginseng in water", it can proceed blood cycle and has nourishing aphrodisiac. As for women, eating mudskipper has an effect of beautifying the skin.

Stone crab

There are a lot of stone crabs, their bodies have the camouflage which is similar to the stones. They eat the moss on the stone as their food. The stone cab's shell is more and meat is less, so we usually use it to boil soup, it tastes fresh. So far, there are three kinds of crabs on our island: ganoderma lucidum crab (Lingzhi crab), sand crab and stone crab. Lingzhi crab is systemic palm red, live in the jungle, have high medicinal value, they are very rare. The sand crabs are crystal clear on the beach, look like lovely crystals. However, they change their color immediately when they are in the sun.

Tropical rainforest (Natural oxygen bar)

We are going into tropical rainforest on this island. There are more than 2,000 kinds of plants on the island, and there are more than 1,700 kinds of tropical plants. The forest coverage is over 90 percent, the air is pretty high on oxygen, up to 4,000 negative oxygen ions per cubic meter. Negative oxygen ion is known as "air vitamin" it can improve heart function and has an obvious effect on lowering blood pressure. It can also lower blood lipids and blood glucose, increase calcium content. So it can prevent osteoporosis efficiently.

Guanri Rock (Sun Rock)

Dear visitors, the sun rock is just ahead. Standing on the rock, you can feel the sea wind and overlook, there is a superb panorama of the vast South China Sea.

Then we can sum up the scene in a poem: The sun bathed in the sea breeze, the waves surging heavily. The eagle soars in the sky, and the sky meet the earth! You can find a huge stone if you look down from the Guanri Rock, this stone looks like a "huge turtle" creeping into the sea slowly. It is also called "golden turtle plumped the sea" because the sunshine makes the "huge turtle" become nimble.

Dragon blood tree

Please look at the tree with pungent leaves grow to the sky on your right-hand side, it is dragon blood tree. Why is it called dragon blood tree? It's because when the tree gets hurt, it will came out a dark red fluid like the legendary "dragon blood", so we call it "dragon blood tree". It is also called the "panda of the plants", it has high medical value. It has a magical role of promoting blood circulation and help to alleviate the pain and swelling. It's also the important element of Yunan Baiyao. The older the dragon tree is, the emptier the stems are.

Wangfu Stone

Please look at the strange square stone on the hillside above your right that juts out to face the mountain, it is called "Wangfu Stone". It looks like a pregnant woman, touching her belly, looking towards the sea and waiting for her husband to come home. The Wang of Wangfu Stone is the homophonic of prosperous in Chinese, and wish you all have prosperity, wealth and everything goes well.

Stone of South China Sea

Please look at the special flat stone wall on the left, there are two big characters written on it: Nanhai, and of course, they can be seen as Hainan. It means that looking at the South China Sea in Hainan. The stone wall that we have seen before is very smoothly, it is as smooth as if someone has cut it with a sword. Therefore, it is also called "Jianpi stone".

Feilai Stone

Please look up and take a look at this stone hanging on the hillside which is called flying stone. Although our island experiences many typhoons every year, the Feilai stone is still. It just like a patron saint, blessing the peace of here. Geologists believe that Feilai stone is formed in the process of geological changes. It is the nature of the uncanny workmanship.

Yunhai Villa

In our left hand above are hotel guest rooms of Yunhai villa on the island. There have single rooms and suites and the range of prices is from 1,000 to over 4,000.

Linhai Log Cabin

On the right hand side, the wooden corridor is the promenade of the island. It's excellent to take photos here, especially the wedding photos. On the upper left is the island hotel facing the sea cabins, there are 6 Linhai cabins in total and each design is very luxurious. Every suite equipped with a pool with fresh water and the price is about 2,000 yuan per night.

Daozhu Villa

The set on the left in the middle is the Daozhu villa of our island, the luxury villas are on the both sides. Daozhu villa is equivalent to the hotel's presidential suite. It is also open to the public and the price is 18,800 yuan per night. There are two luxurious villas on left and right sides and the prices are 5,000 yuan per night.

Inner Area

This is the end of our tour of the outer area. And now let's turn to the inner area. Inside the inner area are mainly some artificial scenes and spectacular natural scenery like just now is lost here. This is also belongs to the part of the central leisure resort, with guest rooms and restaurants.

On the right side is a private customized movie location, and the swimming pool is open to the public for free. There is a leisure bar next to the swimming pool called "Pirate Bar", which offers a variety of drinks, barbecues, and more to choose from. On the left is an animal paradise and there are some peacocks, doves of peace, guinea fowl and other tropical birds. In addition, there are also some lovely sika deer. The hillside on the right was dotted with some of the larger wooden houses and those are the seascape wooden ceiling rooms on the island. There are 16 buildings, each has two floors. They use tatami style design and are equipped with a fresh water pool. The price of each floor is 1,350 yuan per night. Coming down the hill ahead is the teahouse and it is the rest zone where includes Gaiwan tea that the deluxe package tour around the island covers. We can taste the tea, watch the crosstalk and have a rest here. In addition, there are free coconut, melon seeds, popcorn and other snacks for you. OK, here comes the teahouse. Please pay attention to your safety when you get off the bus. You can transfer the bus by ticket. Have fun, everyone!

Please look at the leaves that look like hearts at the bottom of our right hand, the botanical name of this plant is the sea taro. People in the north part of China call it Drip guanyin and it can absorb the oxygen pond to purify the air.

On the right is the summer wharf on our island. The wharf we land on is the winter wharf. These two wharfs are used alternately according to the season, wind direction, wave size and tidal relationship. On the right side is the Lover bridge, it's based on a chain bridge. Since the bridge is not safe because of its rickety structure, we changed it to wooden for safety. The sand on our island is mainly coral sand. Look, is the sand on the beach especially white and exquisite? The sand was made of powder that had fallen from coral rock on the seafloor, so it looked extremely white and delicate. The jade green plants on the right are called Scaevola taccada. You see that its roots are bulky, and it can have the effect of moisture, sand-fixation. They form Bonsai state through the artificial pruning naturally, and they are green all year round. This is the only swimming and bathing area on the island, and swimming on the island is confined to the area enclosed by the float ball. In addition, there are beach chairs, sun umbrella swimming rings for renting and children's paradise diluted water locker room. Ahead is the terminal wharf, it is also means that our trip around the island is about to end. Please wait till the bus stop then get off, don't hurry and don't jump out of the bus. Please check your belongings to avoid leaving them on the bus. I hope that the beautiful Wuzhizhou Island has left a wonderful impression on you, and I'm also looking forward you to come next time!

7. Tianya Haijiao

Dear tourists and friends, welcome to Tianya Haijao, which is also known as Tianya Haijiao. May you all have good luck and love!

I'm Xiao Wang, your tour guide. Today I'm very glad to have the opportunity to accompany you guys to appreciate, seek and feel this magical land, Tianya Haijiao, which is full of Chinese emotions and bring you good luck. I hope my explanation can add wonderful enjoyment to your journey in Hainan and leave you an unforgettable memory.

When we mention the name Tianya Haijiao, I believe everybody has been know this name for a long time. Actually, this name is an idiom coming from a poem whose name is Emperor Wu made a heroic letter with the Lingnan chieftain in the last dynasty of the southern and northern dynasties in Chinese history. The poem said that the world is wide, you and I meet speechless, but our hearts is always together. Sanya was called Yazhou in ancient times. The Chinese characters, Ya, it means the end of the land, south of Ya is the end of the world.

And now our journey has officially begun, let's uncover the mysteries of Tianya Haijiao. During the tour, if you have any need, you can contact me at any time, I will try my best to provide you an unforgettable trip with the best service.

The bag deposit services are available in the tourist center and in the five-star toilets. If necessary, you can deposit all your luggage except valuables there, and then we can have a relaxing trip.

Sanya is a tropical coastal city. The sunshine here is as warm as the people here. Ha-ha, just a joke. During the tour, please take good precautions against sunburn. Besides, there are many rocks along the coast. After years of seawater erosion, the rocks were covered with a variety of sharply shells. Considering everyone's safety, please do not climb the rocks.

Tianya cultural origin

Ok, everybody, who can tell me where you learned about Tianya Haijiao? (Tour guides interact with tourists with idioms, ancient poetry, "please come to the Tianya Haijiao" songs, media publicity, etc.)

So everyone has different ways learning about Tianya Haijiao, in your opinion, what kind of tourist it is? Maybe everyone is seeking your own "Tianya in your mind". Today, we are gathered here by destiny, let's take a walk and feel this magic land.

Tianya haijiao has rich and profound historical and cultural connotations and emotions. It has that kind of friendship, "long distance separates no bosom friends" (written by Tang dynasty poet Wang Bo). It has that kind of affection, "Arises above the sea is a bright moon, shared by all of us near or far, and brought us all together at this very moment" (written by Tang dynasty prime minister Zhang Jiuling). It has that kind of eternal love, "love you till the end of time, and the heart will never change." It has that kind of drifting sigh, "both of us in misfortune go from shore to shore, meeting now, need we have known each other before" (written by Tang dynasty poet Bai Juyi)? It also has that kind of warm invitation from our hearts, "please come to the Tianya Haijiao, where spring is always here". For thousands of years, the strong emotions of the literati, the memorial in people's hearts and so on, have enriched the meaning of this place. With such profound cultural origins, "Tianya Haijiao resort" has become the window and carrier of Tianya culture from a frontier beach. If the Great Wall of China is made of bricks, the Tianya Haijiao is made of emotions. And we also regard it as the Great Wall of emotion. So the back of the fourth set of 1 yuan (rmb) is the Great Wall, and the back of 2 yuan (rmb) is the pillar of the south sky in Tianya Haijiao.

Good luck Tianya landscape avenue

This road is called "good luck Tianya landscape avenue". This road facing the sea, is spacious and flat, just like everyone's smooth love and career in the future. As I said, everyone has his\her own "imagination to the Tianya Haijiao". With the change of time and space, nowadays tourism in the Tianya Haijiao has been a fashionable travel, a symbol of happiness and good luck, a good place to release the mood, and the holy land expressing romantic love. Looking forward, there are clear sky and blue sea. Such beautiful scenery indicates our life is full of good vision.

Tianya Haijiao railway station

Looking to the left, you can see a railway sign that says Tongjing — Maling. This place used to be the landing place for the standard railway rebuilt after liberation. The front narrow-gauge railway was left when the Japanese invaded Hainan Island. During the war of resistance against Japanese aggression, the Japanese stole a lot of rich iron ore from Shilu (now Changjiang city) and used this railway line to transport it from Changjiang in the west of Hainan Island to Sanya port in the south, and then shipped it back to Japan for smelting steel and making guns. This railway is proof of Japan's occupation of our land and theft of our resources. After the victory of the war of resistance against Japanese aggression, this railway became the only major transportation trunk line in the south of Hainan Island, which made indelible contributions to the construction of Hainan Island. This railway has a history of nearly one hundred years.

Square of Tianya Haijiao

The square where we are now is Tianya Haijiao square. Statues of two generals who is riding a horse, holding a gold spear and facing to the south China sea stand on each side of the square. Behind them stood a diamond-shaped copper column, a symbol of triumph. The left statue is Lu Bode, and the other one is Ma Yuan. They were all famous Fubo general who is fighting against sea in the Han dynasty.

Lu Bode was a native of Pingzhou in the west Han dynasty. In 110 BC, the king of Nanyue rebelled. Emperor Wudi of Han ordered Lu Bode to be general Fubo. He led the army to put down the rebellion. He won easily because the locals directly surrendered when they heard his name. After the ground was pacified, nine prefectures were set up in Lingnan. Zhuya and Daner, two of the nine prefectures, are on Hainan island. This is the earliest administrative system recorded in Hainan, and from then on, Hainan island has been a part of China. His descendants built Fubo temple as a memorial.

Statue of Ma Yuan

Ma Yuan, a native of Maoling in the west Han dynasty, was a famous militarist. In AD 41, the two sisters of Vietnam, Zheng Ce and Zheng Er, because of dissatisfaction with the tyranny of the local magistrate, rebelled and became the king. Emperor Guangwudi appointed Ma Yuan general of Fubo to march south to Vietnam and cast copper pillars as the southernmost border of the Han dynasty. His spirit of dying in the battlefield and youth was admired by posterity. Many historical sites related to Ma Yuan have been left in Hainan. Danzhou baima well, one of them, is said to be famous for its white horse kicking sand out of a spring. Each dynasty in hainan built a temple to commemorate the Ma Yuan general.

Both generals were responsible for pacifying China's southern border and developing Hainan Island. The animal at the top of the pillar behind them is the rosefinch in the I ching representing the patron saint of the south of China, whose meaning is protecting our land.

Riyueshi

Looking at the sea in front of you, we can see there are two cross and standing stone in the sea, carved Ri, Yue two words meaning sun and moon. The two words were inscribed by Fan Jingyi, former editor-in-chief of the People's Daily. These two stones form the shape of the heart. There are many beautiful and touching love stories around these two stones, so we also called them "love stones". In the 1986 version of the TV series journey to the west, the scene in which the Monkey King emerged from a crack in a stone was shot here.

The star of Tianya Haijiao

Please look back, the sculpture in the center of the square is called the "star of Tianya Haijiao". On the night of June 3rd, 1997, astronomers at the national astronomical observatories Hebei Xinglong observation base discovered an asteroid with the temporary number 1997LK. On July 14th, 2002, the international minor planet center officially granted the planet a permanent official number of 9,668. In November 2006, with the approval of the international astronomical union committee for small object nomenclature, the national astronomical observatory officially named the asteroid with the "star of Tianya Haijiao". In 2008, the "star of Tianya Haijiao" memorial sculpture was erected here. The creator is Jiang Zhiqiang, a professor at Xiamen University. The sculpture uses the image features of the armillary sphere, an ancient astronomical instrument, and the equatorial theodolite, and incorporates astronomical elements. The 24 toads around it represent the 24 solar terms of China.

On November 6th, 2008, the Beijing Olympic Games gymnastics all-around champion Yang Wei and Yang Yun held a sensational, national, and romantic wedding here. On the left and right sides of the square, there are two stone carvings. The left side one is engraved with the word of love, and the other one is the love declaration of Yang Wei and Yang Yun, which engraved with the word "love to Tianya Haijao, love each other forever". The stone carvings, which surround the Tianya Haijiao star in the center of the square, echo the heart-shaped "love stone" on the sea, represent the meaning of a long life together and everyone can share the same moon.

The annual TIanya Haijiao international wedding day attracts countless lovers. For the beginning of a new life, for a promise that love will last forever, for an agreement that their heart will never change, they came to the beautiful Tianya Haijiao hand in hand, the most romantic place in China, to hold the weddings, letting this long love story last forever. Since 1996, Tianya Haijiao international wedding day has been held on December 12 every year. It has been held for 25 consecutive years, attracting a large number of Chinese and foreign couples.

There have been many large events held in Tianya Haijiao square, such as, Tianya Haijiao Mid-Autumn festival, closing ceremony of hainan island festival and the first world tai chi health conference. There also have been host many internationally influential activities, such as the 53rd miss world final, the new silk road model contest, the 2008 Beijing Olympic torch relay at Tianya Haijiao station, and the Fengwu Tianya celebration party.

The relief of Sanya people

The man-made relief in front of us shows the primitive life scene of Sanya people more than eleven thousand years ago. We can see these people are hunting, fishing, gathering, farming and religion. In 1992 and 1993, archaeological experts found human activity relics after two excavations in Luobidong road in Sanya, which is by far the most southerly site of paleolithic culture in China. The Chinese academy of sciences has named these earliest inhabitants of the Sanya area "Sanya people". To commemorate the important archaeological discovery of "Sanya people", the artist created the relief under the theme of "Sanya people".

Tianya Haijiao stone scenery

Tianya Haijiao scenic spot has a 2 km long coastline, the coastline is relatively straight. The boulders piled up along the coastline, the sand is white and the beach is wide. The megaliths were formed during crustal movements more than 100 million years ago, roughly the same time as the formation of Hainan island. The scenic area is surrounded by mountains and sea. The remaining veins of the Xiamaling mountains extend into the sea. After the granite mountain is stripped, due to the external forces such as waves, sunshine, wind erosion, and its own vertical joint development, the mountain eventually broke and scattered into many large pieces of rock scattered on the beach. These boulders are of various shapes, majestic and spectacular, with large and small pits, which is a typical phenomenon of Marine erosion. The extraordinary workmanship of nature makes us marvel and gives us rich imagination space.

Wonders of tropical rainforest

Everyone must have a deep feeling for the sunshine in Hainan. But we immediately feel cool and comfortable as we enter the shade from the sun-baked open air. The cool place we are now is the tropical rainforest biome. This scenic spot is built on the basis of wild tropical vegetation through plant dressing and transplantation. By building artificial streams, a microclimate with moderate humidity and temperature is created and become the miniature of Hainan's tropical rainforest landscape. In particular, the unique parasitic plant "Asplenium nidus" in the tropical rain forest was planted, adding more tropical rain forest landscape characteristics. This place is full of ancient trees, intertwined with vines, and flowing with small bridges, which makes people feel relaxed and happy and easily forget to return. This stream is called "Hainabaichuan" (all rivers run into sea). At the end of the rainforest, there is also a "safe bridge", which means everyone has a safe journey. Walking along this road, you will feel cool and see the bright and dark scenery. Here you can touch the most primitive wild plants, breathe the freshest air, release the most real feelings through the forest plank road, and experience the beautiful mood of being home to all. (There are also plants such as bauhinia and turtle bamboo, which can be introduced when passing by)

Coastal cliff stone carvings group

Please Look at this coast, the sand here is soft and the tide is flat. Those boulders 200 meters away from here are the famous pillars of the southern sky. Do you have a familiar feeling? The landscape here is the pattern behind the fourth set of RMB two yuan. The big black stone in the distance is the stone with the inscription of "Tianya" that we are looking forward to, and the stone with the inscription "Haijiao" is at its right rear. Let's take off our shoes and walk on the beach and the sea towards Tianya Haijao.

Actually, this kind of coast is technically called sandstone alternating coast. Are you a little strange that all these granites are round? That's because they have been here for hundreds of millions of years, under the sun exposure, the erosion of wind and rain and the impact of waves, after the physical action of heat expansion and cold contraction, finally formed this granite landscape. But for hundreds of millions of years they have not been lonely, accompanied by the waves and the plants. As you can see, a banyan tree grows out of the stone, this tenacious vitality is just like us, no matter how bad the environment, as long as there is a glimmer of life, we can survive and develop tenaciously.

Haipan Nantian stone carving

The first thing we can see is the stone carving in the south of the sea. By the way, do you know which one is the earliest cliff carving in Tianya Haijiao tourist area? It is not the stone with Tianya, not the stone with Haijiao, not the pillars of the southern sky. It is the stone in front of us, which named Haipan Nantian. The stone in front of it looks like a roof. You can see clearly that its edges and corners are very clear, smooth and even, showing the traces of artificial carving. It is different from other natural stones in the scenic area.

Actually, the earliest Tianya Haijiao was not here. During the Song and Yuan dynasties, people defined Tianya Haijiao in the "Tianya pavilion" in Qinzhou, Guangdong province and the "Haijiao pavilion" in Hepu Lianzhou. At that time, people thought that South China Sea corresponds to South China Sky, which refers to the sun's moving area, or the south of the Tropic of cancer.

Emperor Kangxi of the Qing Dynasty redefined the boundary of the southern sky according to the Confucian classics book, Shangshu. According to the research, it is found that the Haipan Nantian stone carving was a sign of latitude measurement left in the first national mapping activity in the history of China during the reign of Kangxi in the Qing Dynasty. In 1714, Emperor Kangxi appointed Miao Shou and Chu Erdai, ministers of the Qing Dynasty , and Tang Shangxian, an emissary of emperor Louis XIV of France, as three imperial envoys to preside over the surveying and mapping, and carved the four characters of "Haipan Nantian" on the stone. "hai" is refer to the South China Sea, and "pan" means divide. "Haipan Nantian" means this stone divides the South China Sea into South Sea and South Sky. As we all know, China is known as the holy land of chixian County, and the meaning of "Haipan Nantian" is exactly the dividing line between heaven and earth in China's territory. The south is Chixian County, and the north is Shenzhou.

Actually, "tianya" is refer to the south sky of here. Every year at 12 o'clock in the middle of the winter solstice, the sun will coincide with the half lying stone. Looking at this scenery, do you have the feeling that I will never change myself as time goes by. This stone carving is the earliest one in our scenic area, which has a history of more than 200 years. In 2012, the stone carving was recognized as the remains of China's astrogeodesy during the Kangxi period by the Chinese Academy of Science, the National Astronomical Observatory and other three units. It is the only remains of this astrogeodesy. According to research, these four characters are probably written by Kangxi himself.

Shen Peng's Inscription Stone Carvings

In May 1996, Shen Peng, the famous calligrapher of China and chairman of Chinese Calligrapher Association, visited the Tianya Haijiao tourist area again, and felt the magnificent view. He was invited to write an impromptu poem and carve it here. "Thousands of waves hit the boulders by the sea. From a distance, it looks like a white fairy standing there. Looking at the red font engraved on the first pillar of southern sky, it makes people feel excited." The cursive works lively and image. Shen Peng has created more than 15,000 pieces of calligraphy. His works are not only collected in important places such as the great hall of the people, but also engraved in scenic spots all over the country and widely spread abroad.

A pillar stone in southern sky

Please Look at the towering cone-shaped strange stone in front of you, this is the stone of a pillar in the southern sky. It is about 7 meters high. From the side, it looks like two mast sail rising from an ancient ship. From the front, it looks like a god pillar standing here, as if it is saying let the waves wash away and I will always stand here. According to historical records in 1911, Fan Yunti, the governor of Yazhou, often came back and forth here, because he often checked the people's situation, He saw that the stone was so upright that he made a vow of one day as an official, one life for the people. Later, he arranged people to engrave the four characters of Nantian Yizhu on the stone, in order to pray for smooth governance, national security and abundant food. So the pillar stone in southern sky has a history of hundreds of years.

In 1909, Fan Yunti transferred to the governor of Yazhou. It is said that he posted a pair of couplets written by himself in the Yamen of the state city: The couplets are as long as I am an official, I will do my best for the people, be strict with myself, enforce the law selflessly, and regard the government as my home, and everything has to discuss, don't come here because of lawsuits.

In 1910, Fan Yunti carved a couplet in the capital of Yazhou. The first one is: "there is so beautiful rivers and mountains, which are just called the south of heaven polar region. In the future, we can see that the civilized atmosphere is actually always on the sea." The inscription time is "Autumn Moon in the second year of Xuantong", and the signature is "Fan Yunti, Yongan, Zhili Prefecture, Quanya Prefecture." Another pair of pictures only has the following couplet: "I dare not do the two things of torture and greed. The gods can see my loyalty." In 2009, when Shen Peng, a famous contemporary calligrapher and consultant of the Chinese couplet association, revisited the Tianya Haijiao, he learned about it and wrote a new couplet for it. The new couplet is "There is no fear in gain or loss. Why do I need to do something insidious and cunning? I dare not do the two things of torture and greed. The gods can see my loyalty."

In fact, the scene of "one pillar in the southern sky" has been integrated into every day of our national life. Do you find that the back pattern of the fourth set of "two yuan RMB" issued in 1980 and 1990 is the "one pillar in the southern sky" in front of you. We all know that the fourth set of one yuan back painting is the "Great Wall", two yuan is "one pillar in the southern sky", five yuan back is "Wuxia of the Yangtze River", and ten yuan back painting is "Mount Everest". Therefore, RMB is called "national card". And that means "one pillar in the southern sky" can be compared with the Great Wall, Wuxia of the Yangtze River and Mount Everest. Stone is a symbol of wealth and good luck. As the saying goes, "if you touch a stone, you will have plenty of food and clothing. If you clap a stone, you will get into ten. If you hold a stone, you will get rich." Take a picture or hug with this stone as soon as you can. It will bring you "fortune."

Tianya stone

Please Look at the boulder in the distance. It's the famous "Tianya" stone. It's the sign and symbol of the scenic spot. This stone is 10.8 meters high, with the circumference of about 66 meters. It's surrounded by mountains and rivers. It's square in the center of the circle and round in the center of the square. Facing the East, it's stable in all directions. It has a history of hundreds of millions of years.

In 1727, Cheng Zhe, governor of Yazhou, inadvertently wrote the word "tianya" on a boulder to redefine the boundaries of "tianya". Interestingly, the Tianya pavilion in Qinzhou was built by Tao Bi, the governor of qinzhou during the qingli period of the northern song dynasty (1041—1048). Who would have thought that the "Tianya" written by this little sesame official has set the Tianya in the history of China forever.

Wisdom stone

After seeing the "Tianya" stone, please follow me to see this huge stone. The stone is formed by the long-term scouring of waves. The texture on the stone is very similar to that of human brain. There is a small tree on the stone, like the ornament on the head of a woman. People often joke that busy streets do not grow grass, smart heads do not grow hair.

Attention, please. Progress stone has no safety facilities. So it is not allowed to climb. If you are pursuing progress, please just take a photo with wisdom stone!

Haijiao stone

There are huge granites standing by the sea. You can see a group of towering rocks when you go inside. Those rocks look like natural copper walls and iron walls standing on the South China Sea in the distance, just like the inscription of General Secretary Jiang Zemin when he came to Tianya Haijiao for the third time on December 22, 2000: "let wind and waves rise and fall, I am still here." On the top of the steeple is inscribed the word "Haijiao", which corresponds to the word "Tianya", forming a complete Tianya Haijiao.

In October 1938, after the fall of Guangzhou, Wang Yi, the general of the Kuomintang, was appointed as the commander of QiongYa garrison headquarters to take charge of the defense of QiongYa. On January 8th, 1939, the mobilization meeting of the six thousand li people for the national disaster was held in Maling, now Tianya town. Wang Yi gave a lecture to the li people and called on them to unite to fight against Japan. After that, Wang Yi came to Xiamaling seaside and carved "Haijiao" on the stone. On May 10th, 1939, general Wang Yi led his men to the bank of the Banpo river in Heping town, Qiongzhong county. To encourage his morale, the general fondly carved the words "only war can survive" on a stone by the river. The two stone carvings were signed "Wang Yi."

Among the rocks on the back of the rock is a fort built by Japanese troops after they occupied Hainan Island, a historical witness to Japan's invasion of China.

Standing here, everyone looks up to the mountain. The building on the mountain is the southern lighting platform of the 11th Asian games in 1990. On August 23rd, 1990, the southern Asian games torch lighting ceremony was held here. The Chinese beacon tower (hall of love), which echoes the theme of love in our scenic spot, is under construction and will be one of the places where couples pledge their love in the future.

Just now we saw the wonders of stone trees on Tianya road. From another angle, can you feel the tenacious vitality of small trees from the beach.

Concluding remarks

In the early 1980s, a song "please come to the Tianya Haijiao" made the Tianya Haijiao a yearning in the hearts of hundreds of millions of Chinese descendants. Nowadays, every year millions of Chinese and foreign tourists come to this holy land built up by Chinese talents and feelings. I believe that today's tour has let you really appreciate the unique charm of the Tianya Haijiao. Today's journey is over. I have to say goodbye to you.

As the saying goes, "There is no dinner without an end." Thank you very much for your support for my work. In just a few hours, I was very impressed by you all. Thank you for your cooperation. During the tour, if there is anything unsatisfactory, please criticize and tell me. Your opinion will be the direction of my efforts and your suggestion will be the goal of my improvement. I hope we will have the chance to get together again and enjoy the scenery of "beautiful Sanya, romantic Tianya".

Finally, I wish you all a safe journey! Happy family! Good health!

4A-rated Tourist Attractions

1. Xinglong Tropical Botanical Garden

Xinglong tropical botanical garden as a national 4A level tourism attraction founded in 1957 where it is developed and managed by the Spice and Beverage Research Institute, Chinese Academy of Tropical Agriculture Sciences. The garden cover an area of 645 hectares and is mainly engaged in the research and development of vanilla, coffee, cacao ,black pepper and other typical tropical plants with a collection of over 3,000 tropical plants species. The Garden has become a comprehensive botanical garden which combines scientific research, production, processing, sightseeing and germplasm resources conservation.

Beautiful botanical garden

Xinglong Tropical Botanical Garden is situated at the foot of a hill and beside a stream, with fresh air, great views, fruit flavor and bird's twitter. It is refreshing in the world. The saying "He who does not visit the beautiful botanical garden never been to Xinglong HaiNan" tell us the mystery of this green pearl in the hometown of overseas Chinese in Xinglong.

Strange but unique botanical garden

The Xinglong tropical botanical garden is pregnant with magical rainforest wonders, everywhere to leave you a surprise where you can enjoy magical old stem flowers, beautiful hanging gardens, special root phenomenon, unique interest of the single tree forest. There is also the "mother of chocolate" — cocoa, the "giant panda" — cyclama, the dancing grass swing to music, the "desert spring" — the traveller, the bloodshot throat and iron watermelon growing on the tree, and so on. These marvelous sight is waiting for you to explore.

Experience the botanical garden

At Xinglong Tropical Botanical Garden, you can experience exciting activities such as handmade chocolate DIY, Xinglong coffee grinding and brewing, Southeast Asian pastry making, and natural plant aroma blending. There are also unique Southeast Asian song and dance performances, as well as free coffee and tea drinks, providing you with a tropical plant experience journey that combines learning, leisure, and entertainment.

Historical botanical garden

Founded in 1957, Xinglong tropical botanical garden has grown from nine researchers and more than 10 workers who started from scratch to a research institution with strong research and development capabilities. In the course of 60 years' development, it has received the care and support from party and state leaders, government departments at all levels and people from all walks of life. More than 20 party and state leaders, including Zhou Enlai, Zhu DE, Deng Xiaoping and Xi Jinping, and more than 80 provincial and ministerial leaders, including He Kang, Han Changfu and Luo Baoming, came to the park for inspection and guidance.

Science and technology botanical garden

Xinglong tropical botanical garden is developed and managed by Spice and Beverage Research Institute, Chinese Academy of Tropical Agriculture Sciences. It is mainly engaged in the introduction and trial planting, high-yield cultivation, disease and insect pest control and product processing of tropical fragrant beverage crops such as vanilla orchid, pepper, coffee, cocoa, kuding tea and rice fragrant tea. Since its establishment, the institute has made more than 100 scientific research achievements, including 43 national, provincial and ministerial achievements awards. To formulate 45 technical standards; we have published more than 800 papers and 55 monographs. Applied for and was granted 58 invention patents and 10 utility model patents.

Since its establishment, the institute has developed 10 series of more than 140 technical products of over 140 specifications, such as cocoa series, coffee series, pepper series, vanilla orchid series and other characteristic tropical spice beverage crop products, with an annual output value of nearly 50 million Yuan.

Popularizing the science of botanical garden

Do you know where the chocolate came from? Do you know the difference between black pepper and white pepper? Do you know what are the three beverages in the world? Come to Xinglong tropical botanical garden, we will reveal these mysteries for you one by one. The Xinglong tropical botanical garden is equipped with function of biodiversity conservation, science education, scientific research and plant appreciation and for many years insisted of popularizing scientific knowledge of tropical plants to tourists. They also hold popular science explanation competition,science exhibition, nature notes, garden identification of plants, travel to find incense and so on from time to time. In the development of public science education has been widely recognized by the society. In addition, relying on the scientific and technological advantages of the institute of thermal sciences, hainan agricultural science and technology 110 spice beverage service station, which is established by the Xinglong tropical botanical garden, has also actively carried out a series of scientific and technological consulting and promotion activities for agriculture, rural areas and farmers.

2. Nanwan Monkey Island

Hello, my dear friends! I'm your guide, and my name is Xiao Li, next I will lead you to travel around.

The increasingly developed city brings us endless crowds and the pressure that makes us breathless. We always hope to have a place where we can throw everything away, back to the bosom of nature, retrieve the pleasure of living in harmony with nature as well. So, today we are going to visit a place where the fruits ripen in all seasons and the flowers give off sweet fragrance all year. It is also an ideal place for rhesus monkeys to live and breed as well, Nanwan Monkey Island.

Nanwan Monkey Island is the only rhesus monkey protection zone tropical island all over the world. It is located in the southernmost point of Lingshui county. The monkey on Nanwan Monkey Island, which the scientific name is rhesus macaques, belongs to the primates. Now there are over 2,000 monkeys in total living freely in here.

On the monkey island, the monkeys are the true "masters", we are "guest" who visit them and the managers of this island are the monkeys' "servants", that is the unique management idea of monkey island — "principle of three people".

Nanwan Monkey Island is composed of several parts, the Cross-sea Sightseeing Ropeway, "Wisdom Monkey" Theme Plaza, Huaguo Mountain Rhesus Monkey Sightseeing Area, Monkey Acrobatic Performance Area and Monkey Acting Area.

Cross-sea Sightseeing Ropeway

If you want to enter our monkey island, you can choose take the boat or sightseeing ropeway. However, the longest over-sea cableway in China, will leave us somewhat regretful if we don't experience it. Riding on the ropeway, you can see the mysterious Nanwan Monkey Island, charming tropical bay, and rich "Dan's folk customs". It offers a panoramic view and brings a different feeling to you.

"Wisdom Monkey" Theme Plaza

Stepping into Nanwan Monkey Island, the first thing you will see is the monkey island sculpture square. You will see a monkey sitting on the book of Darwin's "Origin of Species" with holding the human skull and thinking. The bronze statue of Wisdom Monkey is the enlarged copy of the gift that Dr. Hammer, a famous American red capitalist, once sent to Russian Soviet revolutionist Lenin. He was also telling us that human beings should learn to live by natural laws of and respect the nature.

Huaguo Mountain Rhesus Monkey Sightseeing Area

After appreciating the sight of sculptures, we will go to the rhesus monkey sightseeing area of Huaguo mountain to have a close contact with these lovely creatures. Here you can see the cute monkeys holding flags led by their king, this is a special way for them to welcome guests from afar, isn't it very interesting? At the water park of monkeys – "Yushengchi" (it's a kind of pool), you can see monkeys swimming, diving or high building diving to show off their abilities to the tourists. If you want to take pictures with these lovely monkeys closely, you can buy a bag of food, and then these intelligent monkeys will allow you to take photos with them.

Monkey Acrobatic Performance Area

If we describe the monkeys in the Huaguo Mountain tour area are "wild" monkeys, you will see the creatures behave like "human" in our acrobatic performance area. Here, the monkeys with high imitation ability will serve you with feast. They can perform difficult acrobatics under the leadership of their trainers and will amaze you.

Monkey Acting Area

If these still can't make you feel better or make you belly laugh, let's go to Monkey Acting Area to watch monkey shows which will bring you much more fun. These well-chosen, talented, good-looking and best-built monkeys co-starred in a sitcom called "The Monkey King's Family" which guaranteed your troubles disappear immediately.

Nanwan Monkey Island's intoxicating trip

Nanwan Monkey Island has amorous fish rafts which were known as the "offshore market", and "Tonglou's lights on fishing boat", which is one of the eight scenes of the ancient Lingshui as well as other landscapes. Takeing the cableway from Xincun fishing port, acrossing the sea and mountains, and then you will arrive at the charming monkey island. You will be intoxicated in the world which full of monkeys. They will greet you warmly and take pictures with you. They can also express monkeys' natural abilities along with human nature, so they can gain you applause. If you can give them a handful of candies or snacks, they will satisfy.

After having fun in the monkey mountain, follow the cableway down, take a leaf boat, then you can go to the fishing restaurant on the sea directly. The rows of fish rafts are dotted into a unique style of the watery place. No matter which fish raft seafood stalls you stepped in, the warm and hospitable Li and Miao girls will greet you with smiling face, warmly entertain guests from all over the world. If you are lucky enough, you can just feel at home and have a big meal. I promise you will taste countless kinds of seafood that you have never heard in Haikou, Sanya, or the mainland. Among them, there is a kind of conch called chicken leg conch, we also called it "leg of beauty", it tastes delicious and fresh, also the nutrition is rich and abundant.

OK! My dear friends, our tour bus has entered the scenic spot. I think everyone must be eager to play with the lovely monkeys. Let's go to experience the fun of harmonious coexistence of human and nature with good emotions!

3. China Leiqiong Global Geopark Haikou Volcanic Cluster

Hello, dear ladies and gentlemen, sincerely, welcome all of you to China Leiqiong Global Geopark Haikou Volcanic Cluster. My name is Xiao he. I am your tour guide and I will serve for you during the whole journey. It is my pleasure to show you around the attraction. China Leiqiong Global Geopark Haikou Volcanic Cluster is located in Shishan town, Xiuying district of Haikou. The mountain is 222.8 meters above the sea level, which is the highest peak in Qiongbei (the north part of Haikou province). Covering an area of 108 square kilometers, the Haikou Volcano Group is a rare Quaternary volcanic group in the world, dating back approximately 10,000 years. It has 40 volcanic cones and more than 30 karst tunnels, making it the only tropical urban volcanic group world geological park in China.

The Tablet of China Leiqiong Global Haikou Volcanic Cluster

There are three meaningful tablets in China Leiqiong Global Geopark Haikou Volcanic Cluster, including the main tablet of Leiqiong Global Geopark, mark tablet of the main area of park and the main tablet of nation geological park, which are located in ticket office, tourist center and the entrance of park respectively, distinctive and attractive.

The Cactus Garden

Cactus, a native plant from Mexicao, is a peculiar plant with strong vitality, whose branches are tortuous and stems are flat with much thorn. The flowers are yellow and drought-resistant. They are cultivated by cutting propagation. Cactus grow in various forms which is spherical, palmate, cylindrical, four-diamond shaped and so on, with different sorts. Thanks to the porous basalt rock of volcano area and its strong permeability, cactus grow swell here.

There are four small flower beds. The first one named "volcano soul" where precious plants grow, like euphorbia neriifolia and cactus. The second called "volcano affection" cultivating the lively but thornless cactus whose berry can be tasted. The third is referred to as "volcano destiny", with wolftree as well as carissa carandas. The last one is "volcano love" where exist a grape-shaped basalt rock. Its texture is still visible as it was shaped from the magma is forced out of the holes. In geology, it is called crust lava and also known as ornamental stone. The tallest cactus in the cactus garden has been growing for over 20 years, and such a tall cactus is relatively rare.

Volcano Leisure Square

Crater leisure square is optimal place for leisure and entertainment. There are basalt rock tables, tea tables made of hundred-year Litchi wood, some chairs, a small stage and all kinds of Huoshan snack (local food) indoor. Here, tourists can taste delicious snack and watch wonderful show in volcano styles. Various kinds of Huoshan snack like rice noodles, noodles and coarse cereals. Meanwhile, the excellent shows are performed in the stage center of square, like bamboo dancing, leaves playing, folk songs and so on, which makes tourists not only enjoy the delicacy on the tongue but also enjoy a visual feast.

Root Carving Art Park

Root-Carving Art Park was built in 2009, exhibiting root carvings of Litchi, Longyan, Yizuiluo etc. which are precious trees in Huoshan area. Because of the thin soil layer with many stones in the volcano area, their roots extended through the cracks of rocks, which was how roots variously shaped. Million years later, trunks are used as material and the roots of the trees are cleansed into root carvings that become a kind of artwork.

Root carvings in Huoshan area are peculiarly shaped and it is well-known for its ornamental value. Tourists who go into the root-carving garden can visit around and take pictures with root carvings that he/she like, feeling the nature closely. One of the root carvings called "Shandain", looking like a dragon chair, which is so special that attract many people to take pictures for souvenir.

While "the root of universe and earth" and "the origin of life" are handmade root carvings. In the middle of root carving, "Fanyan" (breed) is linked /connected by 7 roots, which means thriving and prosperous with many sons and grandsons.

Volcanic Ecological Landscape Road

Volcano ecological landscape road, called Huoshanshen Road as well, starts from the main tablet of scenic area, extending to the landscape road at Fengluling crater.

The landscape road is beautiful and unique, showing us the ecosystem of crater. The road was paved unevenly with porous basaltic rocks, which is suitable for barefeet walking. Walking on the paves, it helps people improve blood circulation by foot massage. Thus, it is called "Healthy Road" as well. On the both sides of the volcanic ecological landscape road, there are many banyan trees growing and interlacing, which is a special views. When summer coming, tourist can enjoy the cool here without holding umbrella. Besides, you can appreciate unique natural heirographens, tropical plants along the road. The landscape road is so excellent because local volcanic rocks blend with tropical plants.

Basalt Column

Basalt column is a distinct view. Those pillars stand within the volcanic ecological landscape. Actually, they are naturally formed. During the cooling process of homogenous magma, they were transferred into Polygonal column after cooling, contracting and cracking. Normally, they were quadrangle, pentagon and hexagon and most of them are hexagon, extremely unique. It is called "columnar jointing" geologically, which is similar to clod of the paddy fields and lotus ponds after the exposure to sun. The well-known examples of "columnar jointing" are the "magic tower" of America and "The Giant's Causeway" of Northern Ireland. The formulation principles of volcano basalt columns are similar to "columnar jointing".

Cuiqu Garden

Cuiqu garden, a representative of tropical ecosystem, whose most remarkable signature is the tropical ecosystem combines with the volcano. A wooden walkway across the Bonsai garden shows the native people's preference to local ecological culture. A variety of bonsai were carefully cultivated, exquisite, elegant and vivid, with great ornamental value. Bypassing the hundred-years Banyan trees group whose roots are like voluble dragons, with luxuriant foliage, in different forms. The walkway brings all of you to primitive scene to experience its interest. Besides, when you see the towering Chongyang trees, simple but elegant pulmeria, wild jack fruits as well as other knotted climbers, you will feel that as if you are in the rainforest world. Passing by the orchard, you can enjoy the fragrance of tropical fruit such as jack fruit, carambola, guava, wax apple and so on, which will let you indulge yourself into the pleasure moment.Amazingly, this interesting Cuiqu garden is situated on weathered soil of basalt rocks, where the volcano erupted 8000 years ago, leading to extinctions of species, while creatures come back to life over time which showing us a stunning sight. Go ahead, you will see the relic of lava flow after the volcano eruption, which can vividly tell you the process of lava flowing at that time.

Volcano Seasonal Rainforest Walkways

Corresponding to Cuiqu Park, volcano seasonal rainforest walkways has different styles even though they are both wooden walkways. Volcano season rainforest walkways focus on rainforest style, completely presenting not only Hainan tropical rainforest style, but also the unique views of crater. You can see hundred-year vine stretching along a stone road, a stone wall as well as a wooden walkway.Volcanic bamboo, banyan trees, huanghuali wood, jackfruit trees, wild litchi trees, dripping guanyin and so on, are collectively referred as the vegetation of the monsoon forest, demonstrating the beauty of tropical volcano season rainforest, with Island characteristics. When visitors stroll in the open air, breathing the fresh air, enjoying the cool merrily, and you can appreciate the beauty of nature.

Since volcano season rainforest walkway is located in relatively remote area, lots of tourists may miss this view easily. However, it is a perfect place where you can get closer to feel the appeal of volcano. It is an optimal heaven for leisure and healthcare.

Stone Gate and Dragon Water

Stone gate is built according to the former village's gate in volcano area. In the past, the gates of every village were constructed with volcano stone, which mainly used to keep outsiders and wild beasts from invading and attacking. It is said that there was a kind of wild man who had tall figures and strong limbs, in odd shapes, with long nails. Even so, they could not squat. The savages often hurt children and steal stuffs. In case of savages intruding, small gates were built with volcano stone to keep away from wild man. Thus, stone gate also called "dragon gate".

Getting through the stone gate means "rise as dragon and to be successful and prosperous". It is demanding for people in volcano area to get through the gate. Generally, people must follow the tradition that men cross with left feet while women cross with right feet.

Since dragon is considered as a kind of auspicious animal and totem in the volcanic area, every time dragon boat festival is coming, local people come here and queue, to touch the dragon head and wash hands with dragon water for getting good omens. The water is underground mineral water gushing from basaltic layer.

Volcano Stone Culture Exhibition Area

It is said that ancient residents of volcano area already establish houses with volcano stone during Qin and Han dynasty, which was 1,500 years ago. The houses were constructed with stone and wood, whose roofs were paved with tile and house beams were carved into a totem. In front of the house, they built with volcano stone (basalt rock), you can see several water vats. There are lots of household items and producing tools made of volcano stone around the houses, which intensively reappears the people's culture of producing and living in volcano area.

Entering the stone house, you can see wood oil press, bamboo mill, harrow hook, wood plough, iron grip and deck. In the wealthiest families, deck was a sort of household items whose top could be used as bed while its interior was divided into several compartments where important stuffs could be stored. The secret compartment which is the earliest safe was used to preserve valuables.

Around the stone house, you can see stone basin, stone vat, stone mill, stone mortar, stone pestle as well as juicer. Particularly, the juicer is significant. It is used to produce cane juice that will be made into sugar lump after the process of stewing and roasting. These goods intensively displays ancestor's wisdom.

Fengluling Crater

The last time Fengluling crater erupted is 8000 years ago. It is an active volcano or dormant volcano that is one of the most well-preserved volcanoes in the world. It is 222.8 meters above sea level and the commanding height of Haikou. The crater is 130 meters in diameter and 69 meters in depth.

There are two features in Fengluling crater. First, there is no hydrops, which is extremely rare for crater sceneries. Particularly, it is more miraculous in Fengluling crater where little hydrops exist in spite of the wet weather. Second, it is covered with plants and its vegetation coverage rate is more than 85%, considered as "green lung of Haikou". That is a really distinctive point. More amazingly, the plants of crater grow in layers. From top to bottom there are 4 sorts of various plants — arbors, shrubs, ferns and mosses in sequence. When summer comes, this crater even becomes a natural air-conditioned room. There are 40 craters around the volcano with the area of 108 square kilometers. At present, Fengluling crater is the only one that is established as tourist attraction which makes visitor appreciate the charm of volcano from close range.

Dear friends, our trip has come to an end. The beautiful scenery of the crater is always here waiting for your next visit. Have a pleasant journey!

4. Permanent Venue of the Bo'ao Forum for Asia

Ladies and gentlemen, welcome to Permanent Venue Of The Bo'ao Forum For Asia. I'm glad to serve as your guide today, my name is Xiao Chen. Here, please allow me to express our honest greetings to all of you.

Permanent Venue Of The Bo'ao Forum For Asia is a national 4A tourist attraction, located at the mouth of Wanquan river with South China Sea nearby. Every April, this place will become the world-wide focus. Business and academic leaders will gather from all around the world, discuss significance issues. It's globally famous forum site, already hold dozens of annual forums.

It is located on Dongyu Isle, with total area of 178 hectares, contains the International Conference Center, Grand Hotel, Golf Club and Forum Scenic Area. Looking down in the air, the whole Dongyu Isle like a huge slowly walking turtle with head and body are separated, Wanquan River, Jiuqu River and Longgun River converge here and then rush to the South China Sea, landscape integration as an amazing place, also the core of Boao Town. That's why this place was chosen as the permanent location of the Boao Forum for Asia.

The site contains such view as: Fountain Square, Conference Center, Good-Luck-Platform, Sea Turtle Stone Square, Jade Belt Beach, The place of Happy And Beautiful, Sign of Belt and Road, News Center.

Fountain Square

It is a landscape area consisting of a hollow metal globe supported by a fountain and an elliptical fountain pool. The location of Asia on the globe extends directly to the main road of the island road, symbolizing that the Forum for Asia is an open and developing forum, and representing the Boao Forum for Asia International Convention Center to welcome friends from all over the world. A trapezoidal waterfall forms into the fountain, and the water flows spread around the flower and grass, symbolizing the spread of the significance of the BFA to the whole world. The elliptic fountain pool combines with "sea turtle" body shape to make an abstract design, the pool's tube is divided into three layers, from inside out, respectively comprised by 14, 96, 62 different kind of the tube, the rule of fountain gushing are random and distinct.

International Conference Center

From hotel lobby to North gate

Dear visitors, there's the entrance to main conference hall, the opening and closing ceremonies of annual meeting are held here, from 2002 to 2023, this place are successfully hold annual meeting 21 times.

Now we have arrived at the north gate of International conference center, during the annual meeting, the forum guests are come from the north gate walking on the red carpet of the security check into the main venue to attend the meeting, the media reporters gather on both sides of the area, many reporters seize the opportunity to interview the interviewees they wanted during guest check in here.

Main venue

Ladies and gentlemen, now we are entering the main venue, which is the core of the BFA. The total area of the main venue are 2,592 square meters, 11 meters high, east – west 50 meters, north – south 55 meters. It can accommodate about 2000 delegates at the same time, and there are 2 reception rooms for state guests nearby.

President Xi has attended annual meetings in 2010, 2013, 2015, 2018, 2021 and 2022, respectively he attended the BFA more frequently than any other Chinese leaders. It fully represent the importance our country attaches to the BFA.

My dear friends, the annual opening ceremony speech symbolize China's welcome to guests attending the ceremony, it is also China's voice to the world. The national flags on the rostrum represent the 29 states of the BFA. On April 10th, 2018, President Xi had delivered the opening ceremony and a keynote speech entitled "opening up, creating prosperity, innovation and leading the future" on this stage, in front of the white one-man podium. An "It has been a long time since we last met, and I hope it will be a long time before we have to part." become a classic.

Good-luck-platform

It is said that the legend of the Goddess of Mercy conquered Ao (sea turtle), then equipped with the Yin and Yang (yin and yang, the two opposing principles in nature, the former feminine and negative, the latter masculine and positive) ponds on its top. The design applies Wuxing, the concept of the five elements (of metal, wood, water, fire and earth) used in traditional Chinese cosmology, communicate through this cave. Standing upon the cave, looking up and echoing your voice, you could sense the longstanding echoes of the heaven which also sounds like response from the whole universe, which could be rated as one wonder. And Gods of Fortune, Emolument, Longevity, Happiness and Property will favor whoever prays for the platform.

Aoshi Square

The legendary Ao is a spiritual animal with a dragon head, turtle back, and unicorn tail. In the Aoshi Square of the scenic area, there is a Aoshi spirit statue carved from a whole black dragon bone stone, weighing eight tons and standing two meters high. On September 16th, 2006, the famous Taoist priest presided over the opening ceremony.

Jade Belt Beach

Here the Wanquan River, Jiuqu River, and Longgun River interflow and then rush for the South China Sea, Opposite is The Yudai Beach. The Yudai Beach is a long and narrow natural sandy beach peninsula. Vast and boundless South China sea is outside, and the tranquil mirror-like Wanquan River on the other, lakes and mountains on the inside and outside, form an amazing landscape. It takes 8.3-kilometer-long south-north; east-west about 300 meters at the widest, the narrowest only 10 meters. It's the most narrowest place that separates sea water from river water. Such landform of the peninsula bears a strong resemblance to Miami of the US, Cancun of Mexico, and Gold Coast of Australia, making it the only of its kind in Asia. In June 1999, the northern part of the Yudai Beach was recognized by International Guinness Headquarters as a Guinness Record Holder, "the narrowest beach peninsula separating sea from river". The tail of the jade belt beach is the convergence site, it is also the first world's best preserved river estuary land. This beach was linked together. Due to the typhoon petrel in 2013, it was broken across the waist of the tail of the jade belt beach . Attention! The big gap between the middle is not the real mouth of those three rivers. You can go back and look at the direction of my fingers, and that's the "Head of Sea turtle". The so-called are champion,be the first, is originated there.

Le Mei Scenery

The path leads to a secluded summer solstice, with sunlight shining through the gaps between the stars and leaves. The sound of cicadas echoing in the wind, gentle and gentle like whispers.This is the Le Mei Scenic Area, built in 2019, about 618 meters long, 3 meters wide, walking on this quiet LeMei Road, breathing smooth, feel quiet, return to natural. Dongyu Island is close to mouth of east river, its salty waters surround the Dongyu Island, the water and mud flats is very conducive to the growth of mangroves. Therefore, in order to protect the natural ecology and landscape of mangroves on Dongyu Island better, the government has established the Lemei Lake Mangrove Conservation Area, On the shores of Lake Lemei, you can get a close-up view of the rare woody viviparous plant — the mangrove forest. Red trees crisscross each other, with their brownish red trunks winding and intertwined, forming three-dimensional fences that support the massive tree crowns, like a serene and magical fairyland. On the outer side of the Le Mei Scenic Area, there is a 2.5-kilometer-long roundabout road. It starts from Aoshen Pond in the east and ends at Peilan Bridge in the west, forming a beautiful leisure corridor along the river, sea, green grass, and trees. The Starlight Road, with a total length of 888 meters, is dazzling and sparkling at night. In the darkness, lifting one's eyes, the sky was filled with starlight, the Milky Way flickered under one's feet, and the silver light on the surrounding water shimmered, accompanied by the stars and moon, as if walking in a mysterious fairy tale world.

News Center

The building we see now resembling a seagull is our news center. The entire news center is a steel structure, and its design is built according to the most advanced and standardized news center in Asia. This building is called "Seagull Spreads Its Wings". It symbolizes the takeoff of the Boao Forum for Asia, the takeoff of China, and the takeoff of Asia. The total construction area is 5,358 square meters and can accommodate nearly 2,500 journalists. The total investment is 110 million yuan, and the facilities and equipment inside are advanced. It has 6 independent simultaneous interpretation rooms that can simultaneously achieve simultaneous translation in 6 kinds of languages, providing convenient and technological services for media staff. It was officially put into use during the 2016 Boao Forum for Asia Annual Conference.

Dear friends, our journey to Permanent Venue Of The Bo'ao Forum For Asia has come to an end. We will always be here waiting for your next visit. Wishing you a pleasant journey!

5. West Island

Dear visitors and friends, today we are going to visit the world's rare island—West Island, which is the biggest indigenous tourism isle, located in China's only tropical coastal city—Sanya, located eight nautical miles of south of Sanya Bay. Here dust is separated from the sea, abundant style, surrounded by pure blue reefs, beautiful scenery. Because the surrounding waters are crystal clear and blue, the sea land is also beautifully, it has become one of the recognized diving sites. Here not only has the dynamic exciting sea sport, but also hides the quaint hundred-year-old fishing village, the original island scenery, people call it "the sea peach source, dynamic paradise".

Diving Holy Land

The waters of the western isles are crystal blue, the bottom of the sea is beautiful, and there are a great variety of underwater creatures. Here, you can plunge into the bottom of the sea, stay among the corals, and feel the joy of being surrounded by coral reefs and dancing with fish.

Maritime Amusement World

West Island is a collection of sea bottom, sea surface and air entertainment as one of the sea amusement park, surrounded by the sanya bay west island, blue lingering, water width and tide level, is a paradise for sea sports. Here you can fully experience the competition of fast and furious on the sea, place yourself in the blue sea, feel the unique charm of dynamic and exciting, and enjoy the happy time of jumping into the ocean.

Ox King Island

At the southern tip of the island has a adjacent to the tiny island, called the Ox King Island, is composed of two beautiful hill, the whole island is surrounded by blue sea water, the island confrontation overlapping peaks, Rocky outcrop and wind wave drum, such as sea fairyland.

Standing in the ting tao xuan of the Ox King Island, you can close your eyes to listen to the voice of the sea; On the north peak of the Ox King Island, to meet the power to run to the sea of the big bull; Step across the bridge of lovers flying across the sky, in front of the ancient tree love on the viewing platform, with the sea left 360° no dead Angle of the aesthetic photo; The secret of the sea of south China is hidden in the pavilion of vows of eternal love with the wind blowing slowly. Here, you can admire the rocks, listen to the waves and see the picturesque scenery of the south sea of China.

Coastal Landscape Avenue

West Island coastal landscape avenue is a unique romantic characteristics of the island wedding photography base, embracing the poetic romantic coastal scenery, blue sky and blue sea, green grass such as blanket, tree shadow dance. Poetic wooden plaque, heart-shaped pavilion, bird's nest house between trees, romantic flower arch and web celebrity punch-card points of literature and art such as hundred-year ancient well and ancient boat are also gathered here. The whole road is filled with the warmth and sweetness of love.

You can chase the tail of the sea breeze, walk through the sparse coconut forest, listen to the sound of the waves, and step out of the rhythm of joy in the quiet waterfront plank road; or at the sunset, sunset fall in the tide of coral beach, in your eyes, it must be another beautiful scene.

The most beautiful fishing village in 400 years

In this isolated island across the sea, hidden in an ancient small fishing village — west island fishing village. West island fishing village has been hiding in the arms of the sea more than 400 years, amorous feelings of primitive simplicity, quiet mind, was named the best fishing village.

Walking around in the breeze is blowing through the coastal road, on the other side of the sea is charming Sanya bay city, along the coral on the low wall with small and exquisite works of art. You will meet market road corner "big love", found only on the fishing pier is funny but very domineering fish "rebirth", and the art of the ship hanging bottles. There are also fisherman's boats at anchor in the harbor.

In the study room on the sea, you can feel the wind blowing the page which you can read any page, the heart with the sea wide, reading tea elegance; or go to the women's militia exhibition hall, listen to the militia old woman tell a part of their legend; or walk into the quiet alley, look at the ancient coral houses, taste the western island of 400 years of human history; even at the corner of an alley, you will meet those who reposes in fishing villages in the courtyard the warmth of home stay facility. The two courtyards, called the "cultural and creative hall" and the "house of ideas", contain many curious artifacts. Bustling fishing village markets, all filled with the smoke and fire of this land of idyllic beauty.

The women militia of West Island

The west island fishing village has such a group of lovely "fishermen iron girl", they were famous throughout the country's model female militia, known as the "eight sisters gun squad". This legendary red history dates back to 1959. On 1 August 1959, in order to strengthen the defense of the sea of south China defense outpost, the Western Island militia battalion was established. Living on the island of 8 fishermen girls, Chen Linmei, Chen Famei, Su Lanqin, Wang Fuhua, Wang Nailian, Chen Hongliu, Chen Xianglan, Su Rinong, with a love for the motherland, joined the ranks of female militia gunnery. They were in their prime, the oldest aged 19 and the youngest 16. The group of lovely people, in the era of the fiery red, under the glorious banner lead of the party, burning youth, made a great contribution to the South China Sea defense for the motherland, made one after another honor, created one after another brilliant. In the 1970s, the movie *Haixia* became famous in China. The story was based on this group of lovely people, which recorded the glorious red history. From this, also let the island women militia famous throughout the country.

Time ran, when the spirited "fisherman iron girl", now has become a white-haired grandmother, some even have forever engraved in the historical monument, but the red spirit of West Island women militia has been inherited on the west island. In the West Island women's militia exhibition hall, objects bearing the red memories of West Island still tell the legendary story of the West Island women militia in another way for visitors from all over the country.

West Island yard

Cruise in the hundred years of fishing village, you can taste the simple and artistic fishermen customs, in the fishing village costal road across the sea overlooking sanya city scenery inadvertently turned, you can meet the West Island yard. Exquisite island life begins in the West Island yard, where you can escape the hustle and bustle of the city and enjoy the tranquility of the sea.

Alright, dear tourists, our tour bus has already entered our scenic area. Are you all eager to experience it immediately? Let's take a good mood and experience the fun of West Island!

6. Luhuitou Park

Luhuitou Scenic Area is a themed scenic spot that combines Li ethnic culture, love culture, and ecological culture, known as the "South China Sea Love Mountain". It is located in the Lu Huitou peninsula of southwest of Sanya city, which has five peaks of different size, the highest one is 181 meters, with a total area of 88.89 hectares. The park has seas on three sides, and one side adjacent to the Sanya City. So it not only offers a commanding point for seeing the sea, sunrise and sunset, but also a commanding point of Sanya City. Please remember three spirits culture of the park: Take your hand, First Sight Love and overlook the city.

When we mention this destination, it reminds of a lyric poem by Mr. Ma Wanqi:

Don't miss the travel of hainan in your life, Wuzhi mountain is a high place with good views. Its a precious place where the Phoenix love to visit, Lu Huitou park is a hard place to be given up in Sanya.

It narrates the status of this park in Hainan tourism industry. As an ecological civilization mountain, we do our best to maintain what nature has given us. Please don't litter in the course of the tour, don't spit everywhere, follow the arrangement of the worker and line up in an orderly manner. Let's maintain the harmony of nature together.

Now, let me share the beautiful attractions of the park for all the guests.

Fenghuang Island

The five buildings which jump on our sight are Fenghuang Island. The island is 1250 meters long and 350 meters wide, connected to the central city of Sanya by a 395-meter-long maritime sightseeing bridge. The five 100-metre 28-storey curved buildings are the most luxurious seascape buildings in Sanya Bay.

The five buildings are 360-degree sea view rooms, with five rings appearance, which symbolizes the spirit of the Olympic rings. At the same time, the 2008 Olympic torch relay ignited on this Island. The torch passed through the cities and counties along the way to the Bird's Nest Stadium in Beijing which has the auspicious implication of Phoenix's homing.

Three sides of the island rely on mountain scenery, surrounded by the sea, with a unique tourism scenery in mountain, sky and ocean. Four new wharf are planned, including one 100,000 ton berth, two 150,000 ton berths and one 225,000 ton berth. At that time, Fenghuang Island can dock 6-8 ships, with an annual capacity of 2 million individuals, which will become one of the world largest international wharf.

Sanya Bay

Located on the north side of Fenghuang Island is the beautiful beach called Sanya Bay, stretching more than 20 kilometers of coastline make coconut trees into a forest, so also known as the "Promenade displaying of coconuts". Sanya Bay is also the most prosperous part of Sanya City, divided into three sections, one is an amusement and sightseeing roaming area, farther is the public seaside swimming field and the sea activity area, the others are the sea slope leisure resort area with a number of resorts. The end of Sanya Bay just behind Fenghuang Island is our famous scenic spot Tianya Haijiao.

East-West Daimao Island

On the west side of Fenghuang Island situates two small islands, called East Island on the left. Its a military base, heavily guarded, thus the ordinary person can't be allowed. On the right is West Island, a tourist attraction with an area of 2.8 square kilometers, more than 3,000 residents generations lived by fishing, and many young people who are the aficionados of sea projects playing in there after the opening of the scenic spot.

The two islands are called East-West Daimao Islands. The meaning of Daimao is not same as the meaning of "wearing hat", it means a reptile animal that lives in the tropical deep sea belongs to the State Second-Class Protected Animal in our country, the lifetime up to 1,500 years. The shape is extremely similar to the tortoise, but it has thirteen squama in its carapace it also called "thirteen squama", also known as longevity turtle.

The fishermen of the Southern Sea regard it as the mascot, and think that the Hawksbill Turtle is the ninth son of the dragon. So they use the squama on the back of the Hawksbill Turtle to adorn bracelet, pendant and ring for eliminating disasters and avoiding evil.

Luck and Peace Tree

This tree is one of the " eighteen strange " in Hainan, called "Ficus", the roots of the tree grow outside the bark. Let's see the root of it, the scientific name is "Aerial rooting", which absorbs nutrients and water in the air and grows down, when the roots fall down, they stuck in the soil like this branch for a long time, and this branch will slowly form a new tree. In this way the branches take root, and the roots multiply, a tree will form a deep forest.

The Li nationality gave this ficus tree a beautiful name, called "luck and peace tree". Due to the local in Hainan are Li nationality, (at present, the Li population accounts for 17% of the entire Hainan province) they hold the view that ficus tree is spiritual and a kind friend of humanity. The big ficus is a "rain fairy", the more species, the more amply water in this area. The small ficus is considered to be the village's protection fairy that can protect the village people prosperity, harvest and great fortune, so it's also called the "luck and peace tree".

A Friendly Reminder

Firstly, there are wild rhesus monkeys on the mountain of our destination, the national second-class protected animals. It ferocious and wild. If we are lucky enough to meet this group of monkeys in the course of our tour, please don't make fun, stare and cater for them.

Secondly, Luhuitou park is an ecological mountain with lovely environment and deep forest coverage. Our group members should pour attention to the deep forest fire prevention and no smoking.

Moving up the hillside to appreciating the Banshan peninsula tourist resort that what we called "half heaven and half sea".

In the upper right corner of the sea is a white walled cube with purple glow that is Sailing Harbor of Banshan peninsula, its also The World Volvo Sailing Race Points, Docking Point and One of the ports where international sailing events stop. The farthest mountain is our Luhuitou, and it looks like the running Eld's deer overlook the higher position. On the right there's a more densely district with habitation which is Luhuitou village. In the bottom of our eyes, this red roof of the villa group is the Luhuitou State Guesthouse, dedicated reception of national dignitaries and the predecessor is the Luhuitou Hostel, began work before 1959 and was officially opened in 1961. Finally, we look at the far left sea, which known as the "Pearl of the southern sea", Xiaodonghai, is the national coral reserves, scene temperature of water is between 25-26℃ especially appropriate for coral growth.

We have entered the core of the Luhuitou — love cultural attractions groups, the beautiful legend of love, solidified into a meaningful landscape from this place:

In front of our left, there is a heart-shaped stone carving, is the stone of eternal love. It's named for its shape, like a heart, and nature has such magical power to carve the stone into a shape of love. The blue pattern below is the totem of the Li nationality. It is a nation with only language and no words. They usually record things on totem. This totem also symbolizes the meaning of eternal love.

The Loyal Rock

Looking up is a feature of this destination, it called "The Loyal Rock". It was not a granite or marble, but a fossil of the undersea volcanic rock of billions years ago, because of the movement of the earth's crust, the range under the sea gradually rose into mountains, and the stones came to the surface. We usually use word "The Loyal Rock" to describe the long time, as a metaphor to love firm will never change, then the "The Loyal Rock" can reflect eternity of love. It is said that when a deer turns its head, the flowers and trees are full of love also grass and stone. When lovers arrive, their love and affection like stones on the mountain, the sea is dry, the stones are not eroded. It is because the mountains all over this kind of "Loyal Rock", plus the beautiful love legend, and it's known as the "Love Mountain in Southern Sea".

Love Monument

The is Love Monument of "Vows of Eternal Love", then the sea vows are in Tianya Haijao. During the annual International Wedding Ceremony in November, lovers at home and abroad would come here to married and take a vow of loyalty to their love.

The monument has a red sun on it, on the left of the sun is a dragon, on the right is Phoenix, so-called "dragon and Phoenix".

The males hand left and the females right, let's make a "Vows of Eternal Love". We must do it hands in hands because it means "Hold hands then grow old". Now, let's see the word "Meng", it constitutes with the word "Ri" and "Yue", "Ri" represents "Yang" and "Yue" represents "Yin". The monument has been standing here for hundreds years and absorbing the quintessence of the sun and moon that got some spirituality. So the male touch "Ri" and female touch "Yue", we'll know the effect when we're done.

Enjoying in the attractions of love culture, we should not forget the sight of forest vegetation, rare species of fauna. In the course of the tour, we should take good care of nature, protect the environment, don't climb, engrave words, and make civilized travel.

Now we walk down steps to Sea-View Pavilion. This 270 degree view of the sea is the best view of Luhuitou, so downtown can accept to the eye bottom. On the right hand is the whole Sanya City, surrounded by mountains on three sides, one side of ocean, so the whole city is extending the Sanya Bay coastline, in the end is Tianya Haijiao, Nanshan Temple and Dongtian Park.

My dear friends, in front of us is the core scenic spot — Luhuitou Statue that has a beautiful fairy tale spread in thousand years. Let's uncover her beautiful and moving veil.

Long time ago, in the central mountains of Hainan lived a hard-working and kind-hearted mother and son who were the people of Li nationality, her son was a well-known local hunter, who merely hunted venomous snakes and beasts, but friendly of small animals. At one time, the patriarch of their tribe wanted a Eld's deer in the forest to nourish him, and the patriarch knew that only "a hei" had the ability to do so, so the patriarch locked his mother up and forced him into the mountains, and "a hei" had to be forced to look for the Eld's deer.

When he entered a forest, he suddenly saw a beautiful Eld's deer drinking water by a stream, he couldn't bear to hurt him, but remembered that his mother was still locked up for him to return. He set up his heart with hand-held bow and arrow, as he was about to launch, the Eld's deer jumped over the stream and fled. He chase it all the way, if he stop the deer from looking back at you. Once turned over ninety-nine mountains, waded ninety-nine rivers, chased for nine days and nine nights, had been catching up on the edge of Sanya Bay, in front was the massive sea, behind was the chasing hunter. The Eld's deer found no way to go, then stopped on the top of the cliff suddenly and turned her head back with a shout. All of a sudden, the deer was gone, and there was a beautiful girl veins looked at him. She wore a dress as beautiful as the rosy clouds in the sky, and her eyes shone like stars in the night. He was stunned. Then he came to his senses and asked, she was the fairy in the sky. She had taken a fancy to his diligence and kindness, so led him in this way to the place where the water was rich and beautiful.

Then, with the help of the fairy, he returned to his hometown, defeated the sinful patriarch and rescued his mother, they went to Sanya together and lived a happy life. After the story, the mountain is called "Luhuitou", the village is called "Luhuitou Village", the mountain is called "Luhuitou mountain", and the peninsula is called "Luhuitou Peninsula".

The beautiful legend of Luhuitou tells us that born alive, no matter for love, light or truth, we should have an unyielding pursuit of the spirit, even to Tianya Haijao do not give up, perhaps victory is not far away.

Overlooking the rolling hills on the top of the deer's head, the view is spectacular. During the day, mountains, rivers, cities and oceans are all in one, the boundless sea that is melted into the sky. It is getting dark now, from the top we can see the city blazing with lights and the sea sparking. Meanwhile, on the mountain you can see beautiful trees and flowers and the colorful sky.

Dear friends, we see the various stones inscription on both sides of the road are the cultural totem of Li nationality.

Harvest drawing

Li people believe in the original religion of all living beings. Prevailing totem worship, nature worship. The original primitive religion was closely related to ancient production and life. There were fears of the varied of nature, under the influence of the living thoughts of all things, they thought that nature has the same motives as humans like lust and taste. By offering sacrifices you can pray for the joy, forgiveness, and gifts of nature. Li people have the custom of worshiping rice elves, actually the embodiment of the idea of all living things. In order to pray for a good harvest, a series of sacrificial ceremonies are required from sowing to harvesting. In the harvest, the host shall prepare wine and worship the earth's devils in the field then reward him. This kind of natural worship is undoubtedly the legacy of the ancient Chinese people engaged in agriculture.

Sacrificial Picture

The pattern on the stone is the totem of the Li people. This memorial picture is mainly about two kinds of animals that Li people worship. The above one is frog, the Li people think the frog is a lucky animal and the guardian in the rice field. The following is the cow's head, the cow's work from sunrise to the sunset and people inseparable from it in daily life.

The worship of Li people about animals come from the concept of "all things are alive". Totem, ancestor and nature worship together constitute the original ideology of the ancestors of the Li nationality in Hainan which makes a positive influence in conquering and transforming nature.

"Luhuitou cliff in front of the 'ends of the earth', and then the front is the vast sea. It is known that although there are still a few scattered islands in the southern seas, as far as the whole land is concerned, it is precisely the southern tip of the land of China, and thus it has become the true end of the earth for the nation. Chinese emperors sat facing the south, Chinese houses were built facing the south, the compass invented in China was always magically pointing south, and countless stone lions, iron oxen, bronze horses, and pottery figurines were also standing or prolonging themselves facing the south. This kind of vision across the mountains and rivers and lakes, all of them were wondering about the blue sky of the South China Sea and the end point of a grand social psychological trend. A thousand years of struggle and longing for the limits, and that beautiful deer turned back, all eyes..." This wonderful description of Mr. Yu Qiuyu in "the story of the Tianya" reveals the cultural and spiritual realm of Luhuitou.

The beautiful place, enjoy the true love of the world, eulogize the beautiful love, convey the true meaning of life, summon people to return to the harbor of love!

7. Paddy Field National Park

Dear visitors, today we are going to visit Paddy Field National Park. Paddy Field National Park is the largest agri-tourism attraction in Sanya. It integrates together agricultural-ecology, agricultural science education, farming culture, rice cultivating culture, scientific research, popular science education, interactive experience, folk customs, leisurely holiday and so on. The theme scenic spot shows the civilization and excellence of the earth, fields, rice in the human survival and reproduction process and interprets the theme of ecology, life, life cultural.

At present, the scenic spot contains rice culture square, Chinese rice-farming cultural museum, Yuan Longping national rice R&D center, Chinese star dinosaurs area, Night of the Earth high-tech light and sound show, dinosaurs trail, low altitude flight experience area, Chinese farming culture large-scale live show, kids' land, egret wetland reserve, rice culture sightseeing and experience area, flower culture sightseeing and experience area, tropical fruits and vegetables sightseeing and harvest garden, paddy field hot spring spa, paddy field restaurant, caravan campground, rice themed town, paddy field seven-star leisure hotel, etc. Next, I will introduce you through visiting, entertaining, food, hospitality and travelling.

Visiting

Rice Miracle - Yuan Longping Rice Research Base

The origin of rice evolved from the differentiation of the family Gramineae of rice, which dates back to the Cretaceous era. Based on scientific historical research, it is China that first domesticated wild rice into cultivated rice, which has a history of over 10,000 years (there are 7000 years ago in Hemudu, Zhejiang Province, 14000-12000 years ago in Wannian, Jiangxi Province, and 18000-14000 years ago in Yuchanyan, Daoxian County, Hunan Province).

Yuan Longping, who is the winner of the first National Supreme Science and Technology Award, an academician of the Chinese Academy of Engineering and the pioneer of Chinese research and development of hybrid rice, took Sanya as the seed breeding base and successfully developed the “three-line method” hybrid rice, “two-line method” hybrid rice, super hybrid rice phase I, phase II, and deduced the modern epic of rice “domestication”. For nearly half a century, academician Yuan Longping’s research results have promoted the revival of agricultural science in China, solved the starving problem of Chinese people, and made significant contributions to national food security. He is known as “the father of hybrid rice in the world” and “contemporary Shennong”. He also spread the dream of “grains for the world” to five continents, and set up a monument for social progress and world peace.

Searching for Dreams in Rice Fields - Thousand Acres of Rice Sea

Here, you can get close to the earth and approach the soil. You can realize the artistic conception of the unity of nature and man and also feel the visual shock of thousands of mu of rice waves. You can also recognize the entire process of rice from planting to harvest, understand the history of Chinese rice culture civilization for thousands of years and experience the fun of field farming. You can wander in the rice fields, walk through the 24 solar term cultural corridor and land the five-color earth leisure pavilion (red clay pavilion, yellow clay pavilion, black clay pavilion, white clay pavilion, green clay pavilion) that rich in traditional farming culture and five elements of culture. It can make you appreciate the great and profound Chinese rice culture.

Paddy Field Geothermal Hot Springs

Paddy Field National Park has a hot spring belt. Many gurgling hot springs are going all year round, and the average water temperature up to 59 ℃ . Fluorine and metasilicic acid in the water fulfil the standard of named mineral water concentration, the content radon reaches the standard of medical value concentration, and it is rich in some trace elements which are very beneficial to humans, such as strontium and lithium. In addition to the ornamental value, it can also be developed for spa recuperation in paddy field.

Romantic Blossom Garden

There are thousands of acres of flowers which are very colorful and varied! Here we have gorgeous and romantic canna garden, dragon boat garden, bougainvillea garden, crape myrtle garden, Lotus Garden and so on, making you feel the true artistic conception: please come to Tianya Haijao, here the four seasons flowers are always colorful. Paddy Field National Park is also a tropical rain forest area and aquatic flower breeding base for you to appreciate flowers, view flowers, learn flowers and apperceive flowers.

The Fruits and Vegetables Picking Garden

The Fruits and Vegetables Picking Garden is a good place for parent-child experience, family outdoor activity and outdoor team training. Tropical fruits and vegetables planting experience area includes all kinds of fruit, such as pitaya, guava, carambola, wax apple , mango, passion fruit, naseberry, strawberry and different kinds of tropical vegetables which are all adopting ecological planting cultivation technology. The garden gives the tourists the chance to walk into the fruit and vegetables to pick these green, organic and environmentally healthy fruit and vegetables by themselves, experience the pleasure of being a farmer and enjoy healthy and safe organic foods.

Chinese Star Dinosaurs Area

China is a great dinosaur country, and out of over 1000 known dinosaurs in the world, more than 280 have been discovered in China. 277 species and 323 Chinese dinosaurs from over 20 provinces and regions, including Heilongjiang, Xinjiang, Sichuan, and Yunnan, have been restored in a 1:1 scale and have traveled through billions of years to gather in Sanya Rice National Park, becoming the world's largest outdoor dinosaur exhibition and science popularization base. These digitally designed simulated dinosaurs not only have the ability to flexibly rotate their bodies but also simulate sound production. The small ones are less than one meter high, while the large ones can reach up to 38 meters high. As night falls and the stars twinkle, beneath the sky, these ancient life forms are adorned with dazzling lights, either roaring or roaring loudly, bringing absolute visual and auditory shock to people!

Dinosaur Trail

The 1.5 km long Dinosaur Trail crosses rice fields. Hundreds of motion-simulated dinosaurs brought you into ancient times to explore the meaning of ecology and life.

Parent-child Paradise

It's children's dream world nested in the rice paddies, there are a dinosaur mini-train, dinosaurs pulling straws vehicles, a space post office, dinosaur cars, a science popularization center and so on, appeasing children's imagination to learn in an educational and entertaining environment.

Entertaining

Field Carnival

This is the first large-scale landscape reality show in Sanya, written and artistic director by Mei Shuaiyuan, the famous founder of landscape reality shows in China, and directed by Yan Wenlong, the famous director of landscape reality shows. It tells the cultural context of Chinese agricultural civilization, rice cultivation civilization, sun windmill and other totem civilizations, as well as local Li ethnic customs, and tells the story of spring, summer, autumn, winter, and the 24 solar terms; Tell about rural areas, rice, labor, and dreams; Tell about the sun, moon, land, windmill, and scarecrow; Tell the story of a girl and a young man, labor and love; Telling the seemingly small but actually very big story of eating. The performances are: Preface; Act I, Spring Farming and Transplanting; Act II, Sun and Moon; Act III, Water Girl and Spring Boy; Act IV, Scarecrow and Clouds; Act V, Autumn Harvest and Sun.

Rice Field Carnival is a natural open-air theater covering about 40 Mu. What's more, there are 300 impressive performers act on the ultra-large landscape stage with the scenery of starry natural mountain, growing rice field, panoramic Li village, amazing sound and light. It will bring you a gluttonous feast of spirit, culture and art.

Night of the Earth

The sound and light show Night of the Earth displays combining multimedia, large veil and holographic technology to reappear the wonders of the dinosaurs, as well as call for the ecological civilization and the harmony between human beings and nature. This enables you to fully immerse in the incredibly interactive and immersive scenes and bring you a shocking experience.

Food

Rice Field Feast

Paddy Field Restaurant is an originally developed new ecological catering system by Paddy Field National Park. The restaurant is built up on the rice paddy field covering the area of 23,000 square meters. The architecture is magnificent and broad. It can accommodate over 2,800 diners at the same time. The restaurant also includes a unique seafood square with 72 seafood booths and an ultra-large central visual kitchen. The top master chefs are invited to cook for you through the theme of rice culture when open up the "Rice Culture" corridor, you will enjoy excellent food under coconut trees, beside the paddy fields and near the duck ponds...What a wonderful eating atmosphere that beyond your imagination!

Hospitality

Paddy field seclusion - RV Camp

Rice Field RV Camp is set beside the rice and flowers fields covering an area of 10,000 square meters. There are 20 RVs equipped with five-star internal decorations, one bedroom with one living room, two bedrooms with one living room, and so on. With facilities such as KTV, tea break pub, reception center, children's pool, campfire party, barbecue buffet, folk performance and more, the RV Camp provides a unique leisurely lodging experience for families or self-driving tour and group tour, and also provides private customized service for all kinds of parent-child activities, gathering activities, parties, study tours, and summer or winter camps.

Travelling

There are 6 kilometers of colorful tour-car lane crossing the scenic area. The wooden paths in the paddy fields twists and turns with ecological trials close to flower and paddy fields. The area has over 50 eco-tour-cars to provide tourists with the options of both riding and walking tour. A battery ticket can reach the entire park, you can voluntarily get off at each scenic spot. Personalized VIP service is a super nice choice for family, lovers and friends gathering.

Well, ladies and gentlemen, our tour bus has entered our scenic area. I believe all of you can't wait to experience it immediately, then let us take a good mood to appreciate the fun of harmonious coexistence between human and nature together!

8. Shihua Water Cave Geological Park

Hello everyone, welcome to visit Shihua Water Cave Geological Park, I'm your guide Xu Dan, you can call me Xiao Xu. I hope my explanation can bring you a pleasant mood. This scenic spot covers an area of 290,000 square meters at present and is located at 18° north latitude. It is the lowest latitude natural Karst cave successfully developed so far in China. It is known as "the first cave in Hainan Province". Its total length is about 5,000 meters, of which the dry cave is about 2000 meters and 650 meters of the dry cave has been developed. The water cave is about 3000 meters long and 350 meters has been developed. Shihua Water Cave is a Karst cave naturally formed about 1.4 million years ago and the natural evolution has created a unique cave spectacle.

The scenic spot is composed of above-ground stone forest attractions, underground caves, underground river attractions and tropical fruit garden attractions. The Shihua Water Cave is not an ordinary cave. The scenic area inside the cave consists of a dry cave and a water cave and the tunnel system is complex. With a total length of about 5,000 meters, it is divided into Yingbin District, Shihua Passageway District, Jade and Pearl District, and Nanhai Dragon Palace District. The "one stone and two flowers" curly stone, aragonite flower, calcite crystal flower and their combination in the dry cave can be regarded as national treasures and the best in the world. Shihua Water Cave is known as "Southern Magic Cave" and "Magic Underground Art Hall".

The dry cave contains stalactites, stalagmites, stone pillars, stone flags, stone waterfalls, stone tongues, antimony crystal clusters, crystal clusters, etc. The water hole has been developed 350 meters, and the deepest depth of water is 17 meters. The twisting and winding underground river is meandering and colorful. The scenery of canoe roaming make you feel like getting into a dragon palace, letting you make reverie.

The periphery of the scenic spot is a 10000 acre rubber forest that is the key construction of the "Bayi" general field. For many years, the output of rubber has been ranked the top of Hainan reclamation area. Rubber forests with tropical fruit forests and stone forests in the scenic spot constitutes the beautiful and harmonious scenery of nature.

Shihua Water Cave Geological Park is a comprehensive garden landscape integrating adventure science, tourism, science education and environmental protection education. It is a living geological textbook, and it is also a good place for leisure and vacation.

Geological conditions

There are many types of geological relics on the mountain of Yingdao in Shihuashui (rock flowers water) Cave. The most important parts are caves, cave secondary chemical deposits, stone forests and the corrosion morphology, originally limestone ore (metamorphic marble) with high quality and calcium oxide content up to 52%. It is mainly composed of Karst landscape. The Karst landscape is composed of a variety of special landforms developed on the widely distributed carbonate rocks. The surface stone peaks are tall and the underground caves are fancy. Not only stalactites are dazzling but also there is a continuous underground river in the cave.

In Shihua Water Cave Geological Park we can see the three major rock types of the earth surface — sedimentary rocks, igneous rocks and metamorphic rocks. Limestone belongs to the sedimentary rock. Diabase veins are mantle magma that intrudes into limestone along faults and structural belts, so the veins belong to igneous rocks. When the ascending veins invade into limestone, limestone is transformed into marble by heating fluid. Therefore, marble is a metamorphic rock. This laid the foundation for the formation of stone flowers.

Features

Although the total length of the tunnel in Shihua Water Cave is not very long, it has a complete set of elements, which could reflect the various causes of the formation of the cave passage. From the history of cave development, there are underground rivers that have been developing, and some dry cave tunnels that have escaped from the groundwater level. From the development direction of the caves, there are horizontally extending channels and vertical wells. In terms of the formation cause of the cave, there are wells that develop in the seepage zone (aeration zone), cave loops that develop in the underflow zone, and underground river tunnels that generate near the groundwater level. From the perspective of the tunnel composition, there are main caves and small branch caves, which form a complex three-dimensional cave network system together. The Shihua Water Cave

Tunnel system, wells and fissures, underground river channels and downstream Karst springs together form an orderly Karst cave hydro-geological system. The organized spatial distribution rules and their generation and development sequence of time provided a natural experimental place for tropical Karst caves and tropical Karst hydro-geological studies.

Wonder

The stone flower in the cave mainly has three mineral components, namely calcite, gypsum and rock salt, so it can also be called calcite stone flower, gypsum stone flower and rock salt stone flower.

The formation of stone flowers in Shihua Water Cave is different from stalagmites, stone pillars, stalactites, stone mantles, stone waterfalls, etc. The latter ones are mostly deposited by dripping, flowing and stagnant water, while stone flowers have infiltration water, splashing water, capillary water is deposited. Its chemical composition is calcium carbonate. After people's determination of carbon fourteen, they thought that the stone flower began to form more than 100,000 years ago. The conditions for the formation of the stone flower require the coexistence of several conditions. At least 400,000 years ago, Danzhou should be located in a place where seabed seashells are very rich. This has caused both the inside and outside of the Shihua Water Cave to be rich in calcium carbonate stone, which has become a prerequisite for the formation of stone flowers. Because the movement of the sea washed away some of the calcium carbonate, a stone cave such as Shihua Water Cave was formed over time. Due to the deformation of the terrain by the internal force of the earth, more or less cracks have been created on the top of the complete rock formations of the SShihua Water Cave, and there are rainwater infiltrates whenever it rains. Meanwhile, for various reasons such as air and microorganisms, some rainwater contains carbon dioxide, and the water and carbon dioxide are synthesized into calcium carbonate and penetrate into the cracks. Some holes have more cracks that make the rainwater flows faster, and it is difficult to form stalactites. But it can gradually crystallize under the conditions of relatively stable temperature and humidity, then form some white crystals. That is stone flower.

The stone flowers in the cave are clusters on the rock wall. Some shapes are like silver needles, some are like jade flutes, some are like chrysanthemums, and some are like corals. Each is crystal clear, purity, beautiful, and as hard as jade. Under the reflection of the lights, the clusters of stone flowers are shinning, and many tourists are attracted. Almost all stone flowers have been deposited for millions of years, and they are still growing, which is rare at home and abroad.

Stone flowers in the Shihua Water Cave have three characteristics:

1. The stone flower is glisten, the crystal coagulation, and it is white like jade.

2. It has various poses, unique and magnificent. It gathers the various forms of the world's stone flowers in one place: needle-like, spherical, tower-like, curly, radial, and shape like lucid ganoderma.

3. Attached to the rock wall, it grows to all sides without being affected by gravity, and feel air become stone, continues to grow, and changes endlessly. And the stone flower was only growing one centimeter long in a hundred years.

Inside the cave is a national treasure-level treasure — Curly Stone. Geological experts accidentally discovered the curly stones here during exploration in the cave. They are located at the top of the middle of the dry road. Curly stone is mainly composed of calcite. It distributes on the sidewall and cave tops of the curly stone channel. Many outcrops and cracks are produced along a rock layer, and they are dense in caves and scattered on the rock wall with many output form. There are a lot of curly stones in the Shihua Water Cave, and the shape is very beautiful. It is a kind of sediment that is very popular in the tourist cave. The growth direction of curly stones is not limited by the effect of gravity. They tend to grow upward and sideways. The color is pure white, and the diameter is generally about 5~6cm. It is only found in a few countries such as the United States, Romania, and China.

Let's have a look at this planting on both sides, it is King Palm, whose upper and lower ends are smaller and larger in the middle. It looks like a missile about to be launched, so we also call it "missile tree". It is an evergreen tree in the palm family and is also the national tree of Cuba. The fruit on it is rich in oil and can be used to feed pigeons.

This road that we walking on is our Shilaiyunzhuan Avenue, and it is also a beautiful scenic line. As we are walking across the avenue, the breeze blows slowly towards us just like the good luck brought by the avenue. Let's take a look at a hundred-year-old banyan tree ahead. The banyan tree can be said to be the symbol of Danzhou. Banyan trees have more than hundred years in Danzhou which can be seen everywhere. The prayer belt hanging under the tree is the meaning that the visitors send wishes to their families, relatives, friends and peace.

Dear visitors, the hibiscus flower planted on both sides of the avenue we are walking now is generally called the big red flower. The flowering season of the hibiscus flower on the summer and autumn are most vigorous. It is said that the local indigenous girl will perform hula dance at the beach with this kind of flower. If she puts the flower on her left ear, it means that she have grown up and hoping for a lover. If she puts a flower in her right ear, it means that she already have a lover.

Let's take a look at a banyan tree on the right hand side. We can see that its characteristic is that these wicking capillary roots absorb water and nutrients from the air and the roots form a scene and become the view is that a single tree can become a forest.

Let's continue to look at a large banyan tree on the right hand side. Its characteristic is that its roots are like a huge claw. Next we are going to walk through this promenade, which is the characteristic love hall in our scenic spot. The hibiscus flowers and banyan trees form it. The branches on both sides hanging down like a curved arch like when we were married. And it is a promenade that continues family, love and friendship. Maybe you have heard eight strange things in Hainan: three bugs can make a meal; three mice can fill a whole bag; one locust as a belt; the roots grow outside the bark; the granny climbs the tree faster than a monkey; one end of the island is raining but the other is sunny; the bucket hat on the head can be used as a lid; fried eggs on bluestone slates.

Let's take a look at the two trees on the right hand side called the Hanging Tree. These two trees are a common phenomenon in tropical rain forests. This hanging tree is wrapped in an oil palm tree and the banyan tree is outside. The palm oil we often eat is extracted from this oil palm. Their formation is that some birds, squirrels or bats have eaten the fruits of the banyan tree, then the dung has the seeds of the banyan tree, and is formed by taking roots and germinating on the oil palm tree. They are still a parasitic phenomenon. Slowly the banyan tree will absorb the nutrient and the water of oil palm and hang it off. This is the Hanging Tree.

When we all walked to the gazebo, we could see a god turtle. There is a saying in China "Touch the turtle's head and don't worry about anything. Touch the back of a turtle, you will never get tired for a lifetime." The general meaning of this sentence is that if you touch the turtle's head, everything you worry about will be resolved; if you touch the turtle's back, then you will have a happy life.

Dear friends, after appreciating the beauty of the road, and have a certain understanding of the formation and development of stone forests, Karst caves, and underground rivers. My explanation has come to a end successfully. As the saying goes in Chinese: "Two mountains cannot meet, two people can always meet." I look forward to seeing you all again and serving you all again! Wishing everyone all the best in the new year, peace and happiness, and a pleasant journey!

9. Dongpo Academy

Hello everyone, welcome to visit Dongpo Academy, I'm your guide Shi Dan Dan, you can call me Xiao Shi. I hope my explanation can bring you a pleasant mood. Dongpo Academy is one of the important relics left by Su Dongpo in Danzhou. Its predecessor is "ZaiJiuTang", which was initially built in the first year of the Northern Song Dynasty, that is 1,098. It was rebuilt in the third year of Taiding period in the Yuan Dynasty, which is 1,326, at the same time, Dongpo Temple was also established here. It was renamed Dongpo Academy (1548) after being reconstruct in the 27th year of Jiajing in the Ming Dynasty. In 1996, Dongpo

Academy was listed as a National-Level Cultural Relics Preservation Unit. It is a well-known cultural tourist destination in Hainan.

Zaijiu Pavilion

The Zaijiu Pavilion was built in the 23rd year of the Wanli Period of the Ming Dynasty (1595). The Zaijiu Pavilion has a double eaves structure, with four corners on the upper eaves and eight corners on the lower, twelve columns propping up the green roof. The entire pavilion reveals an elegant simplicity after a long history of precipitation. There are eight woodcuts in the interior of pavilion, depicting the scene of Dongpo while living in Danzhou. Respectively limn the scenes of his friendship, apprenticeship, departure, and so on.

The Story of "Chunmengpo"

In the engraving, the head wearing a bamboo split hat is Su Dongpo, next to him is a countrywoman. The story tells that one day, Su Dongpo met this woman who went to the field delivering meal to her husband. She has a messy hair, because chewing betel nut all year round makes her mouth black red. When Su Dongpo saw her, he satirized: "Dirty hair, black lips, went to the field every day." The woman was very upset to hear these words and responded impolitely: "You know why the government devalued you to this place, just because you don't care about others when you speak".

Dongpo found that the woman was very smart, so he asked her, "Can you tell something about this world?" The woman said, "In brief, the glory and wealth of this world, it's just an illusion!" Su Dongpo was completely convinced by this outspoken and profoundly sophisticated countrywoman, so he gave her a nickname "Chun Mengpo". This is the "Chun Mengpo's story" that has been circulating since the Northern Song Dynasty.

ZaiJiuTang

"ZaiJiuTang", which was initially built in the first year of the Northern-Song Dynasty, that is 1098, the second year from Su Dongpo to Danzhou. Once, Su Dongpo was invited by Changhua Army Envoy Zhang Zhong (the local governor of

Danzhou at the time) to visit Li Ziyun together. During the conversation, everyone proposed to build a house next to Liu Ziyun's residence as a place to set up lectures and make friends for Dongpo. Su Dongpo strongly agreed with this initiative, and took the lead in donated money, he also used the allusion "Studious and Inquisitive" to name the house. Su Dongpo set up the lecture in "Zaijiu Tang", and trained Jiang Tangzuo and Fu Que, the first people in the history of Hainan to obtain a high position in the imperial examination. The society has also formed a situation of "People know to teach children, Families learn Confucianism, the number of people learning in society is increasing", which will have a profound impact on the future.

There was also have a story about "Studious and Inquisitive": Yang Xiong, the famous poet of the Western Han Dynasty, is a knowledgeable person, but he likes drinking very much, therefore, those who wanted to worship him as a teacher went to his home and brought drinks as tuition. This is the origin of the allusion.

Hall statue

Su Dongpo is in the middle. On the left is Li Ziyun. He is both a student and deepest friend in Danzhou of Su Dongpo. In those days, Zhang Zhong was dismissed for taking care of Su Dongpo, Su Dongpo was devalued from the official house and lost his shelter. At that time, Li Ziyun and other Li people helped him build three shacks. Similarly, it is also Li Ziyun's investment and contribution that led to the present ZaiJiuTang. The handsome boy on the right is named Su Guo, it's Su Dongpo's youngest son. When Su Dongpo was demoted to Danzhou in 1097, Su Guo was only 25 years old, it's a good time for fame. However, in order to take care of Su Dongpo's daily life, Su Guo crossed the sea with his father, and spent time with Dongpo for three years. Because Su Guo was a filial son, the Danzhou people wanted to build a shrine to commemorate him.

Picture of Dongpo wearing clogs and hats

The painter of this painting is Qian Xuan, the people who from the Southern Song Dynasty. One day in the record, Su Dongpo encountered rain on the way to visit Li Ziyun, so he borrowed bamboo hats and clogs from the peasant family.

Because he looked strangely dressed, women and children laughed when they saw him, even the dog barked at him. Su Dongpo also laughed after seeing the scene, then said, "It's strange to laugh, also strange to bark!" In all ages, there are many versions of the painting, which have spread widely, but the real place of this story happened in Danzhou.

Dongpo Temple

Dongpo Temple is commonly known as "the main temple hall", which built in the fourth year (1317) of Yuanyou period in the Yuan Dynasty and located in the south of the city. However, it was relocated to the current site in 1326.

The Dongpo Bronze Statue was designed by the famous sculptor He Baosen, a professor at Tsinghua University. It was erected by the Danzhou Government in 2015. The sculpture carved Dongpo sitting leisurely on a wooden chair, holding a scroll in his hand, and staring into the distance calmly. It shows Su Dongpo's spiritual world in which he faced sufferings calmly.

Han Shi Tie

"Han Shi Tie" is called "the third line of the world", which has a great influence in the history of Chinese calligraphy. This post is now in the National Palace Museum in Taipei.

West Corridor

"Farewell poems to Hainan Li people" is a gift poem written by Su Dongpo to Li Ziyun when he could return to the north after leaving for pardon. The meaning of this poem is: I'm like a Danzhou man who grew up in Sichuan. Because of urgent things, I must leave across the sea. There is no good or bad in the life of a person, either alive or dead or dreaming. I knew that I might not meet you again after this farewell. The government's order must not be violated, so don't keep me.

Su Shi — *Inscription on Jinshan Temple portrait*

In May 1101, Su Dongpo returned home and passed through Zhenjiang. He saw the portrait of Li Gonglin who painted him for 10 years at the Jinshan Temple which was still there. He was very emotional, so he wrote this poem for himself:

My heart is like burnt wood, and my body is like an unrestrained boat. If you ask me what I have done through my whole life, I can only say that I have been to Huangzhou, Huizhou and Danzhou. Su Dongpo summarized his life with this poem. Two months after he wrote this, he died of illness in Changzhou, so this poem is also an extraordinary poem by him.

East Corridor

Since the founding of the People's Republic of China, dozens of party and state leaders have visited here. These are the precious photos of them when they visited.

Mango tree

This mango tree was planted in the third year of the reign of emperor Qianlong of the Qing dynasty (1738). It is leafy and making the entire courtyard quiet and refreshing. Every summer, the tree will be filled with mangoes, which locals think is a very precious gift.

QinShuaiQuan

This ancient well is called "QinShuaiQuan", reportedly, it was the well where Su Dongpo used to make tea with the students. In the Ming Dynasty, it was dredged and officially named "QinShuaiQuan". All year round, this well never dries up, and the taste of the well water is clear and sweet. You can put on a bucket of water, take a sip or wash hands. This can also be considered "holy water". You can feel the talent of Dongpo indirectly. If you are a student, you can have a bright future; If you are already working, then you will be able to achieve great achievements!

"QinShuaiQuan" is also called "Liquor Well", there has an interesting story about it. It is said, there is a poor woman nearby. One day, she came to "QinShuaiQuan" to pick up water, sighing, "If the water could be turned into wine, how nice it would be!" At night, Su Dongpo appeared in her dream and made a request: "From tomorrow on, the water will turn into wine, so you can choose to sell money for life." The next day, the woman came to the well with her doubts, she was surprised that the well water had really turned into a fragrant wine. Since then, she has become richer, also become greedier, so she complaining: "Although it is a good thing for the well water to turn into wine, it would be better if you could give me some vinasse to feed my pigs." Hence, Su Dongpo appeared in her dream again and said, "Heaven doesn't feel high, greed is higher than heaven, let you sell water as wine, you do not feel enough, you even want vinasse in the wine." Since then, there has been no more wine in the well. It warns people not to be too greedy.

Spring Bull Sculpture

During the Northern Song Dynasty, the local Li people were backward in thought and superstitious. They exchange agarwood for cattle from the inland, and they often obey the rule that "one cow for once agarwood", but the cattle they exchange are not used for farming. They set up altars, kill cattle and worship gods. This behavior also directly caused the local agricultural production to remain in its original state. Su Dongpo was very distressed by this, so he wrote a series of articles about the value of cattle to agriculture, in order to persuade Li people to eliminate the vulgar and cherish the cattle. With his spare no effort in enlightenment, this vulgar was put to an end. The word on the sculpture is a poem written by Dongpo for the people of Danzhou. He cheerfully described the splendid spring of Danzhou, also entrusted his good wishes to the people of here:

The cattle and plow rods expressed the feeling of welcoming spring, breeze blew from the sea, begging the god of spring to create the work of all things, even the peach blossoms were dyed red and bloody.

Flags and paper-cuts fluttered wildly in the spring day, and a breeze woke me from drunkenness. The scenery of Hainan is different from the inland. The catkin rolled up in the beginning of spring seems like snowflakes.

General Secretary Xi Jinping quoted Su Dongpo's poems to praise the natural scenery of Hainan. At the same time, he pointed out that Hainan's ecological environment is a precious wealth given by nature and must be treasured and carefully protected to make Hainan truly a four-season garden for China.

Dongpo Private School

Su Dongpo set up a lecture in ZaiJiuTang to spread the culture to the people in

Danzhou. This behavior also attracted many inland students to come to study, and made Danzhou become the cultural and educational center of the island at that time.

What you see now are all used by Su Dongpo in that year, this old-style private school restores to the greatest extent the stationery supplies, textbooks and varieties of Northern Song dynasty ritual instruments. In 2018, Dongpo Academy was successively designated as the "Hainan Province Primary and Secondary School Students Research Practice Education Base" and "National Tourism Education Base for Primary and Secondary School Students". We also set up lecture here, you can wear Song suits, enter old-style private school, learn etiquette, worship Confucius, and recite Dongpo's poetry. When you come here, you can experience a realistic time travel.

Paparazzi flower

Paparazzi are very special. This kind of flower can only be seen in Dongpo Academy. It is not only rare but also wonderfully blooming. There is also an interesting story about it.

Once, Wang Anshi wrote a poem: "Bright moon barks in the sky, five dogs lie on the stamens." After seeing it, Su Dongpo thought that the poem was not written in accordance with reality. Thus, he changed the poem to "The bright moon shines in the air, and five puppies lie in the shade." Later, Su Dongpo was exiled to Danzhou. He saw paparazzi flowers with his own eyes in Zaisha Hall, and also saw the bright moon bird (a type of mountain sparrow) soaring in the sky under the bright moon at night. It was then that he suddenly realized that he had made a mistake in correcting Wang Anshi's poem back then. "Paparazzi Flower" also became famous worldwide due to this iron incident.

When the paparazzi bloom, there are 5 small stamens in the blooming petals. It looks like 5 puppies sitting together head to head, so they are called "paparazzi".

Exhibition Gallery

The word "Exhibition Hall" was inscribed in gold by the famous calligrapher Shang Chengzuo. The whole gallery introduces the life story, chronogram and whereabouts of Su Dongpo. It highlights the great achievements of Su Dongpo for Danzhou.

Bronze statue of Dongpo wearing clogs and hats

The bronze statue is drawn from a painting of the same name. In the picture, he wears a bamboo hat on his head and a clog on his feet. This optimistic and easy-going image will always live in the memories of the people of Danzhou. The creator of the bronze statue is Li Hanyi, a famous sculptor in China. The words "Dongpojushi" on the front of the marble base are Guo Moruo's calligraphy.

Refreshment Stands

You can take a break here, drink some lotus tea, taste Danzhou-style snacks, and buy some souvenirs. You can also wear Song Dynasty costumes and take pictures. The ancient banyan tree here is regarded by the locals as the "sacred tree" and they have the custom of praying to the tree. Tourists are tied to the tree with prayer belts to show their respect for the old tree, and ask it to bless family and friends.

On weekends, you can enjoy the song and dance performance of "Dongpo Music Square" here, you can also enjoy the tunes of Danzhou, which is included in the national intangible heritage, and you can feel the fiery Li style through such performances.

Dear friends, our trip to Dongpo Academy is now over. The scenery is always here for your next visit. Wish you have a happy and safe journey!

10. Mu Rui Shan Revolutionary Base Area Memorial Park

Dear friends and tourists, Welcome to Mu Rui Shan Revolutionary Base Area Memorial Park, the cradle of Hainan's revolution. I am today's tour guide Xiao Tang. Murui Mountain is a mountain range extending from Wuzhi Mountain to the northeast. It is the cradle of the Hainan's revolution. During the two low revolutions in Qiongya, Murui Mountain twice preserved the revolutionary fire. It has also made significant contributions to the Hainan people's persistence in armed struggle.

Preserve the revolutionary spark

At the end of 1928, during the first downturn in Hainan, Comrade Wang Wenming led more than 600 people from Qiongya Special Committee, Qiongsu government agencies, Red Army soldiers, Red Guards, Red Army hospitals, and traffic departments to break through the enemy's blockade from the 4 blocks in Lehui. After crossing the Wanquan River and achieving to Mu Rui Mountain, they opened up a revolutionary base.

When they first arrired the mountain, the conditions were very difficult. There was no house, no food, no clothes and no medicine. In order to solve these problems, Comrade Wang Wenming went to the Miao Village in the mountain to mobilize the Miao people. With the support of the seedlings, more than 40 thatched houses were built to solve the housing problem.

What about eating? Comrade Wang Wenming once again mobilized the military and civilians, carried forward the spirit of self-reliance and hard work, and opened up wasteland for farming. Three Red Army farms around more than 300 acres were set up. Rice, mountain orchid, corn, cassava, sweet potato, melon and vegetables were planted. After about half a year, the crops were harvested. The supply and the life of the Red Army have gradually improved, and the problem of food was solved.

What about the clothes? They secretly sent people down the mountain to buy the coarse cloth in nearby villages and towns such as Hanlin, Linkou, and Shibi, and organized a sewing team to sew into clothes to solve the problem of wearing. The masses were mobilized to solve the problems of food, clothing and shelter, and the Red Army gained a firm foothold on Mount Mu Rui.

With the development of the revolutionary situation, two red regimes were established in the hinterland of Murui Mountain and more than 40 surrounding villages. That is, two township governments, one named Dashan Township and the other named Murui Township, which launched a vigorous struggle for the Agrarian Revolution.

In June 1929, the Red Army Independent Group was born in Mount Mu Rui. On this basis, the Red Army hospital, ordnance factory, military and political school, consumer cooperatives, and grain processing factories were simply set up. The Red Army Troupe also rehearsed folk songs, Hainan Opera and other programs to activate the spiritual life of the Red Army. Although life was so hard at that time, the Red Army soldiers still maintained a high degree of optimism, and they were full of confidence in the future of the revolution. So far, Mu Ruishan has become a small society with everything available.

After more than a year of hard work, under the leadership of Comrade Wang Wenming, the Mu Ruishan Revolutionary Base was established. The establishment of the Mu Ruishan Revolutionary Base area preserved the fire of the revolution and also marked a new stage in the development of the armed struggle in Hainan.

Secondary preservation of revolutionary sparks

In the autumn of 1932, during the second downturn in Hainan, Comrade Feng Baiju led more than 100 people from the special committee department and the Qiongsu government department to insist on an arduous struggle for more than 8 months on Mount Mu Rui. They have overcome all kinds of unimaginable difficulties, and have passed through one difficulty after another.

The first is food difficulties. The Kuomintang adopted a policy of merging villages and emigrating. In an attempt to turn Mu Rui Mountain into a no-man's land, isolate the Red Army from the people, and starve the Red Army to death in this revolutionary cradle. Comrade Feng Baiju and more than 100 people have not eaten a full meal in Mu Rui Mountain for months. At the beginning, each person can get a fist-sized rice ball for each meal. Later, there was less and less food, and the rice ball became a coconut shell porridge. In the end, they can only drink rice soup cooked with rice crust. The food is gone, and they can't even eat porridge anymore. People had to go up the mountains to find wild vegetables, pick wild fruits, go down to the river to catch fish and shrimps, and go up the trees to catch birds and bird eggs. They ate everything they can find on the mountain, as long as it is not poisonous. At that time, there was a wild vegetable on the mountain, with tender leaves, crisp stems and a bit bitter taste. The Red Army used this wild vegetable as a "staple food" to sustain life. But no one knows what the name of this wild vegetable is. In order to name this wild vegetable, Comrade Feng Baiju hosted a naming meeting. Some comrades at the meeting said that this kind of wild vegetables can satisfy your stomach, so call it "satisfactory vegetables"! Some comrades also said it can be called "mountain treasure"! Comrade Feng Baiju finally summarized everyone's opinions and said with earnest words: "This kind of wild vegetables saved our lives when the revolution was most difficult. Let's call it 'revolutionary' dish"! This nature of dish is very cold, and the Red Army eats this kind of dish without oil and salt every day. Over time, many comrades have got edema, night blindness, dysentery and any other dieases.

Second, there is no house to live in. In the autumn of 1932, more than 1,000 members of the army of Chen Hanguang in Kuomingtang occupied the Mu Ruishan Revolutionary Base under the cover of airplanes. Burned all the huts where the Red Army lived, robbed all the supplies, and destroyed all the crops on the farm. There is only one piece of clothing left on each Red Army. They had to live in a low and damp cave, where they often changed. In order to avoid the enemy's investigation, sometimes the Red Army has to sleep in several places in one night. In the autumn and winter seasons, the wind and rain were harsh, and the cold wind was biting. At night, the Red Army was too cold to sleep in the cave and had to burn the fire to keep warm. The Red Army went to the mountains to cut banana leaves and put them on the fire to heat them up as quilts and mats. They spent one long night after another in the deep mountains and old forests and caves.

Third, there is no clothes to wear. There was only one piece of clothing on the Red Army, and there was no change of clothes for several months. After a long time, all the clothes rotted and turned into cloth strips and pieces of cloth hanging on the body. In the end, the rotted clothes could not be worn again. The Red Army had to wear leaves and bark. Later, they went to the mountain to find suitable leaves as clothes. Regardless of whether it is a man or a woman, as long as they can wrap the key parts of their body with leaves and bark. What if the hair is too long to be trimmed? The Red Army had to lie on the ground and cut the hair with a machete. Comrade Feng Baiju led these more than 100 people to live a primitive life on Mount Mu Rui for more than 8 months.

Fourth, on the mountain, they must not only fight the enemy, but also fight the harsh natural environment. At that time, many people died on Mount Mu Rui. There were countless people who died of war, starvation, disease, freezing, and being bitten by poisonous snakes. More than 100 people died of illness and starvation in the coffin ditch north of Mount Mu Rui. One day under a big banyan tree in Ma'anling, 9 comrades starved to death. When the Red Army soldiers came to sit and rest under the shade of the tree, they no longer had the strength to stand up, and finally starved to death under the tree.

The more than 100 people led by Comrade Feng Baiju finally left 26 people, including 4 cadres and 22 fighters. Two of the 22 fighters were women, one was Feng Baiju's wife Wang Huizhou, and the other was cook Li Yuefeng. At this time, Feng Baiju considered that if he continues to stay in the mountains, avoid contact with the masses, it will be detrimental to the survival and development of the revolution. Therefore, the Special Committee decided to break through and go down the mountain to find a way to survive. They organized four groups of people to break through and descend the mountain, but none of them succeeded. Either he was found and killed by the enemy on the way, or because of the bad environment, there was no way to come back down the mountain. It lasted until the Spring Festival of 1933, taking advantage of the opportunity for the enemy to relax his vigilance during the Spring Festival. Comrade Feng Baiju personally organized these 26 people, led by Comrade Li Yuefeng, to break through in the emerging direction of Chengmai.

When the team broke out and arrived at Comrade Li Yuefeng's hometown, Feng Baiju sent her into the village to check the situation and find some water and food. The other comrades waited for news in the woods near the village. Unexpectedly, soon after Comrade Li Yuefeng entered the village, he was informed by the bad guys and caught and killed by the enemy. At this time, Feng Baiju and other 25 comrades had to leave the village in grief and anger. They endured hunger and thirst after a two-day trek to return to Mount Mu Rui.

The days on the mountain are even more difficult at this time. The fire in the cave has been extinguished, and there are very few wild vegetables, fish and shrimps. Coupled with the fact that the enemy sends dogs to search for mountains every day, the Red Army has already lost its basic living conditions. This period is also the most difficult period of the Qiongya Revolution. The 25 people united as one, under the leadership of the special committee, supported by faith and will, and persisted until April 1933.

The spirit of Mount Mu Rui

Comrades Wang Wenming and Feng Baiju also forged the spirit of Mu Ruishan in the two struggles of Mount Mu Rui to preserve the fire of the revolution. This is: lofty ideals, firm beliefs; not afraid of sacrifice, bravely to sacrifice; trust the masses and rely on the masses; self-reliance and hard working.

Dear tourists, in the past revolutionary war years, the revolutionary elders made revolutions, fighting the country, seeking liberation, and seeking happiness. Ushered in the birth of the People's Republic of China, it relied on the spirit of Mount Mu Rui. I hope the spirit of Mount Mu Rui shines in the future!

11. Coconut Grand View Garden

Hello everyone, welcome to visit Coconut Grand View Garden, I'm your guide Li Dan, you can call me Xiao Li. I hope my explanation can bring you a pleasant mood.

The Coconut Grand View Garden is a reconstruction of the original coconut germplasm resource bank of the Coconut Research Institute of the Chinese Academy of Tropical Agricultural Sciences, Ministry of Agriculture. It is located in

Wenchang City, Hainan Province, China, known as the "hometown of coconuts", adjacent to the famous coconut forest in the eastern suburbs of Hainan. The park was founded in 1980 and covers an area of 54.4 hectares. It is an ecological scenic area with strong coconut culture characteristics, with coconut forests as the main background, integrating scientific research, popular science education, tourism and sightseeing, as well as leisure and entertainment.

The park gathers 217 types of palm plants and 130 rare tree species with Hainan characteristics. It is currently the most preserved and complete botanical park in China for palm plant species, with a wide variety and peculiar shapes of plants that make people marvel. Relying on the scientific research strength of the Coconut Research Institute, the Coconut Grand View Garden has collected and exchanged coconut germplasm from all over the world. It has now collected 17 coconut germplasm, ranking first in the national collection of coconut germplasm and is praised as the "World Coconut Expo, Window of Chinese Coconut".

In 2021, the Coconut Research Institute of the Chinese Academy of Tropical Agricultural Sciences and Hainan Aiye Cultural and Tourism Development Co., Ltd. will jointly create a coconut themed comprehensive tourist attraction with the core of promoting the integration of coconut industry and tourism development. The Coconut Grand View Park is committed to promoting the spirit of coconut trees, building a first-class palm germplasm resource science popularization and research base in China, integrating the agricultural technology strength of the Coconut Research Institute, extending the coconut industry chain, and developing a coconut industry development platform. It aims to create a comprehensive themed scenic area that integrates the functions of coconut tree spirit, coconut culture, science popularization, cultural tourism, and industrial upgrading. After the completion of the project, it will become the main tourism product of Qiongbei Tourism, including the Coconut Warrior Camp, Coconut Culture Science Popularization and Study, Starry Sky Campsite, Moe Pet Park, Love Coconut Square, Coconut Forest Maze, Strange Coconut, Coconut Spirit and other characteristic theme attractions.

Coconut Warrior Camp

The Coconut Hero Camp is an expansion activity organization center tailored for the Coconut Hero IP in the Coconut Grand View Park scenic area, aimed at promoting the spirit of coconut trees and practicing the development concept of "youth is strong, China is strong". The camp has related supporting facilities such as expansion equipment and expansion venues, which meet the comprehensive functions of enterprise team building, ice breaking expansion, parent-child expansion, and family sports and leisure. Following the footsteps of Coconut Man, parents and children are encouraged to participate in activities such as jungle magic nets, rock climbing and wall climbing, and interlocking in the Warrior Camp. They immerse themselves in a challenging training environment and are refined in the camp, cultivating excellent qualities of perseverance, hard work, and positivity. Through various interactive communication methods such as parent-child games, parents can learn to communicate with their children, continuously improve their ability for communication, and make the parent-child relationship more harmonious.

Coconut Forest Maze

Crossing the "time and space coconut wall", awakening the dormant "treasure", following the footsteps of Coconut Man, exploring the unknown maze world, and searching for hidden "treasures" in the depths.

Moe Pet Park

The Moe Pet Park is located next to the Strange Coconut Area, with the theme of interaction between cute pets. It integrates intimate contact with cute pets, leisure activities, parent-child interaction, science education, and cute pet performances, creating a new vacation experience for the Moe Pet Theme Park. Here, tourists can see adorable squirrels, touch silly and mischievous rabbits, feed clever parrots, interact and take photos with lively and lovely guinea pigs, inspire people's love for nature and the spirit of exploration, and immerse the cute pet park in the coconut forest, aiming to create a way of immersive and close to nature interaction for tourists.

Strange Coconut

The carving art of "Ghostly Axes and Divine Craftsmanship" is a surprise left by nature to humanity. In the Strange Coconut Area, tourists can admire the Y-shaped forked coconut tree, which is "straight trunk, without branches or vines" and generally does not branch or fork. Folk people often use "coconut tree branching" to metaphorically describe impossible things. The probability of multiple embryos appearing in the coconut trees of "Three Yang Kai Tai" and "Five Blessings at the Gate" is lower than that of humans. Or it can be the "coconut fairy" that does not bloom and does not bear fruit. "Coconut fairy" is rare in the world and unique in China, with extremely high research value. These strange coconut trees are all naturally formed and cannot be intervened by humans.

Coconut Tree Spirit

The Coconut Spirit Area is the main tourist area of the Coconut Grand View Park scenic area, and also the core area for showcasing the spirit of Hainan Coconut trees. The area is filled with coconut trees that have been blown down by typhoons but still grow tenaciously. These coconut trees still love this soil, and their intricate air roots support the bridge of life, continuing to protect a piece of land and feeding back nature. Its inability to withstand strong winds represents the spirit of rooting and defending the soil; The fallen body still grows straight towards the sunlight, representing a resilient spirit; Devoting everything to people throughout one's life represents the spirit of selfless dedication, which inspires the people of Hainan to persevere and build a better home together!

Coconut Science Popularization Hall

The Coconut Grand View Park aims to develop a coconut industry development platform as their mission, and they aim to create a comprehensive themed scenic area that integrates coconut spirit, coconut culture, science popularization and research, cultural tourism, and industrial upgrading. They have established a research base with "Nine Zones and One Pavilion": National Tropical Palm Germplasm Resources Nursery, Coconut Warrior Camp, Coconut Forest Maze,

Coconut Tree Spirit, Strange Coconut, Coconut Forest Dance, Coconut Forest Lake Light, Tourist Station, Starry Sky Campsite, and Coconut Science Popularization Hall as their core resources. In November 2022, they were recognized by the China Association for Science and Technology as the "first batch of national science popularization education bases from 2021 to 2025".

Tourist Station

The unique design style, adhering to the concept of harmonious coexistence between humans and nature, not only reflects green environmental protection, but also highlights the coconut theme characteristics.The meticulously crafted aerial garden is mainly composed of various tropical rare plants such as Wenxin Orchid, Pitcher Plant, and Bird's Nest Fern, supplemented by rockeries, rocks, and water systems. It is distributed throughout the relay stations, forming a tropical southern characteristic garden and outdoor ecological park. The station integrates tea breaks, scenic views, and unique coconut water tasting functions, providing tourists with a high-quality viewing experience.

Dear friends, our journey to the Coconut Grand View Garden has come to an end. The beautiful scenery of the Coconut Grand View Garden is always waiting for your next visit here. Have a pleasant journey!

12. Qixianling Hot Springs National Forest Park

Dear tourists,welcome to the beautiful Qixianling Hot Spring National Forest Park for sightseeing and sightseeing. The Qixianling Hot Spring National Forest Park is located in the northeast of Baoting Li and Miao Autonomous County, including two parts: the hot spring area and the forest area. Its charm lies in the hot springs, unique peaks, ethnic customs, and tropical pastoral scenery. In 1998, it was jointly approved by the State Council and the National Forestry Administration as a national forest park. On December 29, 2016, it was officially approved as a national 4A level tourist attraction.

Qixianling Hot Spring National Forest Park is one of the few well preserved tropical rainforests on Hainan Island. The forest park features towering ancient trees and intertwined vines. At present, more than 500 rare plants and over 500 wild animals have been discovered. At a distance of about 700 meters on the mountaineering stone plank road, there is a concentrated distribution of fern fern communities, with poles over 9 meters high. The fern fern is known as the "living fossil of plants" and is a nationally protected ancient relic plant, dating back to the dinosaur era. Strolling through the primitive tropical rainforest of Qixianling, you can fully appreciate the flora and fauna landscape, and absorb the high concentration of oxygen and negative oxygen ions in the primitive tropical rainforest, which can have a health effect.

The scenic area has abundant tourism resources, spectacular and vivid landscape, complete with hydrological, plant, and climate tourism resources, as well as numerous social and cultural tourism resources. It is a large-scale ecological tourism area that integrates peaks, hot springs, customs, countryside, climate, and forests.

Natural environment

The climate in Qixianling area is warm and humid, with an average annual temperature of around 23 ℃ , the highest monthly average temperature of 27 ℃ , the lowest monthly average temperature of 18℃, and an annual rainfall of 1900 millimeters. The entire mountain is densely covered with primitive tropical rainforests and is a natural kingdom of flora and fauna. This includes rare and protected animals and plants such as Hainan yellow pear, butterfly wood, Alsophila spinulosa, bloodthirsty, and king cobra. In Hainan, Qixianling Hot Springs National Forest Park is the only forest park that combines hot springs with tropical rainforests. The park has a negative oxygen ion concentration of up to 8200 per cubic centimeter, which is very beneficial to human health.

The seven peaks of the Seven Immortals Ridge stand like human palms, pointing straight to the sky, or like fairy pavilions, hence the name of the mountain range. The front peak is tall, with an altitude of 1126 meters, while the back six peaks are interdependent and small. Between the three and four peaks of the Seven Immortals Ridge, there is a small stone peak that stands opposite the fourth peak. The small stone peak is shaped like a child, and when viewed from a distance, the four peaks resemble Guanyin. People call this scene "the child worships Guanyin". Climbing to the top of the Seven Immortals Ridge can bring endless joy of traveling with immortals, enjoying with people, getting drunk with scenery, and enjoying life with mountains.

When the morning fog is floating, the Seven Immortals Ridge looks like the seven sisters standing upright in gauze, dignified and graceful; As noon approached, the clouds and mist dissipated, and at this moment, the Seven Immortals Ridge was like seven sharp swords pointing straight at the clouds, with a very majestic momentum.

Mythical legends

Legend has it that in ancient times, hot springs were scattered throughout the Baoting area of Hainan Island. In addition to their work, the common people used orange leaves to soak in hot springs and bathe, which could eliminate fatigue, cure various diseases. Playing water games in hot springs can make people more beautiful and energetic. This matter spread to the Heavenly Palace, and the Queen Mother sent seven fairies down to earth to determine whether this place could be comparable to the Yaochi in the Heavenly Palace.

When the Seven Fairies descended to Baoting, they saw a scene full of green mountains and clear waters, with auspicious clouds swirling around, hot springs rising, birds singing and flowers fragrant, creating a beautiful fairyland on earth. The Seven Fairies were intoxicated, playing in this landscape every day and staying for a long time before returning to the Heavenly Court. This beautiful job was known by a magical Fengshen at sea, who also wanted to occupy this place as a place to live, but every time he came here to play, he would bring storms, submerge large areas of land, and damage large areas of beautiful countryside.

The Seven Fairies saw it in their eyes and were filled with anger. They petitioned the Jade Emperor and engaged in a fierce battle with the Wind God. In the end, they defeated the Wind God and drove him to the depths of the ocean. In order to prevent the Wind God from harming here again, the Seven Fairies were determined to protect this beautiful land and settle in the world forever. Later, it turned into seven beautiful peaks, which is now the magical Seven Immortals Ridge.

Nine Wonders

The tropical rainforest is home to nine wonders, including tall roots, roots holding stones, ancient vines entwined with trees, old stems producing flowers, aerial gardens, plant strangulation, dragons crossing the river, decaying trees producing mushrooms, and towering trees.

Tall trees are determined to compete for sunlight. In order to avoid being too heavy and unstable, some of them try their own ways to solve the problem. They grow thick and wide roots like walls, constantly extending to both sides to help reinforce their roots. The humid air and fertile soil in tropical rainforests provide sufficient conditions for their growth. Some tree species do not have the ability to grow long roots, so they stretch their thick roots and tightly embrace the giant rocks beside them. Their foundation is also stable like a chime stone, forming the wonder of high roots and roots embracing stones.

The spectacle of old stems blooming takes place on the body of Juguo banyan trees, where the flowers and fruits do not bloom on the branches but on the stems of the trees, making it a unique sight among the trees.

The aerial flower basket originated from the masterpiece of birds, which inadvertently brought the seeds or seedlings of orchids or ferns to tall tree crowns or hanging vines in the air, where they took root and bloomed, forming the wonder of aerial flower baskets, adding a lot of color to tropical primitive forests. “A tree piercing through a flower” is very typical. But if birds accidentally bring the seeds of the tall banyan tree to a tree, it will play the role of an accomplice to the forest killer. The tree will eventually be slowly strangled by the support roots of the tall banyan tree, which supplies all its channels for water and nutrition.

From this, it can be seen that not only do animals in the forest kill each other for survival (such as praying mantis catching cicadas and yellow sparrows behind), but the tall banyan in the trees is also a terrifying plant killer in tropical primitive forests. Therefore, it seems that the peaceful forest is not peaceful, but there are hidden dangers behind it. It can truly be described as natural selection, survival of the fittest.

List of Scenic Spots

Legend has it that the Li ethnic hero Liege, who was born with divine power, set out to fight against the wind and demons, and bid farewell to his beloved tribal leader's daughter Yagan with tears under this stone. Day after day of waiting, Yagan couldn't hope to come to Hunt Brother, but was taken back to the mountain stronghold by the coveted foreign leader Dong Zhu.

The longing for her lover, the tears merged into a lake, and her unwavering loyalty to love finally earned the help of the mountain god. With her silver hairpin transformed into wings, she transformed into a bird that broke through the clouds and flew towards her home. Hunter, who defeated the Wind Demon, was seriously injured and spent his days watching under the stone where he broke up. One day, a bird flew in from a distance, and the totem on its feathers made Liege understand that it was his beloved Yagan. So he leaped into a bird and followed Yagan, and the watchstone became a place for young men and women of the Li and Miao ethnic groups to protect their love.

Various strange shaped boulders scatter in the mountains, creating a unique and spectacular scenery in the rainforest wonderland. The worship of natural divine power has led the Li ethnic group to form a mountain god worship ceremony with giant stones as totems for generations.

Legend has it that a long time ago, the Seven Immortals Ridge was coveted by the South China Sea Wind Demons for its abundant production of rare and exotic herbs. The once prosperous Li ethnic homeland has become a mess of life. At the call of the clan leader Di, the young hero Hunter and the tribe's warriors began a defensive battle against the wind and demons. The mountain god who guarded one side also came upon hearing the news, endowing the giant stones with magical spirituality. One by one, the incredibly large "giant spirit stones" climbed up the mountaintop, and the "tree elves" firmly tied them together with tough vines. The tall stone wall temporarily blocked the wind, and the brave warriors of the Li ethnic group finally had a chance to breathe. The scattered people were able to reunite, and all living beings were able to recover.

The huge banyan tree has a history of more than 100 years. It was broken by lightning because it was too tall. But because of the unique climate of Qixian Mountain, the banyan tree sprouted new shoots at the fracture, growing five thick lateral branches, and the ancient vines twined and enjoyed the essence of the sun and the moon. The mountain people around Qixianling have formed a custom of praying in front of this banyan tree for any wish they have, and their wishes are often fulfilled. This place is also a holy land in the hearts of the residents of Qixianling.

In Chinese legend, waterfalls are the link between the mortal world and the immortal realm. The ancient people's longing for the sky gave waterfalls a beautiful imagination. According to legend, the source of Tiantan Waterfall comes from the "Immortal Spring" in the South China Sea fairy world. Long term bathing and drinking can make one's appearance immortal and youth eternal.

There are two towering trees growing in Qixianling, with the same root and double stems, embracing each other. In the eyes of the Li people, they are known as the "lover tree" or "couple tree" that guards love. The Li ethnic group still has a beautiful and touching story about its formation.

Legend has it that the hero of the Li ethnic group, Liege, and the daughter of the clan leader, Yagan, have been childhood sweethearts. One is incredibly brave, and the other is skilled in singing and dancing. Wherever they go, Liege always guards by Yagan's side. They bury the seeds of love in the mountains, and as the sun and moon change, they become a token of their vows to the mountains and seas. Now, they are the big banyan tree that covers the sky and the sun. The two vigorous roots are working hard to absorb nutrients, supporting and intertwined without separation, Like lovers in love. The magical Valentine's Tree has spread throughout the tribe, and people believe it must be arranged by God, sending them sincere blessings.

Dear visitors, if you want to climb the ladder to the summit, you should be prepared for the cold. The mountains here are steep, and the ladder is also very steep. During the climbing process, one should step on it firmly and try to support the railing next to it to avoid crowding. The ladder will become steeper and more dangerous as it goes up, reaching its highest point as if it is walking between vast clouds, and there may even be a sense of instability.

Dengxiantai is located on the top of the second peak of the Seven Immortals Ridge, and is also a legendary place where the Seven Immortals were born and fossilized, achieving enlightenment and soaring. On the Immortal Ascension Platform, the atmosphere is diverse, and the scenery changes and is unique in all four seasons. It is an extraordinary realm, but some who have achieved enlightenment say, "Seven Immortal Ridges in a day are better than a thousand days". Ascending to Sendai, as a sacred mountain and sanctuary in the hearts of the Li people, guarding a peaceful and peaceful place, is not only a totem of spiritual beliefs, but also a place to pray for beautiful expectations.

Scenic Area Planning

The planned area of Qixianling Scenic Area is about 22 square kilometers, including two parts: hot spring area and forest area. The Qixianling Hot Spring National Forest Park is mainly divided into three tourist areas. The first area is the Qixianling National Park Experience Tour, and the other two areas are the Tropical Rainforest Adventure Tour and the Peak Adventure Tour.

The service area of Qixianling Scenic Area covers an area of 70 acres, with facilities including a 3,000 square meter tourist center, a 4,500 meter long and 13 meter wide shuttle lane, a 7,800 square meter parking lot, a 1,300 meter wooden boardwalk, a 2300 meter stone boardwalk, 10 connected shops with a construction area, 10 landscape service platforms along the way, 6 environmentally friendly ecological toilets, and 1 tourist center toilet, a 1,000 square meter Chinese restaurant, a 700 square meter coffee shop, and a 700 square meter large shopping mall.

Dear friends, our trip to Qixianling Hot Springs National Forest Park has come to an end. The beautiful scenery of Qixianling Hot Springs National Forest Park is always waiting for your next visit here. Have a pleasant journey!

13. Hainan Wenbifeng Pangu Cultural Tourism Area

Hello everyone, welcome everyone to visit the Hainan Wenbifeng Pangu Cultural Tourism Area. I am Xiao Wu, the tour guide for this journey. It's my pleasure to serve you and I hope my service will add luster to your pleasant journey. Below, I will introduce to you the Hainan Wenbifeng Pangu Cultural Tourism Area.

The Hainan Wenbifeng Pangu Cultural Tourism Area is located at the foot of Wenbifeng Mountain, No. 6 Dinghu Road, Longhu Town, Ding'an County, Hainan Province. It is about 20 kilometers southeast of Ding'an County, with flat terrain and beautiful mountain scenery. It is one of the eight famous scenic spots in Ding'an. This place has been regarded as a feng shui treasure trove with dragon heads and turtle backs since ancient times. In the tranquil and pristine natural environment, ancient cultural relics shine brightly. The landscape of the unity of heaven and humanity integrates excellent cultural concepts such as Pangu culture, Taoist culture, and historical culture, and has built a national level large-scale cultural tourism area that integrates tourism, leisure and entertainment, Taoist health preservation, religious pilgrimage, and cultural research. In October 2012, it was rated as a national 4A level scenic spot.

The Hainan Wenbifeng Pangu Cultural Tourism Area covers an area of only 3 square kilometers, with the main peak at an altitude of 188 meters. It stands out like a flying peak on the northeast plain of Hainan, and is named Jianling due to its appearance. There are a small mountain range in the east, west, north, south, and other distances, resembling four protective gods. In the late Tang Dynasty, General Li led his troops through this peak and found that it had an extraordinary momentum. When he climbed to the peak, he was amazed. Therefore, he submitted a memorial to the emperor and named this peak Li Jialing. With this peak as the center, he divided it into Li Jiadu for thirty miles, which was considered a royal treasure. In 1488, Chen Ying, the deputy envoy of the Inspectorate General of Guangdong and Guangxi, learned of the many wonders of Lijialing and changed it to Wenbifeng to boost cultural prosperity. Afterwards, there were many literati in Ding'an where Wenbifeng was located, and Qiu Jun, Hai Rui, Wang Honghui, and Zhang Yuesong were recognized as the "Four Famous Figures of Hainan" in national history. The latter two were all born in Ding'an, with Zhang Yuesong being a first-class scholar and a visiting scholar. Ding'an was both ranked first that who passed the imperial examination and passed the imperial examination in the entire island. The Wenbifeng has become a symbol of Ding'an culture, and many juren jinshi have attached their success to this peak.

Bai Yuchan, the fifth ancestor of Taoism and founder of the Nanzong Neidan School, was born in Qiongshan County, Hainan Province. He is young and intelligent, proficient in poetry and books. At the age of 12, he went to Guangzhou as a special recommendation to take the "Child prodigy" exam, and the examiner asked him to write a poem on the topic of "Weaving Machine". Bai Yuchan blurted out and said, "The mountains, rivers, and earth make weaving machines, and flowers are like brocade and willows. In the void and white space, make a horse, and the sun and moon shuttle outside the sky." The young man's broad mindedness is so bold that he should be selected. However, the examiner believed that he was arrogant and did not take it. Bai Yuchan failed the exam and devoted himself to the path from then on. In 1231, Bai Yuchan suddenly retreated during his fame. Legend has it that the giant stone platform at the top of the Wenbifeng is where he ascended to heaven, and there are still footprints and palm prints on the side of the giant stone to this day. When people come here and look back, there is indeed a feeling of Lingxu riding the wind.

Wenbifeng is mainly composed of basalt and schist from the mountainside to the mountaintop, with lush vegetation and often shrouded in clouds and mist. Wenbi, also known as Wenhao Ridge. Wang Honghui, the Minister of Rites of the Ming Dynasty, was born in Longmei Village, Leiming Town and had written works such as "Nanming Qiju Lu" and "Shangyoutang Draft". So far, there is also a Ming Dynasty memorial archway built in memory of Wang Hongxiao, which is full of Hainan architectural characteristics. The architectural design is simple, grand, solid and generous, called "Taishi Archway".

According to legend, Wenbifeng was transformed by the nose bridge of Pangu and was the earliest mountain peak to appear in the world after Pangu created the world. Pangu is the beginning of all things in the universe and the root of world culture. Pangu's nose is naturally a place to absorb the essence of heaven and earth, and is regarded as a auspicious place by the local people. It has been revered and worshipped by generations of Hainan people. Between the peaks and mountains and the sea of clouds is the Nanzong Holy Land Jade Chan Palace, which worships hundreds of ancient Chinese ancestors. There is the Pangu Chan in the ever-changing fields above, and inside is the True Cave Heaven where immortals practice. To the east is the Beidou Seven Stars guarding the verdant sky, and to the west is the Nine Palaces and Eight Trigrams protecting the heavens and earth. The smoke and clouds are vast, and the halls and pavilions are ethereal, like a fairyland of Penglai falling into the mortal world.

According to Sima Qian's "Book of Heavenly Officials", the Pangu Cultural Tourism Area of Wenbifeng corresponds to the South Pole Star in the sky. The South Pole Immortal is also known as the South Pole Star. As the South Pole Immortal presides over longevity, it is known as the Old Longevity Star in ancient myths and legends. This is why the people of Wenbifeng are outstanding and the earth is spiritual.

The Wenbifeng Taoist Culture Park held its grand opening ceremony in 2006 and has the largest architectural complex in Hainan, with a Song Dynasty style. The Yuchan Palace, Wenbi Academy, Cihang Hall, Seven Star Pavilion, Transfer Hall, Bell and Drum Tower, and Health Preservation Hall in the garden are all characteristic landscapes. The park takes "harmony on the main road" as its cultural core and carries out various characteristic tourism activities.

Ladies and gentlemen, please take a look. This is Yuchan Palace, the only legitimate temple of Taoism in Hainan, revered by Taoism as the "Southern Ancestral Altar". Yuchan Palace has the world's largest Taoist architectural complex, consisting of nearly 20 halls including the Cihang Hall for praying for peace, the Yuelao Hall for reconciling marriages, the Yuanchen Hall for reminding one's own destiny, the Wenchang Pavilion for opening wisdom, the Medicine King Hall for health and longevity, and the God of Wealth Hall for wealth and prosperity. The building has a complete structure and distinct style, systematically showcasing the cultural characteristics of Taoist themes. The beauty of the palace and the exquisite carving reflect the outstanding talent and artistic creativity of the ancient laboring people.

The natural trend of the southern slope of Wenbifeng is roughly on the meridian of the various halls of the Yuchan Palace. Taking the natural trend of the southern slope as the central axis, relying on the towering rocks and high points at the summit as the background, with the east and west sides as wings, embellished with garden art, extending between the ancient Chinese architectural complexes, the overall layout is vivid and harmonious. Vividness is the overall meaning of soaring, standing at the peak and overlooking it will give people a feeling of riding cranes and soaring clouds; Harmony is the density and harmony of ancient architectural complexes, with solemnity and affinity complementing each other. Architecture and gardens complement each other to expand the viewing and imaginative space for tourism, without a sense of heaviness, showcasing the cultural connotation of the unity of heaven and humanity.

Dear tourists, that's all for the introduction of the Hainan Wenbifeng Pangu Cultural Tourism Area. Now you can freely visit it and return here according to the planned time. Wishing you have a pleasant time.

14. Mission Hills Resort Haikou

Dear tourists, hello! Welcome to visit Mission Hills Haikou Tourist Resort. I am your tour guide Xiao Yang, it is my honor to accompany you to visit together, I hope my service can bring you a happy mood. Next, I will tell you about Mission Hills Haikou Tourist Resort.

About 10,000 years ago, the Qiongbei Volcano Group in Hainan erupted, with lava surging and pouring for thousands of miles. After experiencing the vast and magical craftsmanship of nature, this place has formed a vast and magical black rock geological heritage. Yangshan, just a short distance from the center of Haikou, is the hinterland of a rocky desert area formed by volcanic rocks for thousands of years. The Mission Hills Resort Haikou is built here, located at No. 1 Guanlan Lake Avenue, Longqiao Town, Longhua District, Haikou City, Hainan Province. It is an international leisure tourism resort that integrates sports, business, health, tourism, conferences, culture, cuisine, shopping, housing, and more. The resort is equipped with a variety of facilities, including a golf course, Haikou clubhouse, Haikou Golf Academy, Mission Hills Resort Haikou, mineral hot spring spa center, Mission Hills International Convention Center, Languifang Entertainment Street, Haikou Mission Hills Huayi Feng Xiaogang Film Commune, and specialty stores. This is an excellent tourist destination for tourists from all over the world. In 2014, it was rated as a national 4A level scenic spot.

Golf club

Haikou Mission Hills Golf Club has the world's largest number of golf holes, and 10 international golf courses form the world's largest public volcanic rock golf course group; All the stadiums here are located on the volcanic rocks formed by volcanic eruptions 10,000 years ago, preserving the natural and cultural primitive scenery of the volcanic area to the greatest extent possible. There are both stadiums with volcanic rock features and sandy stadiums resembling Melbourne's sand dunes. There is an endless skyline here, vast black bare rocks, lush ancient lychees, low old stone walls, and a water landscape wetland transformed from a quarry. Being in it is like being on the moon, and the feeling of weightlessness and relaxation arises naturally. The Mission Hills World Star Game, Mission Hills Golf World Cup, World Women's Golf Championship, Tiger Woods VS McRoy Mission Hills World First Challenge, and other exciting events are taking place here. Top players and cultural and sports giants from all over the world are flocking, and Haikou Mission Hills has become a new landmark for sports and leisure tourism in Hainan.

Leisure and Healing Holy Land

Mission Hills Resort Haikou is also a place of physical and mental recovery that global leisure travelers aspire to. The Mission Hills Hot Spring Hotel is an ideal place to stay, combining tourism and vacation, golf sports, exquisite cuisine, and hot spring spa. The most noteworthy thing is the natural volcanic resources that the hotel possesses. 168 large and small hot and cold spring pools, rich in health preserving mineral elements, gather the Guinness World Record's largest hot spring resort in the style of five continents. Bamboo and volcanic stone are extensively used as decoration materials here to create a simple and natural atmosphere. A 500m long bamboo corridor meanders forward, setting off layers of bluestones, surrounded by a steaming bathing pool, and embellishing the sound and color of the hot spring world. Here, you can experience different hot spring customs from five continents around the world, while also showcasing unique styles.

A new world of film tourism

This is also A new world of film tourism. Mission Hills Group collaborates with Huayi Brothers and renowned director Feng Xiaogang to create a unique film themed tourism commercial project in China — Haikou Mission Hills Huayi Feng Xiaogang Film Commune, which integrates architectural tourism, film tourism, and commercial tourism. The Film Commune includes eight theme areas: 1942nd Street, Nanyang Street, Fanghua Military Region Courtyard, Old Beijing Street, Church Square Area, Feng's New Year Film Landscape Area, Cinema Star Avenue, and Large Studio Shooting Area. It includes the world's largest 8,000 square meter indoor photography studio, which was a gathering place for Chinese stars to bloom.

Sports and leisure characteristic town

Haikou Mission Hills is focusing on building a sports and health characteristic town, and has become one of the first demonstration projects for sports and leisure characteristic towns in China. Mission Hills Sports and Health Characteristic Town, relying on Hainan's three major advantages of "ecological province, international tourism island, and largest economic special zone", with "football, golf, and basketball" as the core sports, with sports and health as the theme and feature, to create a comprehensive tourism industry aggregation function, sports training and experience function, health and health leisure function, sports events and sports activities function The largest sports and health characteristic town in China, which integrating sports and cultural exchange functions.

The three major sports cores of Haikou Mission Hills Sports and Health Characteristic Town include: (1) golf, mainly featuring the world's largest public golf course group, golf academy, and related facilities such as event clubs; (2) football, mainly featuring the Chinese Football (Southern) Training Base, Barcelona Football School, and Barcelona Football Museum, which includes 30 football training fields, offices, accommodation, swimming pools, gyms, medical centers, changing rooms, media centers, and other facilities, are the main football sports; (3) basketball, mainly featuring the Haikou Mission Hills NBA Training Center, NBA Museum, and Experience Center. Thirty sports suitable for nationwide participation include table tennis, badminton, tennis, swimming, etc. In addition, the town has also been established as a national level sports training base for football, golf, skateboarding, rock climbing and other projects, providing a base for training Olympic athletes, professional athletes, and sports reserve talents.

After the completion of Haikou Mission Hills Sports and Health Characteristic Town, it will become a health and leisure characteristic town with a complete sports industry chain, rich sports projects, balance between professional sports training and family sports, distinct sports culture, and reasonable spatial layout. It will integrate national fitness base, sports training base, sports culture base, and Olympic champion cradle, becoming a model of "tourism+sports".

Cultural, tourism, business, and leisure destinations

This is still a cultural, tourism, business, and leisure destination worth visiting. Mission Hills Group has invested billions to build the Haikou Mission Hills New City, including the Mission Hills Lan Gui Fang Fashion and Entertainment Block, International Duty Free Shopping Center, Wild Water World Theme Park, Hainan Overseas Chinese Middle School Mission Hills School, Wanli Hotel, Ritz Carlton Hotel, and Hard Stone Hotel, becoming the true center of Hainan's new fashion city.

Mission Hills Lan Kwai Fong Bar Street is a new fashion entertainment landmark jointly built by Mission Hills and Lan Kwai Fong. It integrates entertainment, shopping, leisure and catering, so that tourists can enjoy the fun of fashion trends.

The Haiwu Mission Hills International Shopping Center is jointly built by Mission Hills Group and Hainan Duty Free Products Co., Ltd., with a first phase operating area of 50,000 square meters. International shopping centers not only introduce first tier international brands, but also rich fashion trend brands. In terms of operation philosophy, they focus on combining online and offline channel resources, becoming a high-quality benchmark for Hainan's one-stop shopping journey.

Mission Hills Group has also built a world-class water park project — Haikou Wild Water World. This is the first water park in China that combines "outdoor and indoor" elements. The indoor water park, covering an area of 8,000 square meters, can break through seasonal and weather restrictions and provide a high-quality entertainment experience similar to outdoor activities. The entertainment projects of Wild Water World not only satisfy family entertainment, but also have extreme excitement, bringing tourists different styles of water amusement experiences.

International education is another highlight of Haikou Mission Hills New City. Mission Hills Group and Hainan Overseas Chinese High School work together to create a first-class and internationally distinctive high-quality school in China — Hainan Overseas Chinese High School Mission Hills School. The school will provide high-quality degrees for Hainan Province and Haikou City, and will also introduce international education methods. With the abundant resources of overseas renowned schools from Mission Hills Group, Hainan Overseas Chinese High School Mission Hills School will establish a platform for Sino foreign education cooperation, promote international exchange and cooperation, and play a positive role in expanding international perspectives and cultivating international talents.

Dear tourists, that's all for the introduction of Haikou Mission Hills Tourist Resort. Now you can freely visit it and return here according to the planned time. Wishing everyone a pleasant time.

3A-rated Tourist Attractions

1. Wugong Temple

Hello everyone, welcome to visit Wugong Temple, I'm your guide Xu Xin, you can call me Xiao Xu. I hope my explanation can bring you a pleasant mood.

The Wugong Temple is a place of nostalgia and nostalgia in Hainan. This temple is composed of a group of ancient architectural complexes, including the Wugong Temple, the Sugong Temple, the Guanjia Hall, the Xuepu Hall, the Wugong Jingshe, and the Qiongyuan. People usually refer to it as the Wugong Temple. This ancient architectural complex was first built during the Wanli period of the Ming Dynasty (1573 — 1619) and continued to be built until the beginning of this century. The Wugong Temple Scenic Area covers an area of approximately 7 hectares. This place is surrounded by strange flowers and trees, and is close to the bustling city, with a unique tranquility. It has been known as the "Qiongtai Scenic Area" since ancient times.

Wugong Temple is the main building of the building complex. It is a two-story wooden structure with a single arch of wooden architecture. It covers an area of 560 square meters and is 9 meters high. It is known as "the first building in Hainan". This temple was built in memory of five historical figures, Li Deyu, Li Gang, Li Guang, Zhao Ding, and Hu Quan, who were exiled to Hainan during the Tang and Song dynasties. It has been more than a hundred years since then. The stone carvings of the Five Officials in the temple are lifelike and full of thoughts. A golden horizontal plaque with the words "Hainan's First Building" hangs high above. On the pillars inside the temple, there is a sound of the Qing Dynasty's long couplet landing, praising the five famous officials, which is quite an addition to the "first floor".

On the right side of Wugong Temple is Xuepu Hall, which is the former site of Guo Wanxiang, a famous scholar from Zhejiang Province in the Qing Dynasty, who came to Qiong to give lectures. It now displays ancient cultural relics such as copper bells and drums since the Han Dynasty. To the right of Xuepu Hall is the Wugong Jingshe, which is a place for Hainan students in the late Qing Dynasty to study classics and history. Today, it displays calligraphy and painting from various dynasties. On the left side of the Wugong Temple is the Guanjia Hall, which refers to the scenery of "floating gold in the Su well" and "thousands of acres of golden ears". The hall is named in memory of Su Dongpo, who carved the well spring.

The Su Gong Temple is adjacent to the Wu Gong Temple. A batch of Su Dongpo's poetry and inscriptions are displayed in the temple, and in front of the temple, there are stone tablets, arch bridges, lotus ponds, and wind pavilions. To the east of the temple lies Qiong Garden, covering an area of 10 acres. Within the garden, there are famous scenic spots such as Fusu Spring, Suquan Pavilion, Xixin Pavilion, and Xianyou Cave.

Fushu Spring is known as the "Number One Spring in Hainan". According to legend, in 1097, Su Dongpo was exiled to Danzhou and stayed overnight here. He saw residents drinking the turbid water of the city river, so he surveyed the terrain and pointed to the ground, saying, "If you dig according to the ground, you should get two springs." The local residents dug it and indeed got two clear and turbid springs, both sweet and sour. Clear is a spring of floating millet, turbid is a spring of washing the heart. Later generations built buildings such as the Su Gong Temple around the two springs. The Heart Washing Spring disappeared in the early Ming Dynasty. The existing Fushu Spring was rebuilt into a square ancient well by the Qing Dynasty (1793) governor Ye Rulan.

Suquan Pavilion has been around for over 300 years and was first built by the governor of the Ming Dynasty (1614), Weng Ruyu. This pavilion was suspended due to the promotion of the governor of Weng County, and was completed by the successor governor Xie Jike.

Xixin Pavilion is a long flat house originally named "Shiyuan Pavilion". It was built after a poem by Su Dongpo and has been renovated and preserved through generations to this day.

Xian You Cave was built by Zhu Weichao, an observer to Hainan in 1916. Legend has it that when he built Qiong Park, he dreamed of drinking with Liu Dun, a Taoist priest and the first poet in the history of Hainan in the Song dynasty, at Suquan Pavilion. Liu pointed outside and said this is the site of his birth, then he flew away. Zhu woke up, quite with emotion, in the place where Liu pointed to build a rockery cave, and according to Liu Dun poem "No one in Xian You Cave" named. Now rockery hole "Xian You Cave" is Zhu Weichao wrote for the title.

Many precious cultural relics are on display in Wugong Temple all year round. Among them, Zhao Ji, the founder of Huizong of Song dynasty, wrote in calligraphy the stone tablet of Sheng Xiao Yu Qing Wan Shou Palace, and his Slender Gold calligraphy was vigorous and elegant, which had important reference value for the study of Taoism and calligraphy. The ancient Tang poetry and calligraphy of Hai Rui, a famous honest and upright official, is also very popular. Many of the above scenic spots and temples are linked into one, become the best scenic spot in hainan. Across the bridge from the Temple of Five Lords and other ancient architectural complexes is the exhibition halls of Wugong Temple, with a floor area of 4,200 square meters and eight exhibition halls.

Biography of Wugong

Li Deyu (787 — 850), a native of present-day Hebei province, was a talented politician who served as prime minister twice in the seventh year of the reign of emperor Wen Zong (838) and the fifth year of the reign of emperor Wu Zong (840). Being framed by the treacherous party, he was demoted again and again. In 848, he was demoted to secretary of the prefecture of Ya Zhou. He arrived in Hainan in 849 and died the next year. After his death was appointed supreme government official in charge of military affairs and presented to the duke of Wei.

Li Gang (1083 — 1140), a native of Fujian province, was a national hero in Chinese history, a talented and heroic prime minister in Song dynasty. He arrived in Hainan in 1129 after being demoted by malicious gossip. Posthumous name is Zhong Ding.

Zhao Ding (1085 — 1147), a native of Shanxi province, was a famous official in the Song dynasty. He served as the right remonstrance, counsellor and assistant administrator. Support Yue Fei anti country Jin, and recommend him as the general. He was banished to Hainan in 1145 for opposing Qin Hui's surrender. After his death, he was granted the title of duke of Feng by Song Xiao Zong, who gave him a posthumous award for loyalty.

Li Guang (1073 — 1157), a native of Zhejiang province, was a famous minister in the Song dynasty. He was once a assistant administrator and counsellor. He was repeatedly disparaged for opposing the peace agreement of Qin Hui's surrender. He was banished to Hainan in 1131 and lived there for more than 10 years, posthumous teputation to Zhuang Jian.

Hu Quan (1102 — 1180), a native of Jiangxi province, used to be a secretary and served as a house clerk. Because of the letter please behead the main surrender sent Qin Hui and so on and was demoted. Because of the false accusation of Qin Hui private party was confiscated to Hainan, live in hainan for 10 years. After his death was appointed to Zhuang Jian.

2. Phoenix Hill Park

Good morning ladies and gentlemen. My name is Xiao Wang. I am your tour guide in Sanya Phoenix Hill Park. At first I welcome you for coming to have a visit in Sanya Phoenix Hill Park. Now, let me show you the Sanya Phoenix Hill Park.

Sanya Phoenix Hill Park is the first "Tropical Rain Forest Mountain and Sea Landscape Tourist Attraction" in China which based on "love". The theme of the whole tourist attraction is "love". We have a particular gesture for greeting here — "Wa-Ai-Lu". Now let us make this gesture together (teach tourists to make the gesture) and say "Wa-Ai-Lu" to our sweethearts, family members or friends loudly at the same time. Do you know the meaning of "Wa-Ai-Lu"? "Wa-Ai-Lu" in Hainan's local language means "I love you". It means welcome and blessing. So I think you have to remember "Wa-Ai-Lu" and say it to the person who you love.

Four characteristics

What will we see here? First, Phoenix Hill is the highest mountain in Sanya. You can see the whole landscape of Sanya — Four Bays and Eight Scenes here. Second, we will use rope-way to go to the top of the mountain. The rope-way comes from Austria. It is 1,624 meters long and it is called "the Rolls-Royce in Rope-Way" for its advanced, safe and stable. Third, this is the thickest rainforest in the central of Sanya. The content of negative oxygen ion here is higher than any other place in Sanya. So, it is called "the Lung of Sanya" and "Natural Oxygen Park". You can breathe the highest quality of oxygen here. Fourth, the most special part of this place is the crystal temple at the top of the mountain. The temple is lucency. You can see the scenery of the mountain and the sea there. The scenery there is very beautiful. Please pay attention, you can not use fire in this tourist attraction. So, you can not smoke after you walk into the tourist attraction. Now, we are going to take the rope-way. The rope-way is provided in your trip. Please stay close to me in order not to get lost. Let us start the trip now!

Gather at the rope-way station

Now the rope-way in front of us is the best sea-view rope-way in Asia. Its country of origin is Austria, and it is really advanced and safe. One carriage is able to take 8 tourists. It will take 10 minutes to go to the top of the mountain. You can see the scenery of Sanya in it. Please do not stand up and shake the carriage in the carriage. Also do not keep your arm or head outside the carriage. Now I am going to take the first carriage with the tourists in the front. Other tourists please take the rope-way one by one with the help of the staff.

Attraction NO.1 — Four Bays and Eight Scenes

The square of a solemn pledge of love

Now, we are arriving at the scenery square — the Square of a Solemn Pledge of Love. And this is the first scene of the "Four Bays and Eight Scenes" of Sanya. You can see the scenery of mountain and sea here. You can also see there are four big words on the stela in front of you. These words mean "the solemn pledge of love". And the small words below the big words are the name of the writer. The writer is "Yinghui". He is the vice-chairman of Chinese Calligraphers Association. He had once came to this tourist attraction with his wife. He was shocked by the scenery here. And then he wrote these words and sent them to this tourist attraction. The words at the other side of the stela mean "18 degrees north latitude". "18 degrees north latitude" is the latitude of Sanya. And "18 degrees north latitude" is called "the latitude of love". Why? Because there are lots of famous tourist attractions on this latitude. Such as Sanya and Hawaii. These are all the best places for honey-month holiday and wedding. People think these tourist attractions full of "culture of love", so this latitude is called "the latitude of love".

Jin Mu Cape, Yu Lin Bay

The azure bay below the stela is the first bay in "Four Bays and Eight Scenes". It is called "Yu Lin Bay". It is a traditional naval base in China. The Chinese navy is stationed there. I can not tell you more because of the politics. Please do not send the picture here on the Internet. On the sea you can see the sea dam of Sanya. It is used to prevent and control the flood. It is the south door of China. Outside the dam is the South China Sea. There is a hill at the left of the dam. It is another scene in "Four Bays and Eight Scenes" — the place where Jin Mu goes in to the sea. It is called "Jin Mu Cape". It is the southern part of Chinese continental shelf, and it is near the South China Sea. So, it is the place where Chinese navy station. There is a beacon at the top of the hill. Chinese soldier patrols the South China Sea and navigated ships on that beacon. There was once an old man in our group. He climbed this mountain and stood here stared the bay for a long time with tears on his face. He told us he was a soldier here 50 years ago when he was young. The things were still there, but people were no more the same ones. Fifty years is a small amount of time for the sea. But for the old man it is whole youth. There are many young soldiers stay here to protect China. They are really great. Let us pay our respects to them!

The guide map of "Four Bays and Eight Scenes"

This is the guide map of "Four Bays and Eight Scenes" where we will go to visit. This is the highest point of Sanya. The Sanya's television tower is here because the signal cover here is very wide. You can see the whole "Four Bays and Eight Scenes" here in 360 degrees. We had already seen "one bay and two scenes". And the better scenery is at the top of the mountain. Now we are at "the square of a solemn pledge of love". Later we will arrive at Lai Yi Square, Phoenix-View Square and Deer-View Square through Concentric Bridge. These three squares are the best places for observing the scenery. And they are the source of Sanya's culture. The whole tour will take about one hour. Please stay close to me in order not to get lost in the rainforest. Now let us go to the next place.

We can see the scenery of "Four Bays and Eight Scenes" of Sanya at Sanya Phoenix Hill Park. You will know what belongs to "Four Bays and Eight Scenes" later. We go on trips because we want to expand our horizon. And more importantly we need to get more knowledge. You can see the scenery which you want to see and I can tell you the knowledge which you want to know. It is better to know the story behind the scenery. Sometimes the story is more amazing than the scenery.

Ficus altissima

The name of this kind of tree is "Ficus Altissima". It is one of the 18 special things in Hainan. The special part is its root. Its root grows outside the bark. After the root grows in to the soil, it becomes stronger and finally grows into a tree trunk. It can grows in any kind of bad environment. Hainan is an island which influenced by strong typhoon frequently. And no ficus altissima was destroyed by typhoon. This ability is adored by the local Li-nationality residents. Li-nationality residents adore nature, such as rock and tree. Li-nationality residents think ficus altissima is sacred. When the festival comes, Li-nationality residents blessing and worship under the ficus altissima. They write the name of people who they love on red tapes and tie the red tapes on ficus altissima. They use this way to bless for safety and happiness. This is the highest point of Sanya. And here is at the border of the South China Sea. The geomantic omen here is great. It makes here special. So, many local residents and tourists willing to bless here. They bless for family's safety and happiness, children can be successful in the future, lovers can keep together for a longtime, friendship can stay for a long time and so on. Now in front of us is the Concentric Bridge. Lots of lovers lock concentric locks on this bridge. It means the lovers can keep together for a long time and live a happy life. We may meet different kinds of problems in our life. But we have our families and lovers keep together with us to walk though the problems. Such as the concentric lock, lock the friendship and love together, and face the problems together.

Luobi Hole

Now we are walking through the Concentric Bridge. This bridge was built by the direction of mountains. There are eight bends on the bridge. It means "with one heart together". In front of us (in the middle of two mountains) is one of the "Four Bays and Eight Scenes" — Luobi Hole. Luobi Hole is a big karst cave with a huge stalactite inside. The stalactite is hanging on the roof, looks like a pen hanging on the roof. It is the reason why this hole is called Luobi Hole. (Luobi in Chinese means a pen drops down from sky) Luobi Hole is the place where ancient Hainan ape man lived. The archaeologist had found the skull of ape man in Hainan. The skull comes from 7,000 years ago. It shows the ancient ape man had already appeared here 7,000 years ago. Now, Luobi Hole is recognized as the place where the earliest Hainan local residents live. And here is the historic site of ancient Hainan ape man. There are many old trees surround the Luobi Hole. And there are not too many people here. The nature environment here is great. And cultural atmosphere here is great too. There are many sanatoriums and universities here. You may ask: Sanya is near the sea, why ancient ape man did not live on the coast? The coast is usually wet. It is bad for body. And there are more natural disasters on the coast. It is hard to keep safe. It is different to live in the mountain. The altitude is high and the air is great. More importantly, there are caves in the mountain. They can be used to resist the natural disaster and the wild beast. And the mountain can provide the place for hunting and picking food. So, living in the mountain is a good choice for ancient Hainan ape man. It shows that the ancient Hainan ape man is really clever.

The Beautiful Crown

The hill in front of us is the “Hubao Hill”. There are nine tall buildings behind the “Hubao Hill”. These buildings are “Tree Hotel”. These buildings look like trees. There is a white building which shape is a crown located under the “Tree Hotel”. It is one of the “Four Bays and Eight Scenes” — “the Beautiful Crown”. The Beautiful Crown looks like a blooming delonix regia. And it still looks like a crystal crown. It is the place for the final of Miss World. The Beautiful Crown had been chosen to be the place for the final of Miss World six times since 2003. It made Sanya famous. In 2007, Chinese lady Zilin Zhang got the final champion in Miss World in Sanya. She is the first Chinese who gets that achievement. At the same time, Sanya got the name:“Capital of Beauty”. In the final of Miss World in 2015, 30 ladies all around the world climbed the Phoenix Hill to enjoy the beautiful sight of Sanya. Now the slogan of Sanya is “Beauty Sanya, together with the Romantic Horizon”. “Beauty Sanya” refers to the Beautiful Crown. And “Romantic Horizon” refers to “Tianya Haijao”.

Yuelao Spring

Now, the spring in front of us is “Yuelao Spring”. Yuelao is a Chinese God who works for marriage with a book of marriage in his left hand and a piece of red string in his right hand. For the singles you can worship him if you want to find your lovers. And for marrieds, you can still worship him to thank him for giving you your lovers.

There is a green plum tree near the Yuelao Spring. April and May is the season of plum. In these days rain comes frequently. Plum is full of Alpha Hydroxy Acid and Vitamin C. It is good for spleen and stomach. You can see there are some bamboos growing below the green plum tree. Bamboo always grows below the green plum tree. So, Chinese use "green plum and bamboo" to describe the friendship between boys and girls.

Now we will walk through the 360 degree annular wood viaduct. The viaduct is through the rainforest. There are many different kinds of plants and animals inside the rainforest. Please walk at the middle of the viaduct. Do not touch the plants and do not interrupt the animals.

The Door of Dragon and Phoenix

Now in front of us is the Door of Dragon and Phoenix. Chinese people think dragon and phoenix together means good luck. So, the Door of Dragon and Phoenix is "the Door of Good Luck". There is a tradition here: The friends, families or lovers have to walk through the Door of Dragon and Phoenix hand by hand together. It means walking through the way of happiness together. Please remember, do not look backwards until you walk through the Door of Dragon and Phoenix. Your good luck may leave if you look backwards.

The most important thing in Phoenix Hill is taking a deep breath. Phoenix Hill is the highest point of Sanya. It has the densest rainforest in Sanya. The content of negative oxygen ion here is higher than any other place in Sanya. Phoenix Hill is called "the Lung of Sanya". Especially the friend who smokes needs to take more deep breaths to clean your lung. The nature environment here is great. So Hainan is called "the Province of Longevity". The secret of longevity is the wonderful nature environment here.

Laiyi Platform

Now we are at the best sightseeing platform in Phoenix Hill — Laiyi Platform. We can see the best scenery of Sanya here. You can see there is a bay in front of us. It is the longest bay in Sanya — Sanya Bay. It is the second bay in "Four Bays and Eight Scenes". Sanya Bay is 22 kilometers long. The beach there is flat. The sunset is the famous scenery in Sanya Bay. There are many coconut palms on the beach, which full of tropical coast style. Chinese chairman had once wrote "Coconut Dream Corridor" for Sanya Bay. Many visitors like to see the sunset and see the night view of Sanya Bay. On the right side of the Sanya Bay is "Tianya Haijao" and "Nanshan Park". The farthest mountain there is Mount Ao. The white statue below the Mount Ao is the famous "South China Sea a Buddism Goddess Guanyin". It is the biggest Guanyin statue in Asia. It is 108 meters tall. It has three bodies, separate means "wisdom", "mercy" and "peace and quiet". It completes the building in 2005. At that time, 108 eminent monks perform a ceremony for its completion. It is said that at that day, the cloud gets together and shapes like a lotus. It is a great event in Chinese Buddhism.

There are two small islands in the distance. These are the one of the "Four Bays and Eight Scenes" — East and West Hawksbill Islands. The left one is "East Island" and the right one is "Right Island". Many years before these islands teem with hawksbill. Now the West Island is a famous tourism island and the East Island is a military base. Many years before Chinese militia women were stationed in East Island. The militia women in East Island are well-known in Hainan island. They had left many heroic stories. Chinese chairman had written poem to glorify the spirit of them by defend the country.

There are five buildings look like fingers in front of Sanya Bay. It is the landmark of Sanya — Phoenix Island. It is an artificial island which takes ten years to build. You can see there is an international seven star hotel. It is called "Eastern Dubai" because its shape looks like "Burj Al Arab" hotel in Dubai. These four buildings at the right are hotel apartments. These are the most expensive buildings in Sanya. The price of ground floor is more than 80,000 RMB per square meter. Higher floor has higher price. The highest price comes in 2012. At that time the price was 100,000 RMB per square meter. These apartments are 360 degree seascape apartments. And in 2008, Phoenix Island was the first station of the Olympic torch in China. Olympic flame came from Greece and then transmitted to other places in China. In the end the Olympic flame transmitted into National Stadium (Chinese name: Nest) in Beijing. So it is called "phoenix goes back into the nest".

Now the tree in front of us is the most noxious tree in Hainan — upas. Its bark is very thick and tough. There is no poison in its bark. But its pulp is full of strong poison. Its pulp can let people die by making the blood solidification in 30 minutes if the wound on the body touches its pulp. We had just said its bark is thick and tough. So many years before local residents use its bark to make clothes. At that time not every local residents had new clothes to wear. And a bark clothes can be used to wear for a very long time. It is said that: "One bark clothes can be used for three generations of the family." We can find out local residents are really clever. Unfortunately, the method of manufacture bark clothes had already been lost for many years. We can only find out these clothes in museums or tourist attractions.

Phoenix Dance Platform

Now we are at "Phoenix Dance Platform". The landscape here is similar to Laiyi Platform. So I am going to tell you something about phoenix culture in Sanya. I had just told you that the name of the landmark of Sanya is Phoenix Island. And you know the name of Sanya airport is Phoenix Airport. The highest mountain in Sanya is Phoenix Hill. Besides, we have Phoenix Road, Phoenix Town and so on. You may find out local residents love phoenix very much. Especially the logo of Sanya is a phoenix. Why local residents love phoenix? Because phoenix is the omen of good luck in Chinese traditional culture. In Chinese culture, phoenix is the symbol of fire. The location of fire is south. And Sanya is located at the south corner of China. So Sanya is called "Phoenix City".

Deer-View Platform

We had just said Sanya is called "Phoenix City". But in early 1980s, Sanya was usually called "Deer City". Deer culture is an important part in Sanya's culture. Deer culture comes from "Lu Hui Tou Peninsula" which is in front of us. Lu Hui Tou Peninsula is a basin between sea and mountain. It is one part of Phoenix Hill.

It is one scene of "Four Bays and Eight Scenes" — Peninsula's Legend. Why it is a legend? In 2009 the policy of "International Tourism Island" of Hainan came out. At that time "Peninsula Group" launched some seascape apartments at Lu Hui Tou Peninsula. On the first day of the sale, the saleroom is more than 3 hundred million RMB. In three days, the saleroom is about 1.5 billion RMB. It cuts the record of saleroom in Chinese realty business. So it is called Peninsula's Legend.

In the whole process of the tour, I had already told you about the "Four Bays and Eight Scenes" in Sanya. Do you still remember what is included? Now we are at the highest point of Sanya city. We can make promises here in the witness of mountain and sea. The scene in front of us is real "the Ends of the Earth". Love is a promise. Lovers stay together is one kind of great happiness. So, let us make promises of love at the southern part of the land and take this promise with us during our whole lives.

Attraction NO.2 — Crystal Temple

Now we are at the second attraction — Crystal Temple. We will walk through Luxin Kiosk, Ruyin Tower, Zhishou Platform and in the end arrive at the first mountain and sea sightseeing crystal temple in China. It still means the process from "know each other", "stay with each other" to "love each other", and finally walks into the temple of marriage. In order to give you a better experience to feel the nature, we will walk through the annular wood viaduct. The first station is Luxin Kiosk. It means the first time when young boys meet young girls. We may both have that moment. It is one kind of situation which is hard to explain. It is also a kind of happiness which can not be hid.

The stone tablet we see now is in the form of imitation bamboo slips. It records the first poem in the Book of Songs of the Han Dynasty and also the first love poem in China, "Guan Ju". Guan Guan is an onomatopoeia, which describe the water birds make joyful and joyful sounds on the water surface, while Ju Jiu is a type of water bird. In fact, in ancient times, the Book of Songs was not read word for word like we do now, but needed to be sung with rhythm. Have you all heard of Teresa

Teng's song "On the side of the water"? It comes from the Book of Songs.

The bottom of the stone tablet is engraved with the words "love" in different colors, representing that love is colorful. Let's take a look at the big love character below. Can we see what the heart character is when I cover it in the middle? The word is "receive". Love needs to be felt with heart, love also needs to be accepted by each other, and love also needs to be tolerant and endured.

Everyone, please follow me forward. Suddenly look back, we can see the tree on the roadside standing tall and graceful like a sika deer, which looking back with deep affection. This is the wonder bestowed upon us by nature, which has led to the idiom "the heart is like a deer colliding".

The path we have taken is a journey of love, and the plants on both sides are also products of nature's gifts. We see, this plant is called the red mulberry, symbolizing red and fiery fire. Love is like a fire, burning the hearts of all of us. This plant is called Bian Ye Mu, also known as "Lao Lai Qiao". When it sprouts, it is green, symbolizing the bitterness of first love. When the leaves become colorful, it also indicates that the fruit of love has matured.

Today's trip of "love" is going to be over now. From enthusiastic first love to walk into the temple of marriage happily and finally stay together calmly. It is life. So you have to take care of your love such as you take care of your belief. You have to remember: The farthest distance is not the lovers can not see each other, the farthest distance is two hearts can not stay with each other together. If you can shake hands please not just stand side by side. If you can hug each other please not just shake hands. If you can hug, please do not separate easily. Now I wish you sincerely: Have a wonderful love, have wonderful friendships, have a happy family, have a wonderful career and have happiness with you all the time.

Now we have finished our trip in Sanya Phoenix Hill Park. Let us go back by rope-way, eight people in one group. The scenery here is waiting for you to come to have a visit again. I wish you have a safe and wonderful trip.

3. Historic Qilou Culture Streets

Dear friends, today we will visit the "Famous Chinese Historical and Cultural Street": Historic Qilou Culture Streets. Historic Qilou Culture Streets, commonly known as Haikou Qilou Old Street, has a history of more than 100 years. There are about 600 historical buildings of Qilou, and 331 buildings have been listed for protection. It is the largest and most well preserved group of Qilou architecture in China today. The existing arcade buildings are mainly concentrated on 12 streets, with a total length of 3,919 meters and a total area of 121.3 hectares.

The first floor of the arcade building is made into a colonnade or walkway for shelter from rain, sun and passage, and the second floor and the upper floor are straddled on the walkway. This kind of building is very consistent with the climate characteristics of strong sunshine and rainfall in the southern coastal areas of China, and its architectural form of "front shop after factory, lower shop on house" is very convenient for business and trade. Since modern times, this kind of building has been distributed in Hong Kong, Macao, Fujian, Guangdong, Hainan and other places along the southeast coast of our country.

Sotto portico architecture was first introduced to Spain from Britain and then to southeast Asia. In modern times, Hainan overseas Chinese, were active in southeast Asia, brought such architectural styles to Haikou city as Eurasian mixed Renaissance style, Eurasian mixed Baroque style and Nanyang style, then combined them with traditional dwellings of northern parts of Hainan province. The single sotto portico buildings are connected with each other, and the single riding corridors on both sides of the road form a long corridor, connecting the entire commercial street as a whole, forming an unique combination of Chinese and western dual-use buildings. In modern times, Haikou city has also formed a distinctive Eurasian mixed city style, as well as an "open and inclusive" spirit and temperament, and become a window for modern China to open to the outside world. In the early 20th century, ten consulates (consuls) from the United States, Japan, Britain, Germany,

France, and Norway were established in Haikou sotto portico old street.

Haikou sotto portico old street as cultural quintessence in developing process in long accumulated history, concentrates on the cultural connotations together such as citizen culture of Haikou, architectural culture, southeast Asian culture, Confucian culture, Buddhist culture, Red culture, maritime culture. And many kinds of traditional cuisine, folk art was born here. There were many touching revolutionary stories, southeast Asian stories and so on. Haikou sotto portico old street is also the “homesickness” place of overseas Chinese. It is a must for people who return home.

Haikou sotto portico old street was initially formed in the 1920s to 1940s, with a history of more than 100 years. Among them, the oldest building, the four archways, was built in the South Song dynasty, with a history of more than 600 years. Haikou sotto portico old street is mostly built in the early 19th century by groups of overseas Chinese who came back from southeast Asia countries and borrowed the architectural style from there. At that time, Hainan people who go sailing to southeast Asia usually have a belief with “leaf return to the roots”, carrying a lifetime of hard-earned money back home to build houses. Hainan, from then, appeared many European arcade architectures with southeast Asian style.

OK, my dear friends, we have arrived at Zhong Shan road. In 2010, the work of the protection and comprehensive renovation of the old arcade block in Haikou was officially began. Zhong Shan road, together with the old block of De Sheng road, Bo Ai road, Xin Hua road and Jie Fang road, has been renovated.

On Zhong Shan road, I recommend several key places for you to visit:

The first is Tai Changlong. It is said that the guests from southeast Asian who came to Haikou will immediately be dragged to the hotel where they thought you should go as soon as the guests landed. If the guest has an accent of local Qionghai area, then you probably be introduced to the Da Ya hotel, since the the owner of the hotel is from Wenchang city. And if the guest has local Wenchang area accent, he or she must go to Tai Changlong, because the boss of Tai Changlong is local Wenchang people.

The second is "700 years old Mazu temple" at 87 Zhong Shan road. Haikou The temple is commonly known as "Mazu temple" and "Big temple"(Damiao). It was built in the Yuan dynasty and has a history of more than 700 years. Whether it's architecture or faith, you will definitely gain something. Every Mazu birthday (lunar March 23rd), the residents here will hold Mazu parade activities.

The Third is the old street cultural exhibition hall of Haikou southeast Asian sotto portico on No.35 Zhong Shan road. The exhibition hall is divided into two floors: On the first floor is the schematic diagram of Hainan maritime silk road transit station; The second floor is composed by two parts, the first is through pictures, material objects, audio and video materials, showing Haikou's hundred of years of history and humanities. The second part is the repairing technology exhibition hall of Haikou sotto portico old street, showing the famous craftsmen, the material collection and operation process in the renovation project. Maked the traditional craft lovers learn and inherit, so that the long-standing traditional Chinese culture and technology can be carried forward.

On June 10th, 2009, Haikou sotto portico old street, with its long history and culture and strong southeast Asian arcade style, won the title of "one of China's top ten historical and cultural streets" in the first session of appraise and elect in Chinese historical and cultural street. In August of the same year, the protection and comprehensive renovation project of Haikou arcade building historic cultural block was approved. In September 2010, Haikou municipal government started the protection programme of Haikou arcade historic building. In April 2014, Haikou arcade street was selected as "2014 key cultural industry project" by the ministry of culture. Up to now, Haikou arcade old street still plays the main commercial function in old city, which vividly records the history of Haikou's development from nothing to a prosperous coastal metropolis, and reflects the tropical local characteristics of Haikou and integration with southeast Asia.

Sotto portico old street is a charm of the old Haikou, it has witnessed the vicissitudes of the history of Haikou, preserving and continuing of a precious memory of this city. Now let us go into the arcade, touching the history, feel the culture, inherit the spirit of the “all rivers run into sea.

4. Jianfengling National Forest Park

My dear friends, hello! I am Wang Li who is your tour guide this time, it is so nice to service you and I hope my service can bring warmth and happiness to you! Jianfengling is the largest and best preserved original tropical rain forest in China. Located in the southwest of Hainan island, it covers two li autonomous cities and counties in Ledong and Dongfang, with a total area of 600 square kilometers and a main forest area of more than 260 square kilometers. The main peak is 1,412 meters above sea level, it is only 50 kilometers northwest of Sanya, China’s southernmost coastal city.

The natural ecological environment in Jianfengling area is unique. Within a horizontal distance of about 15km from the coastal area to the highest elevation in the hinterland of the forest region, the annual average temperature drops from 25℃ in the coastal area to 17 — 19℃ in the high-altitude area, and the annual average rainfall increases from 1,300mm to 3,500mm.

Into the Jianfengling, you can see the sight of ancient trees towering, profound wood. Strange-shaped roots in the forest, tangled vines each other, forming a natural barrier. Even those dead trees, there are epiphytes cleverly reproduced, a variety of beautiful. At the bottom of the rainforest, there are numerous fungi and a variety of flowers and plants. In the elevation of six or seven hundred meters of the river valley, dense growth of hard as iron, thousands of years do not rot stone catalpa, sandalwood and other high-quality trees. There are dinosaur contemporaries of the “living plant fossils” — tree ferns, a few meters or more high trunk out of the mountain stream. This pristine tropical rainforest is also an animal world. There are 16 species of black-crowned gibbons, one of the four great apes, and clouded leopards. There are nearly 150 kinds of birds and more than 4,000 kinds of insects. There are more than 300 species of butterflies alone, comparable to Taiwan province, which is known as the "kingdom of butterflies". Blue sky and white clouds, valley streams, towering ancient trees, birds and animals, strange flowers and grass, rare species, Jianfengling everywhere reflects the theme of "returning to nature". In the current world tourism boom, the forest tourism with the theme of "returning to nature" is very promising. Visitors are amazed by the cold jungles of Alaska, the tropical forests of the Indonesian archipelago, the "countryside tours" of Spain, the "forest elephant rides" of northern Thailand, and the "rainforest camping tours" of subic bay in the Philippines. Zhangjiajie national forest park in China receives more than 600,000 visitors annually. With an area ten times larger than that of Zhangjiajie, the pristine tropical rainforest of Hainan Jianfengling has attracted more and more attention from China and the world in recent years.

Jianfenglin national forest park, established in 1992, in 2000 the provincial government approved area expanded to 20,000 hectares, Jianfenglin forest coverage is 96%, concentrated the tropical parts of the world almost all vegetation types, abundant species resources in the area, its biological diversity index and the tropical forests of South America, Africa, Asia phase approximation, the district has more than 2,800 kinds of vascular plants, which accounts for 8% of plant species, by domestic and foreign experts and scholars as "tropical north rim rich species gene pool", is China's largest existing, the best preserved tropical forests and has the important scientific research, the popular science, the teaching and the forest ecological tourism value. Because tropical rain forest is protected strictly, the water quality of almost all the streams in the forest area meets the national water quality standard of class 1 and can be drunk directly. The park is rich in landscape resources, such as millennium sleeping Buddha, general Junyan, tiger roar longyin, Fengming valley, rainforest valley and other 35 ecological tourist attractions. Deep in the rainforest, there are big planks, hanging gardens, strangling and other characteristics of the rainforest, explaining the mystery of the rainforest, the law of nature.

Jianfenglin has 18 unique peaks surrounded around the Tianchi, rippling, like fairyland, here four spring-like, 19℃ , annual average temperature of the air pure, negative oxygen ion concentration is as high as 50,000-100,000/cubic centimeter, forest health care function significantly, the park has a visitor center, all kinds of hotels, water village, forest villa, perfect facilities, can meet your various needs for the trip. It is an ideal place for tropical forest leisure vacation, adventure, summer shelter, scientific research and popular science, conference and training, medical care.

The scenic area characteristic

In the forest park, there are more than 300 tropical rainforest species, of which 70 species are most precious, such as pobi, zijing, huali and youdan. Slope base, green plum tree trunk straight, tough material, bright color, immortal. The tree is as hard as iron, nails can not be hit into the "green steel" reputation. Torreya torreya contains 21 monomeric alkaloids, four of which have anticancer properties and can be used in pharmaceuticals. Jianfenglin and aloes wood, XiaoGui, alpine sabal, dacrydium, mother gave birth to tropical precious trees, there's a strange form of tree — ficus altissima, old can reach more than one hundred, and the trunk of a tree can have dozens of sizes, overlapping each other, constitute a set of sculpture design, deer or prance, or for a walk, or crouching, or lower the head to drink, vivid, so this kind of ficus altissima, also known as "the Hainan deer tree".

Jianfenglin natural wonders in addition to the forest, there are clouds, wonders of the sea. Into the Jianfenglin, as in the sea of fog, fog transpiration, a confusion. Deep in the mountains, high on the peaks, where the forest is dense, the fog is thickening. Mountain wind blowing, the clouds around the wind roll, will appear waterfall clouds, like the waves of the sea, momentum pound. To the east of Jianfenglin, there is a basin surrounded by mountains, which is called "Tianchi" because it is shrouded by clouds and clouds all day long.

Summer resort — Tianchi

Tianchi, 810 meters above sea level, is the main scenic spot of Jianfengling national forest office. In *the master plan of Jianfengling national forest park* by

Tsinghua university and *the tourism development plan of Jianfengling tropical rainforest tourism area* by Hainan tourism development research institute, Tianchi is regarded as the starting area of the park construction.

Forest tourism and exploration

The park is the largest and most fully protected tropical rain forest area in the country, containing rich biological resources, known as "the north edge of the tropical biological species gene pool." Among the 2,800 species of vascular plants in the park are 78 rare and endangered species of living fossils contemporary with dinosaurs, such as tree-ferns and upas, and nearly 100 species of valuable timber species

It is also a paradise for animals. Black gibbon, clouded leopard, bear, peacock pheasant and other 54 kinds of national protected animals and 24 kinds of provincial protected animals, more than 400 kinds of butterflies, 215 kinds of birds in this living and breeding. Jianfengling national forest park, ancient trees towering, winding vines, rare birds and wild animals play among the forest, fully show the simple, remote, magical charm of the tropical rain forest. "Hanging garden" is a great wonder of tropical rain forest, dozens of kinds of flowers, grass, ferns and other ornamental plants epiphytes in the same millennium trees, clusters of fragrant. Park has more than a kilometer of peak 18, climb the peak overlooking, clouds and clouds, the weather; There are "millennium sleeping Buddha", "general rock", "monkey peak", "dragon cave" and other landscape, which make visitors feel shocked.

The main peak for the birthplace of the river, ancient trees block out the sun, the stream murmurs, clear to the bottom. In this place, the stone and water set off into an interesting, and there are "jade women pool", "dragon temple", "forest baths", "yuanyang waterfall", "nine dragon creek" and other attractions.

Tropical beach

Jianfengling seaside tourism area is adjacent to lingtou port, with 16 kilometers of jinsha coast, where the summer is endless and the sun is abundant. The annual average temperature is 25℃ and the annual average water temperature is 24.5℃.

The beach gently open, the sand white and fine, the water is clear and blue, the bay and the wind and waves are soft, and the sea is densely wooded. It is a natural beach and ideal for water sports such as sailing.

Strong ethnic customs

Jianfengling area is the place where the li people in Hainan live. Following the origin of history and cultural tradition, it still retains the honest folk customs and unique folk customs. Festival activities such as "March 3rd" of the li ethnic group, with dances, songs and wonderful traditional sports competitions with strong li ethnic color, attract a large number of tourists from home and abroad to come for sightseeing every year.

Dear friends, after enjoying the beautiful scenery all the way, we have a certain understanding of Jianfengling, my explanation is complete. As the saying goes: "two mountains can not meet, two people can always meet!" I look forward to seeing you and serving you again! I wish you all the best in the New Year. Wish you have a safe and happy journey!

5. Bawangling National Forest Park

Dear tourists, hello! Welcome to Bawangling National Forest Park. I am your tour guide Xiao Yang, it is my honor to accompany you to visit together, I hope my service can bring you a happy mood. Now I will tell you about Bawangling National Forest Park.

Hainan Bawangling National Forest Park is located in the southwestern mountainous area of Hainan Island, spanning between Changjiang Li Autonomous County and Baisha Li Autonomous County. Its geographical coordinates range from 109°03′ E to 109°17′ E and 18°57′ N to 19°11′ N. With a total area of 8,444.30 hectares, it is the only national nature reserve in China that protects the Changjing ape and its living environment. Within the protected area, there are connected mountains, lush peaks, vast forests and towering ancient trees. The natural ecosystem is well preserved, and tropical biological resources are extremely abundant. There are more than 60 kinds of rare animals, such as giant pandas, clouded leopards and black bears, and precious plants, such as tropical orchids, Mantou fruits, pomegranates, mountain bamboos, black ink, green fruit banyan, mountain olives, hairy peonies and wild litchi.

The terrain of Hainan Bawangling National Forest Park is complex, mainly mountainous. The altitude is between 100 — 1,654 meters. The representative type of soil is brick red soil developed from granite and sandstone as the parent material, which gradually transitions to mountainous red soil with increasing altitude.

Hainan Bawangling National Forest Park belongs to a tropical monsoon climate with no obvious four seasons and is greatly affected by the monsoon. The average annual temperature is 21.3℃ , the hottest month is 22.8℃ , and the coldest month is 13.5℃ . The average annual rainfall is 1657 millimeters, with the rainfall mainly concentrated from July to October. As the altitude increases, the rainfall gradually increases and the relative humidity increases. The annual average relative humidity is 84.2%, and the soil in the forest is moist all year round.

Plant resources

As of 2011, the complex habitat conditions in Hainan Bawangling National Forest Park have become an ideal place for wildlife to live and multiply. There are 2,213 species of vascular plants, 2 species of Cycas hainanensis and Bolei which belong to the national first level protection, and 17 species of national second level protection, such as Youdan, Hainan Fengchuannan, wutong hainanensis, Phalaenopsis and Bauhinia hainanensis.

Animal resources

As of 2011, there are 365 species of terrestrial wild vertebrates in Hainan Bawangling National Forest Park. Among them, 6 species of Hainan gibbons, clouded leopards, Hainan mountain partridges, peacock pheasants, pythons, and giant lizards are listed as national first-class key protected animals; 46 species of animals listed as national second level protected include Hainan water deer, Hainan spirit cat, macaque, Hainan green weasel, Hainan rabbit, giant squirrel, etc.

Hainan Long Arm used to be widely distributed in Wuzhi Mountain, Yingge Ridge, Diaoluo Mountain, Limu Mountain, Dongfang and Baisha on Hainan Island. Currently, it is only distributed in the Bawangling Nature Reserve in Hainan Province. Hainan Gibbon is a medium-sized primate with a robust body, weighing 7-10 kilograms and a body length of 40-50 centimeters. Its forelimbs are significantly longer than its hind limbs and it has no tail. The coat is short and fluffy. The chest and abdomen are light grayish yellow, often stained with black and auspicious colors. The name "Hainan Black Crowned Gibbon" is also derived from the fact that they have an "black hat" on their heads. The entire bodies of the male ape are black, and their bodies are slightly smaller than female apes'. They have short and upright coronal tufts on their heads, like a raging crown. Mother apes have a golden body and a gray yellow, brown yellow, or orange yellow back, with angular or polygonal black crown spots on their heads, resembling wearing a women's black hat. Both males and females have no tails or cheek pouches.

The Hainan Gibbon is one of the four major anthropoid apes in the world, inhabiting the tropical rainforest of the Bawangling National Nature Reserve on Hainan Island. It is a nationally protected endangered species. They are naturally alert, agile in action, and have no fixed abode, making field observations very difficult. It is not only a rare species on the brink of extinction, but also an important object for studying the origin and evolution of human beings. Its rarity is no less than that of the national treasure giant panda.

Yaga Scenic Area

Tourists, please take a look. This is the Yaga Scenic Area, which is mainly distributed with three tourist walkways: "Emotional Path", "Dominant Path", and "Heavenly Path". There is also a unique ecological Yaga vacation (conference) center built in the scenic area. "Qingdao" is a scenic spot in the Yajia Scenic Area of Bawangling that combines mountains, water, forests, and rocks well. In "Qingdao", you can enjoy the Yajia Couples Waterfall, which has a drop of 150 meters and a rock surface width of 30 meters. There is a saying that "if you don't watch the Yajia

Waterfall, you won't come to visit Bawangling in vain"; "Dominance" is a great place to appreciate the dominance of Bawang Ridge; The path of heaven is the pursuit of success, which combines length, height, and steepness.

Baishitan Scenic Area

Dear tourists, this is Baishitan Scenic Area, located in the tropical low mountain rainforest 11 kilometers away from the Bawangling Forestry Bureau. The internal landscape of Baishitan Scenic Area is diverse, distinctive, and one step at a time. The Baishitan Scenic Area has built a sightseeing boardwalk called "Qiandao". The way of money is the way of wealth in life. On both sides of "Qiandao" are scenic spots such as Vine Trees Competing for Beauty, Ju Bao Feng, Yuan Bao Bao, and Bu Bu Gao.

Yaga Falls

Dear tourists, what comes into your sight now is the Yajia Waterfall. It is located 8 kilometers from the centerline of the Bawangling Forestry Bureau Highway, in the middle reaches of the Yajia River, with a drop of 150 meters and a waterfall width of about 30 meters. The top of the waterfall is a group of cascading waterfalls, with a total of 5 levels, a drop of 2–20 meters, a width of 15–20 meters, and the same stone vein, with a length of about 400 meters. The water scenery during the rainy season is like the legendary "Wangniang Beach", and during the dry season it is like natural large stone beds. In addition, there is a deep pond at the entrance of the waterfall, which is about 5 meters deep, 30 meters long, and 20 meters wide.

Bawangling National Forest Park has many beautiful scenery, and at the same time, there is also a legend. Below, I will tell you about it. A long time ago, there was a malicious uncle who, in order to compete for the throne, brought a group of people to the Emperor's Cave and killed his own nephew. When my uncle chopped off my nephew's head with a knife, the earth shook and the mountains shook. In an instant, three blood columns rushed out from my nephew's head, shooting straight out of the emperor's cave and falling far away. At that time, my uncle's face turned pale and his whole body trembled with fear. He immediately ordered his subordinates to lift him away from the Emperor's Cave and settle down on a dam in the vicinity of Bawang Ridge. After the malicious uncle retreated to the area around Bawangling, he self proclaimed himself as a great king. Due to his residence on the dam, the locals call him the King of the Dam. After the wicked uncle became the king, he was always lazy and did nothing wrong. Even one year, due to severe drought and poor grain harvest, the local people couldn't survive anymore, so they went up the mountain to pick wild lychees from the Bawang Ridge. However, when the malicious uncle found out, he occupied the lychee tree and not only refused to let the local people pick it, but also beat the people. Later, the local people did not call him "Ba Wang", but instead called him "Ba Wang", in which "Ba" means overlord. And the original "Bawang Ridge" has also been changed to "Bawang Ridge".

Alright, after seeing so many beautiful scenery and listening to legends, I will introduce to you the management system implemented in the scenic area. Hainan Bawangling National Forest Park implements a three-level management system of "Management Bureau Management Station Management (Monitoring, Inspection) Station"; Firstly, the daily work of the protected area consists of six departments: administrative office, protection publicity department, scientific research and education department, community affairs department, planning and finance department, and police station; Secondly, four management stations were established, including Yaga, Dongyi, Dongliu, and Qingsong; Thirdly, This place has established two management points, including Gaofeng and No.2 Bridge, two monitoring points for Hainan gibbons, including Kuiyegang and Shizi Road, and two inspection stations, including No.2 Bridge and Nanya. The implementation of these management systems provides guarantees for the sustainable development of scenic areas at the environmental protection level.

Dear tourists, that's all for the introduction of Bawangling National Forest Park. Now you can freely visit it and return here according to the planned time. Wishing everyone a pleasant time.

2A-rated Tourist Attractions

1. Hai Rui Memorial Park

Dear tourists, good morning! Today we are going to visit HaiRui Memorial Park. To meet Hai Rui, a statesman and thinker of the Ming Dynasty who was integrity and outspoken. Hai Rui Memorial Park is located in Binya village, Haikou city. Hai Rui Memorial Park is also known as "Hai Rui 's Tomb".

Before arriving at the memorial park, let's learn about Hai Rui's life. Hai Rui, from Qiongshan (now Haikou City), Hainan, whose style name was Ru Xian, first courtesy name was Guo Kai, and pseudonym was Gang Feng. He spent most of his life as an official in Fujian, Zhejiang and Nanjing during the Jiajing, Longqing and Wanli dynasties. He was known as "Hai Qingtian" and "South Bao Zheng" by the world for his integrity and uprightness, and was deeply loved by the people. In 1589, Xu Ziwei came to Hainan by order of the emperor to supervise the construction of the Tomb of Hai Rui. It is said that the coffin rope was suddenly broken when Hai Rui's coffin was transported to the tomb site. People thought that Hai Rui had chosen this geomantic treasure land, so he was buried on the spot.

The entire Hai Rui Memorial Park is rectangular in shape with a five-storey framework. The first floor is a stone arch; the second floor is the tomb of Hai Rui; the third is the stone sculpture of Hai Rui and the fan shaped Veranda of Incorruptibility; the fourth is a three-storey round building, called "Pavilion of Breeze", and the fifth is a rockery barrier and Octahedron Pavilion. It gives a sense of clarity.

OK, guys, now we have arrived at Hai Rui Memorial Park. The stone archway we can see is the main entrance of Hai Rui Memorial Park. Engraved on the concave horizontal scroll are four characters of "Yue Dong Healthy Tendency" (Yue

Dong Zheng Qi), which is given by emperor Wanli of the Ming Dynasty and is a true portrayal of Hai Rui when he was an official.

Entering the main entrance of the stone archway, a long passage paved with granite leads to the tomb of Hai Rui. In the middle of lattice road (path) lies a stone turtle, which expresses people's great love for Hai Rui. Unfortunately, this stone turtle was destroyed in the past. Now what we see is a replica. Every year on February 22 to 25 of the lunar calendar, Hai Rui's tomb scenic spot is full of people, many people come to worship, and last for 400 years without interruption.

At the end of the tomb passage is Hai Rui's tomb, there is a tombstone in front of HaiRui's tomb, the main meaning of the engraved text on it is "The tomb of Hai Gong, whose posthumous name was Zhong Jie. The emperor gave the order to bury Hai Rui luxuriously, granted he as the minister of Zishan (a senior official in feudal China), the Youdu Censor of Nanjing Procuratorate, and the teacher of princes", this is Hai Rui's official title during his life and honorary title after death. The rear part of Hai Rui's tomb was expanded in the 1990s. There is a statue of Hai Rui to commemorate him. His spirit inspires and illuminates future generations.

All right, guys. The rest of the time, you are free to visit, to understand the lifetime of Hai Rui which was free from corruption. That's all for my introduction. Thank you!

2. Red Detachment of Women Memorial Park

Dear friends, I am your tour guide Zhang Jun,You can call me Xiao Zhang. I am very glad to serve you. I hope my service can give happiness to you!

The Red Detachment of Women Memorial Park combines a variety of factors such as tropical gardens, large-scale themed statues, precious pictures and cultural relics of the Girl Army, song and dance performances, and leisure shopping. At the same time, the Red Detachment of Women Memorial Park is a large red tourist area with attractions such as the flag-raising square, peace square, memorial square, memorial hall, sing and dance square, women's army headquarters, artificial lake, coconut forest, Nanbatian former residence and other attractions. First, let us walk towards to the Peace Square.

Peace Square

Dear friends, this is Peace Square. This is the statue called the Liberation Statue. The Liberation Statue is 8 meters high, 12 meters in length, and 4 meters wide. It consists of chains, bamboo hat, horns, and peace dove. Chains are a symbol of the suffering of the people of the old society. Horns are the symbol of the Chinese Communist, and the ideal of communism. The bamboo hat represents the scene of the Red Detachment of Women fighting in the blood. The peace dove symbolizes our good life today. War and peace is an eternal theme of human history, and peace is the goal of human that have been struggled for generations.

Relief

Now let's look at this relief, it is 60 meters long and 3 meters high, It records the extraordinary fighting process of the Red Detachment of Women.

The First relief: Summon of truth. In the past, the majority of women were oppressed by the multiple oppressions of regime, clan, theocracy and husband hood. They were deprived of many rights as humans. Women who lived near the Wanquan River were also in dire straits. It was the Communist Party of China that awoke women with the voice of truth, the women devoted to fight against imperialism and feudalism.

The Second relief: Liberated with a gun. In May 1st of 1931, the communist party of China in Qiongya. On that day, more than a hundred young women joined the women's army, they carried guns and used the revolution to be liberated, began to play the most glorious movement in the Chinese revolution and women's liberation.

The Third relief: Fighting in Shamo Ridge. Shortly after the establishment of the Red Detachment of Women, they cooperated with the Red Army to bring the enemy into the Ambush Circle of the Red Army. Within an hour of this fighting, they wiped out more than 100 enemies, captured more than 70 people, and seized a large number of guns and ammunition. At the same time, they captured Guiyuan Chen, the commander of the Kuomintang Party Association in Lehui county. The third relief vividly showed the victory of the Red Detachment of Women.

The Fourth relief: Burning the Wen city turret. After the fighting in Shamo Ridge, the Red Detachment of Women cooperated with the Red Army attack on Wen city turret. Women's Army soldiers pretended to attack while addressing the enemy politically. At the same time, the main force enemy excavated the tunnel. After three days of hard work, the tunnel was dug through, and the Red Army used fire to attack the Wen city's turret.

The Fifth relief: Catch Chaotian Feng. Chaotian Feng is a squadron leader in Wen city's turret, he was very arrogant. After the Red Detachment of Women and the Red Army attacked the turret of Wen city, they caught Chaotian Feng.

Banyan Tree

The banyan tree can grow on high and steep mountains, and also can grow in the corner of the tree, it is luxuriant and evergreen. Has anyone seen the movie or ballet "Red Detachment of Women"? Party representative Changqing Hong was caught by Batian Nan after being injured in the fighting. He was tied to a big banyan tree and burned to death. The artistic image of this party representative is moving, so people call the banyan tree "hero tree" and "evergreen tree". In 2001, the crew of the "Red Detachment of Women" from the China Ballet Troupe performed in our memorial garden. Four actors who acted Changqing Hong took photos together under this "evergreen tree". Everyone can take an "evergreen" picture here to commemorate our visit to the memorial park.

The statue of Red Detachment of Women

The statue of the Red Detachment of Women is carved from granite stone, 10 meters high and 4.5 meters wide. The statue is with red army octagonal cap, back bamboo hat, shoulder gun, feet wear straw sandals, the eyes sparkled, and the image is realistic. The statue recalls the glories years when the Red Army fighting. The five glittering words "Red Detachment of Women" on the base of the statue are

Yaobang Hu's inscriptions. The inscription on the bottom of the statue records the establishment of the Red Detachment of Women and the glorious journey of valiant battles.

Memorial Hall

The Red Detachment of Women Memorial Hall was allocated 3 million yuan by the Publicity department of the CPC central committee and invested a total of more than 6 million yuan. Consisting of "Bayi" five stars, the appearance is very majestic and spectacular. Group sculpture at the door reproduces the image of the Red Detachment of Women who killed the enemy bravely. The Red Detachment of Women was established on May 1st, 1931. It was a company of 100 female soldiers at first, and later developed into two companies which consist of more than 140 female soldiers. Behind this is the list of 140 soldiers of the Red Detachment of Women.

When the company of the Red Detachment of Women was formed, the company commander was Qionghua Pang, then was Zengmin Feng, and political instructor was Shixiang Wang. After developing into two companies, the commander of the first company was Zengmin Feng and the political instructor was Shixiang Wang; the second company commander was Dunying Huang and the political instructor was Xuelian Pang.

In Qionghai, Hainan Island, why did the Red Detachment of Women born, how did the Red Detachment of Women born? Please visit the picture exhibition.

After the May 4th Movement in 1919, some progressive young people from Qiongle and Lehui propagandized new culture and new ideas, engaged in the women's liberation movement. In June 1926, members of the Communist Party, Yi Lu and Ming Wu, went to Qiongle and Lehui to carried out revolutionary activities, set up schools, and trained women's backbone. Women stepped out of their homes to participate actively in peasant associations and to went to school, Qiongdong and Lehui women's movement was booming, and many women had joined the Chinese Communist Party.

This was the first female member of the Communist Party — Lin Yiren. In the past, women had no right to have their own name. Her husband Shanji Yang gave the name "Lin Yiren" to her, it meant that woman should be a true person.

In the autumn of 1927, Shanji Yang, Wenming Wang, and Yongqin Chen led the Qiongya people in armed struggle, the first shot of the Qiongya armed revolutionary riots started in the coconut village on the Wanquan River in Qionghai. Since then, the Qiongya people's armed forces under the leadership of the Communist Party of China had been born. In the Coconut Village fighting, the founders of the Qiongya revolutionary armed forces Shanji Yang and Yongqin Chen gloriously sacrifice. In August 1930, the second independent division of the Qiongya Red Army was established.

On March 26th, 1931, the Qiongya Special Committee approved the establishment of the Red Detachment of Women Company of Lehui County. On May 1st, 1931, the Red Detachment of Women was established in Lehui County. In the celebration conference of ten thousand people, 100 red army women soldiers in full dress lined up in the playground, company commander Qionghua Pang took over the company flag from the division commander Wenyu Wang, all the company soldiers took solemn oath in front of the flag. From that day, the Red Detachment of Women began the most legendary fighting life in the history of the Chinese revolution.

These Female soldiers conducted military training in hard environments, stood guard and guarded the prisoners. On the one hand, they studied cultural knowledge, publicize and mobilize the masses, on the other hand, they fought against the enemy's attack and suppression. In two years, the Red Detachment of Women fought more than 50 times. Major battles mainly include:

The war of Shamo Ridge. The female soldiers cooperated with the Red Army's Third Regiment to seduce the enemy in Sha Mao Ling, they killed more than 100 enemy forces, captured more than 70 enemies, seized 146 guns and more than 1,000 rounds of bullets. They also captured Guiyuan Chen, the commander of the

Kuomintang Party Association, and there were no injuries or deaths in the Red Detachment of Women. Since then, the reputation of the Red Detachment of Women had awed Qiong island.

Burning the Wen city turret. After fighting of Shamo Ridge, the Red Army's Third Regiment cooperated with the Red Army to attack the Wen city turret. They attacked the Wenshi Fortress by digging tunnels with the main force army, and captured the leader of the people's league — Chaotian Feng. They also cooperated with the red army to fight the turrets of Yangjiang, Xuedao, Zhongbai, Fenjie and 18 places in total. The female army also fought in the Wenkui ridge by themselves.

The most famous fighting is the Maan Ridge Sniping Action. In August 1932, the Kuomintang sent a large number of troops to siege the Qiongya base area in order to cover the transfer of party safely, the Red Detachment of Women's First Company and Red Army Battalion stubbornly blocked the enemy for three days and nights in Maan Ridge. The bullets were used up, and the soldiers used the stones and sticks as weapons to fight the enemy, they did not transfer to Murui Mountain until they received an order from the superior on the fourth day. In order to cover the entire company retreat, 10 female soldiers engaged in fierce hand-to-hand combat with the enemy when the ammunition was cut off, 10 female soldiers all sacrificed on the battlefield. Their bodies were surrounded by broken-smashed guns, and their bodies were covered with blood. The body of these female soldiers still retained the posture of fighting, their clothes were shredded, and it can be seen that they had fought a fierce battle with the enemy before sacrifice.

In the spring of 1933, in order to preserve the force of revolution, the Special Committee of Qiongya decided to allow the regiments belonging to the Second Red Division to evacuate to various regions to start a secret struggle. The Red Detachment of Women's revolution in just two years worth praising. Seventeen of them were killed in the fighting by the enemy's guns. Eight soldiers, including the company commander and the instructor, were arrested and jailed, they were tortured and coerced into intimidation, but no one surrendered. After the Anti-Japanese

War broke out in 1937, the Kuomintang and the Communist Party done the second cooperation, they were released from prison and still engaged in revolutionary struggle in various ways.

In 1956, Wenshao Liu, a propaganda cadre of the Political Department of the Hainan Military Region, was the first to discover and publicize the revolutionary deeds of the Women's Army. He first referred to the Women's Army as the "The Red Detachment of Women". Chairman Mao and Premier Zhou spoke highly of the Red Detachment of Women. In recognition of the revolutionary spirit of the Red Detachment of Women, and in 1960, Chairman Mao met with Zengmin Feng, the company commander of the Red Detachment of Women, and gave her a semi-automatic rifle.

Movies, Ballet, Peking Opera, and Qiong Opera of The Red Detachment of Women reflect the fighting history of the women's army. The Red Detachment of Women has become an extremely precious spiritual treasure of our time.

Song and Dance Square

Dear friends, now we are going to the Song and Dance Square to watch a sing and dance performance that reflects the Red Detachment of Women fighting and living fragment. The singing of "Step forward! Step forward……" is the fight song forever and maintain besides the Wanquan River and coconut grove. It also inspires us to fight for our bright future.

Home of Batian Nan (Nanfu)

In the movie "The Detachment of Women", there is a vicious landlord who named Nan Batian What does the place he lived look like? Let's go to Yelin Village!

There are 2 main houses and 9 side houses in Nanfu, with a total area of more than 1,000 square meters. Nan Batian was here to live the luxurious life. The left room is the living room, Changqing Hong, who was disguised as a Nanyang merchant had a deal with Nan Batian here. Of course, this is a duplicate. The Red Detachment of Women Exhibit Hall on the right side displays lots of goods and pictures, they vividly reflects the extraordinary fighting course of the

Red Detachment of Women. Here are stills from the 2001 China Ballet Troupe performed in our Memorial Garden. You will have some new feelings about it after visiting.

Dear friends, after visiting the Red Detachment of Women Memorial Park, I think everyone have a deep understanding of the heroic and brave fighting process of the Red Detachment of Women. Let us carry forward the spirit of the Red Detachment of Women, and contribute our life-long strength to the comprehensive realization of a well-off society in China and the advancement of our modernization drive.

Part III

Other Tourist Attractions

1. Sanya Romance Park

Hello, everyone! Welcome to Sanya Romance Park. I am Xiao yang, your tour guide. It is a great honor to show you around this charming park. Sanya Romance Park is designed by Songcheng Performing Company , one of the top 30 Chinese cultural enterprises and the first Chinese cultural performing arts group, with an investment of 1 billion yuan. The unique gardening technique and artistic expression style combined with the particular cultural characteristics of Li and Miao in Sanya, which condens the transformation of Sanya in the long history of thousands of years, and showed us the historical and cultural changes from the Luobi Cave ruin to the international tourism island.

Totem Avenue

We are now located on Totem Avenue, surrounded by eight totem with Gangong Bird, snake and frog god, which tell the story of the origin of the Li nationality. According to legend, Li's female ancestor — Mother Li, is born by lightning snake eggs, so the snake is one of the Li nationality totem. And the frog god is Li auspicious beast. It means that people hope to get a fine weather, a good harvest and a prosperously growing family in the protection of it .

A pattern on the ground of the square is also related to Li culture taken from Li's traditional handicrafts — Li Jin. This kind of brocade also has a laudatory name — "Hainan double-sided embroidery" because of exquisite workmanship, various color and rich in characteristics.

The statue of South China Sea

This magnificent sculpture is our South China Sea Statue, it is the first gate into the scenic area. It is 28 meters high and 60 meters wide, as the embodiment of Mazu Lin Mo is not only the spirit totem of Sanya, but also the embodiment of Hainan women and the patron saint of Hainan. There is also a Mazu Temple in the scenic area constantly incensing.

King's Hall

The four elephant gods represent our four heroine in Hainan: Ma Zu, Mrs. Xian, Li Mu, Huang Dao-po. Li Mu is highlighted here.

Li Mu: The folk beliefs of Li nationality include mountain god and stone ancestor worship. The worship of stone progenitor of Li nationality is connected with the worship of reproduction, which embodies the simple view that Li people live in harmony with nature. In history, the Li clan in the matrilineal society is longer, so the first one to gain worship is the female ancestors. Nowadays, the social status of Li women is still very high, which is unparalleled by other groups. For thousands of years, the reason why Li people worship the Li Mu is based on such social conditions and folk beliefs extremely.

(1) God of Guardian. Li Mu is the protection god of Li Mu mountain and the Li nationality. She controls the mountains and rivers to make Li Mu mountain beautiful while blessing Li nationality who live on this area with happiness and longevity.

(2) God of Fertility. Li Mu god is the first ancestor of the Li people, in charge of the Li people's marriage and fertility. Under her protection, the Li people are growing strong generation after generation in this land. In the long history, the people of Li nationality placed their expectation of the continuation of their blood on LI Mu, and their piety was fully expressed in the worship. So, her status is almost the same with Guanyin Bodhisattva.

(3) God of Longevity. There is a uniquely good environment in Li Mu mountain. The people of Li nationality live and work here and they are all longevity. According to the records in different literature of all times, in the Song dynasty, in the record of Zhou Qufei's peom shows that "Those who live in mountain Li Mu are all happiness and longevity." Qianlong's article also contains: "there is a village under the Li Mu mountain, women are always longevity, at the foot of the mountain spring is extremely sweet." Because of the protection of the mother god of li, the good natural environment, high-quality water resources, original ecological food sources, and the open-minded and optimistic character of the Li people, they have a

happiness and healthy life. So, Li Mu is a veritable longevity god.

(4) God of Harvest. After Li Mu settled in Li Mu Mountain, she had many children, so it is necessary to open up wasteland to meet the needs of children's lives. Farming and hunting are dominant in Li society. Also, planting crops is particularly important for the survival of a nation. There is a farming ceremony in Five Finger mountain to sacrifice "rice duke" and "rice mother". The Li people hope to pray for a good harvest by offering sacrifices to "rice duke" and "rice mother". It can be seen that Li mu was the first one to lead the descendants open up the mountains and plant crops. Thanks to the protection of Li Mu, the crops can be harvest and people can have a happy life.

(5) God of Spinning. Li women's textile techniques are world-famous. If a woman of Li nationality does not master it, she will lose her position in the society of Li nationality. This technology is passed down from mother to daughter. When they are weaving, the tool mustn't be touched by men, otherwise they will not be able to make beautiful patterns. As the ancestor god of the Li nationality, the textile, dyeing and embroidery technique inherited by her descendants are also invented by her. So she is the textile god of the Li people.

(6) God of Wealth. As mentioned above, the Li Mu God governs all the things of Li Mu Mountain. The endless treasure in Li Mu mountain provide the material base of life for local people. So, Li Mu is not only the Wealth God of Li Mu mountain, but also the Wealth God in people's heart.

Love Valley

Love is the eternal theme of mankind, the love square in front of you is built for this, Destiny Temple is located here. In the up-right corner is the wind bell corridor, and the Holy Censer is in front of you directly. Since the opening of the scenic spot on September 25th, 2013, the fire in the burner has never been went out. I wish every tourist here to have a prosperous life in the future. If you like, you can also add a fire in it, pray for your family and friends.

Destiny Temple

The night of north is white, all things were silent and quiet, matchmaker celebrates for everyone, and the fairy also comes with smile. This poem describes the matchmaker in China, now we are in the Destiny temple. This temple was built to commemorate the love story named "Luhuitou" in Li nationality. There is a legend that a long time ago, there was a cruel leader who wants to take a pair of valuable deer antler, so he forced the youth Called Brother Black of Li nationality, Black to capture a deer. Once when Black was hunting in the mountains, he saw a beautiful deer chased by a leopard. He started to catch the deer after killing the leopard. He wasn't successful during the nine days and nine nights after climbed the ninety nine mountains until they went to the north of coral reef in Sanya bay. The deer has no way to run. But at the moment that he was ready to kill the deer, the deer turned back suddenly and stared at him affectionately, then became a pretty girl coming to him. Eventually, they get married. Later, they were respected as the god of love of Li nationality. When you walk into the temple, the kind sculpture in Destiny Temple is Yuelao, Chinese god of love. He plays a very important role in Chinese folklore who is a little bit familiar with matchmaker, the main manager of love. It's said that he usually use red rope to tie the feet of men and women to help them fall in love with each other in fate. The legendary image of the Yuelao as we saw now, sitting in the hall and watching the Song city to pray for eternal love.

Wind chime corridor

In Sanya, wind chime is a token of the magic of calling love. In ancient times, the young girl of Li and Miao nationality would hang a wind chime in front of her own door when she reached adulthood. It means that she could formally fall in love with the boys. Then the wind chime becomes a token of blessing in Sanya. Hanging a wind chime here, it also means that wherever you go, the blessing of people who love you and you love will accompany you forever.

Symbiotic tree (couple tree)

Maybe you think it's just one tree here, but it is actually a Bodhi tree embracing the palm tree closely, so it is named symbiotic tree. Planted around the Destiny temple, it represents that lovers will eventually get married. The Bodhi tree has a deep origin with Buddhism and it is known as the "Buddhist holy tree", which is a symbol of sanctity, auspiciousness and nobility in the eyes of Buddhist believers. There is also a custom in folk which twining a string on the trunk of the bodhi tree to pray for blessing.

Lucky Stone

In love valley, there is a stone called "lucky stone", which has absorbed the spirit of earth for hundreds of millions of years. It was carved into the top of a famous temple pagoda in the Tang dynasty, and later collected by the royal family. About the lucky stone there has been spreading such a saying: the first touch, you will have as much as happiness as the sea; the second touch, you will have a successful official career; the third touch, you will live forever like pine tree; the fourth touch, you will have a harmonious and happy family; the fifth touch, you will have as much money as the water of Yangtze river. "Happiness, success, longevity, prosperity, rich", you are very well-off no matter which aspects. On the back of the lucky stone, a solemn pledge of love was carved on it, which is a symbol of eternal love.

Ocarina

Ocarina is a worldwide instrument, most of the region has a record of the use of pottery flute. There are many material for making ocarina like normal clay, purple clay and so on. This kind of instrument is very light, it can be blown out a very wonderful sound and has a very strong musical performance although it looks not as big as other instruments. And the ocarina playing method is also very simple, after a short period of practice, you can also play a satisfactory tune.

Artisanal pottery

Ceramic craft is a traditional culture in China. China is the ancient country of ceramics. And ceramics always remind foreigners of China. The basic materials for making ceramics are soil, water and fire. Only by mastering the plasticity and rheology of soil and water as well as the molding method and sintering rule when we combine them, the formation and evolution of ceramic forms can be promoted and the beautiful shapes of ceramic can be produced. Also, the organic combination of modeling and decoration can't be ignored, through people's keen inspiration and innovative consciousness, Capturing and revealing the plastic beauty, flexibility beauty, and expressive vitality of soil, a new form of ceramic art has emerged. The sense of beauty and expressive force in pottery can be captured to make fire-new form. With gradually heating up of ceramic art, ceramic art are favored by more and more people. It has become another way to relaxing after work and study. In recent years, the relevant education departments have included pottery art in the teaching curriculum from the point of view of quality education, so that children can be influenced by art from an early age, from which to exercise their practical ability. In the pottery gallery, you can make a piece of pottery for yourself and see it slowly take on life in your hands.

Li brocade

Li brocade is the folk brocade of Li nationality in Hainan island. It can be regarded as a living fossil in Chinese history. Li brocade is exquisitely made and full of exaggerated romanticism. Now we can see that a woman of Li Nationality is weaving Li brocade. The weaving method is very delicate and complicated. Li brocade is mainly made of cotton thread, supplemented by hemp and silk thread. The tools' pronunciation in Hainan are "qiong" and "cai". Nowadays the youth can hardly make it. You can see traditional Li brocade costumes with all kinds of patterns, That is the totems of the Li nationality.

Peanut cake

There is a very famous snack in the Beijing capital named peanut cake we can see in front of us now. Peanut cake is an ancient palace meal and a specialty of ancient Kaifeng city, originated from the Song Dynasty, after the Yuan, Ming and Qing dynasties spread for more than 600 years. It is said that in the Qing Dynasty, when the eight-power allied forces invaded, the empress dowager Cixi took refuge in Xi'an. On her way back to the forbidden city, she tasted the peanut cake sent by Kaifeng officials, then she spoke highly of it. Peanut cake is made with selected peanut kernels as the main material, supplemented by white sugar caramel. It only can be done after many complicated processes such as boil soup, stir sugar, peanut pad, etc. The finished product is flaky, multi-level and fragile. The tasty of it is crisp, sweet and delicious. And now, it is a good gift for friends and relatives.

Straw products

Grass weaving is a kind of handicraft which is made from various flexible herbs. In 2008, it was selected as one of the second batch in national list of intangible cultural heritages. At present, the earliest straw products made by Hemudu people in China have been around for 700 years. The wisdom of the ancients is beyond our imagination, they would use the plants everywhere to weave some daily necessities and handicrafts. In the hot weather of Hainan, people usually wear a hat to shade from the sun when they go out. Besides, you can also pose with a hat, so straw weaving is very popular in Hainan.

Horn comb

Horn comb is made carefully by traditional hand craft with horn as raw material. The texture of horn comb is solid and not easily broken. It doesn't hurt the skin but has a good effect for hair. According to the Compendium of Materia Medica:"Horn is sour, salty, cool and non-toxic." When combing hair with horn comb, its pharmacological action can give full play to massage scalp and head nerve, and promote blood circulation.

African Tambourine

Did you hear a cheerful piece of music? Yes, that's from the Philharmonic. This is the African tambourine. The African tambourine was introduced to our country in the 2010 World Cup, Its surface is made of goat's back skin, and the seat is made of mahogany, which is divided into high, alto and bass. The different places in tambourine have different sounds. There are three ways to play tambourine: the first one is to sit on the chair with your feet clamp the drum to hit it. The second one is to tie the drum to the body with a strap, stand and clip the drum between the legs, the body slightly downward tilt to hit it. The third one is to lay the drum on the ground, sit on it and hit. In particular, it is important to remove the ornaments from hand before playing tambourine to avoid damaging the hand and drum.

Slow delivery

Have you think about what kind of life you will be living ten years later and what kind of scenery you will be looking at? Would you like to talk to yourself after ten years? A creative combination of "time capsule" and "traditional letter" — the slow delivery life can help you achieve this wish. The familiar text of a letter is something that can not be transmitted by using messages in modern instant. Let's stand here and write a paragraph to ourselves. When we receive the letter, we will have a dislocation of time and space, so that the present and the past can be reconnected. Don't forget the most valuable memories and expectations in a fast-paced lifestyle.

Sugar painting

In the Song dynasty, there was a sugar booth in the street. Although the stall is small, it always attracted many people to praise it. That is what you see now-sugar painting.

Sugar painting is a folk handicraft of Han nationality, which originated from "sugar prime minister" in Ming Dynasty. That everyone will wonder why it is called "sugar prime minister", not called "sugar people", it is because in the Ming Dynasty every New Year sacrifice to the gods, the sugar melted cast into a variety of animals and characters as sacrifices, the cast of the characters look like wenchen military generals, so it was called "sugar prime minister". In the Qing Dynasty, it became more popular, the production techniques became increasingly exquisite, and the themes were more extensive. Most of them are auspicious patterns favored by dragons, phoenixes, and the general public.

Sugar painting regards spoon for pen, sugar for the ink. The tool used to make the shape is only a spoon and a shovel. The materials used to make sugar painting are red or white sugar and caramel. Boiling them on the stove with warm fire, you can't use it to cast shape until it can be pulled out filament. When drawing the shape, the artist scoops up the melted sugar juice with a small spoon and casts it rapidly back and forth on the marble slab. Because of the cool nature of marble slab, it is easy to paint but adhesion. After casting, randomly using a spatula knife to shovel up the sugar, stick on the bamboo stick, a sugar painting is finally done. It is easy making and good tasting commonly known as "pouring sugar cake" in folk.

Sugar painting is vivid and colorful, deeply loved by the masses, especially children. In front of the sugar painting booth, maybe you can recall your sweet childhood when tasting this sweet sugar.

Sugar-Figure Blowing

The sugar blowers in our scenic area are deeply loved by tourists and friends because we can not only taste its delicious food, but we can also work together with craftsmen to blow a shape that we like. There are also two photos of "foodies" here, and everyone should be familiar with them. While shooting in Sanya Romance Park, Brother Run, Chen He and Wang Zulan both tasted our Sugar-Figure Blowing.

Li Village

It is one of the most lively blocks in the scenic area. There are not only science and technology museum, but also free amusement areas such as water park. There are also wonderful scenes, such as magistrate Cheng find a son-in-law, Li family wedding parade performances, so that you seem to be in the ancient city thousands of years ago through the whole journey.

Science and Technology Museum

Now we are in the Science and Technology museum. This museum uses the high-tech means to reproduce the storm eye, the sunken ship, the strange street, Mr. Dongpo's house and so on.

Storm Eye

The Storm Eye is on our left. Sanya is often hit by typhoons, in 2014 No .9 typhoon "Wilmson" made landfall with a wind force 17, resulting in 1.311 million people in Hainan are suffering economically. The eye of the storm adopts simulation props, with sound effect, wind, rain, fog, light and electricity system, to reproduce the realistic scene of the dark sky and the collapse of the tree house during the hurricane.

Listening Room

Tourists favorite project — Listening room is cross from the storm eye. The gutty tourist might as well go inside and listen how the thousand-year-old ship sank in the ancient maritime silk road and what strange events happened during that time. The multi-channel surround stereo effect and atmosphere interactive scene in this room can bring participants an immersive sense of stimulation.

Inclined House

All facilities in the inclined house are oblique, but the middle column. It is vertical. This house uses the principle of illusion of reference substance, people have the feeling of weightlessness after entering, must be careful! If you feel dizzy try to stare at the floor.

Inverted Room

This is an upside-down world, the roof becomes the floor, all the furniture is hung on the roof, raising your fingers to take a photo, you will be surprised to find that you actually hung reversely on the ceiling.

Mirror Maze

This is the mirror maze, tourists grope in the maze ahead, all kinds of dazzling mirror reflection makes the road difficult to distinguish. It is said that so far no one has been able to walk through the maze. So, if you want to pass it you need much more than courage.

Peeping Wall

From ancient times to the present, curiosity always induces people to break through that window paper. Look! The window has been punctured many holes, what would be the surprise inside?

Mr. Dongpo's House

Many visitors ask why they build a house in the scenic area? Who is the owner in this house? This house belongs to Mr. Su Dongpo a well-known poet in the Song dynasty, who has a deep connection with Hainan. As we all know, the ancient Hainan was a place of exiled officials, and it is said that in the Song Dynasty, the banishment of Hainan was only a punishment less than the penalty of exterminating an entire family. But Mr. Su Dongpo was not depressed when he was exiled to this place. He regarded Danzhou as his second hometown and said, "I am Daner, but parasitic in west Shu". He ran a school here to introduce his style of study, so that many people traveled thousands of miles to Danzhou to learn from him. In the Song dynasty, hainan has no people who won a place in the imperial examinations. But after Mr. Su Dongpo back to north, here Jiang Tangzuo got it. For this Mr Su Dongpo made an inscription: "the sea never breaks the earth, but a miracle happened on the treasure island." People always regarded Mr. Su Dongpo as the pioneer of danzhou culture and held a deep respect for him. Many things related Mr. Su Dongpo have been inherited like Dongpo village, Dongpo well, Dongpo fied, Dongpo bridge, Dongpo hat and so on, all of these are full of people's remembrance. There is even a kind of "Dongpo dialect" in the language. Actually, Hainan's fortunate development was based on his unfortunate exile. Therefore, Mr. Su Dongpo is very respected and appreciated by local people. There is no doubt that the god is partial to Hainan island, the gentle and exquisite clever natural beauty is valuable enough, but god also gives it a brilliant human origin.

Magic Ancestors Portrayal

Maybe the ancestor portrait hanged on wall seemingly ordinary, but after careful observation you will find that his eyes have been staring at us, no matter where you move, his eyes will always follow you. Sometimes he smiles and nods to welcome us.

Bedroom

Many tourists wonder why Mr. Su Dongpo's bed is red like the color of wedding bed. In fact, this is built specially to commemorate his wife Wang Fu. Mr. Su Dongpo loved his wife deeply, but his wife died early, he missed his wife very much, and once wrote the poem “Ten years, dead and living dim and draw apart. I don’t try to remember. But forgetting is hard.” So this wedding bed also witnessed their steadfast love.

Study Room

This is Mr. Su Dongpo’s study room. Do you want to compose a poem like ancients? As long as stand on the ground footprints, gently drive writing brush to the calligraphy scroll, you can try to write poetry.

Guqin Room

Erudite scholars come in good spirits to talk with me, and among my guests there is no unlearned common man. Aren’t they are all who pass in and out of the house? This is the Guqin which Mr. Su Dongpo usually plays. Put your hands on the string, as long as a gentle touch, a song will float out.

Water Park

This area is our water park. Here is a tourists favorite project, which covers “swing bridge”, “water drift”, “wooden bridge” and so on. On a hot summer day, indulge in this cool water!

Magistrate Cheng finds a son-in-law

This palatial building is magistrate cheng’s house. He only has one daughter who is unmarried at the age of 16. Today magistrate Cheng will be here to find a son-in-law by throwing a hydrangea randomly, the unmarried men have a good chance to try. Tips: a favorable position is easy to get hydrangea, the winner can go to the top of building and marry Miss Cheng.

Yazhou Ancient City

After turning left, we are going to step into Yazhou ancient city. Sanya was known as Yazhou in the past, which city has a long history and bright humanities. As early as the Qin Dynasty, Yazhou had been one of the southern three prefecture established by the first emperor. Yazhou ancient city is also an important transit area of the ancient maritime Silk Road. All kinds of treasures are gathered here. Because of the beauty and vitality of Yazhou ancient city, all officials who have been here say it as prosperous as Suzhou and Hangzhou. It's easy to know the flourish of Yazhou when it was compared to Suzhou and Hangzhou. As you can see, the corners of the streets are full of stone sculptures collected from folk. No matter how the dynasties alternate, those stones with historical symbols seem to tell the story of the times all the time.

Snack Square

In the snack square we can not only taste Wenchang chicken, coconut rice, seafood barbecue, bamboo tube rice and other Hainan traditional snacks, but also drink unique coconut milk cool soup in Hainan. They are all delicious. If you are tired of traveling, you can sit here to experience the leisure time of Hainan afternoon and evening.

On the streets of the ancient city, in addition to the delicious snacks , the story including various kinds of passersby like dignitaries, chivalrous men, beggars, drunkards, western beauties, soldiers, monks and so on is enough to widen your horizon.

Six Rooms Square

In our six rooms square exterior scene performance will be staged every day, like hula Guozhuang, Mrs. Xian training troops and so on. You can heartily release your enthusiasm, dancing and singing heartily with our people.

Guozhuang Torch Festival

Guozhuang Torch Festival is also known as the "carnival of the east". In ancient times, when rice and coconut fruit are ripe in every autumn, Li and Miao's ancestors will gather in the square to dance. Under the moon, around the campfire, women will hold pottery pots, men will hold torches, singing harvest songs to express the elimination of pests, wish timely wind and rain, to ensure the prosperity of the grain and family growing strong.

Shangsi Festival

Lunar March 3rd of each year also named Love Festival, which is the biggest traditional folk festival of the Li people in Hainan province. It is also a wonderful day for the Li people. It is a traditional festival for the Li people in Hainan to mourn their hard-working and brave ancestors and express their yearning for love and happiness.

Water-sprinkling Festival

Water-sprinkling festival comes from the simple folk custom of Li and Miao. It's said that long time ago, the central plains flooded, a group of Li Miao ancestors swam across the sea, drifting to Sanya. After seeing the beautiful environment, ancestors decided to settle down here. The only thing that bothers them is the lack of fresh water. Without water, the food cannot be made, and the people would suffer from hunger. Seeing that the day could not live any longer, suddenly one day, the tribal leader dreamed of seven beautiful fairies, who told him in their dreams where the water was. After waking up, the leader followed the hint of dream and finally found the shimmering river in nearby mountains. The people were overjoyed, splashing water in the stream together. To thank the fairy for the holy water, the ancestors retained this custom. It's as a major festival, has been handed down from generation to generation.

Xinhe Festival

On the sixth day of the sixth lunar month, when the rice is ripe and the coconut fruit is bumper, all the Miao compatriots should celebrate the traditional national festival — Xinhe Festival, a festival whose solemnity is second only for tomb-sweeping is for the Miao people to celebrate the harvest. Under the bright moon, everyone around the campfire sings harvest songs, so as to express the grateful feeling about pests elimination, blessing the good weather for grain, and family peace.

Ai Niu Festival

Every year on the fifth day of the tenth lunar month calendar, is the Miao compatriots to celebrate the love of cattle festival day, this day people do not go to the field, cattle do not pull plows, with the four-square pick up fragrant rice and some meat, to feed the cattle a bumper feast, women weave wreaths around the neck of cattle, men with red maple leaves decorated horns, sharing a year of hard work in exchange for the joy of harvest.

Spring Festival Temple Fair

Spring Festival Temple Fair is Sanya's annual cultural feast. The temple fair is originated from the ancient bazaar. Li Miao and other ethnic minorities sing and dance. They sell daily necessities along the street. The scene is lively and festive, and full of flavor.

Haunted House

Did everyone feel excited as if you were a warrior full of strength after hearing Mrs. Xian's story? Then we might as well take advantage of this courage, to experience the spook house. This super-sized haunted house, using a variety of high-tech means as well as realistic projection technology to create wind, rain, thunder, electricity, miasma, snake, beast, corpse reincarnate and other thrillers. Zombies with a green face and ferocious fangs, dead-cat bounce and even bones under the jingling chain bridge suddenly grasp your ankle. Many realistic experiences are absolutely unforgettable!

Theater

Any encounter is a kind of fate, it is worth be cherished. Today, between you and me, between feelings and scenery, we are lucky to listen to this much told tale. Along the way, we seem to see the human landscape from different times. Perhaps a thousand years ago, we meet here like this, and a thousand years later, we reunite again. I think this is the continuation of the fate. In order to perform this impressive performance, our art team and scenic spot design team with chief director Mr. Huang Qiaoling together went deep into various areas of Sanya to conduct investigation and research, which is also a process for our staff to accept the baptism of Sanya culture. From the crowded beach to the most inaccessible historical heritage, from the canopy of tropical rain forests to the depths of the mountain, there are all full of footprint of hard-working people, We should remove the fog of history and show the brilliant civilization of Sanya in front of every tourist through the unique expression of history and culture in Song City.

There are not only the beautiful love legend of deer, the echo of thousands of years in cave in the Romance of Sanya, but also the rough waves of Jianzhen, a renowned monk in Tang dynasty east-crossing, even the heroine Mrs. Xian. The world's most advanced lighting, sound, stage technology, and more than 390 equipment of stage machinery have been used to create these exquisite scenes so that Sanya's splendid culture, beautiful legends, simple folk customs can be demonstrated adequately. I believe performance is definitely worth seeing in your lifetime, it will certainly bring you a grand visual feast and shock from the bottom of your heart. .

Big Hit "One Sand One World"

In Sanya, we choose "sand" as the medium, sand is an important part of the ocean, with a distinct sense of region and the vicissitudes of history. Sand also represents the elapse of time, a day a sand, a thousand years is the history of The Romance of Sanya.

Preface "Luobi Cave"

What was Sanya like ten thousand years ago? How did the ancient cross the sea and come here, and how did they multiply here? In march 1992, the archaeologists discovered the Sanya site ten thousand years ago in the Luobi Cave. They unearthed fossils of human teeth, stone products, mussels etc., and a large number of fire remains. Ancient human beings lived there, fish and hunt, and engraved the imprint of human existence in the southernmost part of China. In the prologue, the performance of bungee fishing truly restored the life of ancient human beings at that time.

Scene One Luhuitou

"Even phoenix likes this place very much, as a treasured land, Luihuitou will never be forgotten by visitorsbe never given by Sanya." Sanya not only has a long history, but also spreads many affecting love stories. Luhuitou is one of the most beautiful legends. In the "The romance of Sanya" performance uses the film narrative technique to make the love story through the high-tech sound and photoelectric technology, integrated in the ethereal fairyland.

Scene Two Mrs. Xian

History is strikingly similar, and in the land of our theatre today, it was the fief of Mrs. Xian. In 558 AD, the emperor Wen of Sui dynasty began to make China reunification, at this time, war broke out in Lingnan region. In the war, Mrs. Xian had to endure the pain of losing husband, led the soldiers to conquer the Baiyue tribes and restore Hainan island which had been hanging overseas for more than 600 years, making it under the control of central government. In recognition of her achievements, the emperor Wen distributes the ancient Yazhou state to her fief.

Scene Three Maritime Silk Road

In the Song dynasty, Sanya port had become a transit station for the "maritime silk road", from which Chinese porcelains were shipped overseas and spices from the Indian Ocean and the Persian gulf were also collected. On fifteenth day of the eighth lunar month, the governor of Yazhou will hold the Mid-Autumn festival to treat the guests and friends of various countries, the scene is grand and spectacular.

Scene four "Jianzhen East-crossing"

In the Tang dynasty, during the reign of emperor Xuanzong, the eminent monk Jianzhen made the sixth east crossing to Fusang (former Japan's name) to promote buddhist culture. During his fifth east crossing, he encountered a hurricane and was drifted to Sanya, where he was warmly received by local officials. In the performance, the high difficulty acrobatic performance in the air is used to show the dangerous process of master Jianzhen fighting with the wind and waves during the process of east crossing.

The End

Forever Tropical Paradise-Sanya! Sunshine, sea, beach and coconut forest

make Sanya known as "Oriental Hawaii", long history and romantic legend bring people endless reverie. In the company of coconut wind, sea rhyme and beach bikini beauty invite you to feel the wonderful night here.

Ladies and gentlemen, this is the end of my service today. I hope I can meet you later and have the opportunity to serve you again. I wish you a wonderful memory of Sanya. Next is the free time for everyone, during the free activities, please keep your belongings and pay attention to your safety, welcome to visit again, thank you, goodbye!

2. Yalong Bay National Tourism Resort

Hello everyone, welcome to visit Yalong Bay National Tourism Resort, I'm your guide Chen Dan, you can call me Xiao Chen. I hope my explanation can bring you a pleasant mood.

Yalong Bay is the name obtained after the rename. Because it was remote and far away from towns and counties in ancient times so it has fewer records in history. It is said that its original name came from the Li language. It had something to do with the sand here in the bay. Lang and Ya were used to describe the sand as white as jade. Because the bay here was like a crescent, it was later called Yalong Bay. After the founding of the People's Republic of China, it was set up as a military base and closed to the outside for a long time, so few people know.

On October 13th, 1992, the Hainan Provincial People's Government hosted a council on the overall planning of the Yalong Bay Scenic Area. After discussion, people unanimously decided to rename Yalong Bay. The words are spelt the same in English, but they are written differently in Chinese. From the point of view of words, although there is only one word difference, its meaning differs a lot. First, in a narrow sense, "Yalong" is the dragon of Sanya. Second, in a broad sense, "Yalong" is the dragon of Asia. Third, the Chinese nation is a descendant of Yan and Huang, and is also a descendant of Dragon, which is the mascot most admired by the Chinese nation. The new name implies that this beautiful Gulf that has been

sleeping for thousands of years will rise like a dragon and illuminate Asia.

The origin and evolution of the name reflects its tremendous change from primitive backwardness to rich civilization today. The development of the resort in the past 30 years has made Yalong Bay a family and couple's choice of vacation and leisure, as well as a paradise for people. Major state affairs, various domestic and international top-level events, cultural and sports events have been successfully held, making Yalong Bay a destination for all kinds of conferences.

Today, Yalong Bay has become famous and has become a well-known travel brand at home and abroad. In China, choosing Yalong Bay vacation has become a fashion. The beautiful natural scenery, comfortable and perfect resort facilities and unique tourism projects make Yalong Bay a vacation paradise for tourists.

Dear friends, our journey to Yalong Bay National Tourism Resort has come to an end. We will always be here waiting for your next visit. Wishing you a pleasant journey!